Fr. George,
With gratitude for sharing
your love for the WORD during
my time at St. MU.
Shalom, Anne

Women, Wisdom, and Witness

Engaging Contexts in Conversation

04.20.13

Edited by

Rosemary P. Carbine and
Kathleen J. Dolphin

A Michael Glazier Book

LITURGICAL PRESS
Collegeville, Minnesota

www.litpress.org

A Michael Glazier Book published by Liturgical Press

Cover design by Ann Blattner. Illustration: Detail of *Wisdom Woman* by Donald Jackson. © 2007 *The Saint John's Bible*, Order of Saint Benedict, Collegeville, Minnesota. Used with permission. All rights reserved.

1   2   3   4   5   6   7   8   9

Library of Congress Control Number: 2012943790

ISBN 978-0-8146-8064-3 — ISBN 978-0-8146-8089-6 (e-book)

Contents

Foreword

The Birth of New Voices

Rosemary P. Carbine, Whittier College,
and Kathleen J. Dolphin, Saint Mary's College, Notre Dame

Helping women find their voices figures prominently in the history of US feminisms[1] and of US feminist and womanist theologies, both Catholic and Protestant.[2] This goal also has featured prominently in the mission of Saint Mary's College since its founding as a women's college by the Congregation of the Sisters of the Holy Cross (CSC Sisters) in 1844. A college in the Catholic liberal arts tradition, it serves as the sister school of the University of Notre Dame.

The college's Center for Spirituality[3] is an important and promising locus where the mission of the college can be advanced with particular

---

[1] Nelle Morton, *The Journey Is Home* (Boston: Beacon Press, 1985); and Rosemary Skinner Keller and Rosemary Radford Ruether, *In Our Own Voices: Four Centuries of American Women's Religious Writing* (Louisville: Westminster John Knox Press, 1995).

[2] Rebecca S. Chopp, *The Power to Speak: Feminism, Language, and God* (New York: Crossroad, 1989); Mary McClintock Fulkerson, *Changing the Subject: Women's Discourses and Feminist Theology* (Minneapolis: Fortress Press, 1994); Mary Ann Hinsdale and Phyllis H. Kaminski, *Women and Theology*, The Annual Publication of the College Theology Society, vol. 40 (Maryknoll, NY: Orbis Books, 1995); Diana L. Hayes, *And Still We Rise: An Introduction to Black Liberation Theology* (New York and Mahwah: Paulist Press, 1996), and *Standing in the Shoes My Mother Made: A Womanist Theology* (Minneapolis: Fortress Press, 2011); Rosetta E. Ross, *Witnessing and Testifying: Black Women, Religion, and Civil Rights* (Minneapolis: Fortress Press, 2003); and Mary Ann Hinsdale, *Women Shaping Theology* (New York and Mahwah: Paulist Press, 2006).

[3] For more information, visit the Center for Spirituality at www.saintmarys.edu /spirituality.

attention to spirituality considered as both an academic discipline and a way of life. The center offers programs that address contemporary religious issues, creating a network of scholars and practitioners for continuing education in spirituality, especially for women. This introduction reviews the history and current praxis of one particularly effective programmatic component of the Center for Spirituality, namely, the New Voices Seminar, an annual intellectual retreat that is informed by dialogical methods used by the Catholic Common Ground Initiative.[4] The seminar provides a forum to articulate and advance women's voices within Catholicism via dialogue across different social locations and academic disciplines that eschews "hardness of hearing" and exercises collaboration.[5]

The seminar coincides with the annual endowed Madeleva Lecture at Saint Mary's College. Creation of the Center for Spirituality in 1984 carried forward the spirit of the Graduate School of Sacred Theology, which flourished at Saint Mary's College from 1943 to 1970 under the guidance of its legendary president, Sister Madeleva Wolff, CSC. The program granted doctoral and master's degrees in theology. At that time, it was the only graduate theological program that admitted women anywhere. Then, as doors began to open for women at other American colleges and universities, the graduate school at Saint Mary's College closed, its pioneering work completed.

In 1985 Monika K. Hellwig officially launched the Center for Spirituality with an inaugural lecture[6] in what became known as the Madeleva Lecture Series.[7] This anthology of essays from twelve participants in the New Voices Seminar is dedicated to the memory of this remarkable woman. Monika K. Hellwig, former professor of theology at Georgetown University and past president of the Association of Catholic Colleges and Universities, died in 2005. She was an important contributor at the

---

[4] The Catholic Common Ground Initiative (CCGI) is housed in the Bernardin Center for Theology and Ministry at the Catholic Theological Union in Chicago. More information can be found at www.catholiccommonground.org.

[5] Hinsdale and Kaminski, *Women and Theology*, x.

[6] Monica K. Hellwig, *Christian Women in a Troubled World*, 1985 Madeleva Lecture in Spirituality (New York and Mahwah: Paulist Press, 1985). See also Dolores Leckey and Kathleen Dolphin, eds., *Monika K. Hellwig: The People's Theologian* (Collegeville, MN: Liturgical Press, 2010).

[7] The lectures can be read online at www.madelevalectures.org/catalog.php.

reunion of Madeleva lecturers in 2000, where she also helped in formulating "The Madeleva Manifesto: A Message of Hope and Courage,"[8] a document composed and signed by all the Madeleva lecturers between 1985 and 2000 who had gathered at Saint Mary's to celebrate the new millennium. Speaking a message of hope and courage to women in the church, these senior scholars addressed women in ministry and theological studies, women looking for models of prophetic leadership, women tempted by the demons of despair and indifference, women suffering the cost of discipleship, and young women in the church. "We will be with you along the way," the manifesto said, "sharing what we have learned about the freedom, joy and power of contemplative intimacy with God. We ask you to join us in a commitment to far-reaching transformation of church and society in non-violent ways." That document birthed, in part, the New Voices Seminar and continues to inspire it.

History of the New Voices Seminar

The Center for Spirituality celebrated its twenty-fifth anniversary during the 2009–10 academic year, focusing on the topic "Women, Wisdom, and Witness." Drawing its title from that anniversary, this book celebrates women, wisdom, and witness as exemplified in the New Voices Seminar. The seminar is a lively intergenerational and in many ways diverse group of roughly forty to fifty women scholars who take an interdisciplinary approach to the study of Christianity, utilizing ethics, history, law, liturgy, ministry, pastoral care, political science, psychology, Scripture studies, social work, sociology, spirituality, and theology.

The New Voices Seminar was inaugurated in 2004 to commemorate the twentieth anniversary of the Madeleva Lecture Series. Approaching its tenth year, the fully funded seminar has flourished as an annual intellectual retreat for young women scholars to create a community of conversation that "is at once dialogical in process, courageous in its openness, and yet very uncommon in fact."[9] Its purpose is to provide an opportunity for women scholars, particularly those who are at a relatively early stage of their career, to share energetic conversations with each other, to learn

[8] "The Madeleva Manifesto: A Message of Hope and Courage" is available online, along with a photo of the signatories, at www.madelevalectures.org/manifesto.php.
[9] Hinsdale and Kaminski, *Women and Theology*, ix.

from the wisdom of more experienced women scholars, and to create a supportive community of women academics. "New Voices" denotes promising women scholars whose work contributes to the vision so articulately expressed in the "Madeleva Manifesto."

> In the tradition of Sister Madeleva Wolff, CSC, we sixteen Madeleva lecturers have been invited to speak a message of hope and courage to women in the church. Reflecting the diversity of gifts bestowed on us by the Spirit, we speak from our particular experiences and vocations, yet share in a universal vision that is faithful to our Catholic tradition. To women in ministry and theological studies we say: re-imagine what it means to be the whole body of Christ. The way things are now is not the design of God.

To date, over fifty women have participated in at least one New Voices Seminar. All participants are invited to return each year, and several new invitees are contacted to join as well. The average annual number of participants is twenty—a new constellation of scholars each year. A small ad hoc committee, including past Madeleva lecturers, selects the invitees, who must fulfill several criteria. The invitee must have a doctoral degree and must be working in an academic setting or in a field with strong connections to academia. Her area of expertise must be in theology and/or related fields in the study of Christianity. She must have a demonstrated interest in spirituality, either specifically and formally as a scholar who engages the discipline in her professional work, or informally as a scholar who desires to integrate the life of the mind with the life of the spirit in her own personal life.

At the time of this writing, the voices of the seminar members are beginning to be heard in the academy; all contribute new and exciting perspectives (feminist, womanist, *mujerista*, and others) in their professional work. The New Voices Seminar supports its members in these endeavors, encouraging them to reflect on the challenge and promise of furthering the Catholic tradition at its best. Intergenerational and intercultural components add depth and richness to this reflection. Several past Madeleva lecturers participated in the first New Voices Seminar as honored guests, and past Madeleva lecturers have joined the group in subsequent seminars as well. Seminar members express appreciation for the opportunity to get acquainted (or reacquainted) with senior scholars in this informal setting. Since the Catholic tradition at its best fosters ecumenical and interreligious dialogue, New Voices Seminar participants have recently included members of diverse faith traditions. However, given the urgent need for women's voices within Catholicism at this time in history, the New Voices Seminar continues to have a decidedly strong Catholic flavor to it.

New Voices Seminar Format

Each year the New Voices Seminar theme coincides with some themes inherent in that year's Madeleva Lecture. The lecturer stays for the New Voices Seminar as a guest of honor, engaging the members in discussion about those themes. Generally, the seminar format consists of three sessions: (1) confidential sharing of personal concerns, current academic projects, successes, and difficulties; (2) discussion of the Madeleva Lecture; and (3) further discussion of themes and issues that emerged in the previous sessions. For example, at a recent seminar in response to the concern about getting work published, the Madeleva lecturer spontaneously presented a brief but substantive workshop on the topic of publishing.

Prior to each session, one participant is invited to serve as a conversation starter. Her task is first to listen with "head and heart" to that session's discussion, then to formulate a response during the coffee break, and then to present her observations to the group when it reconvenes. Unlike an academic response that involves critique and perhaps constructive advice, the response that the conversation starter offers goes deeper. She identifies themes, issues, and questions that emerged. She notes the feelings that were expressed as well. Perhaps she comments on what was *not* said in the discussion.

This conversational format relates directly to a unique feature of this book: each of the three sections concludes with a conversation, an interactive dialogue among a conversation starter and the authors of the chapters in that section. These conversations took place in phone conferences, which were recorded and then transcribed. By introducing the writings and conversations of selected women in the New Voices Seminar, the book models and stimulates much-needed dialogue between theology and ethics about some of the most salient intersections among women, Christianity, and contemporary US society that revolve around poverty, sexual norms, trauma and slavery, and the roles of women in education, the church, and public life.

Rather than conclude each section of the book with questions for further discussion and lists of books for further reading as in most books designed for classroom use, the phone conferences serve as a methodological and pedagogical tool for doing and teaching theology and ethics more adequately across different disciplines. The phone conferences prompt and model how to engage in conversation in the classroom about issues raised by the essays, and thus they differ from traditional formal academic responses. Although the phone conferences strive for the same intellectual and practical rigor of scholarly discourse, the conversations transcribed at the end of each section of the book prompt the contributors—and readers—to think more deeply about a theme or two or three collectively, which exceeds what any single essay accomplishes, and which demonstrates the benefit of a collaborative dialogical method for doing theology and ethics from a variety of disciplinary perspectives. The phone conferences, then, model civic discourse at its best by showcasing passionate scholars who are engaged in dialogue about complex social issues from diverse and divergent viewpoints and who talk across differences of all sorts in order to reach for tentative, open-to-revision conclusions about those issues. By modeling such conversational exchanges, the contributors and the conversation starters intend to open up spaces within classrooms, churches, and elsewhere for informed civic discourse that harnesses the potential of genuine dialogue to replace a prevalent theo-political view of power as unilateral "power over" or "power to" with a "democratized ideal of co-creativity . . . a sustainable catholicity of creaturely solidarity kin to 'democratic cosmopolitanism.'"[10]

Lastly, concluding each section with a transcript of this interactive dialogue demonstrates the communal and collaborative praxis of doing theology and ethics that takes place at the annual New Voices Seminar. It also invites the book's readers to join in such a dialogue. In this way, the book takes its inspiration from the dialogical method employed by the Catholic Common Ground Initiative (CCGI) and shows its benefit for doing more adequate theology and ethics around some of the most important issues of our time.

Since its establishment in 1996 by the late Cardinal Joseph Bernardin, CCGI has been committed to addressing the pastoral concerns of the church in the United States. The initiative does so by modeling and fostering intrachurch dialogue on issues that are timely and relevant for the

---

[10] Catherine Keller, *God and Power: Counter-Apocalyptic Journeys* (Minneapolis: Fortress Press, 2005), 51, 52.

life and mission of the church. Saint Mary's College has been affiliated with CCGI since 2001. The Center for Spirituality administers CCGI programs, typically sponsoring a Catholic Common Ground Conversation approximately once a semester, utilizing conversation starters to open the discussion. These events take place in a space large enough to accommodate several circles of chairs. At each conversation, four individuals are invited to serve as conversation starters by presenting a five-minute commentary on the selected topic. Every effort is made to gather a balanced roster of four conversation starters. Before introducing the conversation starters, the moderator presents a brief summary of the official Catholic teaching on the topic (without further comment). Then, each of the starters presents a brief commentary. For example, for the conversation on homosexuality, a young woman shared her experience of being a lesbian; another student shared her experience of having a brother who is gay; a psychology professor commented on recent research on sexual orientation; and another participant shared her confusion about homosexuality being defined as a profound "disorder." At the end of this half hour of short presentations, each conversation starter "blends into" one of the conversation circles. In these small group conversations, the conversation starters do not act as discussion guides or facilitators in any formal sense. The moderator reminds the participants that in real life we don't have "facilitators" to guide every conversation. Adults learn by experience how to engage in conversations that are respectful and substantive. To develop the art of conversation, "Common Ground Conversation Guidelines"[11] are distributed to the groups. Refreshments are served and the groups engage in conversation for roughly forty minutes. At the end of the discussion, the moderator thanks the participants for engaging in this conversation and bids them farewell. No reporting to the large group takes place, and no written summaries are submitted to review. Rather, the emphasis is on cultivating a free-floating, respectful, and informal conversation that could mark the beginning of many future conversations, enlightened (hopefully) by the Catholic Common Ground Conversation that the participants experienced.

---

[11] "Common Ground Conversation Guidelines" can be found on the Center for Spirituality website: www.saintmarys.edu/spirituality. These light-hearted "ground rules" effectively put participants at ease and guide them in discussion of even the most contentious topics.

This New Voices anthology breaks new ground by enacting a modified version of the CCGI's method of dialogue across differences as a basis for a collaborative, dialogical method to do theology and ethics around some of the most tragic contexts of women's experiences, especially suffering and resistance; some of the most contested contexts in which women scholars put their wisdom to work, namely, in higher education; and some of the most challenging contexts in which women witness to more just ways of life together in the church and the world, namely, at the intersections of religion and public life. "The presence and voices of women, therefore, still evoke some of the most hope-filled yet also the most contested possibilities for inquiry."[12] Thus, this book emphasizes the rich sociopolitical, dialogical, and interdisciplinary implications of Catholic women's intellectual and social praxis in contemporary theology and ethics.

A Chorus of New Voices

This collection brings together a diverse group of women scholars—Euro-American, Latina, African American, Asian American—who represent diverse approaches to theology and ethics (virtue ethics, social ethics, sexual ethics, constructive theology, practical theology, public theology) and who practice in their essays and in their conversations an interdisciplinary approach, drawing on Scripture studies, aesthetics, globalization, history, pedagogy, politics, psychology, postmodern studies, sociology, spirituality, and race and gender studies. Each chapter combines theology or ethics on the one hand with insights from one or more disciplinary perspectives on the other hand. Each essay's twofold task is (1) to utilize those sources to critically reflect on and confront particular contexts of contemporary women's experiences with regard to suffering and resistance, academia and higher education, and religion and public life, and (2) to explore as well as appraise women's creative approaches, both religious and practical, and to enhance women's and wider human well-being, understood as "reciprocal, collaborative energy that engages us personally and communally with God, with one another, and with all of creation in such a way that power becomes synonymous with the vitality of living fully and freely."[13]

---

[12] Hinsdale and Kaminski, *Women and Theology*, x.

[13] Denise M. Ackerman, "Power," in *Dictionary of Feminist Theologies*, ed. Letty M. Russell and J. Shannon Clarkson (Louisville: Westminster John Knox Press, 1996), 219–20.

The book is divided into three thematic sections, which address particularly significant contexts of contemporary women's experience: suffering and resistance, academia and higher education, and religion and public life. Each section provides interdisciplinary perspectives in theology and ethics on a particular theme and concludes, as noted above, with an interactive dialogue. Excerpts from Monika Hellwig's inaugural lecture grace the opening page of each section in order to provide the reader with an orienting point and organizing frame of reference for the essays in that section.

Section I, titled "Women's Experience in Context: Suffering and Resistance," features Anne O'Leary, Saint Mary's University, San Antonio, TX; Susie Paulik Babka, University of San Diego; Mary Doak, University of San Diego; and Nancy Pineda-Madrid, Boston College. The conversation starter is Maureen O'Connell, Fordham University. O'Leary offers the leading essay, "Mary of Nazareth and the Mysticism of Resistance," in which she engages in a quest for the historical Mary by reclaiming the phrase "bondwoman," often mistranslated as "handmaid" in the Lukan narrative, for a deepened understanding of the reality of bondwomen in Israel and for prophetic resistance to such suffering today. Babka's essay, "Art as Witness to Sorrow: Käthe Kollwitz, Emmanuel Levinas, and Dorothee Sölle," offers a theological aesthetics rooted in postmodern ethics regarding the role of art and prayer as modes of witness to suffering, with particular attention to poverty and to maternal grief. Doak's contribution, "Trafficked: Sex Slavery and the Reign of God," identifies and reflects on the ecclesiological, eschatological, and christological responses to globalized sex trafficking, slavery, and trade in women and children. Pineda-Madrid's "Feminicide and the Reinvention of Religious Practices" explores the Ciudad Juárez feminicide of girls and young women, which demands a more adequate account of historical salvation. Pineda-Madrid's essay argues that practices of resistance in response to the feminicide forge a new, emancipatory space that bears theological and political significance for understanding salvation as a social, collective reality.

Conversation starter Maureen O'Connell opens the dialogue by noting a common theme in these four essays: the power of women's resistance to suffering, both individually and communally. What follows is an energetic, insightful, and respectful conversation among the four essayists and O'Connell. The conversation reflects mainly upon theology and ethics, but the focus varies and includes systematic theology, practical theological methodology, biblical theology, and the interface of theology and the visual arts. Readers will note how effectively they build on each other's ideas and commentaries. For example, Doak appreciates Babka's understanding of theological aesthetics as an affirmation of human dignity. Doak, who explores the theological implications of the tragedy of global sex trafficking, finds Babka's analysis particularly helpful. Indeed, Doak expresses her determination to incorporate the notion of human dignity to an even greater extent in her own work as a result of this conversation. The level of mutual support in this conversation is high; yet it does not prevent the participants from posing challenging questions to each other during the good-natured conversation.

Section II, titled "Women's Wisdom in Context: Academia and Higher Education," flows easily from the first, moving from an identification and analysis of key issues into a consideration of the academic vocation that will address these issues. Featured in this section are Mary M. Doyle Roche, College of the Holy Cross; LaReine-Marie Mosely, Loyola University Chicago; Emily Reimer-Barry, University of San Diego; and Bridget Burke Ravizza, Saint Norbert College. In "Virtues and Voices: Building Solidarity among Women Scholars," Roche offers a feminist virtue theory of "listening for voice," in conversation with sociologist Sara Lawrence-Lightfoot, that enables expansive circles of solidarity among scholars and among students. Roche considers the importance of women's voices, women sharing their experiences, and the moral wisdom discerned through those experiences for feminist theology and ethics. Feminist theorists in other disciplines have also highlighted the importance of voice and narrative for understanding the complexity and nuance of many social issues. The technological age has presented new opportunities and obstacles for communicating experience, and feminist theologians can play a pivotal role in articulating the virtues required to build and sustain relationships of solidarity in this context. Mosely's "The Conundrums of Newer Catholic Women Theologians" analyzes aspects of the postmodern times in which newer theologians are situated—the contested meanings of the Second Vatican Council, the impact of the worldwide clergy sexual abuse scandal on the church's moral and social credibility, and the investigations of perceived-to-be-problematic persons. At this crossroads, there are also positive signs—for example, Elizabeth Johnson's instructive response to the US bishops' doctrinal committee and that committee's invitation to dialogue with pretenure theologians. Turning to the life praxis of Maude Petre, an intellectual friend of George Tyrell, Mosely's essay draws some instructive lessons from English Catholic modernism to shed light on ways newer theologians can navigate the troubled waters of the twenty-first-century church in postmodern times. Reimer-Barry reflects on the context of faith formation not only in liturgical but also in other familial, educational, and social settings. Her essay, "Suffering or Flourishing? Marriage and the Imitation of Christ," provides a feminist response to the US bishops' pastoral letter on marriage, drawing out the letter's implications of Jesus' death on the cross as a model for marital love, particularly the implications of an uncritical acceptance of suffering for women. Ravizza's essay, "Feminism a Must: Catholic Sexual Ethics for Today's College Classroom," outlines components of and concrete examples from a course in Catholic sexual ethics that is informed by feminism and sociology and that speaks meaningfully to both scholars and students alike, without reinforcing theories that either equate girls' moral purity with their virginity or disconnect sexual behaviors from our morality.

The participants in this section are theologians and ethicists with diverse areas of expertise, such as Catholic ethics and social teaching, Catholic feminism, women's/gender studies, and African American studies. They are invited into conversation by conversation starter Michele Saracino, Manhattan College. They begin with a discussion of the distinction between listening "to" voices (listening to those already involved in the conversation in some way) and listening "for" voices (seeking out those who have yet to be engaged in the conversation). Participants reflect on the impact listening has on themselves personally, on their teaching practices, and on their theology or ethics. The conversation is enriched by the racial diversity in the group as they grapple with racial issues. These Catholic women scholars seek ways to remain in dialogue with the magisterium while continuing to explore ways of transforming the tradition with creative fidelity.

Section III, titled "Women's Witness in Context: Religion and Public Life," focuses on the work of Nancy Dallavalle, Fairfield University; Rachel Bundang, Marymount School; Kristin Heyer, Santa Clara University; and Rosemary P. Carbine, Whittier College. Dallavalle leads the section with her essay, "Icons and Integrity: Catholic Women in the Church and in the Public Square." Dallavalle builds on Karl Rahner's insight that the story of women falls to women to tell, in order to recount an institutional history of Catholic women in the church through three key icons: "mother" for the institution of the family, "cantor" for the institution of the laity, and "sister" for the institution of the church. Bundang's essay, "Bridget Jones, Cancer Patient: On Navigating the Health Care System as a Singleton," identifies and explores heretofore overlooked gender and spirituality issues for single women in the US health care system, which too often privileges the worth of attached (i.e., married and familied) women. Heyer's essay, "Reservoirs of Hope: Catholic Women's Witness," reflects on the role of women religious, especially those involved in NETWORK and in current US health care reform debates, with a particular focus on their external advocacy and internal operational witness for conscientious discernment and for prophetic obedience. Carbine concludes the third section with "The Beloved Community: Transforming Spaces for Social Change and for Cosmopolitan Citizenship." In this essay, Carbine examines the emergence of the notion of the beloved community in the Civil Rights Movement and the reemergence of this notion in the New Sanctuary Movement, with particular attention to how these movements for equality across racial and national lines transform political and ecclesial spaces for the purpose of social, gender, and global justice.

To launch a conversation among the ethicists and theologians in this section, historian Mary Henold of Roanoke College identifies three common themes in their essays: individuals and institutions (primarily Catholic) who advocate for the poor, the victims of injustice, or the marginalized; the willingness to enter public spaces that are fraught with risk; and the formulation of particular religious and political constructs that promote human flourishing. As a historian, Henold shares with the group her concern regarding the current attempts by the institutional church to perpetuate misguided understandings about Catholic women's identity—a concern expressed by Dallavalle and others as well. This lively conversation is enriched by the mix of reflections on Catholic sisters and laywomen, both single and in committed relationships. The discussion of ecclesiological issues is particularly enlightening as participants grapple with the highly complex nature of the institutional church's identity and sociopolitical impact.

Concluding the volume is an essay by Colleen Griffith, Boston College. In her "Dialogue, the Pearl of Great Price," Griffith notes that each essay in the book elaborates a way of doing theology and ethics in dialogue with specific disciplines and localities to address women's real-life issues pertaining to suffering and resistance, education, and public life. She explores resources in the fields of practical theology, interreligious understanding, and pastoral care to advance the notion of evocative listening, in part modeled on and by the book's dialogues that conclude each section.

Hope in Dialogue across Disciplines and Differences

This collection of essays about women, wisdom, and witness is the product of a group of women scholars who recognize the potential of genuine dialogue to further the greater good of all. A dialogical process has informed the shape of this book from its beginning. In this respect, members of the New Voices Seminar carry forward the wisdom and witness of the sixteen Madeleva lecturers who gathered at Saint Mary's College in 2000 for their convergence conference. At the dawn of the new millennium, the group formulated the "Madeleva Manifesto." The powerful message emerged from the dialogue engaged in by these senior women scholars over a period of several days.

Both the manifesto and this collection were birthed at historically critical turning points. The manifesto was published a year before the 9/11 attack on the World Trade Center and the advent of the US war on terrorism, as well as the early unfolding of the worldwide sex abuse scandal in the Catholic Church. Ten years later, *Women, Wisdom, and Witness* debuts in a seriously polarized church and in a world wracked with political turmoil abroad and political gridlock at home. Arguably, there has never been a time of greater need for genuine dialogue among Catholics themselves, among nations of the world, or between the Catholic Church and other societal institutions, both religious and secular.

In the 1990s, Cardinal Joseph Bernardin of Chicago was keenly aware of a growing crisis within the church. Shortly before his death in 1996, he established the Catholic Common Ground Initiative primarily "to help Catholics address, creatively and faithfully, questions that are vital if the church in the United States is to flourish as we enter the next millennium."[14] Fifteen years later, the initiative is reenergizing itself. It holds great promise as it affirms and promotes the full range and demands of authentic unity, acceptable diversity, and respectful dialogue, not only as a way to dampen conflicts but also as a way to make conflicts constructive. For those doing theology and ethics and those who are interested, for example, in exploring effective ways for the church to bring its rich

[14] See the CCGI founding documents at www.catholiccommonground.org.

tradition to bear on the public square and also to be appropriately influenced by social change itself, the CCGI has much to offer.

The significance of genuine dialogue about contested contexts functions as the central theme of this book. In the process of writing it, the
contributors themselves became more aware of dialogue as a promising
locus for collaboration, with a view toward effectively addressing and
helping to solve some of the most pertinent crises in the church and
civil society. The emerging new voices speak with clarity, conviction,
and courage while listening to (and for) other voices. Such dialogical
collaboration bodes well for the future of theology and ethics, for the
church, and for society.

Acknowledgments

A book of this kind demands a collective and collaborative effort to reach fruition. The coeditors thank the donors to Saint Mary's College who made possible the annual New Voices Seminar since its inception in 2004 through 2010. Michelle Egan, associate director of the Center for Spirituality, and Kathy Guthrie, assistant at the Center for Spirituality, coordinated all logistics for this annual seminar. Michelle Egan copyedited the entire manuscript, and Kathy Guthrie cooperated with IT at Saint Mary's College to facilitate recording and transcribing conversations among contributors that appear in the book. Kathleen appreciates Rosemary's expertise and learned a great deal about the inner workings of the editing process. Rosemary, together with the contributors, is indebted to Kathleen's insight into gathering resources and creating the cohort for the annual seminar, which originally inspired and sustained this project. To all New Voices who accompanied us in past seminars and who will benefit from future seminars, we say—in the words of the "Madeleva Manifesto"—"You are not alone. We remember those who have gone before us, who first held up for us the pearl of great price, the richness of Catholic thought and spirituality. We give thanks to those who continue to mentor us. To the young women of the church we say: carry forward the cause of gospel feminism. We will be with you along the way, sharing what we have learned about the freedom, joy and power of contemplative intimacy with God. We ask you to join us in a commitment to far-reaching transformation of church and society in non-violent ways."

Women's Experience in Context

Suffering and Resistance

When we try to make such a communal discernment of vocation for Christian women within the North American situation in
our own days, then we must certainly take into account the wealth
that is at our disposal, the extent to which we have been liberated
from back-breaking, soul-destroying, exhausting physical work,
the civic rights and participation which we enjoy, the educational
advantages which we have had, and the world of desperate needs
which surround us in our times. . . . We therefore have unprecedented opportunities to participate actively in the affairs of the
larger society through volunteer work, through professional or
business careers and through political activity. There is also no
doubt that the educational advantages we have enjoyed equip us
for acquiring a good understanding of issues concerning peace
and the continuing armaments buildup, and issues concerning the
plight of the poor, the oppressed, refugees, political prisoners, and
populations undergoing famine.

It is, then, above all a time for individual and communal discernment on the part of Christian women of our times who have
enjoyed a privileged education and are placed within the economically privileged, relatively leisured class in a democratically
organized society that offers women great social freedom and, on
the whole, great respect. Because it is a time of rapid changes in

society and rapid communication across the whole world, the call for continuing discernment moves swiftly from crisis to crisis, opportunity to opportunity, and human need to human need. . . .

The suffering of such systemic exclusion of those who have gone before us with whom we can readily identify, by those in other contemporary cultures with whom we must try to identify, and by those among us whose gifts and calling are not acknowledged or honored, is an experiential basis for working toward a clearer understanding of what it is that is awry in our world. It is an experiential basis for an understanding of compassion as a redemptive answer to all that is awry. To enter deeply into the experience of the other, of any other, without exclusion or discrimination is indeed to unravel the apparently unredeemable hatreds, oppressions, and miseries of our world.

—Monika Hellwig, *Christian Women in a Troubled World*, 32–34, 42–43

Mary of Nazareth
and the Mysticism of Resistance

Anne M. O'Leary, PBVM, Saint Mary's University, San Antonio, TX

In this essay, I invite you to join me in looking through one small "opening" that the Gospel of Luke provides through which we may glimpse something of the person and life context (*Sitz im Leben*) of Mary of Nazareth (b. ca. 10 BCE) and the mysticism of resistance that she proclaims.[1] This opening is first found in Luke's account of the annunciation (cf. Luke 1:26-38), specifically in the metaphor that Mary uses to describe her relationship with God at the time the angel visits her with news of God's extraordinary mission for her. Mary responds to Gabriel's announcement by saying: "Behold, I am the handmaid [lit. "bondwoman"] of the Lord. May it be done to me according to your word" (Luke 1:38).[2]

The author of Luke tells us that after Mary's visit to her kinswoman Elizabeth, she sings a prophetic song, the *Magnificat* (Luke 1:46-55), in

---

[1] The first version of this essay was given as a public lecture at the Church of Saint Peter Chanel, Dunedin, New Zealand (June 11, 2009), in response to the invitation by Sister Noreen McGrath, PBVM, and the Presentation Sisters, New Zealand/Aotearoa, to mark the 225th anniversary celebrations in honor of the death of Nano Nagle (1718–84), the founder for the Presentation Sisters. The second and only other version was written as a lecture delivered during the International Presentation Sisters' Charism and Spirituality Retreat, Aberdeen, South Dakota, August 8, 2010.

[2] All biblical quotations are from the *New American Bible* unless otherwise indicated. Saint Mary's Press, *College Study Bible: New American Bible, Including the Revised Psalms and the Revised New Testament, Translated from the Original Languages with Critical Use of All the Ancient Sources* (Winona, MN: St. Mary's Press, 2006).

which she uses the same metaphor to describe her relationship with the
Lord. Mary sings:

> My soul proclaims the greatness of the Lord;
>   my spirit rejoices in God my savior.
> For he has looked upon his handmaid's [bondwoman's] lowliness;
>   behold, from now on will all ages call me blessed. (Luke 1:46-48)

Thus, Mary is the Lord's "lowly bondwoman."

The Greek term for "bondwoman" (*hē doulē*) has usually been translated as "handmaid," corresponding to the Vulgate's rendition of Mary's
response: *Ecce ancilla Domini*. This translation and much subsequent interpretation, combined with the portrayal of Mary by the artists of the
Middle Ages and the Renaissance as a handmaid of a lady of means or
status, have done much to tame the harsh historical reality of the bondage of Mary's day[3] and to cloak the theological richness generated by the
term "bondwoman" that Luke places on the lips of Mary.

This essay is in part about recovering something that has been lost in
translation, and it will show that a study of the Lukan portrayal of Mary
of Nazareth through the hermeneutic of bondage brings into relief the
prophetic dimension of her spirituality and, in particular, the mysticism
of resistance. I draw on Dorothee Sölle's description of the terms "mysticism" and "resistance." Sölle describes mysticism thus: "As the experience
of oneness with God, mysticism is the radical substantiation of the dignity
of a human being."[4] She describes resistance as the positive, proactive opposition to anything that reduces a human being "into that of a consuming and producing machine that neither needs nor is capable of God."[5]

We begin the quest of recovery and demonstration of the thesis by
engaging in three hermeneutical methods: first, the hermeneutic of social
location[6]—in this case, the world of Nazareth, Galilee. Would bondmen

---

[3] S. Scott Bartchy, "Slavery: New Testament," in *The Anchor Bible Dictionary*, ed. David
Noel Freedman et al., vol. 6 (New York: Doubleday, 1992), 66.

[4] Dorothee Sölle, *The Silent Cry: Mysticism and Resistance* (Minneapolis: Fortress Press,
2001), 43.

[5] Ibid., 44. See also Elizabeth Johnson, *Truly Our Sister: A Theology of Mary in the Communion of Saints* (New York: Continuum, 2003), 255.

[6] The hermeneutical methods employed in this essay are based on the work of Elisabeth
Schüssler Fiorenza, *Wisdom Ways: Introducing Feminist Biblical Interpretation* (Maryknoll, NY:
Orbis Books, 2001). See also Johnson, *Truly Our Sister*, 213.

and bondwomen have come from Nazareth in Mary's day? What did it mean to be a bondwoman then? Was Mary ever a bondwoman, literally speaking? To respond to this question, we will examine the geographical, socioeconomic, and political environment in which this first-century Jewish woman lived. This will provide a context for the second aspect of our quest, which is to engage in the hermeneutic of critical evaluation—that is, we will examine how the way in which Luke tells the story of the annunciation impacts its theological import or message in relation to Mary. This will lead us to respond to the questions: How does the term "bondwoman" that Mary uses function theologically? What does it tell us about her person and her spirituality? We conclude our quest of recovery and demonstration by engaging the hermeneutic of transformative action for change. We will reflect on how the study of Mary's song, or *Magnificat*, can inspire a mysticism of resistance appropriate to our time and place. This will lead us to respond to the question: How can a study of Mary of Nazareth and the mysticism of resistance speak to us today—personally and corporately?

Significance of the Study

The problem of "the missing Bible." Why quest for glimpses into the historical Mary and the historical reality in which she lived? My response to this question is threefold. First, while we have a rich tradition of honoring the person of Mary and presenting her to the world, that tradition is often solely or primarily focused on Marian doctrines, dogmas, and devotions. Understandably, from the Reformation (sixteenth century) up to the Second Vatican Council (twentieth century) within Catholicism, the Bible was regarded as a peculiarly "Protestant book." Instead, Catholic theology stressed the sacraments and what was handed down in tradition. However, all doctrines, dogmas, and devotions to Mary must be grounded in and complemented by an understanding of the historical person Mary of Nazareth as portrayed in the New Testament. In the words of the Pontifical International Marian Academy, "Marian devotion . . . must have a deep biblical imprint."[7] We need to take hold anew of the Scriptures and in doing so find again the biblical Mary. Indeed, one

---

[7] The Pontifical International Marian Academy, *The Mother of the Lord: Memory, Presence, Hope* (Staten Island, NY: Alba House, 2007), 76.

of the hallmarks of Catholicism, especially since the modern period, is attentiveness to approaching theological questions with a historical consciousness. We take as a basic principle that God has in the past worked through human history and the history of the cosmos, continues to do so in the present, and promises to do so in the future. Therefore, the quest for the historical Mary is, in fact, a theological quest, a quest for the God of history who raises up prophets of resistance in history.

The problem of excesses in relation to Mary. Second, non-Catholics who observe the cult of Mary in various parts of the world perceive that Catholics have made Mary the fourth person of the Trinity—forming "a quaternity in God."[8] And while we might smugly dismiss their misunderstanding, we must also hear its challenge. The theologians of Vatican II recognized this issue and furnished us with a wise caution: the church "exhorts theologians and preachers of the divine word to abstain zealously both from all gross exaggerations as well as from petty narrow-mindedness in considering the singular dignity of the Mother of God."[9] Moreover, all believers are asked to "assiduously keep away from whatever, either by word or deed, could lead separated brethren or any other into error regarding the true doctrine of the Church."[10] To those who say that Mary appears to be more important than Christ in Catholic tradition, we take another basic principle of Vatican II, namely, that "the Church does not hesitate to profess this subordinate role of Mary's to Christ."[11] The ongoing study of Mary in the Scriptures is one of the ways in which the church redresses any excesses—theological and devotional—that may have emerged in relation to her. In the New Testament, the portrayal of Mary is always directly linked to the identity of her son, Jesus, as the Christ. Therefore, the quest for the historical Mary is ultimately a christological quest, a quest for the prophetic dimension of the Christ.

The problem of the conflation of the role of Mary and that of the Holy Spirit. Third and finally, the Holy Spirit has sometimes been regarded by

---

[8] John Van Den Hengel, "Miriam of Nazareth: Between Symbol and History," in *A Feminist Companion to Mariology*, ed. Amy-Jill Levine, with Maria Mayo Robbins (Cleveland: Pilgrim Press, 2005), 139.

[9] Second Vatican Council, Dogmatic Constitution on the Church (*Lumen Gentium*), 8:67. All quotations from the Vatican II Documents are from http://www.vatican.va /archive/hist_councils/ii_vatican_council.

[10] Ibid. See the Pontifical International Marian Academy, *The Mother of the Lord*, 68.

[11] *Lumen Gentium*, 8:62.

scholars outside the Roman Catholic tradition as the "poor relation" in the Catholic theology of the Trinity. The weaker promotion of the role of the Spirit in the West, relative to the Eastern Orthodox tradition, coupled with the great Roman Catholic regard for Mary, has led to the problem that sometimes the Spirit's functions become attributed to Mary.[12] John Van Den Hengel observes this conflation and writes, "One needs to look only at the Litany of Loreto to recognize in 'ark of the covenant, seat of wisdom, tower of David, advocate of sinners, consoler of the oppressed' titles that originally pertained to the Spirit (or the Church) rather than to Mary."[13] What Mary achieves for us is through the power of the selfsame Sophia-Spirit that hovered over her in Nazareth. Therefore, the quest for the historical Mary is a pneumatological or Spirit-oriented one, a quest for signs of the presence of the Holy Spirit in and through the agency of prophets in history.

The Phenomenon of Bondage in Galilee

Would bondmen and women have come from Nazareth in Mary's day? Nazareth was an isolated village nestled in the hills of southern Galilee with a population of approximately three hundred to four hundred people at the turn of the century CE. In the Gospel of John, Philip tells Nathanael, "We have found the one about whom Moses wrote in the law, and also the prophets, Jesus, son of Joseph, from Nazareth" (John 1:45). Recall Nathanael's pejorative response: "Can anything good come from Nazareth?" (John 1:46). Why was it that Nazareth was disregarded by Jews from elsewhere?

The Hebrew Scriptures never mention this village, nor does the famous first-century historian Josephus (ca. 37–100 CE), nor does the Talmud. Absence of mention suggests absence of importance. Because archaeologists have found nothing in their digs at Nazareth that "suggests wealth,"[14] we plausibly conclude that Mary and most of her fellow townsmen and women belonged to the lower of the two main classes,

---

[12] With regard to the West, Elizabeth Johnson notes the tendency of "forgetting the Spirit" and comments that, "for whatever reason, theology of the Spirit remained in an embryonic state." See Elizabeth A. Johnson, *She Who Is: The Mystery of God in Feminist Theological Discourse* (New York: Crossroad, 1993), 128.

[13] Van Den Hengel, "Miriam of Nazareth," 139. See also ibid., 129.

[14] Johnson, *Truly Our Sister*, 141.

the peasant class. The lower class constituted 90 percent of the population nationally, and they struggled to survive. The remaining 10 percent constituted the upper class, who lived mostly in the country's urban areas.

Bondage was a widespread phenomenon in Galilee and all of Israel before, during, and after Mary's lifetime and that of her son, Jesus (ca. 4 BCE–26 CE). At Traichae in Galilee, in 53 BCE, just decades before Mary was born, Peitholaus (n.d.), an aristocrat from Jerusalem (and second in command to the high priest Hyrcanus II [79–40 BCE]), rose up against Roman occupation but was defeated by Cassius Longinus (85–42 BCE). According to Josephus, Peitholaus was killed and "30,000 men were reputedly sold into slavery."[15] This degree of enslavement does not seem atypical in the Ancient Near East (ANE). Hebrew Bible scholar Muhammad A. Dandamayev notes that, for example,

> When the Babylonian captivity ended and the Jews returned to their homeland after the Persians had captured Mesopotamia, the adult composition of the repatriated people was as follows: out of 42,360 persons (30,000 of them men), the number of slaves and slave women came to 7,337, i.e., between one-fifth and one-sixth of the number of free people.[16]

In the first century BCE, Galilee was a predominantly rural province populated by communities of peasants (Hb., *am ha-'arets*). Historical-critical scholar Séan Freyne's research finds that "in all probability a good portion of Palestine, north and south, was in the hands of the king [Herod the Great, b. ca. 73 BCE] or his agents."[17] Moreover, as a result of triple taxation, "taxes and rents flowed relentlessly away from the rural producers to the storehouses of cities (especially Rome), private estates, and temples."[18] Taxes included 10 percent of the harvest to be given as tribute to the priests of the temple, to the Roman emperor, and to King

---

[15] Josephus Flavius, *Jewish Antiquities* 14:119f, and *Jewish War* 1:180, Loeb Classical Library, vols. 1 and 3, trans. H. St. J. Thakery, R. Marcus, and L. H. Fledman (London: Heinemann, 1925–65), cited in Séan Freyne, *Galilee: From Alexander the Great to Hadrian, 323 BCE to 135 CE: A Study of Second Temple Judaism* (Edinburg: T&T Clark, 2000), 60; see also 93n13.

[16] Muhammad A. Dandamayev, "Slavery: Old Testament," in *The Anchor Bible Dictionary*, 64.

[17] Freyne, *Galilee*, 156.

[18] Johnson, *Truly Our Sister*, 144; see also 144n21.

Herod, not counting what was demanded by the tax collectors.[19] Though free in theory, the peasants in this province were, in reality, caught up in a type of collective bondage: "These natives are 'bound to the soil' so that ownership of the land in question means ownership of its inhabitants and thus their position is best described as 'bondsmen.'"[20]

The impact of decades of collective bondage was the great impoverishment of families that was compounded for many by their subsequent defaulting on debts. It often resulted in one or more members being sold into bondage. Jewish law scholar Ronald L. Eisenberg notes that there were largely two ways in which a Hebrew male could be sold into slavery. A free man could choose to sell himself to escape from extreme poverty (cf. Lev 25:39), becoming a member of the household of another and earning his food and shelter through his labor. A thief might be sold by the court to raise funds to pay his victims (cf. Exod 21:2). In relation to females, until a girl reached puberty, "an impoverished father had the right to 'sell' her to a wealthy family as a bondwoman,"[21] where she would be "used primarily for household tasks requiring neither skill nor extensive supervision."[22] Removing a member from a household was intended not only to benefit the family of origin economically but to secure a future for the bonded female. Fathers sold their young daughters to the masters of upper-class homes in the designer-built cities of Herod the Great near Nazareth, such as Sepphoris.

Among first-century CE Jews, "an extremely frequent phenomenon was the selling of daughters as slaves by their fathers" (cf. Exod 21:7).[23] As a father may sell his daughter "only when he has no other means of subsistence left,"[24] it indicates the extent of impoverishment at this time. Moreover, by the time of the birth of Jesus (ca. 4 BCE), "the children of women in slavery had become the primary source of slaves."[25]

---

[19] Ibid., 148.

[20] Freyne, *Galilee*, 161; see also 161n29.

[21] Ronald L. Eisenberg, *The 613 Mitzvot: A Contemporary Guide to the Commandments of Judaism* (Rockville, MD: Schreiber, 2008), 135.

[22] Dandamayev, "Slavery: Old Testament," 65.

[23] E. Urbach, "The Laws Concerning Slavery as a Source for Social History of the Period of the Second Temple, the Mishna and the Talmud" (London: Papers of the Institute of Jewish Studies, 1964), 15-18, cited in Bartchy, "Slavery: New Testament," 67.

[24] Haim Hermann Cohn, "Slavery," in *Encyclopaedia Judaica*, ed. Michael Berenbaum and Fred Skolnik, vol. 18 (Detroit: MacMillan Reference USA, 2007), 669.

[25] Bartchy, "Slavery: New Testament," 67.

What did it mean to be a "bondwoman," then? Selling a young (i.e., premenses) daughter offered a way of guaranteeing her virginity.[26] Because "the owner of the slaves owned the bodies and not just the work of the persons in slavery [it] meant that slaves were regarded as sexually available without restriction."[27] Moreover, the initial sale of a young girl into bondage was to result in her marriage to the master or the master's son. Upon marriage, the bondwoman was "not to be treated any differently than a free woman" in the household (cf. Exod 21:10).[28] However, as the story of Sarah and Hagar indicates, likely this was observed more in the breach than in the occurrence (cf. Gen 16:4-6).

If a bondwoman enjoyed an improved domestic status upon marriage, she also carried great responsibilities, especially that of being biologically generative in bearing a son. Any sons born to her were to "inherit her *ketubah*, in addition to their share with their half-brothers in his [the master's] estate."[29] Any daughters born of a bondwoman should receive maintenance until the time came to be betrothed. If, however, a master refused to marry the bondwoman, or to have her marry his son, he must allow her father to redeem her in private for a minimal, token sum of money, which spared the loss of dignity for her and her family.[30] The master could not be permitted to ever forget that his own people were once slaves in Egypt (cf. Deut 24:18).

It is not surprising that the grief caused by the breakup and sometimes remaking of families as a result of bondage, coupled with the crippling burden of taxation, stretched to the limit the social fabric of the com-

---

[26] The attractiveness of girl slaves was centuries old: "As was characteristic of other ANE societies, captive men, boys and even women were often put to death and only girls were sent into slavery (Num 31:9-18). Thus, during one military campaign there were captured 67,500 head of sheep, 72,000 head of cattle, 61,000 asses, and 32,000 girls (Num 31:32-35)." See Dandamayev, "Slavery: Old Testament," 63.

[27] Bartchy, "Slavery: New Testament," 69. Susan Elliot writes: "Part of what it means to be a slave is to have no relational 'nexus,' to relate in one direction only: 'vertically' as an extension of the master." See Susan M. Elliot, "John 15:15—Not Slaves but Friends: Slavery and Friendship Imagery and the Clarification of the Disciples' Relationship to Jesus in the Johannine Farewell Discourse," *Proceedings: Eastern Great Lakes and Midwest Biblical Societies* 13 (1993): 39. See also Johnson, *Truly Our Sister*, 255.

[28] Eisenberg, *The 613 Mitzvot*, 287.

[29] Ibid., 288.

[30] See Cohn, "Slavery," 668.

munities of Galilee and beyond. It evoked resistance among the poor against the authors of their suffering. Freyne observes:

> Lack of access to sources of production can cause not just poverty, but an awareness that the condition "is not merely a matter of *poor* times but of *evil* times."[31] Such a breakthrough of consciousness in which the legitimacy of the existing authority is challenged and the right not to be oppressed asserted seems *a priori* at least, to be more likely among those who have absolutely nothing to lose.[32]

Such breakthroughs of consciousness did occur among the people and resulted in the raising up of dissenting voices, at times with some effect. One aspect that endeared King Herod to Rome, likely to the same degree that it generated hatred among the poor, was his ability to stop at nothing in order to raise extra tribute.[33] However, under pressure "from below,"[34] he granted a tax relief in 20 BCE and "remitted one third of the taxes of the people of his kingdom 'under the pretext of letting them recover from a period of lack of crops.'"[35] It marked a small but significant foreshadowing that the mighty elite would be "cast down from their thrones" (Luke 1:52), albeit sometimes in incremental steps. Such resistance to the oppression induced by the pain of bondage and poverty would explode again (37–34 BCE) upon the death of Herod, when Jesus was but an infant, and during the first Jewish revolt in 70 CE.[36]

So in our quest of recovery and demonstration, we can now ask, *was Mary ever a bondwoman, literally speaking?* The peasant class reflected a certain degree of stratification. While the majority of peasants worked the land, about 5 percent of them were artisans or craftspeople. Joseph, to whom Mary was betrothed, belonged to this class. Matthew records how people in Jesus' hometown dismissed him, asking rhetorically, "Is he not the carpenter's [*tekton*] son?" (Matt 13:55; cf. Mark 6:3).

[31] S. Mintz, "The Rural Proletariat and the Problem of Rural Proletarian Consciousness," *Journal of Peasant Studies* 1 (1974): 315, cited in Freyne, *Galilee*, 197.

[32] Freyne, *Galilee*, 197.

[33] Ibid., 64, 66, 191. See also Johnson, *Truly Our Sister*, 153.

[34] "Jewish resistance to Roman rule, then, was more than a people's generic resistance to a state oppression. In both religious-cultural and economic-political senses, the lordship of Caesar conflicted in a particularly poignant way with the traditional Jewish religious loyalties." See Johnson, *Truly Our Sister*, 166.

[35] Freyne, *Galilee*, 178, citing Josephus, *Jewish Antiquities* 15:365.

[36] Josephus, *Jewish War* 2:56, and *Jewish Antiquities* 17:27ff, cited in Freyne, *Galilee*, 123.

Artisans such as Joseph often had an even lower median income than the tenant peasants, as they could not guarantee continuous labor.[37] Thus, as is often still the case, "class marries class." Mary's betrothal to Joseph indicates that she was certainly on the lower side of the social divide, one step above the degraded class and two steps above the lowest class of all, the unclean.[38]

Was Mary ever sold into bondage, though? Could her father have sold her and later redeemed her from a disinterested owner before making a match with Joseph? Although a possible scenario, there is little evidence to support it. Therefore, when Mary speaks of being "a bondwoman of the Lord" (Luke 1:38) and being the Lord's "lowly bondwoman" (Luke 1:48), it is more plausible to conclude that she is speaking metaphorically. However, her metaphor derives from her social location, from the all too familiar and burdensome reality of the members of her degraded class, who were sold into bondage for their own families' survival or bought back in mock redemptions when their services were no longer required by their masters.

It was in an environment of hardship and suffering that Mary's spirituality and sensibilities were fashioned. In such a matrix, she would have learned compassion[39] and that the essence of the role of a bondwoman was the ability to listen, to listen often, and to listen deeply. A young girl listens to her lowly father arranging to sell her to a wealthy master; upon moving to the master's household, she must learn to listen to the master's instructions and those of his wife, children, sons, and chief bondwomen. In listening and observing, she must anticipate the needs, including those unspoken, of those around her and respond accordingly.

Mary, Bondwoman of the Lord

How does the term "bondwoman" that Mary uses function theologically? What does it tell us about her person and her spirituality? Luke's account of the annunciation (Luke 1:26-38) is fashioned according to the literary conventions used in narratives about the commissioning of a prophet and in birth announcements. From a study of the prophetic

---

[37] See Johnson, *Truly Our Sister*, 192.

[38] See ibid., 146.

[39] Gk., *sumpaschō*, lit. "suffer with." See 1 Cor 12:26: "If [one] part suffers, all the parts suffer with it; if one part is honored, all the parts share its joy" (cf. Rom 8:17).

call narratives of Moses, Jeremiah, Isaiah, Ezekiel, and Deutero-Isaiah, Gerard Meagher detects six constitutive elements that are common to these call narratives. They are as follows: (1) the sign, (2) the divine confrontation, (3) the introductory word, (4) the commission, (5) the objection, and (6) the reassurance. He sets them out in tabular form thus:[40]

		1	2	3	4	5	6
Moses	Ex 3:1-12	1-4a	4b-9	10	11	12a	12b
Jeremiah	Jr 1:4-10	4	5a	5b	6	7-8	9-10
Isaiah	Is 6:1-13	1-2	3-7	8-10	11a	11b-13	
Ezekiel	Ez 1:1–3:11	1:1-28	2:1-2	2:3-5	(2:6-8)	2:6-7	2:8–3:11
Dt-Isaiah	Is 40:1-11		1-2	3-6a	6b-7	8-11	
Luke[41]	Lk 1:26-36	26	27-30	31-33	34	35	36

By using the prophetic call form, Luke is indicating clearly that Mary "is engaged for a prophetic task, one in a long line of God-sent deliverers positioned at significant junctures in Israel's history."[42]

Elizabeth Johnson finds five elements common to the prophetic call narratives and the birth narratives of the Old Testament such as the birth of Samson (cf. Judg 13–16):

> First, an angel or some other form of messenger from heaven appears with a greeting. Next, the recipient reacts with fear or awe and is encouraged not to be afraid. Third, central to the story, the announcement itself declares God's intent and gives a glimpse of what the future outcome will be. Fourth, the recipient offers an objection: How so? Fifth, the story ends with a sign of divine power that reassures the recipient.[43]

[40] Gerard Meagher, "The Prophetic Call Narrative," *Irish Theological Quarterly* 39 (1972): 169.

[41] This row is added by this author. See also Meagher, "The Prophetic Call Narrative," 175.

[42] Johnson, *Truly Our Sister*, 250. See also Meagher, "The Prophetic Call Narrative," 177.

[43] Johnson, *Truly Our Sister*, 249; see also 248, 250.

Notably, Luke's account of the annunciation has an extra element:[44] Mary's *consent* to Gabriel's invitation and her self-declaration that she is "a bondwoman of the Lord" (Luke 1:38).[45] The added element provides a glimpse into Luke's theological agenda.

Luke's added element serves to portray Mary as a "mature woman, who had a mind and will of her own."[46] In the words of Cleo McNelly Kearns, Mary's freely offered and audible consent to the Lord "shows a decided aspect of negotiation."[47] She writes further:

> Although she is giving full consent, the text makes clear that she is not simply writing a blank check in response to this angel and his news of sudden, dangerous, and irregular conception. . . . The phrase "according to your word," with which Mary qualifies her fiat, invokes, then, a covenantal and socially authorized relationship. In countersigning that covenant, Mary indicates her understanding that the assurances she has been given here are not mere promises of the earthly and mortal propagation of the species, but of the propagation of eternal holiness, the child will not simply be a human infant but also the Son of God.[48]

Such audible negotiation contrasts with the silence and absence of any freedom to negotiate or dialogue that bondwomen ordinarily endured, when, from the outset, their lives were determined by the say-so of male authority figures—their fathers, masters, masters' sons, male offspring, and priests.[49] A bondwoman was not granted freedom during the yearlong

---

[44] "In none of the twenty-seven Hebrew commissionings [of a prophet] . . . and none of the nine other New Testament commissionings . . . are the commissioned ones depicted as assenting verbally and directly to their commission." See Jane Schaberg, *The Illegitimacy of Jesus: A Feminist Theological Interpretation of the Infancy Narratives* (New York: Crossroad, 1990), 131, cited in Johnson, *Truly Our Sister*, 254.

[45] *Kyriou* means literally "master" or "lord." Johnson and others have indicated that "the relationship signified by this phrase 'handmaid of the Lord' is thus enormously problematic in feminist and womanist theology." However, a study of the tradition of interpretation of this title for God by Mary is beyond the scope of this essay. See Johnson, *Truly Our Sister*, 254.

[46] Ibid., 256.

[47] Cleo McNelly Kearns, *The Virgin Mary, Monotheism, and Sacrifice* (Cambridge: Cambridge University Press, 2008), 149.

[48] Ibid., 149; see also 154.

[49] See Johnson, *Truly Our Sister*, 256, contra Meagher, who states that the "modification is slight." See Meagher, "The Prophetic Call Narrative," 177. Susan Elliot writes: "Part of

Sabbath rest on the seventh year, nor on the year of the great Jubilee, as the law required that she must become betrothed to the master or his son. Upon marriage, she must become part of her betrothed's household and bear her betrothed's offspring. Moreover, Luke's added element serves to portray something of the nature of God. We learn that "divine freedom does not override created freedom but waits upon our free response which, in a theology of grace, God has already made possible,"[50] thereby substantiating the dignity given us as human beings.

We get a further insight into Luke's theological agenda from the angel's greeting to Mary. Luke has Gabriel (Hb., lit. "strength of God") address her by her Hebrew name, Miriam. Here one might ask, what is in a name? Deirdre Good's interesting study "What Does It Mean to Call Mary Mariam?" finds that "50% of all Jewish women in the Second Temple and early Rabbinic periods in Judea and Galilee were called Mariamme (Miriam) or Salome."[51] However, Luke only uses the Hebrew version of the name for the mother of Jesus and calls the other Marys mentioned in the gospel by the Greek name Maria (cf. Mary Magdalene, 8:2; Martha's sister, Mary, 10:39, 42; Mary Magdalene and Mary the mother of James, 24:10).[52] This naming of Mary requires further attention.

---

what it means to be a slave is to have no relational 'nexus,' to relate in one direction only: 'vertically' as an extension of the master." ("John 15:15—Not Slaves but Friends," 39).

[50] Johnson, *Truly Our Sister*, 254. McNelly Kearns's comment is insightful: "Furthermore, as Robert Magliola has pointed out, to see Mary as having said a simple yes *tour de court* at this point, without any degree of inquiry or understanding or consciousness of the terms at stake, would open that *yes* to serious risk. Such acquiescence would be worse than a *no* because it would suggest implications of naïveté and seduction and present her as entering blithely and without question into a relationship that could result in illusion or idolatry. Mary's position as a servant and woman makes her sexually and socially vulnerable here, but it also makes her vulnerable at a deeper level to religious idolatry and to a failure to exercise what Catholic theology would call discernment of spirits, the testing of apparent revelation against tradition and compassionate humanity." See McNelly Kearns, *The Virgin Mary*, 150.

[51] Deirdre Good, "What Does It Mean to Call Mary Mariam?" in *A Feminist Companion to Mariology*, ed. Amy-Jill Levine with Maria Mayo Robbins (Cleveland: Pilgrim Press, 2005), 101.

[52] Ibid. Good also notes that "the specifically Lucan nomenclature 'Mariam' is also found in one other text reporting Jesus' birth, namely, the *Protoevangelium of James*." See ibid., 104.

By the use of the Hebrew name in the opening greeting of the annunciation narrative and the term "bondwoman" in Mary's response, which forms the closing element of the pericope, Luke evokes a parallelism between Miriam of Nazareth and her "eponymous ancestor"[53] Miriam of Egypt, prophet[54] and sister of Moses and Aaron. As well as a shared name, both women are linked by the reality of bondage.[55] The first Miriam knew the pain and suffering caused by the Hebrews' bondage at the hands of the powerful in Egypt. The second Miriam knew the pain and suffering caused by bondage of her villagers in Nazareth at the hands of the powerful ruling class. By framing the account of the annunciation with references that evoke the ancestor Miriam, Luke gives us a further insight into how the term "bondwoman" that Mary uses functions theologically. Thus, as well as the use of the prophetic call form, Luke's use of the Hebrew name for Mary is further evidence that he wishes to speak to the emergence of a new female prophet from Nazareth.

Susan Ackerman, in "Why Is Miriam Also among the Prophets? (And Is Zipporah among the Priests?)," draws our attention to an aspect of the timing of the prophetic vocation of Miriam of Egypt. Ackerman applies the insights of the French ethnographer and folklorist Arnold van Gennep, in his book *Rites de passage* (1909), to the narrative of the exodus in the Hebrew Bible. His research found that when ethnic groups encounter unprecedented challenges, they undergo three stages: (1) separation, (2) margin or *limen* (from the Latin meaning "threshold"), and (3) reincorporation or reaggregation.[56] Ackerman observes that all three stages can be traced in the account of the exodus journey. Moreover, she explains why Miriam fulfills a prophetic role in Exodus 15:20, a role that was in that epoch ordinarily the preserve of men:

> [It is] because the narrative locates her prophetic identity as belonging to a liminal period of anti-structure. In narrative depictions of

[53] Ibid., 102.

[54] Four other women bear the title "prophet" in the Hebrew Bible: Deborah (Judg 4:4), the unnamed wife of the prophet Isaiah (Isa 8:3), Hulda (2 Kgs 22:14; 2 Chr 34:22), and Noadiah (Neh 6:14). See Susan Ackerman, "Why Is Miriam Also among the Prophets? (And Is Zipporah among the Priests?)," *Journal of Biblical Literature* 121, no. 1 (2002): 49.

[55] We also note that, in all the times Luke mentions servants, the only instances in which he uses the term for female slave or a bondwoman are the two times he uses it in relation to Mary of Nazareth, or Miriam as he calls her (cf. Luke 1:38, 48).

[56] Ackerman, "Why Is Miriam Also among the Prophets?" 64.

liminality, the gender conventions that more usually restrict women from holding positions of religious leadership can be suspended. Therefore Miriam can be described as occupying a position as a prophetic functionary that, outside of liminal time and space, women are generally denied.[57]

By evoking the parallelism between Miriam of Egypt and Miriam of Nazareth, Luke is indicating that this female prophet of Nazareth also stands in a liminal space where old traditions and conventions are suspended to make way for the new. Moreover, she literally becomes a liminal space in which the uncontainable God is for a time contained. She becomes "the threshold" between what God has done in the past and the radically new deed that God promises to do in and through her for the community into the future (cf. Isa 43:19).

"Prophecy implies discernment,"[58] and discernment requires deep listening, dialogue, and critical evaluation. Johnson writes, "Mary's stance is of the utmost attentiveness and the creativity which flows from it, based on a listening life."[59] Mary's dialogue emerges from a desire to discern God's promise to her through the angel. Her ability to critically evaluate has her wonder how she might embark "on the task of partnering God in the work of redemption."[60] Clearly, from the way in which Luke tells the story of the annunciation we are oriented to understand that Mary's contribution to the work of redemption will be effected in huge part through her dual vocation as prophet and mother.

Luke records in the form of a canticle, the *Magnificat* (Luke 1:46-55), a further aspect of Mary's response to the invitation to embark on the task of partnering God. Through the use of this genre, he evokes another

[57] Ibid., 71.

[58] Good, "What Does It Mean to Call Mary Miriam?" 104. Mary's son would grow up to fulfill the role of redeemer (Hb., *goel*). The *goel* is one who intervenes on the part of a family when a member of the family has been sold into slavery. He is the one who buys back that enslaved person. For the portrayal of God as the divine *goel*, see Deutero-Isaiah 41:14; 43:14; 44:6, 24; 47:3; 48:17; 49:7, 26; 54:5, 8.

[59] McNelly Kearns writes: "Later tradition will often assert that the fecundating moment takes place through Mary's ear, rather than her womb. The former is an organ common to both genders and associated with the reception of speech and learning, while the latter is strictly maternal and associated with preverbal stages of development." See McNelly Kearns, *The Virgin Mary*, 149. See also Johnson, *Truly Our Sister*, 257n119.

[60] Johnson, *Truly Our Sister*, 256.

parallelism between her and her ancestral namesake, Miriam of Egypt (cf. Exod 15:1-5, 20-21), and indeed with other female singers of her tradition who "sang dangerous songs of salvation."[61]

That Luke has placed on Mary's lips the longest passage spoken by any female in the entire New Testament is worthy of attention.[62] It says something important about the message and the messenger. Second, Luke fashions the canticle or song in two parts; the first part is fashioned in the style of a psalm of praise, the genre of worship and temple liturgy (Luke 1:46-50), while the second part reflects the genre of a prophetic oracle (Luke 1:51-55), the genre of those whom God lifted up to poke at people's conscience about the injustices of their day.

The first part of the *Magnificat*, Mary's song of praise, interlocks with the account of the annunciation by means of Mary's repetition of her self-description as "a bondwoman of the Lord" (Luke 1:48). In this stanza, she accentuates the metaphor by calling herself "a *lowly* bond-woman" (cf. Gen 29:32). The term used for "lowliness" by Luke (Gk., *tapeinōsis*) was also used to describe the status of her female ancestral bondwoman Hagar when seeking refuge in the wilderness after having been cast out by her jealous mistress, Sarah, upon her pregnancy through her master, Abraham (see Gen 16:9, 11). A cognate term (Gk., *kakōsin*) is used in the book of Exodus "to describe the severe affliction from which God delivers the people (Exod 3:7)."[63] By interlocking narratives thus, Luke magnifies the reasons for praise. To the reasons the Hebrews already had for praising God, including God's care of Hagar and the Hebrew slaves in Egypt, Mary has added one more, one unlike any heretofore. The God who had in the past been intimately involved in the redemption of the Hebrew people has at the present time chosen her to be mother of the Son of God. This is reason for praise indeed!

Reflecting on the link between praise and mysticism, Sölle writes:

> Mysticism's basic idea about what language can do—and what it cannot do adequately but also cannot relinquish under any cir-cumstances—is oriented towards pure praise. While praise may have its reasons—and mingles with thanksgiving in the language

---

[61] Ibid., 263. See also Deborah, Judg 5:1–31; Hannah, 1 Sam 2:1–10; and Judith, Jdt 16:1–17.

[62] See Johnson, *Truly Our Sister*, 263.

[63] Ibid., 265.

of liturgy—in reality it always has the character of *sunder warumbe* ["without a why"].[64]

Mary praises God because God has raised her up without any regard for her earthly status as a lowly bondwoman. In this way God has substantiated her dignity. From a study of her prophecy (below), it becomes clear that she in turn envisions that others of lowly status too will be lifted up through the power of God and, in this way, will come to know the true source of their dignity and worth.

Mary's song of praise is modeled on the canticle of Hannah found in the First Book of Samuel (1 Sam 2:1-10). In this way Luke also interlocks the stories of these two women—Mary and Hannah. In the opening stanza of Hannah's song of praise, she declares her delight in God because he has ended her barrenness. The faith evidenced in the prayer and tears of this bondwoman found favor in God's sight. She who had begged God for a child, who had listened often and listened deeply in the temple for God's response, was in time blessed with a son whom she named Samson (1 Sam 1:9-18). Samson, in turn, became bonded spiritually to God. He became a Nazarite,[65] as Hannah had promised God he would, and was a blessing to the whole of Israel.

Spontaneously extolling God by means of a song of praise like that of Hannah indicates how steeped Mary was in her religious tradition. Moreover, by portraying her delight in and prophecy about her blessedness for all generations, a blessedness first affirmed by her cousin Elizabeth (Luke 1:42), Luke is presenting her in line with other great female ancestors who have partnered with God to deliver the people from suffering: "When Jael dispatches the enemy of the people [of Israel], the prophet Deborah utters, 'Most blessed be Jael among women' (Jdg 5:24). After Judith's spectacular defeat over the enemy general, Uzziah praises her, 'O daughter, you are blessed by the Most High God above all other women on the earth' (Jdt 13:18)."[66] While Leah justifiably cries out with joy at the news of her pregnancy, "What good fortune, because women will

[64] Sölle, *The Silent Cry*, 61.

[65] Nazarites were celibate male Jews, easily recognizable because of their long hair, who dedicated their lives to praising God in the temple. They occupied a special section of the temple in Jerusalem.

[66] Johnson, *Truly Our Sister*, 252.

call me fortunate!" (Gen 30:13), Mary prophesies that "all generations" will call her blessed.

The commendations of these women are similar, and the reasons given are also similar. However, the reason for the self-commendation by Mary is due to something radically greater. Mary of Nazareth delights in the blessedness to be afforded to her because it will come from those who recognize that she is the bearer of Mystery, God's very own Son (cf. Luke 1:32).

Thus, the term "bondwoman" functions theologically to tell us something of the nature of God, that the God of Mary and her ancestors is a lover of freedom. In her person, Mary has been lifted up by God. It is not surprising, then, that praise and blessing are hallmarks of her mystical journey of faith (cf. Rom 1:5).

Mary of Nazareth and the Mysticism of Resistance

How can a study of Mary of Nazareth and the mysticism of resistance speak to us today—personally and corporately? Just as a study of the genre of the prophetic call narrative was insightful in decoding Luke's portrayal of Mary as prophet of Nazareth in the annunciation story, so a study of wisdom genres in the Hebrew and Christian Bibles alerts us to the fact that when blessings are ascribed, they are often coupled with curses (cf. Deut 28:1-6, 15-19; 27:14-26). We find such a coupling reflected in Luke's Beatitudes (Luke 6:20–26).

In the first stanza of the *Magnificat*, Mary prophesies about her blessedness through all ages, a blessedness earned because of the Life she carries in pregnancy; in the second stanza, she prophesies the cursedness of those who, because of greed, diminish the life of others, a cursedness that is echoed later by her prophet Son:

> No! he cries to you who are rich, for you have received your
>   consolation!
> No! he cries to you who are filled now, for you will be hungry.
> No! he cries to you who laugh now, for you will grieve and weep.
> No! he cries to you when all speak well of you, for their ancestors
>   treated the false prophets the same way.

This prophet-mother-to-be, like the prophets of old, hurls indictments at those who stand in the way of the reign of God, and, in this way, teaches us about the potent relationship between mysticism and resistance as a force for good (cf. Luke 1:51–53):

No! she cries to the arrogant of mind and heart.
No! she cries to the corrupt rulers who sit upon their thrones.
No! she cries to the rich who forget their covenantal responsibilities
     to the poor.
No! No! No! This is resistance.

So often, and for so long, scholars have proclaimed the power of Mary's
yes, her *via positiva*. However, a study of Mary from the hermeneutic of
bondage helps us to recover the wisdom of the *via negativa*, a wisdom
given to us by Mary, who models that one of the fruits of discernment
and critical evaluation is to know when a negative response, no, is in the
service of the ultimate yes. Johnson writes: "Here her *fiat* finds its home
in her defiant resistance to the powers of evil. She takes on as her own
the divine no to what crushes the lowly, stands up fearlessly and sings out
that it will be overturned. No passivity here, but solidarity with divine
outrage over the degradation of life with the divine promise to repair
the world."[67]

However, this kind of resistance is not an end in itself. The mysticism
of resistance that Mary is caught up in holds in it a vision for transformation and change. She and many others would see and hear later how
her son, Jesus, challenged Simon the Pharisee not to presume that "the
woman in the city" could not be included in the circle of faith (Luke
7:36-50). In Jesus' parable about the hypocritical Pharisee who was cast
down from his proverbial theological throne and the humble tax collector
who was raised up, many more would celebrate God's power to reverse the
status quo (Luke 1:52; 18:9-14). The five thousand hungry persons would
experience how good it was to be filled with good things (Luke 9:10-17).

The kin(g)dom dynamic desired by this mother and Son is captured
well in the words of Sölle when she states that "mysticism and transformation are indissolubly interconnected."[68] Moreover, what we learn
from these related prophets is that the nature of the transformation is
liberating and often concrete. They knew only too well from their own
Sitz im Leben what such transformations could look like:

> Releasing slaves from legal bondage was a frequent and carefully
> regulated event under Jewish, Greek, and Roman laws, by which
> at one stroke the person in slavery ceased to be a property and

[67] Ibid., 271–72.
[68] Sölle, *The Silent Cry*, 89.

became a legal person. "In juristic terms, he was transformed from an object to a subject of rights, the most complete metamorphosis one can imagine" (Finley 1980:97). No matter how much authority the former owner, now patron (Gk *prostates*; Lat *patronus*), may have retained under Greek or Roman law, the freedman/woman was now unequivocally a human being.[69]

In sum, a study of Mary's oracle provides a window through which Luke allows us to view the positive power of how a negative response is articulated in the service of the fundamental yes, or Good News (Gk., *euangelion*). Such a response can effect a transformation for persons that is healing in body, mind, and spirit/soul and for communities that is healing socially, economically, and spiritually. Out of the joy of the *via positiva* and the often-felt pain of the *via negativa* arises the *via transformativa*—the way of "changing the world through compassion and justice."[70]

Conclusion

First, a study of the Lukan portrayal of Mary of Nazareth through the hermeneutic of bondage brings into relief the prophetic dimension of her spirituality and, in particular, the mysticism of resistance. A study of her *Sitz im Leben* using the hermeneutics of social location demonstrates that while we do not find evidence indicating that she was a bondwoman, literally speaking, we do find strong evidence indicating that her spirituality of deep listening and her compassion for the lowly would have been fashioned and honed from the pervasiveness of bondage in her locale. Mary would have absorbed the wisdom and skill of her female indentured kin, especially the practice of listening, that is, of listening often and listening deeply and of responding from that place of deep listening.

Second, a study of the account of the annunciation and the *Magnificat* using the hermeneutic of critical evaluation demonstrates that Luke portrays Mary as having a dual vocation, that of prophet and mother. The grace given to her by virtue of her prophetic vocation would account for her ability to dialogue and negotiate with the angel about God's proposal regarding her motherhood, an ability that bondwomen were ordinarily

[69] Bartchy, "Slavery: New Testament," 71.
[70] Sölle, *The Silent Cry*, 89.

denied. Poet Denise Levertov writes: "She was free / to accept or refuse; choice / integral to humanness."[71] Moreover, the fruit of Mary's tussle with and subsequent consent to the angel's proposal generates two further hallmarks of her mystical spirituality, namely, praise and blessing—that is, praise and blessing proclaimed by her and of her for the radical and unique substantiation by God of her intrinsic worth and potential and, by implication, that of all lowly persons.

Third, a study of the account of the second stanza of the *Magnificat* using the hermeneutic of transformative action for change demonstrates her practice of the mysticism of resistance. The redemption she envisions is as practical as it is powerful. She is clear that arrogance, corruption, and undistributed riches are to be resisted, and, by implication, the principles and practices related to humility, integrity, and the distribution of resources are to be embraced. This kind of resistance is not an end. Rather, it is oriented to transformation, its hallmark, which is resistance as the positive, proactive opposition to anything that reduces a human being.[72] The ultimate ground of such mysticism is the experience of oneness with God, source of all life, and it is an experience that must be sought after and nurtured faithfully, whatever the challenges.

Mary of Nazareth experienced such mystical oneness. We know this from her ability not only to say yes but also to say no when it was in the service of her ultimate yes. Almost two millennia later, the essence of her spirituality continues to reverberate in the experience of others among her Son's disciples. Theologian Dietrich Bonhoeffer (1906–45), writing during his time in prison, expresses it thus:

> What I mean is that God, the Eternal, wants to be loved with our whole heart, not to the detriment of earthly love or to diminish it, but as a sort of cantus firmus[73] to which the other voices of life resound in counterpoint. Where the cantus firmus is clear and distinct, a

[71] Denise Levertov, "Annunciation," in *A Door in the Hive* (New York: New Directions, 1989), 86.

[72] See note 5 above.

[73] Jill Carattini writes: "The *cantus firmus*, which means 'fixed song,' is a pre-existing melody that forms the basis of a polyphonic composition. Though the song introduces twists in pitch and style, counterpoint and refrain, the *cantus firmus* is the enduring melody not always in the forefront, but always playing somewhere within the composition." "The Cantus Firmus," *The BioLogos Forum* (blog), December 1, 2011, http://biologos .org/blog/the-cantus-firmus.

counterpoint can develop as mightily as it wants. The two are "undivided yet distinct," as the Definition of Chalcedon says, like the divine and human natures of Christ. Only this polyphony gives your life wholeness, and you know that no disaster can befall you as long as the cantus firmus continues. . . . Have confidence in the cantus firmus.[74]

---

[74] From a letter to his friend Eberhard Bethge dated May 20, 1944. See *Letters and Papers from Prison*, Dietrich Bonhoeffer Works, vol. 8 (Minneapolis: Fortress Press, 2010), 394–95.

Art as Witness to Sorrow

Käthe Kollwitz, Emmanuel Levinas, and Dorothee Sölle

Susie Paulik Babka, University of San Diego

The first time I saw Käthe Kollwitz's *Woman with Dead Child*, I was completely arrested. Somehow, Kollwitz had simultaneously captured both the deepest tenderness I feel when I hold my children and my worst nightmare. The work defines a particularly poignant aspect of motherhood: once an investment is made in a child's life, whether biological, emotional, or otherwise, a shadow of catastrophe follows all mothers, providing morbid glimpses into a possible future. Parents are forever changed after having made a commitment to a child; their identity is forever after bound to the child, waging a tenuous battle between the best and worst of all possible worlds.

Kollwitz's *Woman with Dead Child* is so powerful because any distinguishing features on the figure of the woman are absent: her face melts into the child's chest, and her muscular arms and legs wrap around the limp body in a futile attempt to provide a fortress against death. No longer recognizable as an individual, the self of the woman has been swallowed by the grief that ties her to the child, a grief that will forever after define her. The child's head is tilted away, his neck stiff, his eyes closed, his spirit already having slipped wordlessly away. Kollwitz gives us the finality of the relationship, leaving no ambiguity in what is portrayed. The child will never return to her, his eyes will never again open, his skin will never again be warm to the touch. Kollwitz completed this work in 1903, soon after her son, Hans, contracted diphtheria and came alarmingly close to death. She wrote to her closest friend, Emma Bonus-Jeep: "During this night an unforgettable cold chill caught and held me: it was the terrible realization that any second this young child's life may be cut off and the child gone forever. . . . It was the worst fear I have ever known."[1] This premonition shadowed her for years, although she couldn't articulate it until after her youngest son, Peter, was killed in action during World War I. In a letter to Hans, she wrote: "In all this, Peter and you are still present. Loving and having to give up what one loves most dearly, and having it still—always the same. How is it that for years, many years, the same theme was always being repeated in my work? The premonition of sacrifice. But one is enough—Hans—one is enough."[2] She used Peter as the model for the child in the etching when he was seven years old; she remembers, ten years after his death, the moment "I drew myself in the mirror while holding him in my arm. The pose was quite a strain, and I let out a groan. Then he said consolingly in his high little voice: 'Don't worry, Mother, it will be beautiful, too.'"[3]

In the depth of that moment—when a young boy saw the exertion of his mother and could in his patience understand the labor pains of creativity—is a trace of the divine, the beauty that passed through their intimacy and became art. Kollwitz translated a mother's perception into a scene with universal implications, affecting us over one hundred years later, in such a way that begs the theological question: How might the creative impulse of the human being, manifest in the arts, be understood as a passion for the absolute, a way of seeking to make meaning of the pain and beauty of the world with reference to the divine? More specifically, how might the arts provide an opportunity for *witness*, namely, the "prophetic witness," as the Jewish philosopher Emmanuel Levinas describes the exhortation to an infinite responsibility? Although her work rarely contains any explicitly "religious" symbolism, Käthe Kollwitz may be regarded as a religious artist because her work provides witness to the sorrow of loss and the violence of poverty, as well as to the intimacy of the mother-child relationship. Additionally, she was one of the few female artists of her time to document her entire life in self-portraiture, a visual

---

[1] Beate (Emma) Bonus-Jeep, *Sechzig Jahre Freundschaft mit Käthe Kollwitz* (Berlin: Karl Rauch Verlag, 1948), 100 (trans. mine).

[2] Käthe Kollwitz, *The Diary and Letters of Käthe Kollwitz*, ed. Hans Kollwitz, trans. Richard and Clara Winston (Evanston, IL: Northwestern University Press, 1988), 145.

[3] Ibid., 164. From a letter to Arthur Bonus, Easter 1924. Cf. Beate Bonus-Jeep, *Sechzig Jahre Freundschaft mit Käthe Kollwitz*.

diary that accompanied her written one, in which a spiritual journey toward death is portrayed in her characteristic visceral honesty. In her struggle to be authentic to the beauty she found even in the context of oppression, grief, and despair lies the search for "God," the symbol of a future beyond death and catastrophe, the symbol of a hope in defiant mothers bound together in a tower of strength.[4] The witness of Kollwitz to the fragile thread of hope that persists in sorrow is symbolized throughout her work, even in the weak lantern light a mother carries into a field strewn with bodies after battle, illuminating her search for loved ones.[5] If architecture is "frozen music," to paraphrase Wittgenstein, then Kollwitz's sketches, drawings, and sculpture are frozen prayers, fixed witnesses to what Emmanuel Levinas underscored as the responsibility of human beings for one another. In other words, Kollwitz shows us how art serves as a witness to the vulnerable and as such are prayers, simultaneously cries against injustice and calls to action.

Few have understood this dual sense of prayer as a recognition of, or witness to, injustice and a summons to action for change as well as Dorothee Sölle. Born in Cologne, Germany, in 1929, a generation after Kollwitz, ecumenical theologian Dorothee Sölle defines theology as that which "practices narrative and prayer. . . . Whatever is living testimony of the life humans live today cannot be summed up in statistics and press releases. Prayer and narrative shun that form of communication; its inherent frigidity would kill them."[6] Although requiring some aspects found in science, Sölle understands theology as "more akin to praxis, poetry, and art than to science. . . . The better theologians were more artist than scientist."[7] Theology experiments with different forms of communication, in her view, but the recognition that takes place in the act of witness serves in the postmodern era as a critical component in theology because "God is memory, and that is why to remember is to approach God. To forget, to repress, is a way of getting rid of God."[8] The act of

[4] See Kollwitz, *The Mothers*, 1921, pen and brush, Boston Museum of Fine Arts, which was also rendered as a woodcut and a bronze sculpture.

[5] See Kollwitz, *Schlachtfeld (Battlefield)*, plate from *The Peasants' War* series, 1907. Etching, drypoint, sandpaper, softground, and aquatint. Private collection.

[6] Dorothee Sölle, *Against the Wind: Memoir of a Radical Christian*, trans. Barbara and Martin Rumscheidt (Minneapolis: Fortress Press, 1999), 31.

[7] Ibid., 36.

[8] Ibid., 132.

witness can be an act of resistance to the tacit acceptance of suffering, especially of the oppressed, as somehow necessary and inevitable in the dominant narrative. Sölle made it her mission in her theological, political, and personal life to be a steadfast witness to the travesty of fascism, from the Nazi atrocities during her youth to today's corporate infiltration of government policy and the consequent exploitation of third-world labor and the environment.

Sölle's close friend, Beverly Wildung Harrison, argues that Sölle was ahead of her time in her interest to fuse witness to these failures with an interpretation of the Christian tradition "as memory of origin and awareness of human vocation, on the one hand, and as source of an indestructible dream of possibilities not yet realized, on the other."[9] In her effort to "put into practice the statement that faith and politics are inseparable"[10] such that "theological reflection without political conse-quences was tantamount to blasphemy,"[11] she and her future husband, Fulbert Steffensky, founded the *Politisches Nachtgebet*, or Political Evensong, movement in 1968, in response to the escalation of the Vietnam War; over one thousand attended the first gathering. The movement was ecu-menical, bringing Catholics and Protestants together, proceeding by way of information, meditation, and action; celebrating sacraments as well as discussing Scripture; and planning actions of protest and service.

Hence, Political Evensong's liturgical remembering of both the po-litical nature of Jesus' death and the disappeared, especially in Argentina, Chile, Uruguay, and El Salvador, became subversive action. Apprehen-sion without indictment, execution without trial, with no notification to relatives—Sölle recognized these disappearances as psychological as well as physical terrorism: to hear what happens to the tortured but to lack certainty about the outcome is too much for families of the disappeared to bear.[12] Organizing resistance for Sölle meant listening to the family's narrative and sharing pictures and stories of the disappeared when the government tries to erase their lives from history. Witness as a deliberate memory, the persistence of truth that the dominant narrative ignores,

---

[9] Beverly Wildung Harrison, "Dorothee Soelle as Pioneering Postmodernist," in *The Theology of Dorothee Soelle*, ed. Sarah K. Pinnock (Harrisburg, PA: Trinity Press Interna-tional, 2003), 241.

[10] Dorothee Sölle, *Against the Wind*, 37.

[11] Ibid., 38.

[12] See ibid., 114.

becomes a powerful and indispensable theological as well as political instrument in an age of terror and uncertainty. Art, as creative expression, fuels and sharpens this witness, giving theology new articulation and relevance.

The Quality of Witness in the Intersection of Theology and Art

Beverly Wildung Harrison notes that theology in the late twentieth century primarily addressed questions "of what if any justifications for theological discourse exist, whether there really are legitimate forms of theological utterance or any discursive substance to Christian theology."[13] She laments the failure of traditional dominant theology in both Catholic and Protestant academia to recognize the import of "creative and re-creative dimensions of spiritual knowing"[14] and argues that Dorothee Sölle was willing to surrender "noetically privileged claims to Truth" through both mysticism and political engagement.[15] Sölle also recognized the value of art—primarily music and poetry—for fostering human communication and locating collective memory: "Both theology and music make suffering less mute, isolated, animalistic, or petrified. They both move us to let the tears flow."[16] Rational language, the language of academic theology, often fails to "break the ice within us"; Sölle notes that when "words do not affect us in our depth, the soul freezes."[17]

By placing the artist and the theologian in dialogue, we gain a sense of what it will mean to develop a theological language of aesthetics in the postmodern era. Although Käthe Kollwitz was near death as Sölle grew into adulthood, both women share a similar intensity of commitment to the forgotten of this world, a desire to stand as a fortress against death. Sölle and Kollwitz cherish narrative, remembrance, image, attentiveness, and recognition in the creative expression that reveals the suffering of the oppressed. In this sense, motherhood, in the experience of both

---

[13] Beverly Wildung Harrison, "Dorothee Soelle as Pioneering Postmodernist," 240.

[14] Ibid., 239.

[15] Ibid., 245.

[16] Dorothee Sölle, *Against the Wind*, 55.

[17] Dorothee Sölle, "Breaking the Ice of the Soul," published in *Mutanfälle: Texte zum Umdenken* (Munich: Deutcher Taschenbuch Verlag, 1996), trans. Barbara and Martin Rumscheidt in *The Theology of Dorothee Soelle*, 32.

women, contributes to their recognition of what is precious in the world, of what must be preserved and protected. Furthermore, Kollwitz and Sölle's experience as women with demanding and successful careers as well as children is valuable to contemporary women because they are able to hone their personal talents while remaining committed to the decentering of the self in the care of others. The habit of caring for a dependent other enhances one's ability to recognize the plight of even a stranger and to act as a witness to that plight.[18]

Emmanuel Levinas provides a conceptual framework toward understanding the role of recognition and witness in the formulation of a new theological language. For him, the mother-child relationship signifies that the encounter with the Other entails an infinite responsibility.[19] The key idea here is that the encounter with the Other is a locus of encounter with God, and God always defies our best attempts to fashion God in

[18] On this point, Sölle writes: "I have often been asked about my personal reasons for engagement on behalf of Vietnam. . . . Again and again a picture came before my eyes. It was of a Vietnamese woman trying to escape the napalm by wading through a river. On her back she carried a child about five years of age. I thought, even if the child survives, the fear and damage can never be erased. Sometimes when I looked at my own children, who were then fifteen, fourteen, eleven and two years old, I remembered that child. I realized that 'motherliness' is indivisible; one cannot be a mother to two or three children and that's it. One cannot like a few children and forget about the children in a school who were incinerated in an American bombing raid because it was believed that there were Vietcong hiding there. . . . One cannot care for a few children while supporting a policy that incinerates so many children, that lets them starve or rot in camps" (*Against the Wind*, 45–46).

[19] Feminist responses to Levinas's work vary greatly. Simone de Beauvoir famously excoriated Levinas for portraying women as the prototypical other in his early work, *Time and the Other* and *Existence and Existents*. Bracha Lichtenberg-Ettinger, however, sees Levinas as recovering the place of the feminine in the history of Western philosophy. See *What Would Eurydice Say? Emmanuel Levinas in conversation with Bracha Lichtenberg-Ettinger (1991–1993)*, trans. J. Simas and C. Ducker (Paris: BLE Atelier, 1997). Luce Irigaray finds Levinas helpful in articulating the hegemony of the masculine in Western thought: "This domination of the philosophic logos stems in large part from its power to reduce all others to the economy of the Same . . . in its greatest generality perhaps of eradication of the difference between the sexes in systems that are self-representative of a 'masculine subject.'" Luce Irigaray, *This Sex Which Is Not One*, trans. Catherine Porter (Ithaca, NY: Cornell University Press, 1985), 74. Tina Chanter has written extensively on the value of Levinas for feminist philosophy. See *Time, Death, and the Feminine: Levinas with Heidegger* (Palo Alto, CA: Stanford University Press, 2001), and her edited volume, *Feminist Interpretations of Emmanuel Levinas* (University Park, PA: Pennsylvania University Press, 2001).

our image and is always infinitely beyond our desire for rational control. Relationships train us to expect that the other person will always surprise us, because the Other represents a "trace" of the divine defiance of comprehension. Nowhere, perhaps, is the tension between this defiance of comprehension and responsibility to the Other, a responsibility that marks me as the one who *recognizes* the very otherness of the Other precisely because this otherness eludes any attempt by me to control it, more prominent than in the mother-child relationship.

In this, men and women alike are enjoined to bear or carry the Other "like a maternal body"[20] without assimilation into "the same," or the self. This is understood by examining the primal relationship that takes place in the maternal body, the making space for the stranger, a xenophilia. The mother's body, in its rush to provide protection and nutrition to the newly forming person, symbolizes the way in which we are responsible for the Other before we even encounter the Other. That the body has a wisdom to act on behalf of the stranger before the self is conscious of the stranger further underscores Levinas's point that in this wisdom is a trace of the divine. My obligation to the Other is undertaken because something greater directs me toward it, not because my ego is naturally self-emptying or because becoming a mother makes women naturally virtuous. Maternity shows "that human possibility which consists in saying that the life of another human being is more important than my own, that the death of the Other is more important to me than my own death. . . . The value of the Other is imposed before mine is."[21]

Placing another's needs before my own is termed "substitution" by Levinas. More than sympathy or empathy, "substitution entails bringing comfort by associating ourselves with the essential weakness and finitude of the other; it is to bear his weight while sacrificing one's interestedness and complacency-in-being, which then turn into responsibility for the

[20] Emmanuel Levinas, *Otherwise than Being, or Beyond Essence*, trans. Alphonso Lingis (Pittsburgh, PA: Duquesne University Press, 2008), 67. For the most part, Levinas uses "Other" when speaking of radical alterity or the transcendent Other, and "other" as the more specific other person.

[21] Emmanuel Levinas and Bracha Lichtenberg-Ettinger, "What Would Eurydice Say? Emmanuel Levinas in Conversation with Bracha Lichtenberg-Ettinger," *Athena: Philosophical Studies* I (2006), in Lisa Baraitser, *Maternal Encounters: The Ethics of Interruption* (London: Routledge, 2009), 42.

other."[22] Substitution is an essential aspect of the maternal relationship; for many mothers, assuming the overwhelming vulnerability of the newborn child is experiencing responsibility for another in a way that exceeds the boundaries of what is reasonable or even possible. Substitution is for Levinas the blueprint of *human* ethical interaction, not merely the domain of biological mothers. He writes, "In proximity to the absolutely Other, the stranger whom I have 'neither conceived nor given birth to,' I already have in my arms, already bear, according to the Biblical formula, 'in my breast as the nurse bears the nursling' [Num 11:12]."[23]

Subjectivity, for Levinas, is experienced only through the encounter with the Other; the realization that I am utterly unable to fulfill the needs of another, but that I desire and attempt to fulfill them, promotes subjectivity. We become ourselves for the sake of the Other, to fulfill the needs of the Other. Assuming maternal identity in the care of a child means that maternal identity is forever bound to the child, even in death. Such ultimate statements concern the possibility of infinity in the finite. Alterity, the "otherness" of the Other, is experienced as an infinite responsibility, which can never be completed or reciprocated; Levinas believes that only through this encounter can we have access to "God." "God" is then approached indirectly, apophatically, unthematically, as the perseverance of the human person in the face of an unfathomable Other, resisting the more instinctual egoistic tendency: "When can a positive sense be given to this negative notion? When I am turned toward the other [person] and called not to leave him alone. It is a turning contrary to my perseverance in being. This is the circumstance in which God has spoken."[24]

Hence, "the Divine can only be manifested through my neighbor,"[25] and Levinas speaks approvingly of the claim that God is inscribed on the face of every other we encounter, but especially in the hungry, the naked, the sick, and the imprisoned (see Matt 25).[26] Thus, God's existence

---

[22] Emmanuel Levinas and Jill Robbins, *Is It Righteous to Be? Interviews with Emmanuel Levinas* (Palo Alto, CA: Stanford University Press, 2001), 228.

[23] Levinas, *Otherwise than Being*, 91.

[24] Ibid., 101.

[25] Emmanuel Levinas, "Jewish Thought Today," in *Difficult Liberty*, trans. Sean Hand (Baltimore, MD: Johns Hopkins University Press, 1990), 159.

[26] Emmanuel Levinas, "Judaism and Christianity," in *In the Time of the Nations*, trans. Michael B. Smith (Bloomington, IN: Indiana University Press, 1994), 161–62. Matt 25 echoes the exhortation of Jer 22:16, "He judged the course of the poor and needy; / then it was well. / Is not this to know me? / says the LORD" (NRSV).

is placed in the sacred history of human relationship, as the moment "through which God may pass."[27] God is both known and unknown, revealed and concealed, in the Other, in the stranger. "A God invisible means not only a God unimaginable, but a God accessible in justice. . . . The Other is the very locus of metaphysical truth, and is indispensable for my relation with God."[28]

Because Levinas sees the Other as the locus of the encounter with God, he understands ethics, the discipline that contemplates right action, to precede ontology as well as theology; the pain of the Other penetrates the heart of complacent lives, and God is encountered indirectly, negatively, as the pregnant space of this encounter. God is also accessible positively in (or as?) the desire to fulfill the needs of the Other, to alleviate pain, and to work for justice even when the self is threatened. Such self-displacement is a hallmark of becoming human and manifests the image of the transcendent God; when torn from egoistic security, we become a self-for-the-Other and bear witness to the Infinite.

"Witness," asserts Levinas, "is humility and admission; it is made before all theology; it is kerygma and prayer, glorification and recognition."[29] Prophetic witness is the linguistic exhortation that awakens us to infinite responsibility, which is a trace of the divine. The prophets of the Hebrew Bible proclaimed the divine will to strengthen the weak, heal the sick, and seek the lost in such a way as to require the listener's response. According to James Hatley, the prophet uses words that signify the other's vulnerability and settle into the audience's consciousness as a thematic structure that they are now free to interpret.[30] Even if the response is apathetic, and the audience returns to their comforts, the words of the prophets form a thematic structure that they cannot fully escape, presenting them with a ubiquitous opportunity for salvation, accessible as their own humanity. "Before putting itself at the service of life as an exchange of information through a linguistic system, saying is witness . . . a sign given to the other."[31] This sign requires the "Here I am" of Isaiah's call

---

[27] Emmanuel Levinas, in an interview with R. Kearney, in *Face to Face with Levinas*, ed. Richard Cohen (Albany, NY: SUNY Press, 1986), 18.

[28] Emmanuel Levinas, *Totality and Infinity*, 78.

[29] Levinas, *Otherwise than Being*, 149.

[30] See James Hatley, *Suffering Witness: The Quandary of Responsibility after the Irreparable* (Albany, NY: SUNY Press, 2000), 121.

[31] Levinas, *Otherwise than Being*, 150.

narrative (6:8). In the divine-human relationship, there can be no other response, as Levinas understands Isaiah 65:24 literally: "Before they call, I will answer; while they are still speaking, I will hear." He explains, "In approaching the other I am always late for the meeting. But this singular obedience to the order to go, without understanding the order, this obedience prior to all representation, . . . this responsibility prior to commitment, . . . [is] inspiration and prophecy, the passing itself of the Infinite."[32]

The question, then, is whether visual art assists in, or takes the role of, prophetic witness in the possibility of the displacement of the self; might visual art act as prophetic exhortation? Art, especially visual, was historically undervalued in the West as a medium for theology until the twentieth century, when Paul Tillich explored abstract art as a way to dislodge the propositional truth claims of language and representation that formed the matrix in which two world wars became "inevitable." As Theodor Adorno observes, "art may be the only remaining medium of truth in an age of incomprehensible terror and suffering."[33] Art, like suffering, is irrational and incomprehensible; art, like suffering, displaces accepted reality and demands a response of the witness.

However, Levinas cautions against using art to replace the encounter with the Other and against being seduced by the beauty of the image and, in being so moved, exonerating ourselves of responsibility for the Other. Adorno also recognized this danger, since visual art verges on turning the victims themselves "into works of art, tossed out to be gobbled up by the world that did them in. The so-called artistic rendering of the naked physical pain of those who were beaten up by rifle butts contains, however distantly, the possibility that pleasure may be squeezed from it."[34] The work of art survives the horror of the victim and "cannot complete its task" in attempting justice for the victim. We may stop before Picasso's *Guernica*, the canvas a startling 25.6 feet wide, and glance at the history of General Franco's complicity with Nazi bombers on that terrible day, and walk past it into the Madrid sunshine. The ones suffering in the work of art are condemned to always suffer: the anguished grimaces in their

[32] Ibid., 150.

[33] Theodor Adorno, *Aesthetic Theory*, trans. C. Lenhardt (London: Routledge and Kegan Paul, 1984), 27.

[34] Theodor Adorno, *Notes to Literature*, vol. 2, trans. Shierry Weber Nicholsen (New York: Columbia University Press, 1992), 88.

appeal heavenward are now nearly seventy-five years old, but has their suffering dispersed and become less trenchant with the fame and multiple replications of *Guernica?* We were reminded recently of the continuing power of *Guernica* when a reproduction that once hung in the United Nations building was covered with a blue drape during Colin Powell's press conference about going to war in Iraq in February 2003.[35] Discussing invasion and war was unseemly before a painting famous both for its dismembered bodies and for its acknowledgment of the function of the press in disseminating information about the tragedy.

Hence the paradox in art resembles the paradox in theology and the problem of suffering: each is incomprehensible, refers to what is beyond definition, contains claims to truth and purpose, and falls prey to the absurd. But all share the intersection between the apophatic (negative) and the kataphatic (positive); without the discipline of silence and emptiness, the kataphatic is impossible. Theology stands at the crossroads of both providing meaning and negating it; the experience of suffering, especially catastrophic suffering, similarly both negates meaning and gives an occasion for it. Finally, art, as Adorno claims, is ultimately "semblance in that, in the midst of meaninglessness, it is unable to escape the suggestion of meaning."[36]

Careful attention to the demands of this paradox, the dialectic between the affirmative and the negative, between semblance and illusion, between meaning and meaninglessness, is attention to, according to David Tracy, "the formerly forgotten, even repressed, others of the modern tradition—hysterics, the mad, mystics, dissenters, avant-garde artists."[37] Art, when it presents this paradox, engages gratitude for the unknown and openness to the radically new, which entails the possibility of self-emptying. Without the emptying of the self before the Other and the permission of the Other to determine the infinite responsibility by which the self may become a subject, there is for Levinas no glimpse of the transcendent God. Without this glimpse, perhaps, there can be no hope for a new world, one opposed to the status quo that celebrates

[35] See David Cohen, "Hidden Treasures: What's So Controversial about Picasso's *Guernica?*" Slate.com, February 6, 2003, http://www.slate.com/id/2078242.

[36] Theodor Adorno, *Aesthetic Theory*, trans. Robert Hullot-Kentor (New York: Continuum, 2004), 202.

[37] David Tracy, *On Naming the Present: God, Hermeneutics, and the Church* (Maryknoll, NY: Orbis Books, 1994), 16.

war and trivializes poverty. Important to this dialectic is the meaning
of witness in response to those who suffer catastrophe. Because of their
attention to the neglected and forgotten, Sölle and Kollwitz remind us
that all reliable discourse about God originates in solidarity with the
vulnerable, exemplified in *Woman with Dead Child*: Kollwitz gives us the
image of a featureless divine feminine who desperately positions herself
between life and death.

An Unusually Sensitive Child

Even the childhood of Käthe Ida Schmidt, born in 1867 in Königsberg, East Prussia, was marked by intense emotional awareness of the
sorrow of others. She was called a "nervous" child, as her sensitivity
often became anxiety and she was "tormented by frightful dreams" so
vivid that she recalled them in her old age. Her mother, Katharina, did
not provide Käthe the level of affection she craved. Of the seven born
to Katharina, three died young. Käthe's younger sister, Lise, provided
her most intimate familial bond: "We were so merged that we no longer
needed to speak in order to communicate with one another. We were an
inseparable pair."[38] When Käthe was nine, the youngest, Benjamin, died
of meningitis at a year old; her grandfather, Julius Rupp, an influential
pastor of the Free Congregation in Königsberg, pronounced the death
an example of life's impermanence. This, Käthe wrote in her diary, was
a "cruel and unloving" reaction.[39] The weight of these losses contributed
to Katharina's emotional distance and met with an equal and opposite
reaction in Käthe.

Her passions found expression in "a sentimental love for the sea,"
Schiller and Goethe, performing plays with Lise, and enduring schoolgirl
crushes. She "was always in love" and was drawn to women as well as
men, attractions she describes as "states of longing,"[40] the yearnings of
adolescence for recognition and mutuality. Impatient with school ("the

[38] Käthe Kollwitz, *The Diary and Letters of Käthe Kollwitz*, ed. Hans Kollwitz, trans.
Richard and Clara Winston (Evanston, IL: Northwestern University Press, 1988), 19.

[39] Ibid., 20. Käthe grew up with mixed feelings about Christianity because "a loving
God was never brought home to us. God is Spirit, I and the Father are one, such sayings
of Christ made us aware of God. But I did not love God—He was far too remote. I
venerated Him, but I loved Jesus" (from a letter written to Arthur Bonus, in ibid., 163).

[40] Ibid., 22–23.

teachers were completely mediocre"), she turned to art as an outlet. Käthe's formal training began at fourteen, when she took private lessons with the copper engraver Rudolf Mauer because Königsberg's Academy of Art did not accept women; ironically, these lessons prepared her for what would become her medium, the etching.

Artistic training channeled the intensity of her response to others into a heightened awareness of their plight, especially of the laborer. She was inclined toward social justice because her parents, although relatively affluent, were involved in socialist causes. They introduced their children to labor movements and political issues through drama and poetry, such as Thomas Hood's "The Song of the Shirt," which was published in an effort to expose the miserable conditions of factory labor. Concerned that Käthe be able to earn a living, Karl Schmidt encouraged her to focus on "genre paintings," which Käthe saw as "the worst trash"—banal compositions of finely dressed women primarily for decorative purposes. He arranged for her painting *After the Ball* to be sold with an additional commission for a related work. Käthe resisted such compromises to please the marketplace and noted that even in her teens, her socialist upbringing had already taken root in her art: "I was strongly attracted to the workman type—and this bent became even more marked later on."[41] At seventeen, she followed her older brother Konrad to Berlin and studied with Karl Stauffer-Bern at the Woman's School of Art.

In Berlin, her paintings of Russian and Slavic peasants and illustrations of Ferdinand Freiligrath's poems convinced Stauffer-Bern that Käthe's style would fare better as etchings, which led her to Max Klinger. Seeing Klinger's work at an exhibition in Berlin, Käthe fell in love again. Klinger's etchings and stark symbolism, later recognized as the first stirrings of surrealism, constructed a world of dream imagery in which nightmarish bats steal away the living. Klinger's admiration of the etching to deliver both realistic, even photographic, detail and austere emotion came from Francisco de Goya, whose *Disasters of War* series of 1810 formed a strong thread that pulled Kollwitz into her own unforgettable compositions.

[41] Ibid., 39. Mina and Arthur Klein add that Käthe "had no mercy for those willing to compromise or sell out their talents. In the drawings of one younger woman she easily detected the effects of doing commercial art jobs for a newspaper. 'One can see it,' she warned. 'If you don't stop, you will spoil your art work for all time.'" *Käthe Kollwitz: Life in Art* (New York: Schocken Books, 1975), 41.

Her early compositions in Munich tended to the provocative; one was based on Émile Zola's 1885 novel, *Germinal*. Zola's "naturalist" method had been to enter the mine shafts with coal miners in northern France and record their uprisings and the tragic results. Through Zola, Käthe discovered the thrill of authentic proximity to labor and life; barely into her twenties, she sketched the streets and taverns of the worker's districts on the banks of the Pregel River, where "knife stabbings were commonplace occurrences."[42]

She planned to depict several additional scenes from *Germinal*, until a few important milestones postponed the work: in 1891 she married Karl Kollwitz, a physician who practiced for the *Krankenkrasse*, the state-sponsored health program; in 1892 she gave birth to their son Hans, and in 1893 she attended a private performance of Gerhart Hauptmann's drama *Die Weber* (*The Weavers*). The play was banned previously by the Prussian police and was subjected to censorship across Germany. The authorities feared repercussions from certain scenes in which the corrupt and overfed employer Dreissiger blames starvation on the poor having too many children. Based on the experiences of his grandfather in the 1844 revolt of weavers in Silesia (today located mostly in Poland and the Czech Republic), *The Weavers* shows the downward spiral of workers faced with unemployment due to massive imports of machine-made cloth. Hauptmann, who later won the Nobel Prize in Literature, brought compassionate attention to the exploited of the Industrial Revolution while avoiding sentimentalism—*The Weavers* ends in chaos, without resolution.

After four years of work, Käthe presented her father the finished *Ein Weberaufstand* (*Weavers' Rebellion*) cycle in 1898, the year before he died—he was "overjoyed," she writes, pleased she held fast to her artistic vocation. The cycle consists of six works: *Poverty, Death, Council, March of the Weavers, Storming the Gate,* and *End*. In *Poverty*, a woman holds her head in her hands at the bed of her sick infant; tiny and nearly skeletal, the child is as swallowed by the bed as by circumstance. Crosshatches of etch marks become the walls and loom, sharp slivers of light in the weight of darkness. Elisabeth Prelinger points out that in this series, Kollwitz does not merely illustrate Hauptmann's play but rather intends a "self-sufficient visual text. . . . It was not a specific historical rebellion to which she was

---

[42] Käthe Kollwitz, *The Diary and Letters*, 41.

referring, but the general intolerable and unchanging state of these workers and the continual nature of their protest against such conditions."[43]

Beauty as Awareness of Dignity

Weavers' Rebellion made Kollwitz an object of praise and controversy;
she was prevented from receiving the Berlin Salon's gold medal by Kaiser
Wilhelm II, which gained her national attention as a "socialist artist." In
a 1901 speech, Wilhelm argued, "When art shows us only misery, and
shows it to us even uglier than misery is anyway, then art commits a sin
against the German people. . . . [It is] descending into the gutter."[44]
Ironically, the term "gutter art" was embraced by those of the Berlin Secession, an artists' association that promoted art with a social conscience
and interfered with state-driven exhibitions, directly challenging the
emperor's attempt to homogenize Prussian culture. Max Liebermann,
a leader of the Berlin Secession, was a Jewish artist who encouraged
Kollwitz to exhibit with them. After the controversy over *Weavers' Rebellion*,
she realized the power of art in the political sphere; however, her innate
sensitivity to the plight of the poor and her profound desire to affirm the
lives of the marginalized brought her to the conversation in the first place.

> My real motive for choosing my subjects almost exclusively from the
> life of workers was that only such subjects gave me in a simple and
> unqualified way what I felt to be beautiful. For me the Königsberg
> longshoremen had beauty; the Polish *jimkes* on their grain ships
> had beauty; the broad freedom of movement in the gestures of the
> common people had beauty. . . . [They] had a breadth to their
> lives. . . . Unsolved problems such as prostitution and unemploy-
> ment grieved and tormented me, and contributed to my feeling that
> I must keep on with my studies of the lower classes. And portraying
> them again and again opened a safety-valve for me; it made life
> bearable.[45]

Kollwitz's recognition of the exploited, the victims of the violence
of poverty and indifference, is beautiful because her art evokes response

[43] Elisabeth Prelinger, *Käthe Kollwitz* (New Haven, CT: Yale University Press, 1992), 30.
[44] Cited in Peter Paret, *The Berlin Secession: Modernism and Its Enemies in Imperial Germany*
(Cambridge, MA: Belnap/Harvard University Press, 1980), 27.
[45] Käthe Kollwitz, *The Diary and Letters*, 43.

and responsibility—not, perhaps, to the direct extent of Dreissiger in Hauptmann's play, but because, as Levinas points out, responsibility for the Other is not dependent upon guilt. Beauty for Kollwitz is the affirmation of dignity, because the dignity of the Other has been recognized and consequently is elevated to the level of something shared. Art takes this moment of recognition and fixes it, sears it into memory, so that it becomes a part of our worldview and forms the habitus of our existence. Such works can rightly be called prayers because they give expression in the search for "God"; this moment of intimacy and recognition of the other's dignity captures when God "enters into our minds," as Levinas describes it. We experience God when we experience the Other; ethics or, for Levinas, the responsibility we have for each other "is an optic"—"the very vision of God."[46] Sölle describes ethics in terms of an equation between resistance (the political) and mysticism (the internal), citing Levinas: "To know God means to know what has to be done"; "God does not live rigidly, self-sufficiently, and immobile in 'his' being. God's being, that which we can know of God, is the divine will to build up the reign, the kingdom of God."[47]

Viewing Kollwitz's *Storming the Gate* prompts us to wonder which side we take—am I standing outside of the ornate iron gate with the gathered workers, the women hunched over from exhaustion or from prying up cobblestones from the street to throw, or am I within the stone estate, yards away, behind the shadowy window? This gathering is not a mob, feral and agitated, but a group so weakened by hunger that they can barely raise their fists in defiance. The oppressed in this work are incapable of affecting the oppressor; the most violent action of the shadowy oppressor is indifference. Dorothee Sölle asks the same questions: "Only those who themselves are suffering will work for the abolition of conditions under which people are exposed to senseless, patently unnecessary suffering, such as hunger, oppression, or torture. Are we going to ally ourselves with them or are we going to remain on the other side of the barrier?"[48]

---

[46] Emmanuel Levinas, *Difficult Freedom: Essays on Judaism*, trans. Seán Hand (Baltimore, MD: Johns Hopkins University Press, 1990), 17.

[47] Dorothee Sölle, *The Silent Cry: Mysticism and Resistance*, trans. Barbara and Martin Rumscheidt (Minneapolis: Fortress Press, 2001), 199, citing Emmanuel Levinas, *Difficult Freedom*, 17.

[48] Dorothee Sölle, *Suffering*, trans. Everett R. Kalin (Philadelphia: Fortress Press, 1975), 2–3.

The violence of indifference to poverty drives much of Kollwitz's work. Her next series, *Bauernkrieg* (*The Peasants' War*), was based on the peasants' revolts of 1522–25, which occurred in the spirit of the revolt against the Catholic Church during the Reformation. The series forms a narrative sequence of seven works. In *Outbreak*, 1903, a peasant woman named "Black Anna" incites the revolt, releasing the energy and direction of the composition, as the peasants fuse together into a scythe of movement. Martha Kearns notes that while other artists show women defending themselves or their families, no artist had previously shown a woman leading a revolution.[49] Mina Klein writes that Käthe saw herself in Black Anna, since as a child she and her older brother Konrad pretended to be revolutionaries.[50] While we cannot anachronistically call Kollwitz a "feminist" artist, she was among the first to make a successful and public career as an artist, and her confidence in the potential of women to effect change is evident in *The Peasants' War*.[51] At the time of the series's completion, however, she had not yet realized the meaning of her career or her work.

On October 22, 1914, her son Peter was killed at the front in Dixmuiden, Flanders. Her diary reflections on his death reveal her devastation. While she often acknowledges conflict between her roles as artist and mother, her relationship with her children was integral to what she produced as an artist; at no time was this more evident to her than when she lost her son. Her grief became the energy to memorialize Peter and find a new purpose to her art. In her diary entry dated February 15, 1915, she writes:

> I do not want to die, even if Hans and Karl should die. I do not want to go until I have faithfully made the most of my talent. . . . This does not contradict the fact that I would have died—smilingly—for Peter, and for Hans too, were the choice offered me. . . . Peter was the seed for the planting which should not have been ground. He was the sowing. I am the bearer and the cultivator of a grain of

[49] Martha Kearns, *Käthe Kollwitz: Woman and Artist* (New York: Feminist Press at CUNY, 1993), 85.

[50] Mina Klein and Arthur Klein, *Käthe Kollwitz: Life in Art*, 43.

[51] Her fame as an artist meant the call to teach and mentor, and she writes, "I always find myself forced to defend the cause of a woman. . . . I can never really do that with conviction, since most of the work in question is mediocre," Käthe Kollwitz, *The Diary and Letters*, 67.

seed-corn. But since I am to be the cultivator, I want to serve faithfully. Since recognizing that, I am almost serene and much firmer
in spirit. It is not only that I am permitted to finish my work—I am
obliged to finish it. This seems to me to be the meaning of all the
gabble about culture. Culture arises only when the individual fulfills
his cycle of obligations. If everyone recognizes and fulfills his cycle
of obligations, genuineness emerges.[52]

She quotes Goethe and finds solace in his imagery of a seed that never
germinated. She returns to the line "seed for the planting which should
not be ground" multiple times in her writings and uses it to title one of
her last works. Importantly, she expresses a shift away from choosing
subject matter based simply on what moves her to an obligation not only
to preserving the memory of her son but to all grieving parents and the
fallen. This shift further shaped her pacifism.

Kollwitz supported Peter's voluntary enlistment when war was im-
manent; after Peter's death, she wrote an open letter published in *Vorwärts*,
a leftist newspaper, and the *Vossische Zeitung*, a daily newspaper in Berlin,
that children must not be sacrificed for war, that provincial boundaries
and German nationalism should not take priority over the children of
any nation, and that the only remaining honor for Germany in October
1918 was to accept defeat rather than allow more death.[53] Publishing such
a letter, given Kollwitz's prominence as an artist and the government's
attempt to repress all pacifist groups, was a courageous act. Kollwitz saw
no justification for the loss of a child, and although she agreed with many
socialist and communist political ideas, she refused to accept any party's
claims of sacrifice for a greater cause. After the war, she more deeply
explored the meaning of maternity in art, especially in two dichotomous
forms: the image of the mother as fortress, as protector of the child,[54]
and the image of a mother's despair from the failure to shield the child
from death or to provide her family enough bread.[55] Often, these images

[52] Ibid., 64.

[53] See ibid., 88–89. Armistice occurred one month later.

[54] See Käthe Kollwitz, *Mothers*, lithograph, 1919; *The Mothers*, woodcut, 1922; *The
Survivors*, lithograph, 1923; *Death Seizes a Woman*, charcoal drawing, 1923, and lithograph,
1934; *Protecting Mother*, limestone sculpture, 1936; *Tower of Mothers*, bronze, 1937, and *Seed
for the Planting Shall Not Be Ground*, lithograph, 1942.

[55] See Käthe Kollwitz, *Fallen*, lithograph, 1921; *Bread!* lithograph, 1924; *Infant Mortality*,
woodcut, 1925; *Homeless*, lithograph, 1926; *Pieta*, bronze, 1937.

assume bold expressionist strokes and heavy contrasts, but Kollwitz never quite joined the expressionist movement. Prelinger observes of Kollwitz's *Krieg (War)* series of the early 1920s, "Everything is expression, gesture, and iconic form. In keeping with her wish that the series should travel the world with its message, Kollwitz adopted a stark black and white language of signs that could be universally understood. They are unencumbered by particulars that would restrict them to a specific time or place."[56]

By 1921, Kollwitz understood that the revolutionary bent of *Weavers' Rebellion* no longer described the artist who had lost a child; the necessity of violence in revolution she now saw as a "deception," and her work as "evolutionary" rather than revolutionary.[57] Hence, her attitude toward what art can accomplish evolved toward the realization that honoring God means maintaining the connection with the people that avant-garde art loses, being "totally genuine and sincere . . . groping for precious truth."[58] She hoped that work on Peter's memorial would discipline her desire for unsentimental honesty, which she considered as prayer: "I am praying when I remember Peter. The need to kneel down and let him pour through, through me. Feel myself altogether one with him. It is a different love from the love in which one weeps and longs and grieves. When I love him in that way I do not pray. But when I feel him in the way which I want to make outwardly visible in my work, then I am praying."[59]

Conclusion

Dorothee Sölle and Käthe Kollwitz share an understanding of prayer as truth telling, or attentive commitment to the world, resistance against the sentimental self that attempts to conform relationship with the Other to the "same." Kollwitz views loving Peter after his death as moving beyond weeping over the self's loss to a love that preserves his alterity; cultivating the attentiveness to alterity is how Kollwitz saw herself, "the woman watching who feels everything . . . a woman in the background

[56] Elizabeth Prelinger, *Käthe Kollwitz*, 59. A footnote remarks that Kollwitz's woodcut *Sacrifice* was reproduced in China in 1931 and contributed to the renaissance of the Chinese woodcut (85n89).

[57] Kollwitz, *The Diary and Letters*, 100.

[58] Ibid., 69.

[59] Ibid., 64.

who sees the suffering of the world"[60]—but not a woman who is a mute witness, as her substantial artistic legacy attests. Kollwitz took this attentiveness to the Other and turned it into justice for the Other. Because she wanted her works to be accessible to as many as possible, she perhaps chose media that are easily reproduced, such as the lithograph, and employed the poster as an effective intersection between art and social justice.[61]

Sölle underscores the relationship between poetry and prayer in her writings, since language has been cheapened and corrupted by consumerism and the "bosses of this world." Poetry is discipline for the emptiness of language in its attempt to speak about God. Similarly, art that stands as a witness to the suffering of the weak and powerless serves to discipline our sight, as we in the media age have become apathetic to the constant parade of images. Sölle writes, "The idea that every human being can pray is for me an enormous affirmation of human creativity. . . . When people try to say with the utmost capacity for truthfulness what really concerns them, they offer prayer and are poets at the same time."[62] Venturing theological language in a postmodern world means the return of art and narrative, attentiveness and mysticism—the return to the human encounter as the primal locus for a trace of the divine.

This essay began by considering that the relationship between children and those committed to children walks a tightrope between joy and disaster, between life and death. The experience of commitment to a child has been little mined in academic theology. Considering the rich evidence of divine possibility in Käthe Kollwitz, Dorothee Sölle, and Emmanuel Levinas, we might interpret that the woman in *Woman with Dead Child* is a new image of God—featureless yet feminine, strong yet powerless to stop tragedy, champion of the vulnerable, yet hunched in grief.

[60] Ibid., 97.

[61] See, for example, Käthe Kollwitz, *Poster for the German Home Workers Exhibition*, lithograph, 1906, and another in 1925; *Vienna Is Dying! Save Its Children!* lithograph, 1920; *Never Again War*, lithograph, 1924.

[62] Sölle, *Against the Wind*, 153.

Trafficked

Sex Slavery and the Reign of God

Mary Doak, University of San Diego

"Trafficking" is a violent word, bringing to mind illicit behavior, dangerous gangs, and the shady world of illegal drugs and guns. To speak then of "human trafficking" is even more disturbing, as it introduces the repugnant idea of a criminal trade in human beings. For many, human trafficking is a phrase that also produces cognitive dissonance: we find it incredible that human beings in the twenty-first century could be objects of commerce along with guns and drugs, bought and sold by gangs often working in large, international networks. Of course, not all (or even most) human trafficking involves crossing international borders, as people are frequently trafficked domestically, or within national boundaries. "Human trafficking" is, after all, simply another term for modern slavery. Constituted by the use of force, fraud, or deception to harbor or transport people for compelled service in the sex industry or other unpaid labor, trafficking is much more common than is often realized.[1] Despite the widespread belief that slavery has been abolished, by current estimates more than twenty-seven million people are slaves: men, women, and children who live and work in brutal, dehumanizing conditions throughout the world, including in the United States and western Europe.[2]

---

[1] While trafficking studies often focus on the transportation of people for coerced labor, the US State Department clearly indicates that trafficking includes all forms of enslavement regardless of the movement of persons. See US Department of State, "What Is Trafficking in Persons?" section of the *Trafficking in Persons Report 2011*, available at http://www.state.gov/j/tip/rls/tiprpt/2011.

[2] Kevin Bales's 1999 estimate of twenty-seven million slaves worldwide is frequently cited. See the discussion of various slavery estimates by Siddharth Kara in his *Sex Trafficking: Inside*

This modern slavery is not only a horrendous human rights violation but also a theological provocation. What does it mean to proclaim the reign of God in a world of human trafficking? What does the prevalence of modern slavery demand of those communities that claim to be disciples of Jesus Christ, and what hope might those communities bring to the enslaved?

In his defense of liberation theology, Gustavo Gutiérrez argued that the central theological question amid the extreme poverty of Latin America was not how to make Christianity credible to the nonbeliever but how to make Christianity sensible to the nonperson. What, he asked, does it mean to preach God's love to people so brutally oppressed and so deeply suffering that they do not recognize themselves (and are not treated by others) as persons?[3] Given the reality of global slavery in the twenty-first century, Gutiérrez's challenge about the nonperson remains theologically significant and timely: How can the belief that love governs the universe be credible in a world where so many are treated not only as nonpersons but literally as objects to be bought and sold?

Concern with slavery is of course deeply rooted in the Jewish and Christian traditions, notwithstanding the fact that these traditions have accepted the validity of slavery as an institution until quite recently. The central Jewish story of the exodus describes God's powerful intervention to free the Hebrew people from slavery, and biblical law codes call readers to identify with the position of slaves by remembering this past history of enslavement (see Exod 20:2)—even while these codes legitimize certain forms of slavery. The ambiguous influence of the institution of slavery is also evident in the Second (Christian) Testament, as seen in the examples of slavery in Jesus' parables as well as in the epistolary teachings that Christian slaves must embrace their condition and obey their masters.[4] Perhaps most intriguing is the Christian use of the term "redemption," referring to the practice of buying the freedom of slaves, to describe the salvation available through Jesus Christ. If what Jesus brings to humanity is best described metaphorically as freedom from slavery, then we can

---

the Business of Modern Slavery (New York: Columbia University Press, 2009), especially 222. Kara's own estimate of more than twenty-eight million is slightly higher than that of Bales.

[3] Gustavo Gutiérrez, "The Task and Content of Liberation Theology," in *The Cambridge Companion to Liberation Theology* (Cambridge: Cambridge University Press, 1999).

[4] See especially the discussion in Jennifer A. Glancy, *Slavery as Moral Problem: In the Early Church and Today* (Minneapolis: Fortress Press, 2011), 54–61.

scarcely avoid the question of what this redemption offers to the young women and girls enslaved and abused in today's sex industry.

Slavery also intersects with Christian claims about the significance of the human body. Slavery is experienced deeply in the bodies of the enslaved, and, as M. Shawn Copeland has recently argued, bodies matter theologically.[5] Christian beliefs and practices affirm that the human body genuinely participates in the self. As a good creation of a good God, the body is neither insignificant nor an impediment; rather, as proclaimed in the doctrine of the resurrection of the body, the human body plays an integral part in the promised eternal redemption of the person. God further dignified the human body by becoming incarnate, bodily enfleshed as Jesus of Nazareth, according to Christian belief. Slavery instrumentalizes people as bodies subject to violence, physical abuse, mutilation, and even destruction for monetary gain. Thus, slavery attacks not only the freedom of the personal will but also the sacrality of the human body created as an integral part of the person by a good and loving God.

Slavery in all of its forms represents an outrage to the dignity of the human person. Yet there are considerable differences in the types and experiences of contemporary slavery, including various horrific forms of coerced labor, forced begging, and even the harvesting of children's organs. Given the complexity of and differentiation within slavery today, a discussion of the entirety of modern slavery is beyond the scope of this article. This essay will focus particularly on sex trafficking, a widespread and growing form of the increasingly lucrative slave trade, even though sex trafficking is often not recognized as slavery due to common assumptions about prostituted women and children. Sex trafficking is also distinct in that sex slaves are predominantly female, isolated from family and community, stigmatized even after release or escape, and exposed to diseases that often cause an early death.[6] Insofar as the task of theologians includes assisting the church to recognize and to respond adequately to the demands of living Christian faith in every time and place, the prevalence of sex slavery throughout the world presents a theological as well

[5] M. Shawn Copeland, *Enfleshing Freedom: Body, Race, and Being* (Minneapolis: Fortress Press, 2010).

[6] See, for example, the comparison of the situations of Indian brothel slaves with the condition of slaves in brick kilns in Nicholas D. Kristof and Sheryl WuDunn, *Half the Sky: Turning Oppression into Opportunity for Women Worldwide* (New York: Alfred A. Knopf, 2009), 12.

as a practical challenge. Theologians bear the responsibility of assisting the Christian community in determining what the promise of the reign of God offers now to those whose bodies are subjected daily to brutal violation and torture as objects of commerce.

The Global Market in Female Bodies

The common assumption in society and often in criminal law is that prostituted women and even children freely choose to sell their bodies because they are tempted by the money or enjoy multiple sexual encounters (perhaps ten to twelve or more each night!) with strangers. After all, the scantily clad young women and (too often) girls brazenly soliciting passersby appear quite willing and indeed anxious to entice customers. Consider also the enduring themes of "fallen women" and "penitent prostitutes" throughout Western culture, especially in the Christian tradition: guilt is ascribed to the woman selling sex for money without consideration of whether she had any real choice in the matter.[7]

Recent studies of human trafficking and its relation to commercial sexual exploitation have clarified that prostitution is often in reality a form of enslavement in which prostituted women and children do not retain the wages paid for their services. Sold by others, they are forced (as all slaves are) to accept their condition by violence and by the threat of violence. Beaten and mutilated, isolated and closely monitored (if not literally locked up) until they accept their role in the sex industry, prostituted women and children learn to act willing and eager to sell sexual services in order to make the quotas imposed on them.[8]

Although the actual number of people forcibly prostituted worldwide is uncertain, research into human trafficking reveals a thriving global market for young women and girls. The United States Department of State estimates that eight hundred thousand people (over 80 percent of

---

[7] For an interesting discussion of cultural fascination with the penitent prostitute, see especially Jane Schaberg, "Fast Forwarding to the Magdalene," *Semeia* 74 (1996): 33–45.

[8] In addition to the many case studies reported by Siddharth Kara in his *Sex Trafficking*, see also the descriptions of coercion in the sex industry throughout Kristof and WuDunn, *Half the Sky*. For discussions of coerced prostitution in the United States, see especially Rachel Lloyd, *Girls Like Us* (New York: HarperCollins, 2011), and Julian Sher, *Somebody's Daughter: The Hidden Story of American's Prostituted Children and the Battle to Save Them* (Chicago: Chicago Review Press, 2011).

whom are women or children) are trafficked across international borders each year for the sex industry or for coerced labor. Domestic trafficking is even more widespread, as the US State Department acknowledges that "millions more" are trafficked within national boundaries.[9] Globalized economic forces are impoverishing many communities while enriching others, and the relatively low cost of transportation facilitates moving girls and young women to wherever the market demand for their bodies is greatest, within or across national boundaries. Given these realities of contemporary life, it should not be so surprising that, as Nicholas Kristof and Sheryl WuDunn observe, "far more women and girls are shipped into brothels each year in the early twenty-first century than African slaves were shipped into slave plantations each year in the eighteenth and nineteenth centuries."[10]

The horrific details of enormous brothels buying young girls from their families in Kolkata, or the torturing of girls who resist sex work in Cambodia, should not lead one to assume that trafficking for sexual exploitation is primarily a third-world problem. Girls and young women are also trafficked into as well as within the United States and Europe. Criminal gangs in the US, for example, are reportedly turning to prostitution because it is more profitable than selling drugs; after all, female bodies can be sold repeatedly and at relatively little risk to the trafficker.[11] Given that a prostituted woman or girl in the United States may well earn $1,000 per night while being forced to live on $20 per day, there is ample economic motivation for this modern-day slavery and for the tenacious violence with which young women and girls are controlled by their pimps.[12]

Another significant factor in the success of trafficking is the young age of many of its victims. People who work with prostituted females in the United States report that these women and girls were often first prostituted as children twelve to fourteen years old, an age at which they are more easily manipulated and controlled.[13] Consider the cases reported

[9] US Department of State, *Trafficking in Persons Report 2011*.

[10] Kristof and WuDunn, *Half the Sky*, 11.

[11] See "In Oakland, Redefining Sex Trade Workers as Abuse Victims," *New York Times*, May 23, 2011, available at http://www.nytimes.com/2011/05/24/us/24oakland.html. See also Sher, *Somebody's Daughter*, esp. 48.

[12] See Sher, *Somebody's Daughter*, esp. 78–79.

[13] According to Rachel Lloyd, "The estimated median age of entry into the commercial sex industry [is] between twelve and fourteen years old" (Lloyd, *Girls*, 12).

by the Reverend Mary Moreno Richardson, an Episcopalian chaplain to victims of human trafficking in San Diego, California.

> In late 2005, a fifteen-year-old African-American girl came to a neighborhood teen shelter terrified by a local street gang. She reported that gang members lured her into a home in San Diego, where they laid out assault rifles and handguns on a kitchen table. They threatened to kill her grandmother and little sister if she refused to leave with them to be prostituted in Las Vegas. . . .
>
> After being rescued, one fourteen-year-old girl was incarcerated for prostitution—our justice system often overlooks the reality of trafficking and criminalizes the victim. She stated she had been kidnapped off the street on her way to school at the age of nine in Oceanside. She was trafficked from San Diego to Las Vegas to Los Angeles.[14]

Or consider the following description by Rachel Lloyd, founder of GEMS, a New York agency that provides services for over three hundred girls each year trafficked in and around New York City.

> She likes swimming, SpongeBob, Mexican food, writing poetry, getting her nails painted. . . . This Christmas, she really wants an iPod but would settle for some sweatsuits, preferably pink. Sometimes she's petulant—pouting and sullen—but mostly she's open and eager to be loved. . . . She's much like any other eleven-year-old girl in America, except for one critical difference. Over the last year of her life, she's been trafficked up and down the East Coast by a twenty-nine-year-old pimp and sold nightly on Craigslist to adult men who ignore her dimples and her baby fat and purchase her for sex.[15]

These cases involving the coercion of very young girls, while shocking, are unfortunately not as rare as we would like to believe. Young girls are abducted, sold by their families, tricked by false promises, or otherwise forced into the sex industry around the world. Even if the majority of commercially sexually exploited women and children in the United States are not kidnapped but are more commonly enticed by a pimp

---

[14] Rev. Canon Mary Moreno Richardson, "Human Trafficking: Victims Don't Always Fit Stereotypes," at http://www.diocal.org/index.php?option=com_content&task=view&id=375&Itemid=215.

[15] Lloyd, *Girls*, 1. See ibid, 16, for the number of trafficked girls per year at GEMS.

feigning love and offering a home, the coercion is no less real for these young girls who are constantly monitored, who learn to expect violent beatings if they fail to behave and to earn as demanded, and who are threatened with worse violence if they try to leave. One study of victims of the sex industry in Portland, Oregon, found that 84 percent had been violently assaulted (many to the point of requiring hospitalization), 53 percent had experienced sexual assault and torture, and 27 percent had been mutilated.[16] Other studies have found that prostituted women and children experience posttraumatic stress disorder at levels equivalent to combat veterans and survivors of state-sponsored torture.[17]

Living with violence and threats of violence, faced with social rejection for having been involved in prostitution, and often lacking a stable home to return to, these girls and young women are often as imprisoned in the sex industry in the United States as those who are literally locked in cages in Thailand or kept under guard in Malaysia. While there may be some women who more or less freely choose to enter and to leave the sex industry, Kathleen Mitchell, an activist working with prostituted girls in Arizona, has rightly noted that "in order to have a choice, you need to have two viable options to choose from."[18] However much some may affirm that they chose to work in the sex industry, most of these girls did not have and did not perceive themselves as having any other real option. Furthermore, girls who begin sex work before they are legally allowed to drive a car (or to consent to sex!) do not have sufficient age, maturity, or awareness of the reality of prostitution to be capable of making a responsible choice in this matter. All prostituted minors are thus appropriately recognized in US law as victims of sex trafficking.

The very serious obstacles to ensuring that young girls and women around the world have real alternatives to sex work should not lead to the assumption that prostitution is a stable and persistent reality about which nothing can be done. Siddharth Kara's recently published analysis

---

[16] These statistics are based on a study conducted by the Council for Prostitution Alternative in Portland, Oregon, as cited by Janice G. Roberts, "Health Effects of Prostitution," in Donna M. Hughes and Claire M. Roche, eds., *Making the Harm Visible: Global Sexual Exploitation of Women and Girls Speaking Out and Providing Services*, available online at http://www.uri.edu/artsci/wms/hughes/mhvtoc.htm.

[17] As cited by Melissa Farley, "Prostitution: Factsheet on Human Rights Violations," at http://www.prostitutionresearch.com/faq/000008.html.

[18] As quoted by Sher, *Somebody's Daughter*, 53.

of the supply and demand cycle of contemporary sex slavery is particularly enlightening about the economic dynamics that fuel the modern trade in sex slaves. As the world's economy has become more thoroughly interconnected, many local economies have been destabilized, resulting in a rapid increase in poverty and desperation in some countries (especially in former Soviet nations such as Moldova). The poor and the daughters of the poor are particularly vulnerable to entrapment in sex slavery, lured by the promise that they will be transported to desperately needed jobs in service industries among the distant wealthy when in reality they are sold to brothel owners. As Kara's analysis demonstrates, this channeling of slaves into the sex industry lowers the cost of buying sex acts while ensuring ample profit for slave owners and traders (at nearly a 70 percent margin of profit, according to Kara's research). As prices for sex acts decrease due to the use of slaves, more men are inclined to purchase sex and to do so more frequently. Buying sex thus becomes a more common practice, fueling the spiral that increases the demand for sex slaves around the world (including in major cities such as Rome, a common destination city for sex slaves from Nigeria and eastern Europe).[19]

Kara's economic studies of sex slavery have led him to join those who conclude that sex trafficking can be successfully combated by raising the costs to the madams and pimps (and thus cutting into their profits) through higher prosecution rates and stiffer penalties for sex traffickers.[20] Increasing the costs associated with sex trafficking causes prices for sex acts to rise and thus lowers the demand, eroding the profit margin to the point that sex trafficking becomes unprofitable. As Kristof and WuDunn document, brothels have gone out of business and sex slaves have been released when government action and the resultant legal problems made prostituting women and children in an area unprofitable.[21] Sex slavery today is not simply an inevitable facet of human life but is rather a fluid and opportunistic practice integrally related to contemporary socioeconomic and political structures.

[19] Kara, *Sex Trafficking*, esp. 16–37, 83–94.

[20] Ibid, esp. 212–16. For a similar conclusion, see Kristof and WuDunn, *Half the Sky*, 27–34.

[21] See especially the Cambodian case discussed by Kristof and WuDunn in *Half the Sky*, 40.

Sexual Slavery and the Body of Christ

Reading the gospels with awareness of modern sex slavery, we can scarcely fail to notice Jesus' countercultural interactions with prostituted women and others who were devalued or discounted in his time. The gospels portray Jesus as unconcerned with abiding by the norms that determined prestige in his day; instead, he scandalized people through his intentional contact with those such as prostituted women who were rejected by "respectable" society. At the same time, he taught parables that overturned accepted ideas about whom God favors or rejects. As described in the gospels, Jesus located God's reign first among the socially outcast, the powerless, and the morally disreputable, and then he invited the socially important, the powerful, and the morally virtuous to join them.[22]

Yet the stories of Jesus' radical behavior have become so familiar that their socially destabilizing power has been domesticated. Religious leaders, especially those with societal prestige, were not then and are not now expected publicly to treat sex workers with the same dignity that is accorded the respected members of society. Despite Jesus' witness, wealthy women and women from the streets are seldom received equally and without distinction in churches; priests or ministers who dine as readily with sex workers as with church elders are neither common nor likely to be celebrated for their faithfulness to Jesus' example.[23]

Imagine the difference it would make for prostituted women and children today if Christians, like Jesus, valued most those that society values least. After all, women and girls in the sex industry, whether they choose or are coerced to be sex workers, are among those least valued in many societies (including in the United States). As Lloyd observed while working with women in Rikers Island prison in New York, "To have been on the street, to be in 'the life,' as the girls called it, was to be on the lowest

[22] Jesus' disregard of social boundaries and commitment to the excluded is noted by theologians, biblical scholars, and general readers of the New Testament. See, for example, Virgilio Elizondo, *Galilean Journey: The Mexican-American Promise*, rev. and expanded version (Maryknoll, NY: Orbis Books, 2000), esp. 58–66; John Dominic Crossan, *Jesus: A Revolutionary Biography* (New York: HarperCollins, 1995); and Garry Wills, *What Jesus Meant* (New York: Viking, 2006).

[23] See, for example, the reaction to dining with sex workers as described by Virgilio Elizondo in his *A God of Incredible Surprises: Jesus of Galilee* (Lanham, MD: Rowman and Littlefield), 85–86.

rung. It didn't matter how old they were; they were shunned and mocked as dirty, nasty, hos, whores, hookers, dumb bitches."[24] Or course, it is not only the incarcerated who devalue sex workers. Consider the reported practice of labeling US police reports of crimes against prostitutes or drug dealers "NHI," an abbreviation for "no humans involved."[25] Today as in Jesus' time, prostituted women and girls are discounted even to the point of having their humanity questioned. Christian faith in the God revealed in Jesus of Nazareth surely requires Christians to cooperate with the work of the Spirit to bring new life and recognized dignity to the despised and devalued victims of the modern sex trade.

In addition to the radical challenge of Jesus' ministry among the rejected and the prostituted, there is yet a deeper—and disturbing—demand suggested in the kenotic Christology cited by Paul in Philippians 2:5-8.

> Let the same mind be in you that you have in Christ Jesus,
> who, though he was in the form of God,
>   did not regard equality with God
>   as something to be exploited,
> but emptied himself,
>   taking the form of a slave,
>   being born in human likeness.
> And being found in human form,
>   he humbled himself
>   and became obedient to the point of death—
>   even death on a cross.[26]

Translations of *morphēn doulou labōn* as the "form of a servant" rather than more accurately as "the form of a slave" have diluted the disruptive power of this passage, as Jennifer Glancy has recently argued.[27] Paul here instructed Christians not merely to help each other a bit more but rather to emulate Jesus' example of voluntarily relinquishing the highest status (equality with God) to join those of lowest status, even to the point of accepting his end as a stripped, tortured, pierced, and broken body exhibited for public gaze.

---

[24] Lloyd, *Girls*, 23.

[25] Ibid., 147.

[26] As translated by Glancy in her *Slavery as Moral Problem*, 25–26.

[27] Jennifer A. Glancy, *Slavery in Early Christianity* (Minneapolis: Fortress Press, 2006), 100–101.

To grasp what New Testament statements about becoming a slave might have communicated to the audience of the first century, it is important to recognize that slavery was a brutal institution in the Greco-Roman world of that time no less than in the antebellum American slave system or in slavery today. To be a slave then (as now) meant that one was deprived of the right to bodily integrity, as Glancy's work has clarified; the horror and shame of Greco-Roman slavery was premised on the fact that slaves by definition could not defend the boundaries of their bodies. As owned bodies, first-century slaves were not only regularly beaten to ensure compliance but were also considered sexually available to their owners or to whomever their owners decided to make them available.[28] As Glancy has further noted, in the first century prostitutes were often slaves who were prostituted to make money for their owners.[29] When the reality of first-century slavery is not sugarcoated as a form of genteel servanthood, the letter to the Philippians is quite troubling: Jesus is described not merely as concerned for the oppressed and rejected but as having become himself one of the most powerless, like a slave without the right to bodily integrity and subject to whatever abuse those with power chose to inflict on his body. Moreover, those who would follow Jesus are instructed similarly to divest themselves of power and privilege even to the point of sharing in the powerless physical vulnerability of slaves.[30]

Feminists and others have rightly identified the problematic implications of this kenotic Christology, especially when invoked to reinforce unequal relations of power. This emphasis on Christ-like obedience and self-emptying has been used to teach women as well as slaves and other oppressed peoples that there is virtue in submitting to those who have assumed positions of authoritarian power over them.[31] Nevertheless, Jesus' suffering as one of the discounted and devalued may be a powerful and positive message when presented not as a reason to accept the denial of

[28] Ibid., 9–29.

[29] Ibid., 54–57.

[30] See also the discussion of Christians instructed to become slaves of all, in Glancy, *Slavery as Moral Problem*, 23–27.

[31] See, for example, the excellent discussion in Colleen Carpenter Cullinan, *Redeeming the Story: Women, Suffering, and Christ* (New York: Continuum, 2003), esp. 16–19. See also the sympathetic summary of feminist critiques of atonement theories in Adam Kotsko, *The Politics of Redemption: The Social Logic of Salvation* (New York: T&T Clark International, 2010), esp. 27–32.

agency but instead as God's identification with the devalued in protest against their suffering and oppression. Jesus' crucifixion might then be understood as the result of his deep solidarity with those who suffer the physical abuse of the sex trade, who are reduced to bodies to be daily raped, tortured, and exhibited as a spectacle for others.

Further, Jesus directs his disciples to seek him among the broken and degraded, which surely include the victims of sex trafficking. As the Body of Christ in the world, the communities of Jesus' disciples must continue Jesus' self-emptying by locating the church among these modern slaves, emptying themselves of social prestige in order to share the danger and the social opprobrium faced by these prostituted and discounted human beings. "In order to be worthy of his [Jesus'] name, the name in which it gathers, the church cannot help but open its heart and embrace those bodies that empire abuses, negates, and crucifies," as Copeland incisively argues.[32]

That the church should endeavor to spread God's reign in solidarity with and among the victims of the sex trade seems obvious, yet what this would mean in reality is rather daunting. The world of sex trafficking is ugly, violent, dangerous, and far removed from respectable society, whereas many of our churches have achieved considerable social esteem and are valued as havens of comfort and support, often by and for the middle and upper classes. To be sure, some Christian ministries in the United States and around the world are actively engaged in opposing sex trafficking and are doing valuable, even heroic, work to support and free the victims of the sex industry.[33] Yet to follow Jesus' example and Paul's kenotic Christology in the context of the modern slave trade would require a reversal of priorities for most of our churches. Rather than building communities among the privileged and then occasionally reaching out to the enslaved, abused, and oppressed, should the church not embrace the risks involved in locating itself primarily among the despised and rejected of society with occasional outreach to the powerful and secure?

Indeed, sex trafficking demands a further development of the church's understanding of its mission in the world today. The Catholic Church at

---

[32] Copeland, *Enfleshing Freedom*, 58.

[33] See especially Dawn Herzog Jewell, *Escaping the Devil's Bedroom: Sex Trafficking, Global Prostitution, and the Gospel's Transforming Power* (Grand Rapids, MI: Monarch Books, 2008), for references to the work of various Christian anti-sex-slavery ministries around the world. She lists the various ministries her research uncovers in her *Escaping*, 201–3.

its Second Vatican Council declared that the church is called to be a sign and instrument of union with God and unity among humanity, a theological perspective affirmed also by the World Council of Churches in the Faith and Order Commission's Paper no. 198.[34] What sort of practical ecclesiology best fits this aim to unite the human community in a world where millions of women and children are trafficked for commercial sexual exploitation? How can the church foster true unity among trafficked victims, their abusers, and those who are unaware of or indifferent to this horrific enterprise?

One hopes that few church members today would agree with the border guard who explained his indifference to the trafficking of kidnapped Nepalese peasant girls for enslavement in Indian brothels: he assumed that this slave trade is simply the (somewhat regrettable) price of social harmony and of the protection of "good" middle-class Indian girls.[35] Although this defense of prostitution as necessary for the protection of virtuous women is no longer commonly espoused by Christian leaders (as it once was), privileged Christians and their church communities in Western societies still too often seek an easy harmony and the appearance of middle-class morality by condemning the sex industry from a position above the fray, without risking active solidarity with its victims. Painful and even divisive changes will surely be required of most church communities if they are to offer support to prostituted girls and women as readily as they now welcome the upper-class (but usually secret) consumers of pornography, strip shows, and prostitutes.[36]

As noted above, Jesus began to unite humanity by very disruptively locating himself with and among the most vulnerable and devalued, a witness that continues to challenge his followers. The violence of the

---

[34] See especially the Vatican II document *Lumen Gentium* (Dogmatic Constitution on the Church), no. 1, available at http://www.vatican.va/archive/hist_councils/ii_vatican_council/documents/vat-ii_const_19641121_lumen-gentium_en.html. See also the Faith and Order Commission's Paper no.198, "The Nature and Mission of the Church: A Stage on the Way to a Common Statement," especially 9–11, available at http://www.oikoumene.org/resources/documents/wcc-commissions/faith-and-order-commission/i-unity-the-church-and-its-mission/the-nature-and-mission-of-the-church-a-stage-on-the-way-to-a-common-statement.html.

[35] Kristof and WuDunn, *Half the Sky*, 23–24.

[36] See, for example, the story of the prostituted woman invited to a church she refused to enter when she recognized too many former customers in the congregation, as related in Jewell, *Escaping*, 192.

sex industry, along with society's reluctance to recognize its coercive brutality, should interrupt any ecclesial tendency to seek a harmonious unity in society without first confronting the reality of damaging power dynamics and the socioeconomic structures that render the poor and people of color especially vulnerable to abuse. Unity in the church and in the world cannot be established without first accepting and even perhaps inviting the conflict inherent in opposing the cultural attitudes and socio-economic and political structures that treat some people as expendable for the good of others. A true unity in God cannot be developed without disturbing the false unity that masks the oppression and dehumanization of the modern sex industry.

In addition to a willingness to share the dangers of opposing the criminal industry of slave profiteers and of disrupting the social harmony predicated on keeping this injustice at a safe distance from "respectable" Christian churches, seeking the reign of God in a world of sex slavery requires sustaining hope within a situation where hope is not easily maintained. After all, hope is a crucial and eminently practical Christian virtue in these situations. As Siddharth Kara reports,

> The slaves I met in victim shelters were the bare few who had managed to escape, and even then their lives offered little hope. Most were infected with HIV, suffered acute drug and alcohol addictions, had been shunned by families, and had little prospects for employment or any form of self-sufficiency upon departure from the shelters, which invariably had to limit their duration of residence due to resource shortages.[37]

Kara's observation is echoed by others who work with rescued sex slaves. Trafficked people have difficulty adjusting to life outside of the sex industry for a variety of reasons, including drug addiction, low self-esteem, psychological trauma, and the stigma (including often a criminal record) of having been involved in sex work. For those unaware of the extent of the trauma and damage inflicted on trafficked people, the return of freed slaves to the sex industry is perplexing and may reinforce stereotypes about the character and proclivities of prostituted women and children. Yet a Christian affirmation of the body as integral to the person ought to inspire Christian attentiveness to the depth of damage to the self sustained through the bodily assaults of sex slavery. People who

---

[37] Kara, *Sex Trafficking*, 15.

have survived the levels of abuse and torture that sex slaves experience cannot reasonably be expected to make the kinds of choices that people can make who have been protected, loved, and nurtured throughout their lives.

When trafficked victims are too traumatized to leave the sex industry, Christians must respond with patient solidarity and accompaniment in hope of healing rather than with condemnation of what is perceived as immoral sexual behavior. Perhaps a helpful precedent is suggested in the nevertheless problematic response of the early Christian church to slavery. While affirming that the reign of God initiated by Jesus required that in the Christian community there should be "neither slave nor free" (Gal 3:28), the early church did not demand the freedom of slaves. Although this acceptance of slavery is disturbing, interesting implications arise here for those caught in the sex trade today. If early Christian communities accepted slaves as full members of the church, even while these slaves lacked control over whom they served sexually, then does this not suggest that currently prostituted people might be accepted as full members of the church—without undue judgment or vilification—even before they are able to break free of the sex industry? Given the extent of damage inflicted on a self that has been reduced to a body bought, sold, and frequently tortured, perhaps the inclusion of slaves as full members of the church in its first centuries could inspire the welcome and full inclusion of prostituted children, women, and men in the church today.

Conclusion

Acknowledging and affirming the discounted human beings of this inhuman global sex trade provides a stark reminder that the church is integrally a part of an unjust world, a world in which natural resources, animals, and even human beings are used and abused for the benefit of others (often including church members). As market values increasingly become the dominant source of publicly recognized value in the United States and worldwide, little is exempt from reduction to monetary value. An ecclesial mission to unite all in God requires something more in the face of this global buying and selling—even of human beings—than is provided by the commonplace ecclesial bromides against consumerism or nonmarital sexual activity. Called to cooperate with the divine Spirit in transforming this world, the church itself is in need of a transformation through which it might come more fully to recognize and to witness against the devastating costs of this market dominance, including costs to other human beings, to the planet's ecosystem, and to our capacity for true community. The mission of the church cannot be fulfilled unless Christians are formed to witness actively to their faith in the reign of God as redemption from *all* that enslaves and constrains. This faith must therefore be lived as an active hope in concrete—and kenotic—resistance to the destruction and degradation created around the world by a merciless global economy reducing so many to lives of desperation and early death.

Gregory of Nyssa, one of the early opponents of slaveholding within the church, notably proclaimed that "it is only in the union of all the particular members that the beauty of Christ's Body is complete."[38] Citing Gregory on this point, Copeland further warns, "Unless our sisters and brothers are beside and with each of us, we are not the flesh of Christ."[39] When human beings are treated as bodies to be abused for profit and pleasure, the church cannot be fully the Body of Christ until it responds as Jesus did, emptying itself of privilege to share, in solidarity and in hope, the plight of the enslaved.

---

[38] Gregory of Nyssa, "On the Making of Man," 13, as cited by Copeland, *Enfleshing Freedom*, 82.

[39] Copeland, *Enfleshing Freedom*, 82.

Feminicide and the Reinvention of Religious Practices

Nancy Pineda-Madrid, Boston College

The contemporary tragedy of the Ciudad Juárez feminicide presses upon us the need to consider anew how we encounter the salvific process in history. The brutal sexual trauma that has cut short the lives of girls and young women affects not only victimized families and friends but the wider community of Juárez in which no poor woman feels safe. It further demands of us, all of us, some account of historical salvation. Indeed, how does the context created by this feminicide recast our understanding of salvation? To engage this question, we need to turn our attention to the public response of those most directly victimized, the families of the murdered girls and women. Mothers of many of the victims, several other women, and some men have developed practices of resistance that command our attention. While any evil of this magnitude raises a multitude of theological questions, here I focus on the ways that the practices of resistance not only seek to subvert the social trauma of feminicide but also bear soteriological significance. These practices of resistance break open for us new ways of thinking about salvation.

The reality of feminicide produces an enormous challenge because of the difficulty in believing that human beings are capable of such evil. Yet we must face this evil directly lest it continue unabated. The first section describes the meaning of "feminicide" and its manifestation in Ciudad Juárez and other communities. Yet the story of this social trauma cannot be rightly told without a sharp focus on the practices of resistance created by several women (and men) in Ciudad Juárez. This is the focus of the second section. These practices advance a strategy of subversion

61

that not only reclaims women's bodies, public space, and political standing but also transforms our theological sensibilities. Our given patterns of thought about crucifixion are turned upside down by these practices. Accordingly, the third and final section delves into the soteriological significance of these practices.

Feminicide in Ciudad Juárez and Beyond

While gender-based violence against women dates back several millennia,[1] arguably to the beginning of the human race, only recently have the terms "femicide" and "feminicide" been used to identify a distinctive lethal violence against women and girls. These terms need to be understood in the larger context of violence against women today, which, as in the past, takes many forms: rape, sexual torture, domestic violence, disappearances, sexual trafficking, female gender mutilation, and murder, among others. To clarify further, the Women's Caucus for Gender Justice insightfully argued before the International Criminal Court at The Hague that "gender crimes are incidents of violence targeting or affecting women exclusively or disproportionately, not because the victims of such crimes are of a particular religion or race, but because they are women."[2] Feminist scholars from several disciplines have increasingly been using the terms "femicide" and "feminicide" to distinguish the killing of women and girls *because they are female*. Misogynistic violence is here taken to the extreme.

Even though scholars have used these two terms interchangeably, more recently clear distinctions between them have begun to emerge. Femicide is synonymous with "homicide" except that femicide refers exclusively to the killing of women. Feminicide, on the other hand, carries a more particular meaning: it refers to systematic killing based on gender inequalities. Femicide may refer to only one murder, while feminicide invariably refers to a large number of murders, which more closely resembles the meaning of "genocide." Femicide is a term that dates back two centuries in the English-speaking world. However, in the

---

[1] A number of biblical stories offer accounts of violence against women. See, for example, Phyllis Trible, *Texts of Terror: Literary-Feminist Readings of Biblical Narratives* (Philadelphia: Fortress Press, 1984).

[2] As quoted by Rosa Linda Fregoso and Cynthia Bejarano, eds., *Terrorizing Women: Feminicide in the Americas* (Durham, NC: Duke University Press, 2010), 2.

mid-1970s, United States feminist sociologist Diana Russell used it and developed its meaning further.[3] Feminicide, in contrast, owes its origin to feminist activists in the Spanish-speaking country of the Dominican Republic and their term *feminicidio*. These feminist activists used *feminicidio* in their efforts to bring violence against women to an end. In 1987 Mexican anthropologist Marcela Lagarde y de los Rios introduced the term *feminicidio* into scholarly discourse.[4] Many feminist social scientists today who are studying the killing of women in Ciudad Juárez use the term "feminicide." Rosa-Linda Fregoso and Cynthia Bejarano have clarified further the meaning of "feminicide." They write:

> Building on the generic definition of *femicide* as "the murder of women and girls *because* they are female" [the definition advanced by Diana Russell], we define *feminicide* as the murders of women and girls founded on a gender power structure. Second, feminicide is gender-based violence that is both public and private, implicating both the state (directly or indirectly) and individual perpetrators (private or state actors); it thus encompasses systematic, widespread, and everyday interpersonal violence. Third, feminicide is systemic violence rooted in social, political, economic, and cultural inequalities. In this sense, the focus of our analysis is not just on gender but also on the intersection of gender dynamics with the cruelties of racism and economic injustices in local as well as global contexts. Finally, our framing of the concept follows Lagarde's critical human rights formulation of feminicide as a "crime against humanity."[5]

In this definition "feminicide," unlike "femicide," not only is widespread but implicates the state due to the fact that the perpetrators enjoy impunity for their crimes. In addition, feminicidal violence takes into account the structural inequalities of class, race, and ethnicity and the ways in which particular women and girls are rendered acutely vulnerable. Feminicidal violence almost always bears a brutal and vicious character.

In the mid-1990s journalists and other investigators noticed a pattern of ritualized killing of women and girls in Ciudad Juárez. Most agree that these killings started in 1993. Among the first victims was Alma Chavarría

---

[3] Diana E. H. Russell, "Defining Femicide and Related Concepts," in *Femicide in Global Perspective*, ed. Diana E. H. Russell and Roberta A. Harmes (New York: Teachers College Press, 2001), 12–25.

[4] Fregoso and Bejarano, *Terrorizing Women*, 4.

[5] Ibid., 5.

Fávila, who was raped, anally and vaginally, severely beaten, and eventually murdered through strangulation. It is unclear whether she was a young woman or a girl.[6] Diana Washington Valdez, a journalist with the *El Paso Times*, reported in April 2009 that more than six hundred women and girls had been raped, tortured, and murdered.[7] Many more went missing. A database kept by *El Colegio de la Frontera Norte* (COLEF)[8] documents that from 1993 to 2004, 75 percent of the victims were between the ages of ten and twenty-nine.[9] As of this writing, the killings continue. On July 20, 2011, Valdez reported that "Chihuahua state officials said 122 girls and women have been slain in Juárez this year."[10] Almost all the victims are young, poor, thin, and with olive complexions. Juárez, a city of over two million inhabitants, sits right on the border across from El Paso, Texas, a city of about eight hundred thousand. To place the feminicide in a larger context, in 2010 Juárez had over three thousand murders, while El Paso had only five. Over the last several years, various authorities (local, state, national, and international) have undertaken multiple investigations into these killings. Each has ended in failure. Journalists, scholars, public officials, international investigators, and others have offered a wide range of explanations for the feminicide. The most reliable data, interpreted by social scientist Julia Monárrez Fragoso, identifies the forms of the killings as primarily systemic sexual feminicide, meaning serial murders where victims did not know their assassin(s), and intimate feminicide, where the victims did know their assassin(s).[11] In almost all cases, the bodies of the victims reveal severe sexual abuse.

---

[6] Diana Washington Valdez, *The Killing Fields: Harvest of Women* (Burbank, CA: Peace at the Border, 2006), 363; Teresa Rodríguez, Diana Montané, and Lisa Pulitzer, *The Daughters of Juárez: A True Story of Serial Murder South of the Border* (New York: Atria Books, 2007), 38.

[7] Diana Washington Valdez, "Mexico on Trial in Murders of Women," *El Paso Times*, April 30, 2009.

[8] COLEF is a research center with locations in several major cities in Mexico including Ciudad Juárez. COLEF offers graduate degrees (both MAs and PhDs) in various social science fields.

[9] Julia Estela Monárrez Fragoso, *Trama de una injusticia: Feminicidio sexual sistémico en Ciudad Juárez* (Tijuana, Mexico: El Colegio de la Frontera Norte, 2009), 105.

[10] Diana Washington Valdez, "Family Worried about Missing Juárez Teen," *El Paso Times*, July 20, 2011.

[11] Adriana Carmona López, Alma Gómez Caballero, and Lucha Castro Rodríguez, "Feminicide in Latin America in the Movement for Women's Human Rights," in *Ter-*

To unpack the systemic, serial nature of these murders a bit further, anthropologist Rita Laura Segato "suggests that these murders are hate crimes carried out as part of initiation rites among what are called *fratrias*, or brotherhoods of criminals that require proof of loyalty through the commission of these kinds of misogynistic acts."[12] And *Dallas Morning News* journalists Alfredo Corchado and Ricardo Sandoval "attribute these murders to current and former police officers' belonging to a drug-trafficking mafia known as *La línea* (the line), who carry out these macabre orgies as part of their celebrations when they successfully pass a shipment of drugs into the United States."[13] The killers have consistently used women's bodies to mark territory and demonstrate power. These killings are "politically motivated sexual violence"[14] in which the killers use social terror, trauma, and ultimately fear to control territory and overpower any threat to their ongoing work. Moreover, since these killings have been allowed to continue with impunity, the state is also implicated. These killings, then, have given rise to an overwhelming sense of terror and trauma in Juárez. The tragedy of an almost two-decades-long feminicide carries social significance that cannot be overstated, and that cannot be limited, for that matter, to either Juárez or Mexico. It implicates us all.

While Ciudad Juárez has received much international attention, feminicide is not limited to this example in Mexico[15] or in the Americas. The Guatemalan Human Rights Commission/USA has documented feminicide there for years. Between 2000 and 2009, 4,867 women and girls there were brutally killed. Ninety-nine percent of Guatemalan feminicide cases "remain in impunity." Over this nine-year period, the number of killings there has sharply escalated year to year, numbering 213 in 2000,

---

rorizing Women: Feminicide in the Américas, ed. Rosa-Linda Fregoso and Cynthia Bejarano (Durham, NC: Duke University Press, 2010), 163–65.

[12] Hector Domínguez-Ruvalcaba and Patricia Ravelo Blancas, "Obedience without Compliance: The Role of the Government, Organized Crime, and NGOS in the System of Impunity That Murders the Women of Ciudad Juárez," in *Terrorizing Women*, ed. Fregoso and Bejarano, 183.

[13] Domínguez-Ruvalcaba and Ravelo Blancas, "Obedience without Compliance," 183.

[14] Rosa Linda Fregoso, "Toward a Planetary Civil Society," in *Women and Migration in the US-Mexico Borderlands*, ed. Denise A. Segura and Patricia Zavella (Durham, NC: Duke University Press, 2007), 36.

[15] In her groundbreaking work Diana Washington Valdez notes feminicides throughout Mexico. See Valdez, *Killing Fields*, 265.

and then 722 in 2008, and 708 in 2009.[16] From 1960 until the signing of the Guatemala Peace Accords in 1996, sexual violence was used as a weapon of war and with full impunity for perpetrators. A generation of young men enlisted in the Guatemalan military and in the Patrullas de Autodefensa Civil (Civil Defense Patrols) was trained to use sexual violence as a weapon of war, as part of military operations in rural areas suspected of supporting the guerrilla effort. The deadly assault against women continues to this day with several of the same forms of violence that were employed by the military during the internal civil conflict. Many former members of the Guatemalan military currently work for the country's police force, which has seriously compromised communities' efforts to bring violence against women to an end.[17] Horrifically, feminicide threatens the lives of women living in Argentina, Costa Rica, Colombia, El Salvador, Honduras, and Peru, among other countries in the Americas as well as in Africa and Asia.[18] This evil is widespread and tragically growing.

The tragedy of feminicide raises many theological questions: How do Christians continue to affirm the goodness of God in the face of feminicide? In what ways does feminicide call the Christian church to conversion? How has the Christian church denounced feminicide, or failed to do so? What is the relationship between this ongoing crucifixion of women and Jesus' crucifixion? Does feminicide shed new light on Christian understandings of *imago Dei* and *imago Christi*? On understandings of sin and salvation? These and many other questions are raised by this horror. David Tracy once astutely observed that "in the contemporary fascination with evil, as in so many important theological issues, the religious sensibilities of religious peoples—especially oppressed and marginalized peoples in their songs, their endurance and protest, their struggles for justice, their forms of prayer and lament, their liturgy,

---

[16] Guatemala Human Rights Commission/USA, "Fact Sheet: Femicide and Feminicide" (Washington, DC, 2010). See also Amnesty International, *No Protection, No Justice: Killings of Women in Guatemala*, Stop Violence Against Women (London, June 2005), 2–30.

[17] Angélica Cházaro, Jennifer Casey, and Katherine Ruhl, "Getting Away with Murder: Guatemala's Failure to Protect Women and Rodi Alvarado's Quest for Safety," in *Terrorizing Women*, ed. Fregoso and Bejarano, 99–101.

[18] Fregoso and Bejarano, *Terrorizing Women*; Monica A. Maher, "The Truth Will Set Us Free: Religion, Violence and Women's Empowerment in Latin America," in *Global Empowerment of Women: Responses to Globalization and Politicized Religions*, ed. Carolyn Elliott (New York: Routledge, 2008).

their laughter, their reading of the scriptures—are often wiser, not only religiously but also theologically, than the carefully crafted theodicies of the professional theologians."[19] The response courageously developed by women (and men) to the feminicide in Juárez holds theological wisdom and, I contend, sheds light on what salvation should mean for us.

Public Practices of Resistance, Radicalizing Religious Symbols

In the mid-1990s, when Juárez activists detected a pattern in the increasing numbers of murdered women and girls, these activists organized groups of protestors to resist the violence against women and to demand that the feminicide end. By the end of 2001 over three hundred groups existed to raise public consciousness locally, nationally, and internationally; to insist that justice be served; to pressure public authorities to take serious action; to bring attention to the value of women's lives in Mexico; and to support those who had lost loved ones to feminicide. The year 2001 marked a turning point due to two particularly terrorizing events that captured the public imagination. The story of the brutal murder of seventeen-year-old Lilia Alejandra García Andrade became widely known. Over a six-day period, beginning on Valentine's Day, she was kidnapped, savagely beaten, sexually tortured and mutilated, and eventually strangled to death. Second, on the sixth of November five bodies were dumped at a busy intersection in Juárez, specifically at the crossroads of Ejército Nacional and Paseo de la Victoria. The very next day three more bodies were dumped at the same intersection. The perpetrators saw no need to conceal their crime.[20] To a significant degree these events became the tipping point that, in early 2002, propelled some three hundred groups to unify under one umbrella coalition entitled Campaña alto a la impunidad: Ni Una Muerte Más (Stop the Impunity: Not One More Death Campaign), better known as Ni Una Más.[21] The leadership of this transnational coalition organized several demonstrations to call

---

[19] David Tracy, "Saving from Evil: Salvation and Evil Today," in *The Fascination of Evil*, ed. David Tracy and Hermann Häring (Maryknoll, NY: SCM Press, 1998), 114–15.

[20] Fregoso, "Toward a Planetary Civil Society," 55; Kathleen Staudt, *Violence and Activism at the Border: Gender, Fear, and Everyday Life in Ciudad Juárez* (Austin, TX: University of Texas Press, 2008), 85; Rodríguez, Montané, and Pulitzer, *Daughters of Juárez*, 166, 178.

[21] Mark Ensalaco, "Murder in Ciudad Juárez: A Parable of Women's Struggle for Human Rights," *Violence against Women* 12, no. 5 (May 2006): 428–29.

attention to the feminicide, to demand that it end, and to ensure that all women in Mexico freely exercise their full rights as citizens. They organized marches, rituals, protests, and public memorial installations. Political scientist Kathleen Staudt has identified these protests as "performance activism."[22] Yet what is striking about these protests, or what I call practices of resistance, is Ni Una Más's use of religious symbols.

In March 2002 Ni Una Más along with Chihuahua City–based Mujeres de Negro (Women in Black) organized a dramatic march of over two hundred miles from Chihuahua City to Ciudad Juárez and its Paso del Norte International Bridge. They named their campaign and march *Éxodo por Vida* (Exodus for Life).[23] This six-day march started on International Women's Day, March 8. The participants reflected a diverse cross section of society, including "elderly women, campesinas, housewives, factory workers, students, professionals."[24] Many women marchers wore long black dresses and pink hats that came to symbolize their ongoing mourning for Juárez's daughters. As Melissa W. Wright notes, the women marchers chose to dress in "black clothing of mourning, domesticity, and female modesty to express their identities as social justice and human rights advocates. . . . The group's self-portrayal as mothers provided legitimacy for them as women who were on the street not as political subversives or as 'women of the street' but, rather, as women doing what women are publicly sanctioned to do. They were looking for their children."[25] Yet their march allowed them to create an image "of the 'domestic woman in mourning' to express their political opposition to the state government, which was doing nothing about the violence."[26] The marchers carried a large six-foot-tall cross made of railroad ties through the desert and eventually through the streets of Juárez. The numbers of marchers grew to thousands as they processed down main streets toward

[22] Fregoso, "Toward a Planetary Civil Society," 55–56; Staudt, *Violence and Activism at the Border*, 79; Valdez, *Killing Fields*, 75.

[23] Carmona López, Gómez Caballero, and Castro Rodríguez, "Feminicide in Latin America in the Movement for Women's Human Rights," 167–68; Melissa W. Wright, "Paradoxes, Protests, and the Mujeres de Negro of Northern Mexico," in *Terrorizing Women*, Fregoso and Bejarano, 167.

[24] Fregoso, "Toward a Planetary Civil Society," 55–56.

[25] Wright, "Paradoxes, Protests, and the Mujeres de Negro of Northern Mexico," 316.

[26] Melissa W. Wright, "Femicide, Mother-Activism, and the Geography of Protest," in *Making a Killing: Femicide, Free Trade, and La Frontera*, ed. Alicia Gaspar de Alba and Georgina Guzmán (Austin, TX: University of Texas Press, 2010), 224.

the center of the city, defying Chihuahua's then "Governor Patricio Martinez's alleged attempts to stop the procession."[27]

Like the exodus of the Hebrew and Christian Scriptures, these women marched in the desert, in this case the Chihuahuan desert, seeking release from bondage and slavery that shackled them and allowed the ongoing killing of Juárez's daughters to continue with impunity. Many women marchers recognized that governing elites idealize the patriarchal family in Mexico and that this ideal is supported by widespread fundamentalist Christian and Catholic interpretations of family values. This "rule of the father" social system has been used to severely limit if not altogether negate the role of women in public. This social system has grossly undermined the value of women's humanity in general. Moreover, women in this system are denied value apart from their familial roles of wife, mother, daughter, or sister. The freedom these protestors sought was first and foremost justice for the women and girls who have been murdered as well as for their families. Yet their march meant more. It addressed justice for all women, poor as well as rich. It argued for freedom for women to be recognized as full citizens with political standing and with protection under the law. They stood against "Pharaoh's rule" in challenging the imperial power of their circumstance—namely, local, state, and federal government authorities who have refused to take the ritualized sexual torture and widespread serial killing of women seriously. Their march ended at the Paso del Norte International Bridge (also known as the Santa Fe Bridge), where they erected that six-foot cross and affixed it to a large board adorned with hundreds of square-head nails, each carrying a small slip of white paper with a victim's name. These protestors added torn clothing, a mannequin, and photographs to this cross installation and memorial designed to keep the memory of the victims alive. *Éxodo por Vida* served as a public, courageous denunciation of feminicide and of all the ways ruling elites deem poor women's lives negligible. As a practice of resistance to patriarchy, it condemns "rule of the father" in its blatantly evil forms as well as in its seemingly more benign/benevolent expressions. This march challenges patriarchy because the women who organized it assumed for themselves, and on behalf of all women, a public civic and religious role for women, still uncommon in this society. Moreover, the women organizers reinterpreted the conventional negative association

---

[27] Valdez, *Killing Fields*, 74–75.

of "woman" and "public" and transformed the notion of "public" into a place that women belong, a place in which women shape society in ways life giving and constructive.

The exodus was not the only religious symbol employed, nor even the primary one. Pink crosses appeared in many locations. First, the six-foot cross installation erected in March of 2002 at the Paso del Norte Bridge could not have been located in a more public place. Over one hundred thousand people cross the border daily between the two cities, and the Paso del Norte Bridge is one of only three bridges linking Ciudad Juárez and El Paso, Texas. The cross remains there at the entrance to the bridge with a pink Ni Una Mas sign nailed at the crossbar. In addition, a large pink wooden cross was raised where the body of Lilia Alejandra García Andrade was found, with her name written on the crossbar.[28] Eight pink crosses, each standing more than four feet tall, were also erected where the eight bodies were found in November 2001. On each crossbar one of the following names is written: Lupita, Esmeralda, Barbara, Brenda, Veronica, Laura, Claudia, and on the final crossbar "Desconocida," meaning "Unknown." Pink crosses have been erected throughout Juárez to mark the location where a body was found, with the name of the victim written on the crossbar. Moreover, as early as 1999, another group of protestors, Voces Sin Eco, painted electric and telephone poles pink and then painted a black cross on them. As one woman explained, "Black stood for death and pink for the promise of life and youth."[29] A pole was painted for each woman or girl murdered to honor her memory by claiming public space for her and to protest the depravity of justice manifested by the ongoing feminicide. Every time another girl or woman was killed, Voces Sin Eco painted a new cross, ensuring that these girls and women were not forgotten even though most civil authorities have repeatedly ignored, ridiculed, botched, or otherwise destroyed any attempts at a rigorous investigation. Also, Mujeres de Negro erected a large cross in front of the governor's office in Chihuahua City, but it was taken down in 2002. They then had another cross put up there, which was also taken down. Many members of this group have been threatened, had their phones tapped, been followed and watched, or experienced physical abuse.[30] At every march and protest, pink crosses have been used to honor the memories of those so brutally killed.

[28] Ibid., 205.
[29] Ibid., 38. See also Fregoso, "Toward a Planetary Civil Society," 54.
[30] Wright, "Paradoxes, Protests, and the Mujeres de Negro of Northern Mexico," 322–23.

By using the religious symbol of the cross, the women protesting feminicide have drawn connections between the crucifixion of Jesus and the crucifixion of Juárez's daughters. Crucifixion did not just happen two thousand years ago; rather, crucifixion is ongoing today at the dawn of the twenty-first century. With the brutal killings of Juárez's women and girls, we have the tragic murdering of the innocent and the utter culpability of the state because it has granted impunity. Jesus too died an unimaginable, horrific death, in his case at the hands of Roman imperial power. In making this connection, the protestors invite us to rethink crucifixion, to see it as gendered, and thus to move far beyond our conventional understanding. In their use of the cross, they again offer a critique of patriarchal power in its social, political, cultural, theological, and ecclesial manifestations. In the protestors' reinterpretation of crucifixion, we discover not a domesticated Christian message but a piercingly fresh one. In making this connection, the protesters elevate their fight against this feminicidal evil to the level of the transcendent. This is no longer a fight on strictly human terms but now involves God. In making this connection, they likewise push forward the questions of resurrection and salvation.

The protestors—many of whom have lost a daughter, sister, or mother to feminicide—write the story of these killings into the biblical narratives of exodus and Jesus' crucifixion, death, and resurrection. They lift up contemporary women's experiences of enslavement as well as crucifixion, drawing a connection back in history to the biblical period. They claim historical space by insisting that the stories of the victims will not be forgotten. Through their employment of biblical stories, they draw on an external power, a religious authority, which they have made their own by means of the practices of resistance they have created.

Of Soteriological Significance

Two ideas serve as the basis for this third section. First, a foundational anthropological principle in Christianity is that "one may have as radical an understanding of evil and sin as necessary as long as one's understanding of grace and salvation are equally radical."[31] In the face of the horrific evil of feminicide, we need to ask ourselves, where might we turn

---

[31] Tracy, "Saving from Evil," 107.

to discover a glimpse of grace and salvation that counters such evil? This question calls forward a second idea. If we agree with David Tracy that the sensibilities of religious peoples often bear greater theological wisdom than the carefully developed arguments of professional theologians,[32] then perhaps we have much to learn from the practices of resistance developed by the courageous women (and some men) of Ciudad Juárez who have lost loved ones to feminicide. To draw from the wisdom manifest in the practices of resistance developed by these women is akin to following them into "the empty tomb." As Elisabeth Schüssler Fiorenza has argued, this christological tradition supports those who would confront the brutal violence and killing of women and other "nonpersons." As she explains, "The texts of the empty tomb tradition take suffering and death seriously but do not see them as having the 'last word' or a religious-theological value in themselves. Since G*d was absent in the execution of the Just One, the women's presence under the cross is a witness to this absence. The tomb is the brutal final reality that eclipses G*d and vitiates all possibilities for the future. *But* the 'tomb is empty!'"[33] Like the tradition of the empty tomb, the space of the practices of resistance encourages a candid and openhearted reckoning with the feminicide's unimaginable violence and social trauma. Many of the practices lay claim to particular places, locations in Juárez to remember the murdered, to demand that these killings stop, and to infuse and inhabit these places with the memory of the murdered women and girls, in keeping with belief in a God who unceasingly loves and demands justice, particularly in the face of horrific evil. In a tangible way, these places have made visible women's hopes and actions in search of their own liberation. These courageous protestors are engaged in a salvific process.

Their practices of resistance further a salvific process precisely because these women protestors who have suffered the tragic, brutal death of a loved one have not succumbed to hurling their anger and outrage violently against others, nor have they allowed their suffering to consume them so fully that they cannot see beyond it, but they have instead chosen to publicly cry out *against* death and to cry out *for* life. They have chosen to fight for community. They have chosen to bring the crucified

---

[32] Ibid., 114–15.

[33] Elisabeth Schüssler Fiorenza, *Jesus: Miriam's Child, Sophia's Prophet: Critical Issues in Feminist Christology* (New York: Continuum, 1994), 125, italics mine.

daughters of Juárez down from the cross.[34] What their practices of resistance signify is that they are committed to prevail over the effects of evil they know only too well. For the practices are akin to a call to God and a call upon God to act so that the historical trajectory within which the women of Juárez find themselves does not simply continue into the future. Rather, they hope that their cries lead to a "break [in] the process, and that [the hoped-for] break in the process is where something more than history becomes present in history." The something "more" than history is recognition of the possibility of novelty within a given historical situation that "breaks into the normality of the experience. . . . History is the arena of novelty, of creativity; God's self-revelation comes by making 'more' history, that is, a greater and better history than existed in the past."[35] Their efforts enable the "fragments of salvation to gain a foothold within history."[36]

In their response to evil, we discover a praxis of salvation. By "praxis of salvation" I mean the integral relation between human thought and action (or practice) on behalf of the future whole that God intends for all humanity and creation. Through their protests, marches, and public actions, the women of Juárez make more visible the foundational spiritual unity of the world. This spiritual unity of the world becomes more visible because in their practices of resistance they identify their own lives with a trajectory that extends beyond their lifetimes. The symbols of exodus and the cross signal this much larger temporal trajectory. Just as they know the suffering in the loss of a daughter, sister, or mother, they anticipate a better tomorrow through the promise of resurrection. What we come to know through their example is that the transformation of this world is realized when those who are most vulnerable among us, in this case those who have most acutely suffered in this feminicide, strongly desire and actively work to bring about a realization of the reign of God that is greater than what they have known.

---

[34] Ignacio Ellacuría, "The Crucified People," in *Systematic Theology: Perspectives from Liberation Theology*, ed. Jon Sobrino and Ignacio Ellacuría (Maryknoll, NY: Orbis Books, 1993), 257.

[35] Ignacio Ellacuría, "The Historicity of Christian Salvation," in *Mysterium Liberationis: Fundamental Concepts in Liberation Theology*, ed. Ignacio Ellacuría, SJ, and Jon Sobrino, SJ (Maryknoll, NY: Orbis Books, 1993), 258.

[36] Elizabeth A. Johnson, "Jesus and Salvation," in *CTSA Proceedings*, ed. Paul Crowley, vol. 49 (Santa Clara, CA: CTSA, 1994), 11.

In many respects, their vision for the world mirrors the vision that Jesus lived and died defending. "In being condemned personally, Jesus had to learn the road to definitive salvation—a salvation . . . that was essentially a matter of the coming of God's Reign and not a personal resurrection separate from what had been his earthly preaching of the Reign."[37] Analogous to Jesus, many of the victimized have come to see that salvation entails not only a personal release from the horror of the feminicide, but rather, and more significantly, a deliverance that is collective, social in nature—in other words, a deliverance that makes the reign of God more socially real as well as more personally real.

[37] Ellacuría, "Historicity of Christian Salvation," 260.

In Conversation with Maureen H. O'Connell, Fordham University

Each of these rich essays left me with much to ponder. My identity as an Euro-American ethicist increasingly involves work in theological aesthetics, but a "theological aesthetics from below," which echoes Nancy's excerpts from David Tracy in terms of the ways in which the lived experience of theodicy in communities of suffering is far more insightful than we in the academy articulate. In that regard, I draw from Susie's examination of Kollwitz and Sölle that beauty is about the affirmation of human dignity, and that dignity must involve the increased capacity to take on the vulnerability of others in order to resist vulnerability that is not chosen but imposed.

Nancy's essay highlights the importance of following the lead of suffering persons and opening up spaces—much like Elisabeth Schüssler Fiorenza's notion of the empty tomb—in the very heart (physically and geographically) of structural violence where new things can emerge: new ways of being, new ways of understanding, new ways of moving forward. Mary's essay emphasizes the elements of the tradition (scriptural and christological in particular) that speak explicitly to the structural and intrapersonal reality of sex trafficking in the twenty-first century; also, she questions how we literally embody solidarity since this injustice breaks individual bodies as well as the collective Body of Christ. Finally, Anne's essay explores the theological significance of Mary as an indentured servant and not merely a medieval handmaid (as she is so popularly portrayed in religious iconography) and what that might mean in terms of the significance of her yes (for women in Nancy's essay and Mary's essay, for example)—as well as her firsthand experience of the various things to which she says no in her poetic response.

All the essays converge on certain ideas or common themes. All challenge some fundamental theological categories—reign of God, salvation, Mariology, theodicy—and theological language (doctrine, hermeneutics), using experiences of women to deconstruct and reconstruct these ideas. And that's what I'm hoping we can spend some time on during our conversation—elements of that reconstructive move that seem very elusive for those who do not experience directly the brokenness of the world or the brokenness of the Catholic tradition. Also, women are not only distinct victims of both injustice and pain (whether as mothers who face loss the moment they have children or as members of a gender that is a target of structural or institutionalized violence) but also, and more important, women are agents of change for themselves and their communities, and that agency is coming from embodiment and human dignity that stems from relationality. So I really appreciate the sense that we have much to learn from these persons and communities—and not just in terms of what they have to say to us about facets of our current reality that we miss but in terms of how those in positions of privilege (and therefore responsibility) can better respond.

In addition, part of the first two themes, from my perspective, is women's particular capacity for lament—the idea of lament as a form of prayer, an articulation of belief, an expression of resistance via a sense that what is, is not what should be or what God intends, and that women, by virtue of particular capacities for relationship that come from fundamental vulnerabilities—that are chosen or imposed—have a keen sense of this sense of alternative future and therefore have courage to call our attention to it. A few theologians have recently been working on this idea of lament—I'm thinking of Brad Hinze or Bryan Massingale[1]—but you all are opening up space here for a feminist approach to lament: it's embodied, it's a performative practice, it happens in public space, it is a form of resistance. It's probably more things—and I'd like to hear more about that.

I'd also like to pose some questions for our conversation together. What do "nontheological" folks in our tradition—artists like Kollwitz, the women of Juárez, or those who are trafficked and their allies—contribute to theological discourse about mysticism? What do they add to

---

[1] See Bradford Hinze, "Ecclesial Impasse: What Can We Learn from Our Laments?" *Theological Studies* 72, no. 3 (September 2011): 470–95; and Bryan Massingale, "Healing a Divided World," *Origins* 37, no. 11 (2007): 161–86.

this rich and, for me, compelling aspect of the tradition? I don't mean to essentialize here, but do women's forms of resistance—political and/ or mystical—have particular characteristics? What are they? What are their sources? And to what end? How do the arts—visual as in the case of Kollwitz, performative as in the case of the organizations in Juárez, poetic as in the *Magnificat*, or even rhetorical as in the opinion writing of Kristof and WuDunn in *Half the Sky*—expand our sense of what responsibility means and requires? How can we begin to bring some of the insights that you have surfaced here into theological discourse in the academy and in our classrooms?[2]

Maureen: First, let me just say thanks to everybody. The four of you really put together some fantastic essays. And as I said in my initial comments that I sent around to you, they struck lots of different chords in me, and some things I'm already actually thinking about implementing in my classroom this semester, and that is one of the last questions I'd like for us to talk about.

As I mentioned in my written comments to the group, a common theme here in your essays is a notion of resistance, or ways that women both claim an identity and claim a tradition and push against it, particularly pushing against it in trying to respond to the reality of human suffering. Each of you probably unknowingly engaged that idea from a couple different perspectives.

Susie, in your essay, I was really struck by the theme that you tried to hammer home from both Kollwitz and Sölle about beauty being a commitment to affirming human dignity, that we come to know through an increased capacity for relationship with other people. And so the way in which you described Kollwitz's own dealing with suffering and grief and war through her painting, the kind of work that she did and the kinds of relationships she was trying to claim in that work, and then the way you used Sölle as a theologian to unpack that and really think about what it means to resist vulnerability, I thought, was really tremendous.

And again I really appreciated, Nancy, the work that you did in lifting up the agency that we're seeing coming out of communities along the

[2] The following transcript reprints a conference call that took place on the morning of August 29, 2011, among the conversation starter, the contributors in this section, and the coeditors. Opening and concluding parts of the call have been edited or altogether omitted, but without altering the content of the call.

border between Mexico and the United States, communities of women who are trying to, through performative practices and performative arts, open up new spaces in the midst of violence in order to resist it. And I really was compelled by that. And I thought your piece worked so well, in many ways, with Mary's.

Mary, you set the stage to articulate the depth and the breadth of the problem of sex trafficking and the ethical and theological questions it raises. And so, Mary, your piece left me with a question about what solidarity really looks like in the context of sexual violence, when this is something that's happening both to individual, real bodies and to the collective theological or spiritual Body of Christ. So what does solidarity look like there? And I feel like Nancy's and Susie's pieces give us a sense of what that could be.

And then, again, I was so compelled by Anne's essay, in thinking through the notion of Mary as an indentured servant or a bondwoman, and what did that really mean? The implications of that just continue as I am thinking about and have read *The Help* as well as seen the movie, and I'm so perplexed by that book and film on so many different levels. I feel like Anne is bringing up a really important idea about Mary as a servant and what that means for us in the US in light of our history, both of slavery and of domestic labor, and the way we've thought about domestic labor in our past and even in our present, both mostly dealing with folks of color. There was just so much there, Anne, and I have never thought about this in the context of the *Magnificat*, but there is an element of what Mary is saying no to. There's an element of resistance there in that, and I had not ever really pondered that before.

And so, women and agency, women witnessing to a reality, women opening up space to try to rethink what's going on in a reality, and women's agency of resisting and responding were themes that really ran through all of those essays. So, do you all want to elaborate on some of the themes that I touched on in your essays, or highlight or call our attention to them in our conversation? Or even for readers of your essays or of this dialogue in the volume, is there anything you'd want to add to that or amplify a little bit of what I've said in terms of the things that I've noted in your essays?

Susie: I want to thank Maureen for pulling out our common threads. She's absolutely nailed many of the themes in each of the essays, which I found very compelling.

I heard Nancy's paper at CTSA in 2010, and I was amazed by it then. Nancy's essay and Mary's essay, more explicitly, discuss the theme of kenosis. Nancy discusses kenosis in terms of creating the empty spaces where new realities can take place, the sense of the emptying of the self that happens in motherhood or happens for a caregiver or happens for someone who has dealt with violence—the attempt to create a place where safety is possible, a place where resistance to violence is possible. So, thank you for that.

Nancy: I, too, was very struck by all of these essays, and I think one of the things that came forward for me is the agency that comes out of communities, which you picked up on here, Maureen. And that agency and how that is connected to communities, and, this relates to Mary's question and her discussion of the church, how we understand ourselves as church. And for me, that called forward the question of what's the relationship between our churches and the communities that are suffering, the people that are suffering, and how they respond to their own suffering? That relationship, I think, is present in a lot of what we're writing here, and that's a piece I think needs to be developed and considered further.

Mary: I am honored and grateful to have my essay included in this section with these other wonderful essays that touch on and develop further such significant theological and ethical themes. Putting it in this context, I'm really glad to have Susie's essay here, because what motivated me to write this was my strong sense that—in this case of sex trafficking, but also in so many other ways in this globalized situation—it's imperative that we learn to see others as equally human. And, in the histories of our communities and our religious traditions, I think that's long been the challenge: to see the other as human as we are has really been difficult, and yet it's important today. Sex trafficking is a particular case, I think, where these women and girls are discounted as not really like us. So, I think Susie's work on this topic is really helpful in bringing out what I was gesturing toward. Nancy's comments about community are also crucial and reminded me that one of the issues I came up against in struggling with and writing about sex trafficking was the importance of isolating sex traffic victims so that they can't build communities of resistance.

Isolation was a practice that came up over and over in the books I read on sex trafficking. Further, Anne has brought out the importance of saying no as well as saying yes, so that women's voiced outrage doesn't simply become the outlet that makes it now OK because we've marked the pain and now we can just integrate injustice into the status quo with women as the professional mourners. Instead, women are actually saying no to this and not just cleaning up that part of reality, so we can go on.

Anne: First of all, I too am thrilled that the genesis of my work is in this contribution. And I too was amazed by what Sölle has called the mysticism of resistance reflected in the essays by Susie, Nancy, and Mary. Living in the context of south Texas, especially in the context reflected in Nancy's essay on feminicide—am I saying that correctly, Nancy?

Nancy: Yes.

Anne: When people talk about their blood relatives who have disappeared, I really feel grief in myself. And the point which Maureen brought out about lament resonates with me. Often grief has to be "internalized," as people do not have spaces where they can lament in their newfound communities. Where do the relatives here in San Antonio gather to lament their missing or dead loved ones in Mexico and elsewhere? Some of the undocumented people here cannot return to help in the search for missing relatives, or to walk in the marches, or to place pink crosses. So I suppose it was a reminder, again, that context does matter.

I would like to bring something out that I've been acutely aware of, and that Nancy especially brought to the fore, which I was sharing with Rosemary and Kathleen earlier. In fact, all of your essays have helped me clarify what I have had an intuition about for some time, namely, what is lost in terms of translation in the Lukan narrative in relation to Mary. I too have been struggling with the more positive portrayals of Mary as a bondwoman and an indentured servant that arise in part out of the study of manumission and so forth. I have been grappling with the portrayal that servants like Mary were really middle class and well treated. That is one reading. I think what is reflected in my essay when I critique it in the light of the other essays is that Mary of Nazareth and others practiced and articulated a type of resistance in order to name just how awful the reality of bondage was. So luckily, I came across again recently the work of Séan Freyne of Dublin,[3] along with that of J. Massyngberde Ford,[4]

---

[3] Séan Freyne, *Galilee: From Alexander the Great to Hadrian, 323 BCE to 135 CE: A Study of Second Temple Judaism* (Edinburgh: T&T Clark, 2000).

[4] J. Massyngberde Ford, *My Enemy Is My Guest: Jesus and Violence in Luke* (Maryknoll, NY: Orbis Books, 1984).

whose work portrays a reality far closer to what is reflected in the other three essays. So I am, I suppose, very grounded by that.

I am also stunned by my own blindness, and that of scholarship in general, not to see more clearly (because of the lack in translations or conditioning) that Mary stands in a line of other great women of resistance. Looking at Mary as a bondwoman and prophet of resistance, and reading her canticle in that light, I now see in the first stanza of praise and in the declaration of her as "blessed" that there is a continuum between her story and what Deborah proclaimed of Jael and what was true of Judith, and between her and other great women and great canticles of the Hebrew Bible. Moreover, if we were to read the second stanza of Mary's canticle outside of its Lukan context, we might guess that it was taken from Amos or Isaiah, that it belongs to the prophetic corpus. Not only has the language of "handmaid" tamed the portrayal of Mary, but the categorization or use of her canticle primarily as a song of praise for liturgy has tamed what is a really severe and timely indictment.

So you can see, I'm a little bit passionate about this, but I'll just finish with a quote that I want to put into the conversation from Susan Ackerman. She says, and she's speaking of prophecy, particularly of the five named female prophets of the Old Testament: "Women, for example, seem to have held the exclusive responsibility for singing victory songs, or songs of resistance, after an Israelite triumph in holy war, and appear also to have assumed a principal position as ritual musicians upon occasions of lament."[5]

Now, apart from the mystical element, the portrayal of prophets, women prophets, who sing songs of resistance as well as tend to the occasions of lament or grief took me back to the story of the marches through Juárez in Nancy's essay. So these are some of the things that are unfolding for me in this dialogue among us.

Maureen: That's great. I appreciate the comments that you all made because, again, I think it deepens the point that you are making in your own essays but also starts to highlight some key points of convergence.

And maybe we can start to delve a little bit more into some of those key points. Each of you challenges or engages some fundamental theological categories. So, your essays are inherently theological in that you're

---

[5] Susan Ackerman, "Why Is Miriam Also among the Prophets? (And Is Zipporah among the Priests?)" *Journal of Biblical Literature* 121, no. 1 (2002): 47–80.

pondering ideas of salvation, Mariology, theology, even theological language and how it functions. So, I appreciate your serious engagement with these things. And you are using the experiences of women to deconstruct some of these fundamental and very familiar categories, but then I think also it's the way of feminist theology to try to reconstruct them.

And so that's where I'd like to spend the time that we might have remaining on the call—to talk a little bit about what you see from the scope of your essays in terms of women engaging around a deconstruction but also reconstruction of these fundamental theological categories.

And one place that I—and Anne brought this up in that comment that she made about lament—would be curious to hear a little bit from you about is this idea of lament. I do think we're returning to the significance of lament. There are several scholars, particularly in ethics, scholars like Bryan Massingale, who are saying that justice can't just be something that we know intellectually. It has to be something that we experience, and that we need things beyond just straightforward language to help us tap into that experiential dimension of justice. We need things like poetry, dance, and the visual arts to help us tap into what justice feels like, and not just what we know somehow justice to be.

So I'm wondering if there's anything that you see in the work that you did in your essays that says, "Here's a feminist take on this concept of lament." Given what you've worked on, how do women claim to understand lament differently, and if so, then what is lament, coming from the experiences of women?

Susie: Terrific question. The use of lament is something I've been thinking about for a long time, because I have always wondered why, in the midst of this world's chaos, that there isn't a more effective liturgical way to deal with lament on a regular basis. We have feast days and certain holiday periods in which we may incorporate lament as a church, but we don't have a weekly liturgical way to respond to the tragic headlines that confront us on a daily basis. One of the things I attempted in the essay was discussing the notion of the recognition of the other; recognition of the other and what the other needs is crucial to any movement in terms of resistance or any movement in terms of justice. Lament helps us do this.

Art enables the recognition of the other, just as Maureen said. Lament helps a community take the next step. From a liturgical perspective, art and lament make us aware of the tragedies happening right outside our doors and give us the impetus that we can somehow—once we know what's going on, once we can recognize the plight of the other—hopefully, act and join in the sorts of activities that can effect change.

Maureen: So do you think—Susie, to follow up on that point—do you think Kollwitz as an artist functions with the notion of lament, or is there something particular that artists and women artists bring to the idea of being able to know the other, to recognize the plight of the other?

Susie: What struck me about Kollwitz is her insight into what people who weren't necessarily in her circle had to endure; she was willing to go to the neighborhoods where dock workers lived and sketch them. She was willing to enter into the lives of the weavers and the lives of those other resistance movements, even though she actually had a relatively comfortable life. She was willing to find out about the lives of those in this other world, and she was able to bring this insight into her art, even when people advised her that she would make more money if she just painted pretty pictures.

Dorothee Sölle had a similar insight, in the sense that she could have had a comfortable academic position, but she didn't go that route. Her activism landed her in trouble many times. To be willing to recognize the plight of the other even to the point of accepting the other's hardship is such an inspiration to me, because it is something that I wrestle with all the time.

Nancy: I think that's so important, that recognition. Through my own work, I have come to know some of the organizing being done by women in Juárez, particularly those who have known loss. In many respects, the pink crosses going up around the city of Juárez and the cross installation at the bridge are public rituals, symbols, and installations that I think make lament an ongoing public prayer, one that claims pockets of physical space in the city.

And I see these women as popular artists. In creating these installations, the women are employing religious symbols to combat the evil that they experience. One image, that I happily discovered since I wrote the article for this publication, was produced by a woman named Laura Molina.[6] She takes Michelangelo's classic image of the Pieta and transforms it by using Guadalupe as the Mary figure holding the body of a

---

[6] This image is called *Justice for the Women of Juárez* and is depicted in Alicia Gaspar de Alba and Georgina Guzmán, *Making a Killing: Femicide, Free Trade, and La Frontera* (Austin, TX: University of Texas Press, 2010).

Juárez woman who's been killed and shows the graphic violence on her body. In this depiction the murdered Juárez woman takes the place of Jesus. A great example of the creativity that's going on here.

You were asking, Maureen, about theological language and how it functions. Many of these depictions in Juárez involve reinterpreting Jesus the Christ as the murdered women of Juárez. The women in Juárez are putting this together in some profound ways. I find this very rich. And to put forward these depictions in public as they are provokes and pushes the people of Juárez and all of us to think differently about Christian symbols. It keeps them fresh and doesn't allow them to become domesticated. With regard to the image created by Laura Molina, I intend to work with it further, because it is so provocative in the best sense. I think it connects up with what you were doing, Anne. It's very interesting that artists like Molina are drawing connections between Jesus and the violence against women in Juárez. For the most part, connections are not being made between Guadalupe or Mary and the violence against women, with this one exception. The Mary or Guadalupe figure here is not in the place of the women who've experienced violence, but in the place of Jesus. I find this a very interesting connection.

Maureen: Yes, that's fantastic. And the question that comes to mind in terms of the sacramental imagination, and keeping the sacramental imagination of the people alive—doesn't that, in a way, open up possibilities for meeting what Susie named a liturgical need to deal with lament? Aren't these folks in many ways creating sacred space and engaging in a practice of using imagery that is very familiar to us in certain contexts, and then making it unfamiliar to create new ways of thinking about what's going on?

Anne: The hermeneutics of bondage and resistance takes us also to the end of Luke's gospel, to what is usually called the Way of the Cross, where we read of the large crowd of people present, including many women. I find it interesting that Mary is not named, although the hermeneutic of suspicion would indicate that she was there in solidarity with the many women who were there, who mourned and lamented Jesus.

And Jesus seems to turn to them with an indictment. He turns to them and says, "Daughters of Jerusalem, do not weep for me. Weep instead for yourselves and for your children." In the light of what we are talking about, I now hear in this an indictment for our community, our church, and it goes something like this: "Do not weep at the cross on

Good Friday only, but weep for yourselves and your children and what is happening through sex trade and through the destruction of human beings and human dignity at places like Juárez, for the disappearance of girls and the savage treatment of them."

And then with a type of reversal, Jesus continues by giving the women a blessing: "Blessed are you who are barren, the wombs that never bore, the breasts that will never nurse." There is a twofold reading here which connects to the Hebrew genre of blessings and curses: blessed is the emptiness, because out of that—we talked earlier about the empty spaces—out of your barren wombs will come positive resistance.

And, equally, woe to those who because of their actions cause young girls to never have babies and mother them, cause sisters to no longer have sisters, and mothers and fathers to no longer have their daughters. So the whole project and orientation is changing the reading not only of the beginning of the Lukan narrative in relation to Mary but of the end in relation to the gathering of women. The whole collection of the women of Luke are gathered there and note what Jesus says—"Do not weep for me. Weep for yourselves and your children"—and that's what is reflected in all your work.

Mary: Thank you, Anne. That was really powerfully put. I deeply appreciate Maureen's question, because it challenged me to think about lament. What's going on in these other essays has been helping me think through whether there's something happening with these women and their way of lamenting that overcomes the divisions of public and private and, at the same time, the divisions between justice and mourning. So we don't have the dead mourned privately by women while men are out working for a new, better, just world publicly, but rather have all of that together. I've always been really deeply influenced by Johann Metz's argument that we have to remember the dead in order to have true justice in the future.[7] This is what I see developing in these essays—the idea that women's work for justice for the future includes memory of the specific dead. And in doing that, the attention to each individual is important to reinforce so that everyone's life is of value. Future justice is very important, but not just for the living. This was developed powerfully in Nancy's work, but I think it's also there in Susie's and Anne's blurring

[7] Johann Baptist Metz, *Faith in History and Society: Toward a Practical Fundamental Theology*, trans. and ed. J. Matthew Ashley (New York: Crossroad Publishing, 2007), esp. 60–84.

of those categories, challenging us to think more broadly and to build a
future public justice inspired by our specific and personal memories of
the dead and of past suffering.

Anne: If I can add, one point that strikes me is the embodiment of lament, and how Jesus spoke straightaway—after saying "Weep for yourselves"—about the body and that aspect of the body that is peculiar
only to women, the womb. Lament is the universal element that in many
cultures, especially in the East, is women's work—women wail and lament
in times of grief, aloud, and in my experience, in my own Irish culture,
women did this in the past. This grieving or lamenting was part of the
culture and the ritual of grief. Today, however, we are no longer regarded
as sophisticated if we cry out, vocally or in and through body gestures,
personally or collectively. And so that element has, in my experience,
been tamed in our tradition in the West.

Nancy: I think that's a very provocative comment. And it leads me to
think about the fact that we can't really deal with and face tragedy if
we don't lament. And some have argued, I believe Cornel West[8] has
and others, that in many respects we don't deal well with tragedy in this
country. In the United States, tragedy isn't really a concept that we engage
well. And in many respects, the experience of women has an enormous
amount to contribute here, because we in our bodily selves really do
know tragedy, a tragedy that many of these chapters address. We know
tragedy, and yet in some ways, our ability to address it and create a more
just society is fundamentally dependent on our recognition of the fact
that that's what we're dealing with here, tragedies that are horrific.

Maureen: Well, I think your comment is great, Nancy, for getting into
a second question. And I recognize that these are related, and in a lot
of ways speak to Mary's point about all of your work muddying the
dichotomy—the public-private, justice-mourning dichotomy that's cut
down gender lines—in thinking through justice. Both of your comments
lead me to this next question that I want to put to the four of you. At
the risk of essentializing, and I don't want to essentialize, I do think we
might be able to claim certain forms of resistance that women embody
or enact or bear witness to. And I'm wondering if in thinking through

[8] See Cornel West, *The Cornel West Reader* (New York: Basic Civitas Books, 1999).

the folks that you examined in your essays, can we name what some of those forms of witness or resistance are? What are some of those forms of resistance, and what are they contributing perhaps to this tradition that I think Mary rightly names as the mystical-political tradition? Here I am thinking of Metz and Dorothee Sölle as another major thinker in that tradition, talking about a deep relationship with God and with the other in the context of suffering that empowers one, compels one to act. So, any characteristics or ideas about the resistance that we could claim as being distinctively feminist or coming from women's experiences?

Anne: The first one that comes to my mind has to do with the matter of the different natures or statuses, if you will, of the partners of the covenant. The only angelophany or call narrative in the whole of the Christian Bible where an audible consent is given in response to a divine messenger is that given by Mary in the account of the annunciation. So the assertiveness of one's place and the dignity of one's response irrespective of the scale, if you will, or the degree of difference between the partners is a characteristic of the way women naturally relate or desire to relate. (Alas, this is not always possible in circumstances where women are oppressed.)

Mary: I have one or two things that I would add here. One, and maybe I've already said this or hinted at it, is women's tendency to remember the particular. Susie, of course, has brought this out especially well. My mom, who had eleven children, always rejected the idea that she would feel the loss of one child less because she had others. She insisted that a parent would mourn each child, and each child would be mourned differently. And so I think that lamenting the individual and the refusal to let go of the particularity of loss is something specific to women. Their movement for justice brings in the particularity of the specific person, the name of this woman dead, that child gone, this life cut off.

A second relevant point that I didn't write much about is what I've read about people trying to build solidarity to overcome sex trafficking with a consistent emphasis on reestablishing relationship. Often very little can be done except to accompany trafficked women through the long process of struggling to survive and to heal. This attention to being there with women in a personal relationship of support and accompaniment is a dimension that I think women particularly contribute, while they may also be working to change laws and structures to make it easier for women and girls to achieve freedom and harder for them to be trafficked.

Attention to the particularities of relationship and of persons is a crucial part of what's needed, and women are addressing this.

Anne: The other thing—and I'll be brief—is the ability to rejoice, to celebrate. Even as women bear what is deeply painful or tragic, the ability to combine tragedy and canticle, or more accurately, lament and canticle, is very peculiar to women. I think it is.

Susie: In terms of the particularity that Mary indicated, I think that women have a particular ability to recognize an individual story, an individual narrative, and focus on the value of that story. I don't mean to generalize, but often men think in terms of statistics, how many affected, what are the numbers, while women have a tendency to ask relational questions: What did she face at the end, or what was something that gave her joy, or what's a story to remember from her childhood? Women have a tendency to focus on these sorts of relational details, perhaps displaying a tendency to be more focused on the needs of the other. In terms of women's experience, of what they know as women and their roles as mothers or as caregivers, they have opportunities to exercise this ability in ways that men usually do not. This sense of being aware of the particular story or narrative of the other was a particular talent that Sölle displayed. When she visited with the Mothers of the Disappeared, she listened to their narratives, contemplated the pictures of their loved ones, in a way that the men probably did not. Perhaps the men wanted to immediately march in the street, which is a good thing, but it is also valuable to sit with the women and hear their stories.

Nancy: I think, too, that in terms of forms of resistance—and this is really provoked by what you're saying, Susie—women, because they give birth, have a tendency to be in tune with the thread of life as multi-generational, as extending well before their own lives and well after. Because women tend to appreciate this extension, rich possibilities emerge. Women—in depicting and focusing on the particularity of suffering, for example, in Juárez—think about their community and what it will be for their children and for their children's children, and on into the future, as well as a connection back into the past. The women in Juárez, in connecting their own stories to the story of Jesus, are connecting their lives today to an event of two thousand years ago and are anticipating, in many respects, the resurrection—the bodily resurrection of us all in the future. So there's that larger extension of life that is important for us to consider.

Maureen: I am wondering if any of you have thoughts about how to bring the insights that you have come to in your own essays, and even those that we have surfaced here collectively about lament and resistance, into our classrooms? Is there any sense of how we might start to talk a little bit about women's ways of lamenting, women's ways of resistance in our classrooms, in our theology classrooms—and potentially the academy? I do think that this book project and the very process of the project is starting to actually model some of the things that we might talk about in this last question. But thinking about this in terms of teaching, how do you take this to the classroom? How do you take this to undergraduates?

Mary: I'm going to jump in with a general point here, because I think the rest of you have some powerful and specific insights, but one thing I need to keep reminding myself of is to resist the claim that theology is predominantly about abstract or general ideas. I've always been absolutely convinced by Paul Ricoeur's hermeneutical claim that if you don't understand what something means for you in your context, then you simply don't understand what it means.[9] So the idea that we can teach beliefs about God, the Trinity, salvation, or the reign of God as abstract doctrines and then leave students to determine what, if anything, those doctrines might mean in their lives is a huge mistake, as though the application is something apart from the academic discussion of theological meaning. We're not teaching them what Christian beliefs are if we're not exploring with them where those beliefs challenge their own life situations. (That was to give you all a chance to compose your thoughts and say something really good.)

Maureen: That was really good, Mary.

Anne: Something I do a little of already, but this will then help me to move it further, when I do the abstract theology, is that I ask the students to apply the narratives to their personal experiences that arise from the community, from their ethnic grouping, and then nationally and internationally. So, whether it is embodiment of resistance or lamentation, one aspect would be to ask our students to apply narratives to lived experience in a dialectical fashion. All of our theology is generated ultimately from

---

[9] Paul Ricoeur, *Interpretation Theory: Discourse and the Surplus of Meaning* (Fort Worth, TX: Texas Christian University Press, 1976), esp. 80–88.

the experience of God and of community, and of the woundedness and the blessedness of life. So, one suggestion is that as part of an assignment, they use their own experiences, or they research the experiences of others, and link these with the texts that reflect the more abstract theological ideas.

Nancy: I do something similar to what's already been said. Whatever theme or concept I'm trying to teach on a given day, I always launch the class with a question, or perhaps an article from the newspaper, or a small clip from a film, or a work of art, very much like what Susie has given us. That was such a wonderful introduction to Kollwitz's work! This launches them into their own experience, to get them to turn to their personal experience or their experience with the community that they live in or someplace where they can look at an experience of suffering, for example, and then we move into what we're discussing or reading for that day. But to start there with their personal experience is something I always try to do.

Kathleen: Are there some closing remarks that we could invite right now, and then move into Rosemary's reflection?

Anne: I'm not sure if this is a closing remark, but it is one last thought that I didn't share already. For the women at the tomb in Luke, their stories seemed to be nonsense, and they were not believed. One characteristic of women's experience which seems to be almost universal is that the initial response to their stories is dismissal. Of course, the response of women to such dismissals is to say, "You may dismiss us now, but we're not going to go away." So I'm just connecting that reading of Luke again with the hermeneutic of resistance.

Nancy: I think, Anne, what you're saying is on target. As I've presented work on the feminicide in Juárez, a lot of times one of the first reactions is disbelief, that this can't possibly be real, that this couldn't possibly be happening, and a dismissal of the reality of this tragedy. So I think the point is, and this has been true throughout history, that it's important to pay attention to the reaction of disbelief.

Mary: Yes, I'd be very happy to let Anne's comments about the dismissal of women, of their experiences and their suffering, stand as a closing remark on what I've tried to say.

Susie: Yes, in Mary's essay there's the reminder that women are often criminalized for prostitution when they're the ones forced into it. That dismissal of their suffering Nancy brought out as well. One statement highlighted in her essay cites the testimony of the Women's Caucus for Gender Justice at The Hague: women are victims of violence for no other reason than because they are women. This statement indicates a world blind to this violence, which I find chilling. Anne's essay places Mary in the tradition of the Hebrew Bible prophets such as Miriam of Exodus and Hagar—whom I've always considered the first female theologian because she runs into the wilderness and demands that God answer her. All of us have contributed to articulating the demand that women must not be silenced, that we will continue to tell the stories of the disappeared, and we will continue to bring violence against women to the attention of the world. Thank you all.

Kathleen: And thanks to all of you.

Maureen: Well said, really. Thank you very much; it was just a rich, rich conversation, and your essays are fantastic. And I don't want that to be the last word, but I wanted to acknowledge that.

Kathleen: Thank you, Maureen; thank you all. Rosemary, would you conclude with a reflection?

Rosemary: Sure. Let me remind everybody that each of the sections of the book will begin with an excerpt from Monika Hellwig's inaugural lecture of the Madeleva Lecture Series. Her first lecture in the series, given in 1985, was titled "Christian Women in a Troubled World." And each section of the book, as I've said, will print an excerpt at the beginning in order to provide an orienting point or a frame of reference for the essays in that section. So, let me conclude by reading the excerpt that I've chosen for our section in light of the topics raised by your essays. And if you'd like to make any comments about the excerpt once I've concluded, I invite you to do so.

[Rosemary reads the excerpt.]

I know that's a lot to absorb, but I think that we in this section embody parts of what Hellwig analyzed in 1985. I'm wondering if you have interpreted your vocation explicitly in the way that she describes it. Do you interpret your theological, ethical, and scriptural work in the way that she describes it, or are you pushing that work in different directions? I invite your responses.

Susie: This is a terrific passage. I struggle with the dissonance between my own comfort and privilege, the advantages I've had my entire life, and the level of suffering and injustice in the world. This dissonance is an ongoing part of spiritual life, of theological life, of teaching life, and she voiced that problem well.

Mary: I also agree that the issues of being elite and privileged are very important to consider. One of the things that I've been thinking about lately is that the global economy is tying us all into a vast competitive system in which our privileges and liberties are increasingly, again, being implicated in and depend upon other people's oppression and the destruction of their communities. And that globalization actually makes individual and communal discernment of the demands of justice much more difficult, because it's awfully hard to give up our standard of living. It's hard to see the cost of our lifestyle when we're in a global system, and it's a lot easier not to see the cost. So, I think our churches as church have a role to play, but it's a big task for us to face, the communal discernment of injustice, especially for those of us who are the elite and privileged in this system.

Anne: I would absolutely concur with Hellwig's perspective on the responsibility of our vocation and the privilege that I enjoy. Two things come to mind: one is the challenge of bridging the gap. It is a reminder to me to reflect on the question, "How do I bridge the gap between my writings, my study, and the women whose lives I want to be improved because of the work I do?" I am reminded of Dorothee Sölle's reflection about what she calls, if I recall correctly, the *via media*, "a mysticism of the middle way"[10]—namely, that when our lifestyle and commitment is not so far removed from what or whom we are writing about, our textual response bears more integrity.

And the second thing I am reminded about comes from the Leadership Conference of Women Religious (LCWR) that I attended in August. For the session on immigration, rather than bring in a theologian to address us, the organizers invited three women, two of whom had been undocumented in this country and one who still is. All three are working toward immigration reform for undocumented people. I imagine that if we ever do an exercise like this again, that some of the women that

---

[10] She writes: "This resistance does not necessarily have to assume the shape of radical possessionlessness, but the recollection of the craziness of the mystical tradition helps in finding the truth that some things cannot be possessed, bought, and sold." See *The Silent Cry: Mysticism and Resistance* (Minneapolis: Fortress Press, 2001), 254.

we are writing about and for are part of the conversation. So it just calls forth in me that response, insofar as that is possible.

Nancy: Yes, and I agree with what all of you have expressed. What it lifts up for me is the fact that bodies matter in our world. All the essays that we've contributed, and certainly Monika Hellwig's passage, reflect that point. And I, too, struggle with trying to be committed, at the expense of my privilege, to those who are in much more dire circumstances than I am. So amen to these reflections.

Kathleen: I think we've heard from all the contributors now, so picking up on that word "amen," amen to all. And Rosemary, thank you for reading that reflection from Monika Hellwig. It's so remarkable how that reflection actually emphasizes what this conversation has been about for the last hour or so. So thank you all. Are there any parish announcements or anything before we'd like to end?

Mary: I have really enjoyed this very stimulating, thought-provoking conversation. I'm grateful to all of you, especially Maureen, Rosemary, and Kathleen, as well as my fellow contributors, whose essays are so challenging.

Susie: That's amen again.

Nancy: Amen to that, yes.

Anne: Thank you.

Maureen: Thanks.

Women's Wisdom in Context

Academia and Higher Education

To be deprived of the power of domination, to have little or no access to bullying power, to be unable to compel or persuade by threat or use of institutional sanctions, is necessarily to be thrown back upon other resources. And that may well be to discover that divine power, the power of grace, is of a very different kind, effective inasmuch as it empowers and liberates human freedom—freedom for self-transcendence, freedom for true community with others, freedom for God and for God's purposes in creation and history. On the other hand, to have access to bullying power is inevitably to be sorely tempted to use it. But it is not Christ's way. Because of our Church organization, Christ's way by empowerment of human freedom to transcend is likely to be more immediately apparent to women.

Looked at positively, the characteristic possibilities for a spirituality of Christian women that can really make a Christian difference in a troubled world seem to be concerned particularly with prayer, compassion, solidarity and creative imagination. . . .

Redemptive compassion issues in solidarity, and the structures by which redemption is brought about, are structures of solidarity. If sin is the centering of private projects to the disregard of what these do to other people, and with consequences of feuds and wars, oppression and needless sufferings, fear and insecurity, violence and chaos, then redemption is the process of undoing all of this by the reconstruction of a society, a world, a network of relationships that respect the solidarity of the human race as created and destined by God. We are far from this reconstruction and it may seem that the project is quite hopeless, yet quiet observation assures us that every small effort or initiative in this direction is almost immediately immensely fruitful.

—Monika Hellwig, *Christian Women in a Troubled World*, 25–26, 43–44

Virtues and Voices

Building Solidarity among Women Scholars

Mary M. Doyle Roche, College of the Holy Cross

Wisdom calls aloud in the streets,
    she raises her voice in the public squares;
she calls out at the street corners,
    she delivers her message at the city gates.

—Proverbs 1:20[1]

In the autumn of 2005, I received an invitation to the New Voices Seminar and the annual Madeleva Lecture at Saint Mary's College that coming spring. I had read the "Madeleva Manifesto" and had treasured copies of the series of pocket-sized gray volumes, the published versions of previous lectures.[2] Even so, I had little idea of what to expect when I arrived in the small regional airport in South Bend the following April. A recently minted PhD, desperately hanging on to my sanity as the first year of full-time teaching was coming to a close, I was greeted by the hospitality of Kathleen Dolphin, the director of the Center for Spirituality—already a different experience from any other academic conference I had attended. The warm welcome continued as I met colleagues

[1] Passages from the Bible in this section are taken from the New Jerusalem Bible translation.

[2] An excerpt of the "Madeleva Manifesto" is available at http://www3.saintmarys.edu/madeleva-lecture-series (accessed May 1, 2011). The Madeleva lectures have been published by Paulist Press, Mahwah, NJ.

from Saint Mary's for the first time and familiar faces began to arrive on campus.

Since that time, I have been present for lectures and conversations with Susan A. Ross, M. Shawn Copeland, Anne E. Patrick, and Wendy M. Wright—a veritable backstage pass to dialogues with leading members of the scholarly community to which I had recently been inducted.[3] We talked long and leisurely about beauty, creativity, race, gender, images and imagination, bodies and souls, work and vocation, faith and life in the church. Each year, even newer voices join in and others return for more. The New Voices Seminar has become in many ways a safe space for scholarly creativity, mentoring, solidarity, questioning, shared frustration, and vulnerability.

Yet this essay is not an ode to the New Voices Seminar. I begin with this brief narrative because it is an experience that has sparked my interest in thinking critically and practically about building solidarity among women scholars, including women theologians and ethicists, today. The first part of this essay focuses briefly on the importance of *voice* for feminist theorists and builds on an insight that scholars should not only listen *to* voices but listen *for* voices as well.[4] This is an imminent (effecting its primary change on the agent), transformative practice. The second part moves to articulate a feminist virtue ethic that stresses the practices necessary to live solidaristically in the academic community. Solidarity as a virtue is often associated, quite rightly, with social justice practices and a commitment to a preferential option for the poor. However, solidarity among women scholars might also require practices that cultivate the virtue of fidelity. Finally, the third part explores the possibilities and challenges of expanding circles of solidarity in global perspective. Technology will have a crucial role to play in these endeavors, but solidarity in cyberspace has limits that must be acknowledged, including access and technological literacy as well as the implications of disembodied voices in virtual communities.

---

[3] Susan A. Ross, "For the Beauty of the Earth: Women, Sacramentality, and Justice," 2006; M. Shawn Copeland, "The Subversive Power of Love: The Vision of Henriette Delille," 2007; Anne E. Patrick, "Women, Conscience, and the Creative Process," 2009; Wendy M. Wright "Le Point Vierge: Mary and the Catholic Imagination," 2010.

[4] Sara Lawrence-Lightfoot and Jessica Hoffman Davis, *The Art and Science of Portraiture* (San Francisco: Jossey-Bass, 1997).

Voices

Her lips were moving but her voice could not be heard.

—1 Samuel 1:13

In 1982 Carol Gilligan published her groundbreaking feminist critique of dominant theories of moral development, *In a Different Voice*.[5] With other feminist theorists Gilligan alerted us to the limits of prevailing theories of moral development that failed to account for the ways in which women and girls tend to frame and resolve moral dilemmas. Because the responses of women and girls to various ethical cases resisted conforming to the researchers' expectations, their reasoning was deemed less developed, their moral growth stunted. Gilligan pointed out that while a principled commitment to justice may be important for ethical action, women and girls viewed the case narratives in terms of how the context shaped and was shaped by relationships among the moral actors. Women and girls made moral decisions in light of attempts to remain faithful to key particular relationships, as opposed to strict adherence to universal, abstract principles. An adequate moral theory would have to incorporate these experiences and voices as legitimate sources of moral wisdom and would value maintaining human relationships as a key element of moral living.

In Margaret Farley's essay "A Feminist Version of Respect for Persons," the value that modernity places on autonomy is set in the context of the relationality that is constitutive of human personhood.[6] Without denying the importance of extending the Enlightenment project regarding human autonomy and independence to women, Farley clearly notes its anthropological limits. Human beings are radically social and interdependent with one another. Human beings thrive in relationships that are characterized by justice and fidelity. "Freedom," writes Farley, "then, rises out of relationality and serves it. Freedom is for the sake of relationship—with ourselves and with all that can be known and loved."[7] The voices of Christian feminist ethics brought this crucial nuance to the

---

[5] Carol Gilligan, *In a Different Voice: Psychological Theory and Women's Development* (Cambridge, MA: Harvard University Press, 1982).

[6] Margaret A. Farley, "A Feminist Version of Respect for Persons," *Feminist Ethics and the Catholic Moral Tradition*, ed. Charles E. Curran, Margaret A. Farley, and Richard A. McCormick (Mahwah, NJ: Paulist Press, 1996), 164–83; originally published in *Journal of Feminist Studies in Religion* 9, nos. 1–2 (Spring–Fall 1993): 183–98.

[7] Farley, "A Feminist Version of Respect for Persons," 179.

table of feminist theory that had emphasized the values of the Enlightenment, in particular the claims to individual autonomy and political rights.

In 1985 Elaine Scarry's *The Body in Pain: The Making and Unmaking of the World* demonstrated what is at stake in voice.[8] According to Scarry, "Physical pain does not simply resist language but actively destroys it, bringing about an immediate reversion to a state anterior to language, to the sounds and cries a human being makes before language is learned."[9] In her analysis of torture, she notes that the aim of the torturer is to separate body from voice, self from voice. Paradoxically, torture succeeds in a perverse way not when it elicits important information (which it rarely if ever does) but when it deconstructs, unmakes a world, when it silences and destroys.[10] To silence, then, is to deny humanity, and the silencing extends beyond the individual victim to the wider community, including the dehumanization of the torturer.

In 1991 Dana Crowley Jack wrote *Silencing the Self: Women and Depression* in which she describes the corrosive effects on women's mental health of keeping silent about one's experiences of suffering and isolation.[11] Silencing imposed by one's relationships or by the wider culture can become internalized. Reclaiming one's voice is crucial for healing. Jack's work has become instrumental for practices of community-based participatory action research, education, and intervention among HIV+ women of color in the Boston area. Sharing voice through writing and discussion has been a fruitful avenue for healing among these women and has empowered them to educate others in an incredible act of courageous disclosure in the film *Women's Voices, Women's Lives*.[12]

Studying women's voices through different fields of psychology, ethics, and medicine translated into studying women's voices in academia itself.

---

[8] Elaine Scarry, *The Body in Pain: The Making and Unmaking of the World* (New York: Oxford University Press, 1985).

[9] Ibid., 4.

[10] Ibid., 20.

[11] Dana Crowley Jack, *Silencing the Self: Women and Depression* (Cambridge, MA: Harvard University Press, 1991). Jack's theories were introduced to me by Rosanna DeMarco, PhD, PHCNS-BC, ACRN, FAAN, of Boston College Connell School of Nursing, who has incorporated the concept of silencing the self into community-based participatory action research with HIV-positive women of color in Boston, MA, in collaboration with Sistah Powah and the Women of Color AIDS Council.

[12] Rosanna DeMarco, *Women's Voices, Women's Lives*, Boston College Connell School of Nursing.

Though some strands of feminism highlighted the distinctive "experience of women," many women did not see themselves or their experiences honored in articulations of white academics from North America and Europe. Is there such a thing as "women's experience" or a different "women's voice?" Feminist ethics subsequently resisted essentialism based on sex or gender and challenged the notion that there is unity of experience among women. The "different voice" raised by Gilligan became a chorus of different voices speaking from many experiences shaped by multiple axes of difference (race, ethnicity, socioeconomic status, sexual orientation, religion, etc.). Voices from history long ignored even by feminist scholars were brought into relief so that the wisdom wrought from experience could inspire women today.

A classic example in this chorus comes from Madeleva lecturer M. Shawn Copeland. In "Wading through Many Sorrows: Toward a Theology of Suffering in Womanist Perspective,"[13] she immerses us in the narratives of women in chattel slavery who clung to voice and empowered themselves through *sass*. A womanist theology of suffering attends to the "differentiated range of Black women's experiences" and "retells the lives and sufferings of those who 'came through' and those who have 'gone on to glory land.'" The exercise of voice in sass became a powerful means of resistance to the obliteration of the self under slavery and torture: "Enslaved Black women use sass to guard, regain, and secure self-esteem; to obtain and hold psychological distance; to speak truth.[14]

As personal uniqueness came to the fore, the postmodern interest in difference made any hint of universality, whether of experience or of moral norms, extremely suspect. Christian feminist ethicists (particularly those whose roots have been both nourished and choked off by the natural law traditions in Catholicism) have struggled to strike a balance that could remain open to a vision of shared humanity.[15] The multitude of voices

[13] M. Shawn Copeland, "Wading through Many Sorrows: Toward a Theology of Suffering in Womanist Perspective," originally in Emilie Townes, ed., *A Troubling in My Soul: Womanist Perspectives on Evil and Suffering* (Maryknoll, NY: Orbis Books, 1993), 109–29; later reprinted in *Feminist Ethics in the Catholic Moral Tradition*, ed. Charles E. Curran, Margaret A. Farley, and Richard A. McCormick (Mahwah, NJ: Paulist Press, 1996).

[14] Copeland, "Wading through Many Sorrows," in Curran et al., eds., *Feminist Ethics in the Catholic Moral Tradition*, 155 and 152.

[15] Margaret Farley, "Feminism and Universal Morality," in Gene Outka and John P. Reeder, eds., *Prospects for a Common Morality* (Princeton, NJ: Princeton University Press, 1993). Susan Parsons, "Feminist Ethics after Modernity: Towards an Appropriate Universalism," *Studies in Christian Ethics* 8, no. 1 (1995): 77–94. On feminist ethics and the natural law

need not end up in a cacophony. The desire for solidarity grounded in a common human experience remains. A question rises to the surface: How to hear this voice among the many voices, and beyond that, how to hear the "still, small voice" of the Lord in all creation? The scholarship of Sara Lawrence-Lightfoot may provide insight into how women theologians might endeavor to hear this voice in their research and collegial practices.

Sara Lawrence-Lightfoot is a sociologist and MacArthur Fellow who has written on United States school culture. I first encountered her work in my research on ethical issues involving children and childhood. Lawrence-Lightfoot pioneered a method in sociological research called portraiture. Like the revival and renewal of the method of casuistry (reasoning through the use of case studies) in Catholic moral theology, Lawrence-Lightfoot emphasizes the role of narrative in informing research.[16] She takes her lead from Oliver Sacks's 1985 book, *The Man Who Mistook His Wife for a Hat*. She picks up on his insight that clinical storytelling declined as medicine sought recognition as a science, becoming "increasingly routinized, codified, and impersonal." This loss was not without serious ramifications: "The efforts to increase the rigor and the *science* led to caricatures and distortions in seeing, hearing, and healing the patient, in defining doctor-patient relationship, and in identifying points of intervention and sources of strength leading to the patient's recovery."[17]

In her articulation of portraiture in the social sciences, Lawrence-Lightfoot elaborates on listening for voice.

> We focus on the *actors'* voices; we listen for the timbre, resonance, cadence, and tone of their voices, their message, and their meaning. We make a subtle distinction between listening *to* voice and listening *for* voice, the latter a more assertive stance than the former. When the portraitist listens for voice, she seeks it out, trying to capture its texture and cadence, exploring its meaning and transporting its sound and message into the text through carefully selected quotations.[18]

---

traditions, see Cristina L. H. Traina, *Feminist Ethics and the Natural Law: An End to the Anathemas* (Washington, DC: Georgetown University Press, 1999).

[16] See, for example, James F. Keenan and Thomas A. Shannon, *The Context of Casuistry* (Washington, DC: Georgetown University Press, 1995).

[17] Lawrence-Lightfoot and Hoffman Davis, *The Art and Science of Portraiture*, 5–6.

[18] Ibid., 99. Lawrence-Lightfoot borrows the phrase "listening for voice" from American author Eudora Welty. See Eudora Welty, *Eye of the Story: Selected Essays and Reviews* (New York: Vintage, 1990).

Listening for voice differs from listening to voices, or hearing. Listening for voice is active and engaged. It is transformative of the listener and the speaker alike. It involves listening for meaning, for the "through" line, the narrative unity amid the fractures in one voice and amid the plurality of voices. Portraiture asks that scholars listen for "repetitive refrains," "resonant metaphors," as well as themes that are "contrasting and dissonant."[19] It entails listening for what is genuinely human.

Lawrence-Lightfoot presents a challenge to her field of sociology that could be taken up by feminist theologians as well, in both our research and our own practices of scholarly and social interaction. As Lawrence-Lightfoot states, "As newcomer and stranger to the setting, the researcher inevitably experiences surprises: events, experiences, behaviors, and values that she had not anticipated, and to which she must adapt and respond."[20] The surprises encountered in research also pop up in other interactions among scholars. I recall my first academic conference: entering an elevator at some hotel, near some airport, and seeing familiar names on name tags, names I had only encountered in books. I was surprised by physical appearance, the sound of a voice, a sense of humor, a spouse, the makeup of various groups headed out to eat. We may be surprised too by questions raised in conference sessions, or a new direction for a well-known scholar. The New Voices Seminar also provides space for surprise within a distinctive atmosphere of trust that is born not only of familiarity but of solidarity as well.

However, as members of a scholarly community, we are not simply adapting and responding to what is happening around us. As Lawrence-Lightfoot remarks, "It is not only important for the portraitist to paint the contours and dimensions of the setting, it is also crucial that she sketch herself into the context."[21] We are shaped by and actively give shape to the context in which we find ourselves; Lawrence-Lightfoot reminds us that "context is not static."[22] With respect to the theological disciplines, feminist scholars are alert to the many voices that have been silenced, omitted, erased from the sketches of Christian community. Even feminist scholars must also be alert to their own practices of silencing, omission, and erasure in a global church. Women are writing themselves into the

---

[19] Lawrence-Lightfoot and Hoffman Davis, *The Art and Science of Portraiture*, 193.

[20] Ibid., 43.

[21] Ibid., 50.

[22] Ibid., 57.

story of the theological disciplines, and our guilds need to engage in what ethicist John Wall refers to as "narrative expansion."[23]

Both raising voice and listening for voice are transformative of both speaker and listener. My story has new meaning once it has been spoken; I am new for having spoken it. In listening for voice, I not only receive a story but have become a participant in the narrative. The danger, of course, for any scholar—and for any colleague, family member, friend, spouse, parent, or child, for that matter—is not to receive the story on its own terms but rather to impose meaning on the narrative that effectively silences the speaker and co-opts the story. Practices of Christian listening for voice and narrative expansion do not have competing selves at the center of the narrative. Rather, the gospel story sits at the center; it is this voice for which we are listening as it is spoken, healed, crucified, and risen. This is the story into which we speak and write ourselves in responsiveness to others and to the Other, the One who creates with the Word.

This is far from an exhaustive look at the importance or the complexity of voice for feminist theologians. These few examples of feminist contributions do, however, provide some cues for practices of authentic solidarity in feminist perspective. Listening for voice strives to be active and engaged without being oppressive. Stories are not spoken out from or into the ether. They are shared by embodied people in concrete sets of circumstances with others who in some way shape and are shaped by those circumstances. The stories are intertwined in the telling. The human story is at once shared and diverse beyond imagining. So our practices of solidarity will likewise be diverse, but recognizable to those who are shaped by the gospel narrative.

Finally, if voice, sharing experiences and reflection on experiences, is central to the moral self, then one way of responding to the other in solidarity will be to create spaces for voice and narrative. While solidarity resists silencing, it must also cultivate a level of comfort with silence.[24] As the poet Mary Oliver says in "Praying," we make room for other voices

---

[23] John Wall, *Ethics in Light of Childhood* (Washington, DC: Georgetown University Press, 2010).

[24] Thomas Merton, *No Man Is an Island* (New York: Harcourt Brace, 1955), and *Contemplative Prayer* (New York: Herder and Herder, 1969); Anne D. LeClaire, *Listening below the Noise: A Meditation on the Practice of Silence* (New York: Harper Collins, 2009).

by cultivating silence.[25] In the space of that silence, others raise their voices on their own terms and in their own time.

Virtues

Each mortal thing does one thing and the same:
Deals out that being indoors each one dwells;
Selves—goes itself; *myself* it speaks and spells,
Crying *Whát I do is me: for that I came.*

—Gerard Manley Hopkins, from "As Kingfishers Catch Fire"

In his "Last Lecture" at Boston College, systematic theologian Michael Himes highlights the moral task of speaking our message quite definitely in the world.[26] For Himes, the message is Michael Himes. The self and the message are the same. The questions that guide moral living for Himes include, What is your story? What is the source of your pain? What is the source of your joy? How did you come to be here? The project of human personhood is telling your story. If we are to follow the likes of Himes and Jesuit poet Gerard Manley Hopkins, my story is myself. More importantly for this essay, if speaking my unique message is essential to personhood, then listening for the story of another is the hallmark of human solidarity.

In the field of moral theology, this approach is consistent with two inter-related strands of the Catholic tradition: casuistry and virtue. Casuistry is a practice of relating case narratives in order to reveal patterns of wisdom and right action. Casuistry alerts us to the details and texture of a particular case even as it draws analogies to other cases. As ethicist Cristina Traina reminds us, for casuistry to be done well it is crucial to have knowledge of a wide range of case narratives that have been resolved successfully.[27] Feminist ethicists have demanded that an even wider range of cases and possible resolutions be included in moral deliberation. While precedent is important, stare decisis (standing by previous decisions) is not a value in itself. James Keenan has noted that casuistry's history has been marked by an attempt to balance the letter and the spirit of moral principles as

[25] Mary Oliver, "Praying," in *Thirst* (Boston: Beacon Press, 2006), 37.
[26] Michael Himes, "Last Lecture," given November 18, 2008, available at http://frontrow.bc.edu/program/himes2 (accessed June 6, 2011).
[27] Traina, *Feminist Ethics and the Natural Law*, 105.

communities confront the chaos that often characterizes life, especially the life of the poor.[28] Casuistry is well suited as a moral methodology for thinking in times of change and even social upheaval.

Casuistry employed with a feminist lens will seek out the stories of the poor and vulnerable and so nurture the habits of solidarity and compassion. This method of moral reasoning will attend to both the particular and the universal. Casuistry must respect the moral agency of all people; it is not a substitute judgment; ethicists are not superior arbiters of the moral culpability of others, undermining the agency of those involved or twisting their narratives. Casuistry is not practiced in the abstract; rather, it is practiced in the concrete daily lives of real people as they share their stories of joy and suffering, of human failing and right living. Casuistry practiced in Christian feminist ethics will be undertaken in community formed by the good news of the gospel story, aiming at ever-greater justice and freedom for relationships and responsibilities.[29] The aim of casuistry is the "incarnation of virtue."[30]

Virtue is a person-centered, rather than an act-centered, ethic. According to moral theologian James Keenan, a virtue ethic presents the moral agent with three central questions: Who am I? Who do I want to become? How ought I get there? These questions are founded on several assumptions drawn from the work of Thomas Aquinas: every act is a moral act, and we become what we do.[31] Resembling the lines of Hopkins's "As Kingfishers Catch Fire," the just one "justices" and keeps all of her "goings just." Cultivating a habit of just actions and decisions makes one just. If we become what we do, then what I do is me; the story I tell is me in my becoming.

Virtue ethics alerts us to the moral challenges and opportunities we face in everyday life. The habits we form and the practices in which we engage transform us. Moreover, moral agents—and I would add moral

[28] James F. Keenan, "Applying the Seventeenth-Century Casuistry of Accommodation to HIV Prevention," *Theological Studies* 60, no. 3 (September 1999): 499–512, and "The Return of Casuistry" *Theological Studies* 57, no. 1 (March 1996): 123–39.

[29] Mary M. Doyle Roche, "Casuistry: Moral Method for an Ethics of Childhood," paper delivered at the Catholic Theological Ethics in the World Church Conference, Trento, July 2010.

[30] Traina, *Feminist Ethics and the Natural Law*, 105.

[31] James F. Keenan, "Ten Reasons Why Aquinas Is Important for Ethics Today," *New Blackfriars* 75 (July-August 1994): 354–63.

communities—need a proactive plan. Virtue is not a reactive ethics; the virtuous person or community does not wait paralyzed until a new moral dilemma emerges. It is an ethic of growth, of striving out of love to do the right. Otherwise, moral agents live in a moral minefield, remaining perfectly still for fear of sinning.[32]

As Keenan sketches cardinal virtues for our age, he is clearly influenced by developments in feminist theological ethics, particularly the emphasis on relationality. Relationship is at the heart of the life of virtue and is the lens through which we discern particular virtues. For Keenan, human beings desire *union*, being together, being one—with one another and, ultimately, with God. Many of our moral struggles reflect this desire. Keenan identifies three spheres of relationality and their corresponding virtues. We are in relationships generally, with a great number of others with whom we must live justly. We are in particular, specific relationships with those who are near and dear to us. With these we must live faithfully. And we are in relationship with our very unique selves to whom we owe self-care.[33] How can these virtues advance solidarity among women in academic settings in the concrete?

Building solidarity among women scholars requires certain habits of virtue. Listening for voice is a key practice for solidarity with women scholars. The practice of casuistry, listening to and for the wisdom in and across narratives, is a fruitful moral method for those who desire solidarity with others. Solidarity is, I think, most closely associated with the commitment to justice found in Catholic social teaching.[34] Solidarity involves standing with others in their struggle and making common cause with those who seek justice. For scholars, solidarity may mean teaching about and devoting our research and scholarly endeavors to the concerns of many people whom we may never meet, especially those who are poor and powerless, those whose voices have been silenced in familial, political, academic, and ecclesial communities.

---

[32] James F. Keenan, *Moral Wisdom: Lessons and Texts from the Catholic Tradition*, 2nd ed. (Lanham, MD: Rowman & Littlefield, 2010).

[33] Keenan, *Moral Wisdom*.

[34] See Kenneth Himes, ed., *Modern Catholic Social Teaching: Commentaries and Interpretations* (Washington, DC: Georgetown University Press, 2005). Jon Sobrino has been among the most influential articulators of the importance of solidarity for Christian theology and ethics; see Stephen Pope, ed., *Hope and Solidarity: Sobrino's Challenge to Christian Theology* (Maryknoll, NY: Orbis Books, 2008).

Yet this notion of standing *with* others suggests some proximity as well. Thus, solidarity among women scholars may move closer to the practices of fidelity—faithfulness to particular others. This has been the genius of practices like the New Voices and other gatherings of colleagues. Fostering solidarity is facilitated by the fostering of friendships. Friendships are encouraged when friends can be together. Friendship is, on the whole, an embodied reality even though it can be sustained through long absences and in our technological age may occasionally be formed and sustained without physical presence.

What began as a way to engage other women scholars in conversation about our theological research and experience in the academy has evolved into the desire for union with these particular women. This is the desire that motivates us to get together at other conferences and in other contexts and has in part motivated the writing of this book. It is good to be together in person and on the written page. Being together has also opened the possibility of listening for our theological narratives in the context of the larger narratives of our lives. Social location and context influence scholarship and are full of details that can be known only among friends with whom there is trust and faithfulness.

The circles of solidarity, fidelity, and friendship have a way of expanding. At a recent conference, New Voices members and others laughed about the "six degrees of Suzy" (names have been changed to protect the innocent). Friendships have opened the way to forge new relationships among colleagues. On several occasions I have met other scholars with the expression "I feel as if I already know you." We have shared stories and engaged each other's writing and lectures with a keen sense of the person behind the page and the podium. We may read each other's work—but we are also present to one another in a different way when we are gathered together. We share our stories with particular others with whom there is trust. There is a generosity of spirit that calls us to be our best and to think well about pressing theological and moral issues. It would be a mistake to think of this as soft or "touchy-feely." The hermeneutic of suspicion is alive and well, as is intellectual rigor. But many unchallenged assumptions are best faced and explored with company.

Solidarity among and with women theologians will require, then, several concrete practices. First, we theologians must listen to and for voice in each other's scholarship. Second, we ought to share those voices with others in our teaching and in our writing (expanding our reading lists and syllabi beyond the "classics"). A third practice involves engaging voices with a hermeneutics that is both critical and generous. A posture of generosity may be especially crucial for Catholic Christian theologians who have a unique and often strained relationship with the episcopacy's magisterial authority. Our responsibility as theologians, ethicists, and so on entails critiquing one another so that our articulations improve—moving closer to what is right and true. Women scholars do so because we desire the best for one another and the church, the people of God in the world.

The fourth and perhaps most logistically challenging practice of solidarity involves being together, physically present to one another, whenever possible. The New Voices Seminar embodies this grace of being together and thereby fosters a host of virtues: justice, fidelity, and self-care among them.[35] Listening for voice in these more intimate moments of laughter, tears, and table fellowship opens a space for a deepening solidarity akin to the virtue of fidelity, as well as a broadening solidarity associated with justice. If the community of women scholars aims to be a solidaristic community, with secure relationships that are ever opening onto new relationships, this will take deliberate planning, institutional forms of support, and commitment to the practices of virtue.

Expanding Circles of Solidarity

No utterance at all, no speech,
not a sound to be heard,
but from the entire earth the design stands out,
this message reaches the whole world.

—Psalm 19:3-4

In July of 2010, I would find myself on another small plane, arriving in another small airport, Verona, on my way to Trento in the Alto Aldige region of Italy for the Catholic Theological Ethics in the World Church Conference. The list of events incorporated a dinner for women scholars. Madeleva lecturers and New Voices members attended, and the conversations we enjoyed in South Bend were picked up again over espresso and gelato. Trento provided a feast for the senses, full of history and the possibility for transformation and renewal.

---

[35] Keenan, *Moral Wisdom.*

Women may still have been in the minority, but women were present and had travelled from all over the globe: the Americas, Europe, Africa, Asia, and Oceania. Once again, familiar names appeared in the flesh. As we shared stories and ideas, the desire to continue on in this way grew. Global solidarity that moves toward the practices of fidelity as well as justice presents a challenge. But is it impossible?

Technology makes maintaining all sorts of relationships, professional and personal, much easier. However, it presumes ready access and technological literacy. Among the stories shared in Trento was the difficulty that scholars faced, particularly women in Africa and parts of Asia, in accessing technology in order to do scholarly work. What many of us take for granted in the United States and Europe appeared quite arduous for our sister scholars. Even confronting this limitation presented well-meaning scholars of privilege with more questions and the need for more details to the story: hardware requires software, and communication requires Internet access. Carrying laptops might invite theft and its related dangers.

While technological questions come with technological answers, the deeper challenges of structural injustice and gender inequality remain (and they are not limited in any way to specific contexts). Another danger also continues to present itself. As we globalize solidarity and seek to build friendships across great distances via technology, we may risk settling for a cheap imitation: "globalizing superficiality."[36] Jesuit Superior General Adolfo Nicolás has reflected on the "cut-and-paste" culture promoted by technological advances.

> When one can access so much information so quickly and so painlessly; when one can express and publish to the world one's reactions so immediately and so unthinkingly in one's blogs or micro-blogs; when the latest opinion column from the *New York Times* or *El País*, or the newest viral video can be spread so quickly to people half a world away, shaping their perceptions and feelings, then the laborious, painstaking work of serious, critical thinking often gets short-circuited.[37]

---

[36] Adolfo Nicolás, SJ, superior general of the Society of Jesus, "Depth, Universality, and Learned Ministry: Challenges to Jesuit Higher Education Today," remarks for "Networking Jesuit Higher Education: Shaping the Future for a Humane, Just, Sustainable Globe," Mexico City, April 23, 2010, http://www.ajcunet.edu/Shaping-the-Future-Mexico-City (accessed December 30, 2011).

[37] Ibid.

Technology thus poses serious consequences for the habits of critical thinking. Nicolas suggests that the rapid and easy access to volumes of information will lead people to think less, and less well. He also highlights the potential for the globalization of superficiality to both corrode relationships and hinder building new, lasting, and deep relationships: "When one can become 'friends' so quickly and so painlessly with mere acquaintances or total strangers on one's social networks—and if one can so easily 'unfriend' another without the hard work of encounter or, if need be, confrontation and then reconciliation—then relationships can also become superficial."[38]

Such superficiality impacts voice and virtue for women scholars. E-mail and text message function ideally for quick communications, but they are not suited to sharing stories. Emoticons cannot convey complexity of thought, depth of emotion, or horizon of vision. Globalizing solidarity will rely on a creative use of communication technology and expanding access to its riches. It will, however, need to be critical of the very same technologies and resist allowing the limits of that technology to put limits on how we build and sustain relationships. Scholars may paradoxically communicate more and know less about one another. As Sherry Turkle, director of MIT's Initiative on Technology and Self, has noted, we may begin to expect more from technology and less from each other.[39]

Building solidarity among women scholars requires the cultivation of virtue through practices of justice and fidelity. The New Voices Seminar and other international gatherings of women theologians highlight the need for an embodied solidarity that grows in the context of just relationships among a global group of scholars as well as in the intimate context of friendship. These relationships are renewed and transformed when scholars are present to one another. Physical presence comprises an important aspect of solidarity, as well as the presence of the spirit that transcends bodily limits. Such presence and listening *for* voices can be facilitated by the use of communication technologies, especially for global networks. Technology can bridge distance in many ways, but that bridge may not have the sure foundation required to withstand the many stresses and strains fueled by injustice. Women theologians, feminist and otherwise, must work to create space, both physical and cyber or virtual,

---

[38] Ibid.

[39] Sherry Turkle, *Alone Together: Why We Expect More from Technology and Less from Each Other* (New York: Basic Books, 2011).

to live the promise of the "Madeleva Manifesto," "We will be with you along the way, sharing what we have learned about the freedom, joy, and power of contemplative intimacy with God."[40]

---

[40] From the "Madeleva Manifesto," http://www3.saintmarys.edu/madeleva-lecture -series (accessed May 1, 2011).

The Conundrums
of Newer Catholic Women Theologians

LaReine-Marie Mosely, Loyola University Chicago

Those of us who are newer Catholic women theologians find that we are living in truly interesting times. As the fiftieth anniversary of the Second Vatican Council is upon us, people in theological circles are embroiled in debates regarding whether the hermeneutic of this council is one of continuity or rupture. In December of 2005, Pope Benedict XVI offered his reflections on this topic in a Christmas letter addressed to the Roman Curia. He wrote:

> On the one hand, there is an interpretation that I would call "a hermeneutic of discontinuity and rupture"; it has frequently availed itself of the sympathies of the mass media, and also one trend of modern theology. On the other, there is the "hermeneutic of reform," of renewal in the continuity of the one subject-Church which the Lord has given to us. She is a subject which increases in time and develops, yet always remaining the same, the one subject of the journeying People of God.[1]

For Benedict XVI, this fitting hermeneutic is one of continuity, or more precisely, reform in continuity of the church.[2] The manner in which this disagreement is framed will undoubtedly continue to prompt all kinds of responses now and over the next three years as other anniversaries of the council are observed.

---

[1] Pope Benedict XVI, address to the Roman Curia, December 22, 2005, http://www.vatican.va/holy_father/benedict_xvi/speeches/2005/december/documents/hf_ben_xvi_spe_20051222_roman-curia_en.html (accessed February 9, 2012).
[2] Ibid.

In order to better understand this letter to the Roman Curia, it is important to place it in its context. Some scholars believe that Benedict's real dialogue partners are the traditionalists, that is, Marcel Lefebvre et al., since the language of rupture has its origins in communications from Lefebvre and the respective pope.[3] Regardless of where the language of rupture or continuity began, it has surfaced as one compelling way to talk about the council.[4]

As newer Catholic women theologians in the US, many of us consider this discourse in tandem with the events of the past ten years when the clergy sexual abuse scandal became increasingly public.[5] The abuse, and in some cases the cover-up on the part of bishops and cardinals, was like a cancer, consuming all who came in contact with it. Then, when it was thought that things could not get any worse, the scandal "went global," leaving many to wonder if the life of the people of God, the church, could ever be the same.

These years of hearing the stories of those abused and watching litigation unfold have also been filled with mixed messages about who really counts. In February of 2012, an international conference convened at the Vatican, titled Toward Healing and Renewal, and brought together some of the best minds from a variety of fields. Monsignor Stephen J. Rossetti suggested that "the church should listen to victims rather than focus their attention on priests accused of wrongdoing."[6] Such a victims-centered hermeneutic of compassion should characterize all of the church's responses to abuse around the globe. To be sure, the priest perpetrators likewise need to be cared for and treated justly and fairly, but never at the expense of the youngsters and minor adolescents who were wounded and traumatized. These experiences have distorted their experiences of God and church. In Matthew 19:1-15a, Jesus teaches his disciples that "it is to such as these [the children] that the kingdom of heaven belongs."

[3] Sandro Magister, "Benedict XVI, the Reformer," January 19, 2012, http://chiesa.espresso.repubblica.it/articolo/1350146?eng=y (accessed February 19, 2012).

[4] See Joseph A. Komonchak, "Novelty in Continuity," *America*, February 2, 2009. Another way to talk about the council is Richard Gaillardetz, "Conversation Starters: Dialogue and Deliberation during Vatican II," *America*, February 13, 2012.

[5] See Thomas Plante, *Sin against the Innocents: Sexual Abuse by Priests and the Role of the Church* (Westport, CT: Greenwood Publishing Group, 2003), vii.

[6] Elisabetta Povoledo, "Vatican Urged to Give Priority to Abuse Victims," *New York Times*, February 7, 2012, http://www.nytimes.com/2012/02/08/world/europe/vatican-urged-to-give-priority-to-abuse-victims.html?_r=1 (accessed February 9, 2012).

The passage continues, "And [Jesus] laid his hands on them" (NRSV). A victims-centered hermeneutic of compassion adopted by all would contribute to the healing of all those hurt and disillusioned.

Such an approach may have eventually resulted in the contemporary equivalent of sitting in sackcloth and ashes in prayer and penance.[7] As the news covered the revelations of clergy sexual abuse around the globe, many of us understood this pattern of behavior as structural sin. Structural sins "involve the dehumanizing and undignified disregard for others (or oneself) who are treated as objects and used as means to pursue one's own ends."[8] As an institution, how do we face the structural sin that has crept into our church over the centuries? Patterns of sinfulness are systemic insofar as they have reared their heads all over the globe in Catholic churches, dioceses, and archdioceses. In all that we do, there is a call to be in solidarity with the most vulnerable, to practice an option for the poor, since the poor are those who suffer.[9] In this spirit, the hierarchy and clergy can express their sorrow for sins of omission and commission against those minors who have been victimized and make a commitment to come to terms with the culture that "allowed" some of the abuse to continue. The people of God can participate in prayer and do penance with and for those directly involved. Indeed, some of the penance has already affected the faithful, as archdioceses and dioceses have paid out very large amounts of money as a result of litigation. Equally as important as the above practices, the hierarchy and clergy need to embrace a genuine spirit of humility and do all that they can to live out that spirit in concrete ways. Additionally, the hierarchy and clergy need to avoid every appearance of sidestepping responsibility for the sins of their brothers. What might the church look like now if the energy and resources of the worldwide church had been directed toward this goal?

A hermeneutic of humility and compassion would necessitate analyzing and working to dismantle long-standing patterns of clericalism, chauvinism, and "the old boys' club" network in the priesthood and

---

[7] Sackcloth and ashes convey wearing clothes made of coarse material and placing ashes on one's body in a spirit of penance and humility.

[8] Meghan T. Sweeney, "Sin (Social, Structural)," in *An Introductory Dictionary of Theology and Religious Studies*, ed. Orlando O. Espin and James B. Nickoloff (Collegeville, MN: Liturgical Press, 2007), 1289.

[9] Kathleen Anne McManus, OP, *Unbroken Communion: The Place and Meaning of Suffering in the Theology of Edward Schillebeeckx* (New York: Rowman & Littlefield, 2003), 135–41.

among the hierarchy today. An adequate response to the worldwide clergy sexual abuse scandal demands such a prolonged look at systemic issues, beginning with those listed above, because this is likely the context and mind-set that paved the way for some of the abuse of vulnerable minors. One wonders if and how these patterns are being dealt with in seminaries around the world today.

A Hermeneutic in Practice

A hermeneutic of humility and compassion would have a wide purview that embraces all the people of God in relationship with the clergy and hierarchy of the church. One recent case that comes to mind is the exchange between the United States Conference of Catholic Bishops' Committee on Doctrine (hereafter the USCCB Committee) and the writing of one of the church's most celebrated and respected theologians, Professor Elizabeth Johnson, a distinguished professor of theology at Fordham University and a member of the Sisters of Saint Joseph, Brentwood, NY. The writing in question is Johnson's 2007 book, *Quest for the Living God: Mapping Frontiers in the Theology of God*.[10] The USCCB Committee's concerns surround analogies used to talk about God, to which the Catholic Theological Society of America commented that Johnson's approach of using culturally diverse analogies to talk about God is a common approach used by theologians today.[11]

The problems began when the USCCB Committee failed to follow guidelines that they themselves had written and approved, entitled Doctrinal Responsibilities. The first step was supposed to involve an informal meeting with the theologian in question.[12] Instead, the Committee was in the process of issuing a press release, much to the surprise of Johnson, who was unaware that her book was under consideration, when Archbishop (now Cardinal) Timothy Dolan informed her of the situation. The

[10] Elizabeth Johnson, *Quest for the Living God: Mapping Frontiers in the Theology of God* (New York: Continuum, 2007, 2011).

[11] Board of Directors of the Catholic Theological Society of America, November 4, 2011, http://www.ctsa-online.org/BOD_statement_committee-on-doctrine_USCCB.html (accessed February 9, 2012).

[12] Thomas C. Fox, "Theologians Criticize Bishops' Handling of Book Critique," *National Catholic Reporter*, April 8, 2011, http://ncronline.org/news/accountability/theologians-criticize-bishops-handling-book-critique (accessed February 9, 2012).

concerns of the Committee were explicated fully in a communication to which Johnson graciously responded. Some months later, the Committee reiterated their concerns and expressed their belief that *Quest for the Living God* not be used as a textbook in Catholic colleges and universities. While this back-and-forth communication transpired, there still had been no face-to-face meeting of the Committee with Johnson! The chair of the Committee maintains that invitations were extended to Johnson, while Johnson categorically denies the existence of such invitations. Johnson has made public her communications to and from the Committee.[13] A hermeneutic of humility and compassion would put the responsibility of initiating conversations on the bishops so as to witness to positive relationships between bishops and theologians.

These sorts of situations may leave some newer Catholic women theologians like myself full of conundrums—perplexed and wondering what the future holds for Catholic theologians. One sign of hope was an invitation sent by the same USCCB Committee to newer Catholic theologians via college presidents to attend a meeting in Washington, DC, titled "Intellectual Tasks of the New Evangelization," held between September 15 and 17, 2011. While my commitment to other conferences precluded me from attending, the fifty theologians who participated were generally pleased with the gathering.[14] As the bishops and theologians gathered, there was a sense of respect for the important role that each plays in teaching and evangelization. This meeting was planned for some time and was not a reaction to the situation with Elizabeth Johnson; moreover, the group of theologians was not handpicked because of their beliefs. One attendee commented that the gathering would have been more helpful if it had incorporated postconference conversations for all attendees to get to know each other better. This and similar meetings provide bishops and theologians with opportunities to work collaboratively on behalf of the church. I applaud these and other good-will efforts.

[13] See the blog at *Commonweal*, http://www.commonwealmagazine.org/blog/?p=15712 (accessed February 9, 2012).

[14] See Colleen Pollock, "USCCB Session on New Evangelization Inspires Theologians," September 29, 2011, http://www.dioceseofgreensburg.org/accent/Pages/9-29-2011 USCCBsessiononnew.aspx (accessed February 9, 2012). See the *Catholic Moral Theology* blog, http://catholicmoraltheology.com/young-theologians-meet-the-commitee-on -doctrine-a-small-important-step-forward (accessed February 19, 2012).

Strengthened by our own resolve, encouraged by our many theological mentors, together with good-will gestures on the part of theologians and bishops, many of us newer Catholic women theologians will not be deterred or left overly concerned about our conundrums. Far too many women walk with us and have gone before us to show us the way. If a hermeneutic of humility and compassion can permeate the church and encourage bold work to dismantle patterns of domination evident in systems where our bishops and priests operate, many theologians and the rest of the people of God will continue to believe in the spirit of the Second Vatican Council as one of positive and appropriate engagement with the world community.

In some ways, responses to whether the Second Vatican Council represented reform in continuity or rupture may very well elicit "yes and no," as people from around the world give testimony to what this council has meant to them.

Models for Women Theologians, Past and Present

Recently, I was serendipitously introduced to a faithful, Catholic woman theologian while reading a collection of essays on saintly women. There I met Maude Dominica Petre, an English woman who lived from 1863 to 1943 and whose life is exemplary. Petre was always her own woman. As a young adult, she traveled to Rome to study scholastic theology. With this experience in the context of her lively faith life, Petre was ahead of her times as seen in her openness to other Christians and her conversations with the likes of George Tyrrell, Baron Friedrich von Hugel, and Alfred Loisy. Petre collaborated most closely with Tyrrell, a Jesuit priest who was eventually excommunicated for publicly refuting ties to modernism. Unlike Tyrell and other proponents linked with Catholic modernism, Petre was never silenced or excommunicated. In the spirit of her Cisalpine ancestors, who wished to rein in the power of the pope and allow for some autonomy for select regions, Petre's approach can be captured in the phrase "faith and loyalty blended with criticism and discrimination."[15]

In the preface of her book *Catholicism and Independence*, she describes her approach to life and faith: "It is that of the right, the necessity, the duty of every mind to work out its salvation by the courageous facing

---

[15] Ellen Leonard, *Unresting Transformation: The Theology and Spirituality of Maude Petre* (New York and Lanham: University Press of America, 1991), 130.

of its own difficulties, the resolute following of its own lights."[16] In this spirit, Petre negotiated her world at a time when Catholics in England had to endure all sorts of prejudice on account of their minority faith status. Theologian and biographer Ellen Leonard writes of Petre and her fellow English Catholics, "These recusant Catholics had a sense of themselves as part of a universal body with a loyalty to Rome, but also as loyal English citizens." These Catholics were also "marked by fidelity in spite of opposition, by loyalty, and by lay leadership."[17]

In another book by Petre, entitled *Modernism: Its Failure and Its Fruits*, she wrote about modernism's elusiveness.

> Many, indeed most, of those who took part in the movement are yet living, whether they continue to take an active part in it or not. The repressive measures invoked against it are still in full action; its supposed votaries are still objects of pious horror to the orthodox; to deny and repudiate it is still a means of advancement to the ecclesiastic who would make his way; it is still a spectre of undefined shape, of lurid colour and colossal dimensions to the simple believer.[18]

So, Petre agreed with most theologians today who describe modernism as a collection of beliefs held by a diverse group of people. About this era, James C. Livingston wrote,

> *Pascendi Gregis* gives the impression that here was a highly organized school of thinkers with a clear intellectual platform who cleverly sought to undermine the traditional teachings of the Church from within. Actually, Catholic Modernism was not a single movement but a general tendency among quite independent individuals who sought, in the words of Alfred Loisy, "to adapt the Catholic religion to the intellectual, moral and social needs of the present time." What drew the Modernists together, as happened in some cases, was a common concern to adapt the teaching of the Church to the modern age.[19]

[16] Maude Petre, *Catholicism and Independence* (New York: Longmans, Green and Co., 1907), ix.

[17] Ellen Leonard, "English Catholicism and Modernism," in *Catholicism Contending with Modernity: Roman Catholic Modernism and Anti-Modernism in Historical Context*, ed. Darrell Jodock (New York: Cambridge University Press, 2000), 250.

[18] Maude Dominica Petre, *Modernism: Its Failures and its Fruits* (London: T. C. & E. C. Jack, 1918), 5.

[19] James C. Livingston, *Modern Christian Thought: The Enlightenment and the Nineteenth Century*, 2nd ed. (Minneapolis: Fortress Press, 2006), 365.

Suffice it to say, Petre, Tyrrell, and their other conversation partners were concerned when Pope Pius X condemned modernism as the hierarchy understood it, and when priests, bishops, and professors of religious sciences were required to take the antimodernist oath. This practice continued until 1967![20] The notion that the church had much to fear from an engagement with modernity would be turned on its head at the Second Vatican Council. During the opening address of the council, Pope John XXIII prayed that "the work of all may correspond to the modern expectations and needs of the various peoples of the world."[21]

In multiple ways, Maude Petre lived out a similar spirit of engagement with the world, especially with other Christians. Although not a professional theologian by today's standards, Petre was a theologian, scholar, author, activist, and midwife of the church's future. She was a free thinker within the church. Petre exchanged letters with the likes of Friedrich von Hugel and Alfred Loisy, two prominent figures in the movement. Petre also preserved letters of some prominent people, in addition to acting as Tyrell's literary executor. She was grounded and was not beyond expressing her love and admiration for Tyrrell, for which some scholars have attempted to dismiss her contribution to Catholic life in the late nineteenth and early twentieth centuries. Maude Petre's life was spent as a single laywoman, and from that vantage point she lived a meaningful life. Petre understood God's call in her life and embraced it, as well as chose to live a life of "limited obedience" to the church. This perspective enabled her to deal with authoritarian leaders while keeping her integrity.[22] Petre's spirituality was rooted in the world and characterized by great faith and love. She practiced a critical spirituality with truly modern sensibilities that make her particularly relevant to women today.[23]

An author in her own right, Petre wrote mostly on historical and theological topics, but she also wrote about war, peace, democracy, and other political issues of her day. She left a significant record of modernism for future generations. Petre was a woman who understood the primacy of each person's conscience, since "contemporary moral theology and

[20] Richard McBrien, *Catholicism* (New York: HarperCollins, 1994), 49–50.

[21] Pope John XXIII, "Opening Speech to the Vatican II Council," http://www.saint-mike.org/library/papal_library/johnxxiii/opening_speech_vaticanii.html (accessed February 23, 2012).

[22] Leonard, *Unresting Transformation*, 198.

[23] Ibid., 207ff.

church teaching (e.g., Vatican Council II) consider it imperative that persons follow their consciences, even if at odds with particular moral norms, since, again, this is the faculty by which moral accountability is experienced."[24] As theologians who are reading the signs of the times, we need adequately informed consciences to engage some of the significant questions of our time: for instance, health care issues, poverty, preemptive strikes at the time of war, and present sexual mores. With honesty, clarity, integrity, and compassion, we can speak our truth with confidence and humility in keeping with Petre.

Maude Petre is a sister in the struggle in this regard. She lived her faith during interesting ecclesial times and never stopped believing that her faith and intelligence could be reconciled. Petre made choices fearlessly and accepted their consequences. She was a member of a Parisian religious congregation of women whose lives would now be described as members of a secular institute. When her publishing brought her undue attention, Petre chose not to renew her vows and broke her ties with the congregation. In perhaps her most fearless choice, Petre was buried one grave from her friend and colleague, George Tyrrell, in an Anglican cemetery. In doing so, she aligned herself with Tyrrell in life and in death.[25] An ecclesial hermeneutic of compassion prompts me to stand in solidarity with her as she endured suspicion because of her ties with Tyrrell and other so-called modernists. May all those theologians who are enduring a similar set of circumstances because of their work be fearless and walk by faith.

Newer Catholic women theologians like me are also fortunate to be aligned with Sister M. Madeleva Wolff, CSC, who opened doors for women's theological education. We are also accompanied by all the Madeleva lecturers whose voices resound in these interesting times. Because of these women, we are "new voices." The "Madeleva Manifesto," penned in 2000 by the first sixteen lecturers, has been embraced and lived by subsequent lecturers. Their words challenge us and spur us on into the future.

[24] Michael J. Hartwig, "Conscience," in *An Introductory Dictionary of Theology and Religious Studies*, ed. Espin and Nickoloff, 271–72.

[25] Owen F. Cummings, *Prophets, Guardians, and Saints* (New York: Paulist Press, 2007), 190.

"The Madeleva Manifesto: A Message of Hope and Courage"

In the tradition of Sister Madeleva Wolff, CSC, we sixteen Madeleva lecturers have been invited to speak a message of hope and courage to women in the church. Reflecting the diversity of gifts bestowed on us by the Spirit, we speak from our particular experiences and vocations, yet share in a universal vision that is faithful to our catholic tradition.

- To women in ministry and theological studies we say: re-imagine what it means to be the whole body of Christ. The way things are now is not the design of God.

- To young women looking for models of prophetic leadership, we say: walk with us as we seek to follow the way of Jesus Christ, who inspires our hope and guides our concerns. The Spirit calls us to a gospel feminism that respects the human dignity of all, and who inspires us to be faithful disciples, to stay in the struggle to overcome oppression of all kinds whether based on gender, sexual orientation, race, or class.

- To women who are tempted by the demons of despair and indifference, we say: re-imagine what it means to be a full human being made in the image of God, and to live and speak this truth in our daily lives.

- To women who suffer the cost of discipleship we say: you are not alone. We remember those who have gone before us, who first held up for us the pearl of great price, the richness of Catholic thought and spirituality. We give thanks to those who continue to mentor us.

- To the young women of the church we say: carry forward the cause of gospel feminism. We will be with you along the way, sharing what we have learned about the freedom, joy and power of contemplative intimacy with God. We ask you to join us in a commitment to far-reaching transformation of church and society in non-violent ways. We deplore, and hold ourselves morally bound, to protest and resist, in church and society, all actions, customs, laws and structures that treat women or men as less than fully human. We pledge ourselves to carry forth the heritage of biblical justice which mandates that all persons share in right relationship with each other, with the cosmos, and with the Creator.

We hold ourselves responsible to look for the holy in unexpected places and persons, and pledge ourselves to continued energetic dialogue about issues of freedom and responsibility for women. We invite others of all traditions to join us in imagining the great shalom of God.[26]

Feast of Saint Catherine of Siena, laywoman, Doctor of the Church
April 29, 2000
Saint Mary's College, Notre Dame, Indiana

Signed by the 16 Madeleva Lecturers in Spirituality, 1985–2001:

Mary C. Boys, SNJM
Lisa Sowle Cahill
Denise Lardner Carmody
Joan Chittister, OSB
Mary Collins, OSB
Elizabeth Dreyer
Maria Harris
Diana L. Hayes
Monika K. Hellwig
M. Catherine Hilkert, OP
Elizabeth Johnson, CSJ
Dolores R. Leckey
Gail Mandell
Kathleen Norris
Jeanette Rodriguez
Sandra M. Schneiders, IHM

---

[26] "The Madeleva Manifesto: A Message of Hope and Courage" (© Saint Mary's College, Notre Dame, IN) is available online at http://www.madelevalectures.org /manifesto.php.

Suffering or Flourishing?
Marriage and the Imitation of Christ[1]

Emily Reimer-Barry, University of San Diego

Young people today—including the college students I teach—have grown up in an era of high divorce rates and family fragmentation. Social scientists writing about this generation warn us of major shifts in sexual practices; fewer college-educated young people are getting married, and those who marry do so later in life.[2] In addition to these changing realities regarding marriage, upon graduation from college my students will enter a labor market beset by instability, flexibility, and the expectation that for the right job one might have to relocate. Their generation is not following the pattern of "school, job, marriage, house, and children" that earlier generations of middle-class Americans thought normative. While some social scientists see problematic patterns of immaturity and egoism among this generation,[3] we should hesitate to frame this analysis

---

[1] An earlier version of this analysis appeared in Emily Reimer-Barry, "In Sickness and in Health: Towards a Renewed Roman Catholic Theology of Marriage in Light of the Experiences of Married Women Living with HIV/AIDS" (unpublished doctoral dissertation, Loyola University Chicago, 2008), which was written before the release of Marriage: Love and Life in the Divine Plan. I am grateful for the feedback I received from Patricia Beattie Jung, Susan A. Ross, and Aana M. Vigen.

[2] Andrew J. Cherlin, *The Marriage-Go-Round: The State of Marriage and the Family in America Today* (New York: Vintage, 2010). See also Rose M. Kreider and Tavia Simmons, *Marital Status 2000: Census 2000 Brief* (Washington, DC: US Census Bureau, 2003). Analysis of the 2010 census is underway; when reports become available, they will be posted at www.census.gov.

[3] Gary Cross, *Men to Boys: The Making of Modern Immaturity* (New York: Columbia University Press, 2008).

in too judgmental a light. Are these young people rejecting marriage? Or are they rejecting one particular kind of marriage? In this essay, I am interested in whether these changing patterns of behavior might benefit young women. Might there be some positive elements in the fact that college-educated women have more opportunities for fulfilling employment and may choose to delay marriage and childbearing in order to serve the common good through their work outside the home? Given the complex and at times contradictory demands on young women today, the theology of marriage proposed by official Catholic teachings must be reexamined in order to promote the full flourishing of women in this new context.

The United States Conference of Catholic Bishops addressed the current situation of fragmentation and disillusionment in their 2009 pastoral letter, Marriage: Love and Life in the Divine Plan.[4] The bishops argue that marriage is under attack in US culture and explain that they are troubled by rising rates of nonmarital cohabitation, divorce, and contraceptive use.[5] The bishops diagnose a culture that promotes individualistic attitudes toward marriage, and they are disturbed by legislative efforts to redefine marriage to allow same-sex couples to legally marry.[6] Given these perceived threats to marriage in contemporary US culture, the purpose of the pastoral letter was to present God's "divine plan" for marriage.[7] The letter summarizes official church teachings, making them both accessible for a general audience and useful as a resource for anyone interested in official Catholic teachings on marriage.

For the most part, the pastoral letter on marriage does not present any new teachings. Marriage: Love and Life in the Divine Plan draws

---

[4] United States Conference of Catholic Bishops (hereafter USCCB), Marriage: Love and Life in the Divine Plan (Washington, DC: United States Conference of Catholic Bishops Publishing, 2009), available online at http://www.usccb.org/issues-and-action/marriage-and-family/marriage/love-and-life. Page numbers of subsequent references are taken from this online version. The pastoral letter is also available in Spanish. The Leaders' Guide was published in June 2010. USCCB, Marriage: Love and Life in the Divine Plan; Leaders' Guide (Washington, DC: United States Conference of Catholic Bishops Publishing, 2010), also available online at the website given above. There are other resources available online, including a PowerPoint presentation summarizing the document.

[5] USCCB, Marriage, 4.

[6] Ibid., 4.

[7] Ibid., 6.

upon the theology of marriage presented in other official teachings, including canon law,[8] conciliar documents,[9] previous publications from the United States Conference of Catholic Bishops,[10] and papal encyclicals,[11] in addition to the *Catechism*[12] and the Rite of Marriage.[13] It relies heavily on a particular interpretation of natural law for an understanding of theological anthropology, gender essentialism, and moral methodology. Characterized as John Paul II's "theology of the body," this natural law reasoning has been popularized by such authors as Christopher West[14] and is presented in the marriage pastoral as authoritative papal teaching, although the citation given derives from a papal audience.[15] The pastoral letter also cites Scripture, privileging the two creation stories of Genesis 1–2, Paul's household codes of Ephesians 5:22-32, and the prohibition of divorce attributed to Jesus in Matthew 19:3-9. In review-

---

[8] *Code of Canon Law: Latin-English Edition*, New English Translation (*Codex Iuris Cononici*) (Washington, DC: Canon Law Society of America, 1998), cited twelve times.

[9] Second Vatican Council, Constitution on the Church in the Modern World (*Gaudium et Spes*), in *Vatican Council II: The Basic Sixteen Documents*, ed. Austin Flannery (Northport, NY: Costello Publishing, 1996), cited fifteen times; Vatican II, Dogmatic Constitution on the Church (*Lumen Gentium*), in *Vatican Council II*, cited three times.

[10] USCCB, Married Love and the Gift of Life (Washington, DC: USCCB, 2006), cited once; USCCB, Between Man and Woman: Questions and Answers about Marriage and Same-Sex Unions (Washington, DC: USCCB, 2003), cited once; USCCB, *United States Catholic Catechism for Adults* (Washington, DC: USCCB, 2006), cited twice; USCCB, When I Call for Help: A Pastoral Response to Domestic Violence against Women (Washington, DC: USCCB, 2002), cited once; USCCB, Follow the Way of Love: A Pastoral Message to Families (Washington, DC: USCCB, 1993), cited once.

[11] Pope Paul VI, On the Regulation of Birth (*Humanae Vitae*), available online at http://www.vatican.va/holy_father/paul_vi/encyclicals/documents/hf_p-vi_enc_25071968_humanae-vitae_en.html, cited seven times; Pope John Paul II, On the Family (*Familiaris Consortio*) (Washington, DC: USCCB, 1982), cited seventeen times, and On the Dignity and Vocation of Women (*Mulieris Dignitatem*) (Washington, DC: USCCB, 1998), cited three times; Pope Benedict XVI, Charity in Truth (*Caritas in Veritate*) (Washington, DC: USCCB, 2009), cited once, God Is Love (*Deus Caritas Est*) (Washington, DC: USCCB, 2006), cited twice.

[12] *Catechism of the Catholic Church*, 2nd ed. (Washington, DC: Libreria Editrice Vaticana–USCCB, 2000), cited thirty-five times.

[13] Rite of Marriage, in *The Rites of the Catholic Church*, vol. 1 (New York: Pueblo Publishing, 1976), cited three times.

[14] Christopher West, *Good News about Sex and Marriage* (Cincinnati, OH: Servant Publications, 2000), and *Theology of the Body Explained* (Boston, MA: Pauline Books and Media, 2003).

[15] USCCB, Marriage, 12. The pastoral letter cites John Paul II, general audiences, May 30, 1984; January 5, 1983; and January 26, 1983.

ing the document's citations, the bishops take great care to demonstrate that this pastoral letter is consistent with previous Catholic teachings; indeed, it often seems to be an internal dialogue. While writing on issues of grave importance to married couples, the bishops make no mention of consultation with married couples in the preparation of the document. Also, despite many publications by Catholic theologians in the past fifty years—on marriage, sexuality, and feminist theology, some authored by lay married theologians[16]—the only theologian cited is Thomas Aquinas and in reference to the distinction between angels and humans.[17]

Such limited internal dialogue leads the document to paint a glowing picture of Catholic marriage traditions, while failing to acknowledge that Christian marriage traditions arose in patriarchal contexts and have actually developed in significant ways. By ignoring Catholic feminist scholarship on marriage and families, the bishops miss an opportunity to wrestle with the complexities of the Catholic tradition in light of the experiences of contemporary couples. For example, while the bishops assert spousal equality,[18] they do not explain that the affirmation of equal dignity between men and women is actually a major development in Catholic theology of marriage, and they do not mourn the reality that spousal inequality of power remains a major threat to women's flourishing.[19] Thus, the attempt to clearly describe "God's plan" for marriage as

[16] For example, Lisa Sowle Cahill, *Family: A Christian Social Perspective* (Minneapolis: Fortress Press, 2000), and *Sex, Gender, and Christian Ethics* (Cambridge: Cambridge University Press, 1996); Julie Hanlon Rubio, *A Christian Theology of Marriage and Family* (Boston: Beacon Press, 2000); David Matzko McCarthy, *Sex and Love in the Home* (London: SCM, 2010); Richard R. Gaillardetz, *A Daring Promise: A Spirituality of Christian Marriage* (New York: Crossroad, 2002); Florence Caffrey Bourg, *Where Two or Three Are Gathered: Christian Families as Domestic Churches* (Notre Dame: University of Notre Dame Press, 2004); Christine E. Gudorf, *Body, Sex, and Pleasure: Reconstructing Christian Sexual Ethics* (Cleveland: Pilgrim Press, 1994); and Susan A. Ross, *Extravagant Affections* (New York: Continuum, 2001).

[17] "For St. Thomas Aquinas, while angels are, strictly speaking, higher than human beings by nature, the ability to procreate in love makes human beings, at least in one way, more in the image and likeness of God than the angels, who are unable to procreate. In human beings, one finds 'a certain imitation of God, consisting in the fact that man proceeds from man, as God proceeds from God.'" USCCB, Marriage, 38n63, citing Thomas Aquinas, *Summa Theologiae*, I. q. 93, art. 3.

[18] The document interprets the first creation story as evidence of the "fundamental equality and dignity of man and woman." USCCB, Marriage, 9.

[19] Christine E. Gudorf, "Violence against Women in World Religions," in *Violence against Women in Contemporary World Religion: Roots and Cures*, ed. Daniel C. Maguire and

a received tradition and firm foundation, without any mention of patriarchal traditions or authentic development, raises fundamental questions
about whether this interpretation of marital norms is in fact a "truthful
guide, a trustworthy light for the way," as the bishops put it.[20]

One major theme of *Marriage: Love and Life in the Divine Plan* is that
married couples are called to imitate Christ in their marriage.[21] While this
claim is not in itself problematic, the document's emphasis on self-sacrifice
as constitutive of Christian discipleship raises serious concerns for me as
a feminist theologian.[22] The document says explicitly: "Christ's love for
the Church is a love of complete self-giving. This love is most completely
expressed by his death on the Cross."[23] Elsewhere, the document argues:

> Marital and familial love finds its complete expression, following
> the example of Jesus himself, in a willingness to sacrifice oneself
> in everyday situations for one's spouse and children. There is no
> greater love within a marriage and a family than for the spouses and
> children to lay down their lives for one another. This is the heart
> of the vocation of marriage, the heart of the call to become holy.[24]

According to the bishops, married love requires *complete self-giving*, and
Jesus' death on the cross symbolizes that complete self-giving theologically. But what does it mean, particularly for women, to say that holiness
in heterosexual marriage demands laying down one's life for another?
Must a wife sacrifice herself for her husband and children and accept
suffering in marriage without question or challenge? Putting forward a
device for torture—the cross—as a symbol for marital love proves deeply
problematic theologically. This image is used repeatedly and without
qualification throughout the pastoral letter.[25] The document's emphasis
on self-renunciation in marriage recommends an uncritical acceptance

---

Sa'Diyya Shaikh (Cleveland: Pilgrim Press, 2007), 9–28. See also Grace M. Kantzen,
"The Courtroom and the Garden: Gender and Violence in Christendom," in *Violence
against Women*, 29–48.

   [20] USCCB, Marriage, 6.

   [21] Ibid., 32–33.

   [22] A word count reveals the emphasis on this theme. The word "self-giving" appears
twenty-one times in the pastoral letter, while "self-gift" appears twelve times. "Gift of
self" and "sacrifice" appear eight and five times, respectively.

   [23] USCCB, Marriage, 32.

   [24] Ibid., 48.

   [25] Ibid., 18, 21, 31–33, 47–48.

of suffering, which looks particularly problematic for married women. Married women are more likely than married men to be trapped in violent or abusive marriages, and continued emphasis on procreation in marriage carries expectations for multiple pregnancies. The consequences of both are borne by women's bodies.

Rather than downplay the significance of the cross in Christian discipleship, this essay draws our attention to the particular interpretation of the cross depicted in the marriage pastoral. The theology of the cross found within the pastoral letter derives the meaning of Good Friday from the perspective of Easter Sunday, assuming that suffering is always and unambiguously redemptive. In contrast to this simplistic understanding, this essay proposes that we pause a bit longer in the Good Friday context to consider the cross an inadequate symbol for marital love. If Jesus' death on the cross involved humiliation, pain, suffering, tragedy, despair, and loss, is the cross the most appropriate symbol for marriage? Is this the message to convey to young people considering the vocation of marriage? A marriage described as torture is not exactly attractive to young people in general or to women in particular—and for good reason! Are there other motifs within the gospels that provide a more life-giving image for married couples or young people preparing for marriage?

In the following pages, I explain why the bishops' emphasis on self-sacrifice looks problematic for married women and then uncover alternative christological models that offer more liberating biblical symbols for marital love. I argue that the threefold love commandment provides a more fruitful model for the realistic balancing of love commitments required by Christian marriage than the symbol of the cross. As a wife and mother, I know that marriage and parenting require constant self-giving and that often this self-giving proves difficult and sometimes painful. Nevertheless, I find the bishops' document on marriage to be problematic because it does not articulate the possibility of healthy self-concern in marriage. Thus, I argue that imitating Christ as a married person requires a delicate balance of love for God, self, and neighbor, a life-affirming balance based on the norm of mutual flourishing in family life rather than an unqualified demand to accept suffering.

Is Self-Neglect Holy?

Doing God's will means being kind to my neighbors no matter what it takes, following the Ten Commandments to the best of my ability and then some. And loving my husband, loving other people, basically the love thing. No matter what. That's what God basically wants. My husband has stolen from me. My husband has beaten me, and I still love my husband unconditionally.

—Crystal, forty-seven years old[26]

Men are the problem. They do not see us as equal. They say we exist for them. I have watched my mother suffer my whole life. I will never get married.

—Mary, eighteen years old[27]

What does conjugal love require of married women? What does complete self-giving look like in marriage? The personal testimonies of Crystal and Mary have stayed with me, even though years have passed since we met. When Crystal shared her story with me, I was struck by how seriously she took the Christian calls to self-sacrifice and forgiveness of others that had been part of her Catholic upbringing. Her understanding of love—which she names as the central Christian virtue—is complete self-giving. But while her understanding of love is rooted in biblical understandings of sacrifice and attentiveness to one's neighbor, Crystal does not operate with an understanding of her own identity as precious to God and worthy of love. She lacks safety in her own marriage and yet maintains that Christian marriage requires her to love her spouse unconditionally. Mary, a Kenyan secondary school student, reminded me of some of the young people in my US classrooms. Having seen her mother suffer in a dehumanizing and violent marriage, she has decided to not marry in order to protect her own well-being. "Sacrament" hardly seems the right word to describe these two relationships.

Feminist theologians have drawn attention to the ways that God-talk *functions.*[28] In thinking about the adequacy of religious language, Sandra Schneiders explains that "God's presumed masculinity has functioned as the ultimate religious legitimation of the unjust social structures which

---

[26] Crystal (pseud.), interviewed by the author, August 3, 2006, Chicago, IL. Emily Reimer-Barry, "In Sickness and in Health," 135.

[27] Mary (pseud.), interviewed by the author, July 7, 2009, Nairobi, Kenya. Loyola University Chicago Kenya Immersion Project. Excerpt from fieldwork interviews.

[28] For example, see Sandra M. Schneiders, *Women and the Word* (New York: Paulist Press, 1986), 5.

victimize women."[29] I worry that the same kind of theological projection can inhibit the full flourishing of married women reading the US bishops' pastoral letter on marriage. Who is served by a theology of marriage rooted in the call to sacrifice oneself? How does this description *function*? Who benefits? For years, I have been concerned by the subtle process of gender socialization that occurs in Christian moral formation. Whether in liturgical prayer, devotional prayer books, veneration of particular saints as role models for discipleship, or adult education curricula, the ways that we talk about what is natural and appropriate for men and woman have powerful effects on the moral imagination of Christians. In two prior research projects, I had the opportunity to interview women and ask them about their experiences of this moral formation. In those projects, I concluded that some Christian women have been formed to think of discipleship predominantly as a life of self-neglect. I had their stories in mind when I first read the bishops' pastoral letter on marriage, and I felt saddened by the way that this latest document emphasizes self-giving love without also describing appropriate self-concern in marriage.

Marriage: Love and Life in the Divine Plan explains that by participating in the "intimate self-giving of Christ," married persons leave behind "the lustful, self-centered pleasures of our culture."[30] Self-concern is framed simply as selfishness; "selfless" love and "self-gift" are proposed as self-evident goods without qualification.[31] Marriage is described as a school of virtue and a path for holiness.[32] According to the bishops, the sacrament of matrimony offers human fulfillment "through participation in the self-giving love pouring out of the pierced heart of Christ on the Cross."[33] Such descriptions imply that marital love is primarily characterized by renunciation of self and acceptance of suffering. Too little attention is paid to marriage as an egalitarian partnership between two persons who are called not only to give of themselves but also to take care of themselves.

Marital sexuality receives a good deal of attention in the pastoral letter; the sexual act is described as the "act most symbolic and expressive

[29] Ibid.
[30] USCCB, Marriage, 47.
[31] Ibid., 12.
[32] Ibid., 47, 51.
[33] Ibid., 47.

of the marriage as a whole."[34] Here too the bishops emphasize "total self-gift," arguing that artificial means of birth control run contrary to God's design for marriage because contraception involves a "refusal to give oneself entirely" to one's spouse.[35] Without offering any evidence to support this analysis, the bishops assert that the use of contraception "has the potential to damage or destroy the marriage" and that "it results in many other negative consequences, both personal and social."[36]

Without any attention to the unique demands that procreative marital sexuality places on women, including pregnancy, childbirth, and infant care, the pastoral letter on marriage frames holiness in marriage as a willingness to die to self—*totally, completely, entirely.* The virtuous wife gives herself entirely to her spouse and children without care for herself. Readers familiar with the papal documents cited in the pastoral letter will recall that women are singled out as being particularly well suited to receptivity and passivity in John Paul II's characterization of the "nuptial meaning" of the human body.[37] John Paul II described motherhood as the essential vocation of all women, naming motherhood as a vocation of self-gift and sacrifice.[38] Such claims have reinforced the view for many

---

[34] Ibid., 17.

[35] Ibid., 17–21, at 19. See also *Familiaris Consortio*, no. 32; *Catechism*, no. 2370; and *Humanae Vitae*, no 13.

[36] USCCB, Marriage, 19.

[37] Ibid., 10. See also John Paul II, *Mulieris Dignitatem*, 10; and John Paul II, *Theology of the Body: Human Love in the Divine Plan* (Boston: Pauline, 1997).

[38] John Paul II, *Mulieris Dignitatem*, 10, 28–31, Letter to Women, 2, and *Familiaris Consortio*, 22, 23. The point here is that fatherhood is not described as the essential vocation of all men; parenting as a woman's task receives greater attention in the tradition. My intention here is not to disvalue or ignore the real sacrifices that women have made for their families but rather to examine some aspects of their religious formation that encourage women, more than their spouses, to think of sacrifice as constitutive of their vocation as mothers. Some feminist writers would claim that it is true that women have been socialized into certain "nurturing, caring" roles in society but that this trait is not biologically based or in any way inevitable but rather learned. In this view, men too have been socialized into "the masculine" roles, but this too is dependent on cultural context, upbringing, familial expectations, opportunities, and so forth. John Paul II's attempt to name concrete gendered differences in the home and workplace has been critiqued by many feminist scholars. See Christine E. Gudorf, "Parenting, Mutual Love, and Sacrifice," in Barbara Hilkert Andolsen, Christine E. Gudorf, and Mary D. Pellauer, eds., *Women's Consciousness, Women's Conscience: A Reader in Feminist Ethics* (Minneapolis, MN: Seabury, 1985), 175–91; "Encountering the Other: The Modern Papacy on Women,"

Christian women that they should always think of others before thinking of themselves, and that self-care is, at best, unnecessary or superfluous and, at worst, sinful. Rather, we need an ethic that both enhances women's moral agency and encourages proper self-concern in marriage.[39]

Particularly problematic is the pastoral letter's failure to address domestic violence as a fundamental challenge to the nature and purposes of marriage. Intimate partner violence is pervasive in US society: approximately 1.5 million women are raped and/or physically assaulted by an intimate partner annually in the United States, and one in four women in the US said they were raped and/or physically assaulted by an intimate partner at some point in their lifetime.[40] Instead of naming violence against women as a fundamental challenge to marriage, the marriage pastoral focuses on contraception, same-sex unions, divorce, and cohabitation as threats that "are directed at the very meaning and purposes of marriage."[41] While the bishops say in their analysis of divorce that "no one in a marriage is obliged to maintain common living with an abusing spouse,"[42] this statement does not carry sufficient moral normative force, given that this section contains rigid claims about the "binding nature" of marriage: "Jesus himself teaches that divorce does not accord with the binding nature of marriage as intended by the Creator (see Mt 19:3-9)."[43] Thus, while domestic violence is clearly contrary to the dignity and flourishing of married women, what might seem less obvious are the ways that subtle affirmations of gender essentialism, procreationism, and

---

and "Western Religion and the Patriarchal Family," in Charles E. Curran, Margaret A. Farley, Richard A. McCormick, SJ, eds., *Feminist Ethics and the Catholic Moral Tradition* (New York: Paulist Press, 1996), 66–89, 251–77; Lisa Sowle Cahill, *Family*, 91; and Margaret A. Farley, "The Church and the Family: An Ethical Task," *Horizons* 10/1 (1983): 50–71.

[39] Barbara Hilkert Andolsen, "Women and Roman Catholic Sexual Ethics," in *Feminist Ethics and the Catholic Moral Tradition*, 207–39.

[40] P. Thaden and N. Thoennes, *Extent, Nature, and Consequences of Intimate Partner Violence: Findings from the National Violence against Women Survey* (Washington, DC: US Department of Justice, 2000). Intimate partner violence is primarily a crime against women. M. Henneburg, *Bureau of Justice Statistics 2000: At a Glance* (Washington, DC: US Department of Justice Bureau of Justice Statistics, 2000). For an overview of international statistics with analysis, see United Nations Population Fund, "Gender-Based Violence: A Price Too High," in *State of World Population 2005: The Promise of Equality* (New York: United Nations Population Fund, 2005), 65–73.

[41] USCCB, Marriage, 17.

[42] Ibid., 25, citing USCCB, When I Call For Help, 11.

[43] USCCB, Marriage, 24.

biblical fundamentalism create expectations for unequal power relationships between men and women due to implicit understandings about
what is "natural" for women, or about what "God intends" for married women's self-sacrifice or self-gift within marriage. Violence against
women is deeply rooted in cultural traditions of patriarchy sanctified by
Christianity that have denied women equal power with their husbands.
Wife battering, while now explicitly condemned by the Catholic Church,
is rooted in beliefs of women's inferiority, views sustained by the church
in previous eras.[44] Violence against women remains a threat to the stability of marriage. While the bishops rightly offer victimized women
a way out by admitting that divorce may be the only solution in cases
of domestic violence, preventing wife abuse requires both dismantling
patriarchal structures of marriage traditions and renewing attention to
what egalitarian partnerships require. The pastoral letter falls short in
both of these aspects.

In addition, the letter's depictions of married life focusing on the
need for sacrifice and self-denial in marriage miss the opportunity to
describe the possibility for joy and for self-affirming love that can result
from a loving and mutually respectful partnership. While the bishops
describe marriage as a mutual partnership,[45] they fail to affirm proper
self-concern within marriage and do not give sufficient attention to the
messiness of authentic mutuality. Nor does the letter express an awareness of the ways that married love changes within different stages of
a couple's life and marital journey. In fact, the letter tends to speak of
married love in very abstract terms, which results in a failure to deal
with the everyday concerns of most married couples. Spouses are not
counseled to consider their own needs, desires, or vocations, but rather
instructed to focus all their love and attention on their partner and
children. Self-concern and self-love are notably absent in this letter's
interpretations of marital love.

[44] For centuries husbands were duty bound to "discipline" their wives. Rosemary
Radford Ruether, "The Western Religious Tradition and Violence against Women in
the Home," in Joanne Carlson Brown and Carole R. Bohn, eds., *Christianity, Patriarchy, and
Abuse: A Feminist Critique* (Cleveland: Pilgrim Press, 1989), 31–41, at 34–35.
[45] USCCB, Marriage, 7, 11, 17.

Is Discipleship Only about Self-Sacrifice?

Christians look to Jesus as a moral exemplar, and Christology neces-sarily shapes Christian habits of thinking and being. What exactly are Christians called to emulate in the life of Jesus? Is discipleship predomi-nantly expressed in self-sacrifice? Does discipleship require neglect of our own desires, needs, and joys? Is self-concern always problematic? New Testament Christologies vary significantly in addressing these questions.[46] While the Pauline epistles and the Gospel of Mark focus on the cross and resurrection of Jesus, Matthew and Luke give greater attention to Jesus' origins and public ministry, and John's Christology emphasizes Jesus as the Logos, God's Word become flesh. While some of the earliest New Testament authors seem to focus exclusively on Jesus' death as salvific, this is not the only way to interpret the life, death, and resurrection of Jesus. In some interpretations, the salvation Jesus brings is evident long before his death on the cross. While early Christians focused on the pas-sion of Jesus in proclaiming him as the Christ, exclusive focus on the cross is ultimately too narrow, both theologically and ethically. We need attention to the full and complex person of Jesus in the New Testament canon correlated with an expanded Christology that attends sufficiently to Jesus' life and public ministry, passion, and death, as well as the ac-counts of the disciples' experiences of the risen Christ.

One model of Christology that fosters an expansive contemporary theo-ethical imagination beyond the exclusive image of Christ crucified is Jesus the healer. This model emphasizes Jesus' public ministry, focusing on the ways that Jesus brought both spiritual and physical healing. Jesus was concerned not only with people's spiritual salvation but also with their integral flourishing in this life. Daniel P. Sulmasy explains that the Christian meaning of healing can be understood in three ways: healing as restoration of right relationships, healing as encounter, and healing as witness.[47] For many whom Jesus cured, such as the leper of Luke's gospel, Jesus disregarded culturally embedded purity codes and public health practices in order to bring healing.[48] Jesus the healer exhibited special

---

[46] Daniel J. Harrington, SJ, *Who Is Jesus? Why Is He Important?* (Franklin, WI: Sheed & Ward, 1999), 5–15.

[47] Daniel P. Sulmasy, OFM, MD, *A Balm for Gilead: Meditations on Spirituality and the Healing Arts* (Washington, DC: Georgetown University Press, 2006), 21–27.

[48] See Luke 5:12-16; Mark 5:24-34.

concern for the marginalized and for suffering women.[49] A major theme of the healing miracles in the gospels is that the person was welcomed back into the community and into a new relationship with God. Sulmasy explains further:

> Frequently, Jesus states as he heals, "Your faith has made you well" (Mk 10:52). The faith to which Jesus refers is relational. The faith associated with the healing miracles is not assent to the propositions of a creed but to a trusting relationship with Jesus. . . . Jesus frequently heals at the behest of the patient's *relations*. Thus, Jesus restores family relationships when he heals: for the widow who had lost her son (Lk 7:11-17); for Jairus, who was losing his daughter (Lk 8:40-42, 49-56); for Peter, whose mother-in-law was ill (Mt 8:14-15); for Martha and Mary, who had lost their brother Lazarus (Jn 11:1-44); and for the centurion whose household was losing a cherished servant (Mt 8:5-13).[50]

The healing miracles point to a broad understanding of healing that goes beyond the cure of illness to include the restoration of flourishing relationships.

Sulmasy goes further when he invokes Matthew 25:36, "I was sick and you took care of me" (NRSV), as an invitation to reflect on how accompanying the sick is a direct encounter with Christ.[51] It is a radical claim to say that one "finds God" when we embrace those in need of healing. Sulmasy argues that privileging the image of Jesus as healer is an important theological shift but that one must also reflect more deeply on the presence of Christ in the person who seeks healing.

Sulmasy also describes healing as witness to the reign of God, noting the healings performed by the early apostles as examples of their charge to spread the "good news" of Christ.[52] Healing is a "special sign of God's promise," writes Sulmasy.[53] Invoking the christological image of Jesus as healer helps to affirm the claim that God desires the full, integral, relational flourishing of every human being.

---

[49] See Luke 8:43-48; 7:36-50; 6:11-17; 23:55.

[50] Sulmasy, *A Balm for Gilead*, 23.

[51] Ibid., 24.

[52] Ibid., 24. See Acts 3:1-10; 5:12-16; 9:36-43; 20:7-12.

[53] Ibid., 26.

New Testament scholar Daniel Harrington also emphasizes Jesus as a healer in his analysis of the Gospel of Mark, where Harrington explains that the healings and miraculous actions of Jesus are "in the service of his central concern—God's kingdom."[54] Harrington elaborates:

> In Jesus' public ministry the power of God's kingdom is already manifest. The first miracle story—the healing of a man with "an unclean spirit"—in 1:21-28 underlines the close relation between Jesus' teaching and his healing. It begins by describing the warm reception that Jesus' teaching got in the synagogue at Capernaum: "They were astounded at his teaching, for he taught them as one having authority, and not as their scribes." Next a man with an unclean spirit enters the synagogue, and Jesus exorcises the demon and restores the man to health. Then the crowd responds by linking the two aspects of Jesus' ministry: "A new teaching—with authority! He commands even the unclean spirits, and they obey him."[55]

Harrington argues that through the healing miracles, the Gospel of Mark portrays Jesus as a healer whose power over nature, illness, and death makes present the kingdom of God.

Another Christology emphasizes Jesus as the liberator; its central theme is that Jesus' preaching focused on Jesus himself bringing liberation. In the Lukan account of the beginning of Jesus' public ministry, Jesus reads from the scroll of Isaiah, proclaiming his anointment to "let the oppressed go free" (Luke 4:16-21; NAB). Jesus demonstrates special concern for those with limited power, showing God's mercy to all but especially to the poor and outcast. To privilege the role of Jesus as liberator challenges any facile claims about the inherent goodness or necessity of suffering in the Christian life. Dehumanizing suffering cannot be legitimated by claims that it is God's will. Rather, in the words of liberation theologian Jon Sobrino, "We need to present a Christ who, as a minimum, is the ally of liberation, not of oppression."[56]

But Jesus' preaching seems to have posed a threat to those in power. By preaching the coming, even the immediate presence, of the kingdom of God, he challenged the political and religious leaders of his time.[57]

---

[54] Harrington, *Who Is Jesus?* 24.

[55] Ibid., 24.

[56] Jon Sobrino, *Jesus the Liberator: A Historical-Theological View* (Maryknoll, NY: Orbis Books, 1993), 3.

[57] Harrington, *Who Is Jesus?* 12.

His teachings led directly to his execution. But this does not mean that Jesus had a death wish or saw himself as a sacrificial victim. Elizabeth Johnson explains:

> It is not that Jesus came to die; he was not masochistic. He came to live and to bring life abundantly to everyone else. Doing so faithfully, however, put him at odds with the religious and civil powers not tuned into God's ways. In one real sense the crucified Jesus is a victim arrested, unjustly tried, executed. But he is far from passive. His death results from a very active ministry in which love and compassion for the dispossessed led him into conflict with the powerful.[58]

In this interpretation, Jesus' death on the cross is not required by a blood-thirsty God, nor is it the result of Jesus' own desire to suffer and offer himself as a sacrificial lamb. Rather, his acceptance of death was a non-violent response to injustice rooted in his actively compassionate ministry with the people.

Recovering these two portraits of Jesus especially benefits married women today. Contemporary Christian women who pattern their lives of discipleship on the testimony of the biblical witness benefit from a rich and multivalent christological model that is neither focused exclusively on nor ignores the cross. For married Christian women, this expanded Christology suggests that discipleship within marriage means participating in God's healing and liberating presence in the world. African feminist theologian Mercy Amba Oduyoye applies this liberationist message when she explains that for many African Christian women, "Jesus is the brother or kin who frees women from the domination of inhuman husbands."[59] Drawing on the example of Jesus in the gospels, married women can affirm their own self-concern in relationships.

---

[58] Elizabeth A. Johnson, *Consider Jesus: Waves of Renewal in Christology* (New York: Crossroad, 1990), 91–92. See also Leonardo Boff, *Christ the Liberator* (Maryknoll, NY: Orbis Books, 1978); Jon Sobrino, *Christology at the Crossroads* (Maryknoll, NY: Orbis Books, 1978); and Monika K. Hellwig, *Jesus: The Compassion of God* (Wilmington, DE: Michael Glazier, 1983).

[59] Mercy Amba Oduyoye, "Jesus Christ," in Kwok Pui-lan, ed., *Hope Abundant: Third World and Indigenous Women's Theology* (Maryknoll, NY: Orbis Books, 2010), 168.

Married Women and the Imitation of Christ:
Toward a Theology of Self-Care in Relationships

The biblical mandate of the love commandment provides a helpful lens for interpreting appropriate self-care in marriage. When we explore self-love through the lens of the love commandment, we find that self-love is affirmed together with love for God and love for one's neighbor.[60] Based on the writings of a number of theologians exploring this important aspect of Christian discipleship,[61] authentic self-love seeks the well-being of the totality of ourselves as multidimensional persons—bodily, intellectually, spiritually, and emotionally. Self-love requires being honest with, accepting, valuing, and forgiving oneself. Self-love entails caring for oneself by healthful eating, regular sleeping, working, learning new skills, protecting oneself from harm, setting personal goals, and fostering supportive relationships.[62] Self-love also mandates that we allow others

---

[60] See Matt 22:36-39; Mark 12:28-31; and Luke 10:25-28. In the Synoptic accounts of the love commandment, we Christians are called to love our neighbors as we love ourselves, implying a distinct love for self. That this self-love is inferred does not mean it is less important than love for neighbor.

[61] Theologians have begun to emphasize the importance of self-love in recent years. According to Darlene Fozard Weaver, self-love is an independent moral obligation based on regarding all human beings as equals created by God in God's image. See Weaver, *Self-Love and Christian Ethics* (Cambridge: Cambridge University Press, 2002), 47–77, 131–66. James Keenan writes about self-esteem or self-care as a "cardinal virtue" or a "bottomline moral task" sought for its own sake. Keenan proposes four cardinal virtues: justice, fidelity, self-care, and prudence. See Keenan, *Virtues for Ordinary Christians* (Franklin, WI: Sheed & Ward, 1999), 70–75, at 72, and "Proposing Cardinal Virtues," *Theological Studies* 56, no. 4 (1995): 709–29. Stephen Pope calls for renewed attention to a relational anthropology in order to counter the cultural views of self-love as expressive individualism. See Pope, "Expressive Individualism and True Self-Love: A Thomistic Perspective," *Journal of Religion* 71, no. 3 (1991): 384–99. Cheryl Townsend Gilkes remarks that self-love is "probably the most critical task we complete" in our commitment to human wholeness. Cheryl Townsend Gilkes, "The 'Loves' and 'Troubles' of African-American Women's Bodies: The Womanist Challenge to Cultural Humiliation and Community Ambivalence," in Emilie M. Townes, ed., *A Troubling in My Soul* (Maryknoll, NY: Orbis Books, 1993), 232–49, at 247. Edward Collins Vacek, SJ, devotes a chapter to self-love in *Love, Human and Divine: The Heart of Christian Ethics* (Washington, DC: Georgetown University Press, 2004), 239–79.

[62] For a more sustained treatment of basic goods for human flourishing, see Cristina L. H. Traina, *Feminist Ethics and Natural Law: The End of the Anathemas* (Washington, DC: Georgetown University Press, 1999), 44–48.

to care for us, that we attend to friendships that nurture us, that we ask for support from friends and loved ones, and even that we accept praise.

Jesus models such self-love for Christians. He allowed others to care for him,[63] attended to friendships, asked for help and support,[64] and accepted praise from others.[65] He honored his embodiment by taking time to eat and rest, his friendships by dining and conversing with his followers, and God through prayer and ministry.[66] Additionally, Jesus often separated from his followers, especially for prayer, a model that later informed Christian asceticism. He sometimes sent the disciples on missions on their own, without him, and he seems to have required some independent time from social relations in order to better pursue his ministry rooted in righting social relations. Jesus prioritized his relationship with God, whom he addressed as Abba, as he sought to follow God's will in his life. Jesus' relationship with God does not necessarily imply a rejection of self-love, since self-love is properly a response to God's love. At a time when these loves clashed—for example, in Gethsemane—Jesus submitted his will to God's: "Abba, Father, all things are possible to you. Take this cup away from me, but not what I will but what you will" (Mark 14:36; NAB). If we interpret Jesus' agony as a model of the love commandment, then he prioritized love for God by trusting in and remaining committed to God. Although he petitioned God to remove the cup of suffering, Jesus did not lose faith in or reject God.[67] Jesus did not ask God to send suffering into his life. He was willing to accept the consequences of his decision to remain committed to God, including suffering and death.

---

[63] Mark 14:3-9; Matt 26:6-13; Luke 7:36-38.

[64] Matt 26:36-46; Mark 14:33-34; John 12:1-11; 11:2-3, 17-44.

[65] John 12:13-15; 18:36-37; Luke 19:35-40; Matt 21:9-11.

[66] Mark 1:12, 35; 14:32-42.

[67] In two of the four gospel accounts, as Jesus is dying on the cross, in excruciating pain, having been humiliated, tortured, and taunted, Jesus cries out in a loud voice, "My God, my God, why have you forsaken me?" (Matt 27:46; Mark 15:34; NAB/NRSV). These are difficult words to interpret. On the one hand, the expression could mirror the questions of the disciples who wondered how God could let this happen to Jesus. Some also interpret Jesus' final words on the cross as his expression of doubt or abandonment. I interpret them instead as lament, an outpouring of anguish and desolation, a human cry of sense making, but not despair. These words echo the psalmist's cry in Psalm 22:1, concerning the suffering of a righteous person. Assuming the gospel authors were aware of the psalm, which ends in an act of faith declaring that "dominion belongs to the LORD" (Ps 22:28; NRSV), one can interpret the reference to Psalm 22 as the evangelists' way of showing Jesus to be a righteous servant of God.

Because self-love is properly regarded as a response to God's prior loving and affirmation of the self, self-love from a Christian perspective can never be construed as selfishness or arrogance. Selfishness is grounded in an inability to see one's integral good as related to the good of others. At its core, selfishness is contrary to self-love because the selfish person sees everything and everyone as existing for her benefit alone, for her use and pleasure. This attitude is sinful, not because the self is unworthy of love and attention, but because the self exists in a web of relationships to God and others, relationships that demand mutual affirmation. Christian love for self does not necessarily lead to self-centeredness. Affirming and caring for oneself can take place even in relationship with others. Because we are inherently social persons, our true integral flourishing occurs precisely in our mutual relationships. But if I am an "end" in myself, called to love and cherish myself, and at the same time a relational being situated within a web of relationships, how am I to negotiate these multiple loves?

Our love relationship with God spills over into the other relationships in our lives when we begin to respond to God's command to care for others. Love for the neighbor is a central theme of Jesus' preaching and, similar to self-care, is a concrete way that Christians cooperate with God in the world. In his preaching, Jesus called his followers to love their family and friends, but also the outcast, the sick, and the weak. Mercy and compassion for others are not optional for the Christian, who is called to feed the hungry, give drink to the thirsty, welcome the stranger, clothe the naked, care for the ill, and visit the imprisoned.[68]

Some theologians characterize sacrificial agape as *the* radical Christian love to which Jesus called his disciples. These authors tend to give the impression that we can and should choose between love of self and love of neighbor, and some go so far as to name self-love as sinful.[69]

---

[68] Matt 25:31-46; Luke 6:31-36. See also 1 John 3:17-18.

[69] Søren Kierkegaard, *Works of Love*, trans. Howard and Edna Hong (New York: Harper Torchbooks, 1962), 62–63; Anders Nygren, *Agape and Eros* (Chicago: University of Chicago Press, 1982); C. S. Lewis, *The Four Loves* (San Diego, CA: Harvest/HBJ, 1960); Gene Outka, *Agape: An Ethical Analysis* (New Haven, CT: Yale University Press, 1972); Bernard V. Brady, "Christian Love Is Sacrificial Love," in *Christian Love: How Christians through the Ages Have Understood Love* (Washington, DC: Georgetown University Press, 2003), 194–209; Reinhold Niebuhr, *Love and Justice*, ed. D. B. Robertson (Cleveland: World Publishing Co., 1967), 38, and *Moral Man and Immoral Society: A Study in Ethics and Politics* (New York: Charles Scribner's Sons, 1960), 74–75. Reinhold Niebuhr is known for "Christian

Other theologians have been concerned about the problems of subordinating self-love to love for others and have rightly identified problems with excessive self-surrender.[70] Surely the Christian life requires love of neighbor, but the more important question rotates around how to rightly balance the obligation to love one's neighbors with the obligation to love and care for oneself.

Toward an Understanding of Appropriate Sacrifice in Married Life

Love for self and love for others frequently overlap. Because human beings are social and relational beings, our experience of self-love is fostered and made possible in human community. Catholic social teaching has emphasized this inherently social view of the human person.[71] As inherently social persons, we cannot seek our own good without attention to relationships that contribute both to our own flourishing and, necessarily, to the good of others. Nevertheless, Christian life is messy, and sometimes Christians experience conflicting demands among these loves. How might the triple love commandment inform a Christian woman's discernment about such dilemmas?

Sometimes neighbor love requires a gift of self that is experienced initially as a loss to self, as when parents chose frugal living in order to save for their children's education, or when a woman cares for her dying spouse. Not

---

realism," which was closely associated with "political realism" in the context of the Cold War. Scholars of Niebuhr caution against overemphasizing his analysis of pride and the need for self-sacrifice. Rebekah Miles explains that some feminists have mischaracterized and oversimplified Niebuhr's understanding of sin, pride, and self-sacrifice. See Miles, *The Bonds of Freedom: Feminist Theology and Christian Realism* (Oxford: Oxford University Press, 2001), 28–89, 147–53; and Robin W. Lovin, *Reinhold Niebuhr and Christian Realism* (Cambridge: Cambridge University Press, 1995), 142–47.

[70] Martin D'Arcy, *The Mind and Heart of Love* (New York: Meridian Books, 1956); Barbara Hilkert Andolsen, "Agape in Feminist Ethics," in *On Love and Friendship: Philosophical Readings*, ed. Clifford Williams (Boston, MA: Jones and Bartlett, 1995), and "Elements of a Feminist Approach to Bioethics," in *Feminist Ethics and the Catholic Moral Tradition*, 341–81; Valerie Saiving (Goldstein), "The Human Situation: A Feminine View," *Journal of Religion* 4 (1960), reprinted in *Womanspirit Rising: A Feminist Reader in Religion*, ed. Carol P. Christ and Judith Plaskow (New York: Harper & Row, 1979), 25–42.

[71] Charles E. Curran, *Catholic Social Teaching 1891–Present: A Historical, Theological, and Ethical Analysis* (Washington, DC: Georgetown University Press, 2002).

all neighbor love is reciprocal or immediately mutual, even if it has the goal of eventual mutual relationship, as a pregnant woman's love of her child in utero can have the goal of mutuality even while her sacrifices are unrewarded. However, sacrificial love for the other, if freely chosen and affirming of one's own well-being, may be good and moral. On these grounds, we can interpret sacrifice in marriage not as the goal per se of Christian life but as a means to fulfill loving care and devotion to children and spouse, as Jesus' acceptance of suffering was not intended for its own sake but was accepted as a consequence of fidelity to God and to his social ministry.

Christians should not seek out opportunities for suffering, and yet some suffering can be accepted within a larger love relationship. Nevertheless, the Christian life does not require total self-renunciation. Meaningful relationships are built upon mutuality and reciprocity, but we will never discover a mathematically informed ethical calculus to achieve perfect balance between receiving and giving. Rather, in patterns of giving, caring, sharing, and relating to others, we establish trust and enable deeper life-giving connections with others. A relationship of mutuality requires "sharing of power—with, by, and among all parties in the relationship in a way that recognizes the wholeness and particular experience of each participant toward the end of optimum flourishing of all."[72] This understanding of interconnected obligations relies on a relational anthropology and an interpretation of the life of Jesus as a call to transform relationships of oppression into relationships of mutual obligation, justice, and flourishing. Sadly, this more nuanced view of sacrifice-in-mutual-relationships is not found in the bishops' pastoral letter on married life.

Mutuality affirms the person as beloved of God but does not wholly reject the place of self-sacrifice in loving relationships. Instead, as ethicist Dawn Nothwehr claims, "Only when one chooses self-denial toward a goal of greater mutuality (or of mutual love) is sacrifice healthy."[73] Similarly, ethicist Margaret Farley explains how self-sacrifice can be a part of love, but that not all self-sacrifice expresses love.

> [We have] a moral obligation not to relate to another person in a way
> that is truly destructive of ourselves as persons. It does not mean that
> we ought never to sacrifice our own welfare—sacrifice even our home,

---

[72] Dawn M. Nothwehr, *Mutuality: A Formal Norm for Christian Social Ethics* (Eugene, OR: Wipf & Stock, 1998), 233.
[73] Ibid., 221.

our health, our security, our reputation, our professional future, our very life. What it does mean (to say that we must not relate to others in ways destructive of ourselves as persons) is that while we may sacrifice everything we have, we may not sacrifice everything we are. We may not sacrifice in a final sense our autonomy. We may not sacrifice our capability for union and communion with God and human persons.[74]

Christians should not sacrifice to the point of despair, desperation, or loss of identity as a person loved by God with inherent dignity. Social constraints that demand this kind of dehumanizing sacrifice are not of God. Practical theologian Don Browning observes that sacrificial love has an "unavoidable role in the Christian life and Christian families."[75] With feminist ethicists Barbara Hilkert Andolsen and Farley, Browning asserts that self-sacrifice has limits and operates in the service of mutual love.

> Love as equal regard is not something that one individual expresses unilaterally toward another. It is something that people create to-gether . . . through successive attempts to communicate needs and desires, to listen and to understand, to empathize with, hold, and accept, and then to live their mutual agreements.[76]

Browning describes self-sacrifice in the context of mutual relationships, emphasizing the ongoing process of establishing trust, of communicating one's needs, and of knowing that one's love for the other will be accepted, cherished, and reciprocated.

In keeping with these ethicists' reflections, the triple love commandment reveals the heart of the radical call to discipleship—to follow the one who revealed to humanity the fullness of God's love, we are to respond by loving God, our neighbors, and ourselves. For Christians, the starting point is accepting God's love. Each person is loved by and is precious to God. Each person is unique and has inherent dignity as a child of God. From this experience of God's love, the person is called to see herself as beloved. She is called to affirm, forgive, love, and care for herself. This self-love, in turn, prepares her for mutual relationships with others. Self-

---

[74] Margaret Farley, *Personal Commitments: Beginning, Keeping, Changing* (San Francisco, CA: Harper & Row, 1986), 106.

[75] Don Browning, Bonnie Miller-McLemore, Pamela Couture, K. Brynolf Lyon, and Robert Franklin, *From Culture Wars to Common Ground: Religion and the American Family Debate* (Louisville: Westminster John Knox Press, 1997), 127.

[76] Ibid., 276.

love requires that she seek relationships of authentic mutuality. In relating to others, she will need to continue to guard her own self-care, communicate honestly about her own needs, maintain her identity, establish limits on grounds of appropriate vulnerability, and work to ensure that trust builds and that the relationship remains mutual so that she can, to the extent possible, protect herself from victimization.

Thus, I privilege the triple love commandment as the criterion to judge the adequacy of any calls to self-sacrifice that appear to contradict self-love. Self-sacrificial love for one's spouse, to be moral, must coincide with love for God and must derive from radical self-acceptance. Thus, sacrifice can be promoted only if it is willingly chosen, preserves love for God, and is self-affirming. Love between spouses can be mutual, not in the sense of equal amounts of self-gift, but in the sense of unity toward a goal of mutual affirmation in relation to God.

Conclusion

What does this essay's analysis imply, then, for readers of the US bishops' pastoral letter on marriage? In retrieving New Testament Christology for a contemporary theology of marriage, the bishops focus too narrowly on the cross as the primary example of Jesus' self-giving love. As I have argued, when the Christian story of salvation focuses only on Jesus' death while excluding the loving care of God the Creator and rejecting the import of Jesus' own proclamation of the love commandment, the ensuing message of sacrifice and self-renunciation fails to be life giving. Pastoral ministers will need to make distinctions between healthy and unhealthy sacrifice so that women and marginalized persons are not subject to messages that oversimplify this important aspect of Christian discipleship. Much work needs to be done to explain that it is not simply "selfish" or "immature" if young women worry about their own self-care in romantic relationships. Affirmation of spousal equality and the norm of mutual flourishing should be emphasized. Married men and women struggle to balance love for God, self, spouse, children, and the common good in their work for justice outside the home. If the Catholic Church continues to affirm marriage as a foundation for a healthy society, then future documents should take special care to offer nuanced and qualified claims, evidence-based analysis, and a grounded and experiential methodology in dialogue with lay theologians who have much to contribute to a renewed Catholic theology of marriage.

Feminism a Must

Catholic Sexual Ethics for Today's College Classroom

Bridget Burke Ravizza, Saint Norbert College

Catholic colleges are in dire need of meaningful discussion (in and beyond courses) about sexual ethics that are relevant, meaningful, and informed by feminism. In her important study about sexual culture, spirituality, and religion on a variety of college campuses, Donna Freitas notes that many students at Catholic colleges are sexually active and yet experience a troubling disconnect between their faith commitments and their sexual choices. Moreover, these students are largely dissatisfied with the sexual behavior and attitudes on their campuses as well as in the wider American culture. However, they do not look to church teaching and theology for guidance on how that culture—and their participation in it—might change for the better. In fact, Freitas indicates that many students at these colleges are uninformed about Catholic teaching on sexual matters and, when they are exposed to it, consider it "irrelevant" or even "ridiculous."[1]

Two problems are apparent here. First, students are disappointed and dissatisfied with sexual behavior and attitudes on their campuses. Second, students lack education about Catholic sexual ethics and/or regard it as irrelevant in the face of such disappointment and dissatisfaction. Both problems must be taken seriously and addressed by professors and administrators at Catholic colleges, and offering practically and pedagogically

---

[1] Donna Freitas, *Sex and the Soul: Juggling Sexuality, Spirituality, Romance, and Religion on America's College Campuses* (Oxford: Oxford University Press, 2008), 17.

relevant sexual ethics courses is a crucial step in the right direction. Our students deserve nothing less.

Based on interviews with students, Freitas describes a culture at Catholic colleges that is dominated by "hookups" rather than dating. The hookup scene involves casual sexual encounters outside of steady, romantic relationships—ranging from kissing to sexual intercourse and often involving oral sex performed by women on men. Within the hookup culture, double standards operate for men and women. Sexual encounters often are controlled by men and their expectations. Women easily gain a reputation as "slutty" or "dirty" as a result of behavior, whereas men are praised for having multiple sexual partners. The hypermasculine overtones of the hookup culture are illustrated by the dress-up theme parties that students described to Freitas, which assign men "all the power positions" in pairings such as millionaires and maids, jock pros and sport hos, and professors and schoolgirls.[2] At these parties, women usually dress in revealing clothing in an attempt to "be sexy," and many students hook up.[3] Freitas observes that "it is not difficult to make the leap (or small step) from these parties to the male fantasies of pornography. In fact, these parties' themes mimic classic porn scenarios, now widely accessible on the Internet."[4]

While such parties may be limited to certain groups of students, the *sexualization of girls* and the *mainstreaming of pornography* in the United States has nevertheless had widespread effects on how college-aged men and women perceive themselves and their relationships. American girls at increasingly younger ages are getting the message that to be a girl means to be sexy and that their worth is attached to their sexual appeal or "hotness." A 2007 report by the American Psychological Association indicates that the process of sexualization begins in the tween years—that is, from eight to twelve years of age—and is reinforced by the media, peers, even educators and parents.[5] Moreover, American boys and girls

[2] Freitas, *Sex and the Soul*, 145.

[3] Some women claim to appreciate the chance to "dress sexy" and hook up, feeling empowered by it, though they experience difficulty with negotiating the line between "sexy" and "slutty." Freitas, 146.

[4] Freitas, *Sex and the Soul*, 145.

[5] Sexualization, according to the APA document, is distinct from sexuality in the following ways: (1) one's value is equated with "sex appeal or behavior"; (2) one is submitted to a "standard that equates physical attractiveness with being sexy"; (3) one is "sexually

come of age in a highly sexualized culture in which pornography has become mainstream—with the help of the Internet, porn is ubiquitous. Moreover, the lines between the pornography industry and popular media are increasingly blurred by, for example, raunchy music videos and *Girls Gone Wild* ads on late-night TV.[6] Clearly, our students are shaped by a culture that makes "women's worth contingent upon their ability to please men and to shape their sexual identities around what men want."[7] In turn, men are pressured to conform to oppositional and destructive "be-a-man" understandings of masculinity, characterized by femiphobia, misogyny, and male sexual entitlement. Not only are men poorly served by this model of masculinity, but it also too easily justifies sexual violence against women.[8] Such binary ways of assigning gender roles—as active/passive, sexual predator/gatekeeper—sell both men and women short, yet these roles continue to dominate the hookup culture on Catholic college campuses.

Binary ways of thinking about sexuality and relationships also relegate LGBTQ students to the margins. Freitas helpfully notes that while straight students have difficulty negotiating the sexual culture at religiously identified colleges, the struggles of LGBTQ students are generally "more fraught and even more frightening."[9] Too often these students experience difficulties with finding safe contexts in which to openly express and discuss their sexuality. This, too, must be addressed on Catholic campuses.[10]

---

objectified—that is, made a thing for another's sexual use"; and (4) "sexuality is inappropriately imposed upon a person." The study is discussed on p. 147 in Freitas's *Sex and the Soul*. See the "Report of the APA Task Force on the Sexualization of Girls" (2007), http://www.apa.org/pi/women/programs/girls/report.aspx (accessed May 1, 2011).

[6] See Ariel Levy, *Female Chauvinist Pigs: Women and the Rise of Raunch Culture* (New York: Free Press, 2005); Robert Jensen, *Getting Off: Pornography and the End of Masculinity* (Cambridge, MA: South End Press, 2007); and Jessica Valenti, *The Purity Myth: How America's Obsession with Virginity Is Hurting Young Women* (Berkeley, CA: Seal Press, 2010).

[7] Valenti, *The Purity Myth*, 91.

[8] See Valenti, *The Purity Myth*, chapter 8, "Beyond Manliness"; Michael Kimmel, *Guyland: The Perilous World Where Boys Become Men* (especially his chapter on "Predatory Sex and Party Rape"); and Sut Jhally's film *Dreamworlds 3: Desire, Sex and Power in Music Video* (Northampton, MA: Media Education Foundation, 2007).

[9] Valenti, *The Purity Myth*, 190.

[10] And not only on Catholic campuses, of course. A handful of 2010 cases in which gay college students took their own lives, including the tragic case of Tyler Clementi at Rutgers University, highlights the intensity of this problem and the need for education.

Professors thus have important work to do to meet the needs of our students. Theological ethicists at Catholic colleges have a vital role to play in helping students understand Catholic teaching on sexual ethics and exposing them to current conversations in Christian sexual ethics in ways that are accessible, relevant, and that take their experiences seriously. Ideally, such work will enable students to better integrate their faith commitments with their sexual choices. More specifically, feminist theological ethicists have a crucial role in this endeavor. Without feminist voices, Christian sexual ethics will not meet the needs of young people, especially women, who—as argued above—are often the most (but by no means the only ones) negatively affected by attitudes and practices within our hypersexualized culture. Unfortunately, women are also most negatively affected by some of the theological approaches meant to offer an *alternative* to that culture, approaches that equate their morality with their virginity and promote restrictive gender roles. Thus, feminist analysis is required, and the inclusion of feminist voices in ethics is a must. This essay offers suggestions for the development of a sexual ethics course taught at a Catholic college that is pertinent, meaningful, and informed by feminism.

One Way to Connect Faith and Sex: The Maintenance of Purity

Freitas's study shows that while students at Catholic colleges "are seldom influenced by faith or by an identifiable moral framework" when it comes to their sexuality and sexual choices, this is not the case for students at evangelical colleges.[11] Rather, students at these schools readily connect their sexuality and sexual choices to their theological beliefs, and they talk easily about those connections. Evangelical students focus their sexual ethics on the maintenance of sexual purity and often experience a great deal of pressure to conform to that stricture. Whereas students at Catholic colleges deal with peer pressure to "hook up" or lose their virginity, students—particularly girls—at evangelical schools face pressure to stay pure and "keep" their virginity.[12] Sexual activities outside marriage—even kissing—are described by students using the language of sin,

[11] Freitas, *Sex and the Soul*, 217.
[12] Valenti explains the difficulty of defining virginity, noting that it has most often been defined by men and used to enforce traditional patriarchal gender roles.

and are often guilt inducing for women.[13] By contrast, staying sexually pure and controlling sexual desires until marriage is considered a way of being faithful to God's plan for human sexuality and relationships. Evangelical students are actively supported in the effort to stay pure by faculty, staff, administrators, and other students because heterosexual marriage is widely accepted as the proper place for sexual expression by God's design. Sex on these campuses is interpreted publicly, not privately.

Educators concerned about Freitas's findings about the sexual culture on Catholic college campuses may find the "thick" religious culture at evangelical colleges appealing and encouraging. Objective sexual norms are believed to exist, young people make strong connections between their faith commitments and their sexual choices, and they find support and guidance in doing so. Yet educators ought not too easily, or uncritically, appropriate the approach to sexual ethics prevalent at evangelical schools. Freitas identifies aspects of the purity culture on evangelical campuses that make feminists wary. First, many women at these schools are preoccupied with finding a spouse; senior women need to "find a ring by spring" lest they graduate without being engaged. Yet women are expected to undertake a passive search for a man; they are not encouraged to "express feelings about interest" in men, let alone initiate a relationship.[14] Much is at stake for evangelical women since, according to Freitas, "not finding your future husband at college is not only a social failure but also a religious failure. A woman begins to fulfill her role as a good Christian woman when she becomes a wife. Until then, she is simply waiting."[15] In contrast, men on these campuses prioritize academic and professional pursuits. While some men are pressured to find a good woman to marry, becoming a husband does not monopolize their attention. Feminists may object with good reason to women's passive role in the dating, or better, "waiting," game at evangelical colleges, as well as to the fact that women's energies appear inordinately directed at securing their future role as wife and presumably mother rather than toward intellectual and professional goals.[16]

---

[13] Freitas, *Sex and the Soul*, 121.

[14] Ibid., 115.

[15] Ibid., 118.

[16] This is not an either-or proposition, but if finding a husband is dominating the energies of most young women at the expense of academic pursuits, it is cause for worry.

A second concern about the purity culture is its severe ethic, which manifests as "debilitating and often unrealistic."[17] High standards, intense pressure, and inability to meet expectations have devastating effects, both personal and social, especially for women. Third-wave feminist and writer Jessica Valenti offers a scathing critique of the purity movement in the US in *The Purity Myth: How America's Obsession with Virginity is Hurting Young Women*. The sexual ethic at these evangelical schools reflects this wider purity movement, which is characterized by purity balls, where fathers pledge to protect their daughters' sexuality and girls pledge to remain sexually pure until marriage.[18] Valenti criticizes the movement's focus on girls' sexual purity—in particular, on virginity—because it is paternalistic (emphasizing male control of women's sexuality) and because it too simply links a woman's moral goodness to her ability to refrain from sexual activity (emphasizing passivity). Virginity is essentially equated with goodness; in other words, girls are told that all they need to do in order to "be good" is *not* have sex. Although the purity movement's goals oppose our oversexualized popular culture, Valenti argues that they offer another manifestation of the sexualization of girls, whose worth is tied to their bodies, specifically to their sexuality. Within this ethical system, if girls are sexually active, particularly if they "lose their virginity," they experience a loss of goodness and value.

The assumption that a girl or woman loses value as a result of sexual activity follows an androcentric pattern within sexual ethics, characterized by male control of female sexuality and the firm establishment of traditional patriarchal gender roles. Valenti points out that "men, or male-led institutions, have always been the ones that get to define and assign value to virginity."[19] Virginity has traditionally been connected to the establishment of paternity and the use of women's sexuality as a

---

[17] Freitas, *Sex and the Soul*, 219.

[18] The pledges often are symbolized by a ring, given from father to daughter; the ring, in turn, is given to the girl's husband on her wedding day. Studies show that the promotion of abstinence by pledging to maintain virginity until marriage or taking chastity vows is not generally effective. For example, a study by Janet Rosenblum, published in 2009 in *Pediatrics*, found that "the teenagers who took chastity vows were just as likely to have premarital sex as their peers—and significantly less likely to use protection." See Alex Altman, "Do Virginity Pledges Work?" *Time Magazine* (2008), http://www.time.com /time/printout/0,8816,1868990,00.html (accessed February 8, 2011). On the effectiveness of abstinence-only education, see also Valenti, *The Purity Myth*, 119–20.

[19] Valenti, *The Purity Myth*, 22.

commodity. In both cases, "the notion [of virginity] has . . . been deeply entrenched in patriarchy and male ownership."[20] The idea that women are somehow "damaged goods" upon losing their virginity is tied to the definition of women as the sexual property of men, handed on from father to husband and often for a bride price. Moving beyond this idea today proves difficult because popular, religious, and campus cultures continue to assign women's value to sexual purity and equate a loss of virginity with a loss of that value.

Consequently, sexual activity outside of marriage (whether by choice or coercion) is often thought to render women immoral, "dirty," and "spoiled." The idea that having sex (in particular, having intercourse) makes one dirty and damaged is illustrated in certain abstinence-only education messages directed at young people. For example, one abstinence program compares a woman's body to a wrapped lollipop. After having been licked, the woman qua lollipop is nothing but a "poorly wrapped, saliva-fouled sucker," hardly appetizing for the next man with whom she may have sex.[21] Another educational demonstration depicts a girl's body as a piece of tape that is placed on a boy's arm and removed, dirty and more difficult—or altogether unable—to "stick" to the next boy.

Not only evangelical Christians send such messages to girls and young women. A similar message was conveyed, for example, when Christopher West gave a lecture on Pope John Paul II's theology of the body to a Green Bay auditorium filled mostly with teenagers in 2009.[22] West illustrated his message about sexual purity by comparing the body to a piece of paper that he held in his hand, which—having been "used" by another person during sex—was crumpled up and thrown aside. Although he attempted to relay a message about one person's use of another as a "thing" for sexual pleasure (thereby denying their full dignity), I nevertheless wonder how young audience members who were sexually active (again, by choice or by coercion/force) reacted during that demonstration. In this scenario, they are represented by a crumpled piece of trash, or similarly a saliva-fouled sucker, or a piece of tape that is soiled and unable to

---

[20] Ibid., 22. She is drawing on Henne Blank's *Virgin: The Untouched History* (New York: Bloomsbury USA, 2007).

[21] Freitas, *Sex and the Soul*, 41, quoting Darren Washington, abstinence educator.

[22] Christopher West spoke about the theology of the body at the Weidner Center at the University of Wisconsin–Green Bay, October 12, 2009.

adhere or fulfill its function.[23] Educators can and must do better to help young people understand the goodness of their sexuality, particularly in a culture in which girls are already taught—and in harmful ways—to associate their worth with their sexuality.

We should apply a feminist hermeneutic of suspicion to any approach to sexual ethics that simply equates a girl's morality with her ability to abstain from sex or that implies that a girl's value is lost as a result of sexual activity.[24] Valenti ultimately argues that we must learn to trust women to make their own choices about sexual behavior and to move away from paternalistic (strict "father morality") approaches to sexual ethics. Moreover, she argues that girls and young women should be taught that their sexual behavior "has no bearing on whether they are ethical people."[25] While I sympathize with many of Valenti's criticisms of the purity movement, she goes too far when she completely severs sexual behavior from morality.[26] The Christian tradition has consistently taught that our sexual behavior does have some bearing on or is intertwined with our status as ethical people. That tradition maintains that we are called to holiness as embodied persons, and our sexual behavior can be either edifying, thereby contributing to our holiness, or destructive, thereby diminishing our character, breaking communion with God and others. Therefore, educators and in particular ethicists at Catholic colleges have an obligation to help our students consider what kinds of sexual behaviors may lead to flourishing and what kinds diminish self and others. Doing so responsibly demands, at the very least, redesigning courses in sexual ethics.

[23] West does argue that grace in and through Jesus Christ restores a person's dignity and that consequently the goodness of sexuality can be reclaimed. And within the purity movement, there is talk about "repackaging virginity" or reclaiming a spiritual virginity once one's virginity (however that is defined) has been lost. Nevertheless, the message about being damaged, made dirty, or spoiled can be harmful to young women, especially when expectations are so restrictive that even kissing is considered a violation of purity.

[24] Often she is told that she is no longer "marriage material" or is worth less to a man.

[25] Valenti, *The Purity Myth*, 196.

[26] In *The Purity Myth*, Valenti criticizes certain kinds of sexual behavior, such as rape and the objectification of women, which she condemns as immoral. And yet she also argues that if sex is freely chosen, then it does not bear on whether or not we are good persons.

Beyond Purity: Developing a Course, Considering Essentials

In order for a sexual ethics course on today's Catholic college campus to adequately meet the needs of students, I recommend that it do at least the following: help students understand magisterial teaching on sexual matters; incorporate experience, particularly the experience of women and girls; analyze gender; rethink complementarity; and promote Christian virtues. The remainder of this essay will comment briefly on each of these components and offer some concrete examples for approaching them.[27] Included as well will be concrete examples of how students in my classroom have reacted and responded to the strategies and materials suggested.

Understanding Magisterial Teaching

Considering the general lack of understanding of magisterial teaching about sexuality and sexual ethics noted by Freitas, courses in sexual ethics must help students examine key documents of the tradition in order to gain foundational knowledge of official church teaching. For example, students can be lead through documents such as *Humanae Vitae, Persona Humana, Evangelium Vitae,* Always Our Children, and John Paul II's reflections on the theology of the body, which lay out the fundamentals of official teaching on sexual issues and link sexual norms to a theological anthropology. Key theological concepts can be examined with the help of these documents, such as a theology of complementarity, heterosexual marriage as the proper and exclusive context for genital activity, and the inseparable (unitive and procreative) moral meanings of sexual intercourse.

Happily, I find that while students may enter the classroom with a dearth of knowledge about magisterial teaching, they genuinely *want* to know. In my classes, students—Catholic and non-Catholic alike—are eager to read and discuss magisterial documents related to sexual matters and to know the context within which they developed. For example, my students quite readily engage *Humanae Vitae* (HV). In contrast to the trivialization of sexual interaction and the commodification of persons that characterizes the hookup culture, many students are taken by HV's emphasis on the goodness and sacramental depth of sexuality and rela-

[27] Other materials and methods may, of course, achieve these same ends.

tionships as part of God's design for human beings. Generally, students sympathize with Pope Paul VI's argument that sexual relationships are best when they are life giving, even if they question whether sex should be limited to heterosexual married partnership or whether married couples must be open to procreation in each and every act of intercourse. Students are fascinated to learn about the history of the birth control commission and its debates over teaching on artificial contraception—debates that continue today, intensified by the spread of diseases like HIV/AIDS and ongoing gender injustice.

It is easy enough to see how careful examination of magisterial documents benefits the Catholic students in my classes, who are more informed about, and perhaps more thoroughly formed by, the Catholic tradition as a result. But non-Catholic students also express appreciation for a more thorough knowledge of, and ability to articulate, Catholic sexual teachings. Working through Catholic documents together often inspires them to discover more about what their respective tradition teaches on relevant matters, such as artificial contraception or same-sex attraction/relationships. I am gratified when they excitedly share their findings with the class, sparking lively conversations about similarities and differences among religious traditions. In turn, all students are enriched.

Incorporating Experience

Taking the experience of women seriously is a nonnegotiable component in feminist ethics. Helping students think about the intersections between gender, race, and class in the lives of women and girls will serve as a vital component in any course informed by feminism, including sexual ethics. Sexual teachings that are presented as absolute and universal are often challenged when the complexities of everyday experiences are brought to the fore. Experiential ambiguity demands nuance and discernment in ethical thinking.

Official Catholic teaching upholds heterosexual marriage and sex as the ideal and condemns the use of artificial contraception as intrinsically evil.[28] Yet many Catholic ethicists have compellingly argued for the ethical

---

[28] Interestingly, Pope Benedict XVI recently claimed in an interview with Peter Seewald that there may be exceptions to the teaching against the use of condoms, such as the use of condoms by a male prostitute, "as a first step in the direction of moralization, a first assumption of responsibility, on the way to recovering an awareness that not everything

use of condoms to protect against disease in a case in which one or both partners is infected, whether within or outside of marriage.[29] Students ought to examine these arguments, in conjunction with stories of women and girls who—in patriarchal contexts around the world—are particularly at risk for disease and who often have little or no say in what happens to their bodies. Such real-life stories can be found in texts like Nicholas Kristof and Sheryl WuDunn's *Half the Sky*, Kevin Bales's *Disposable People*, and Melissa Browning's "HIV/AIDS Prevention and Sexed Bodies," as well as in films like *The Day My God Died*, which powerfully illustrates the effects of trafficking and sexual slavery in the lives of vulnerable young girls.[30]

Discussing the ethics of abortion also becomes complicated when contextualized. Students might benefit, for example, by examining the recent case in Phoenix, Arizona, in which the ethics committee at Saint Joseph Hospital led by Sister Margaret McBride approved an abortion for a mother of four who suffered from hypertension as a result of her eleven-week pregnancy and who was told by doctors that she would likely (with close to 100 percent certainty) die if the pregnancy continued. Subsequent to the abortion for medical reasons that saved the life of the mother, Sister McBride was excommunicated, and the hospital lost its Catholic status. Or perhaps discussing an article about abortion outside of the US, where the topic is highly politicized and linked to legal debates over choice, can help students consider abortion from different perspectives. For example, Mallika Kaur Sarkaria's "Lessons from Punjab's 'Missing Girls': Toward a Global Feminist Perspective on 'Choice' in Abortion" examines widespread sex-selective abortion in Punjab, India.[31] She illustrates how the "choice" to abort girl fetuses is

---

is allowed and that one can do whatever one wants." John L. Allen Jr. "Pope Signals Nuance on Condoms," *National Catholic Reporter*, November 20, 2010, http://ncronline .org/print/21369 (accessed March 6, 2011).

   [29] See *Catholic Ethicists on HIV/AIDS Prevention*, ed. James Keenan, assisted by Lisa Sowle Cahill, Jon Fuller, and Kevin Kelly (New York: Continuum, 2000).

   [30] Nicholas D. Kristof and Sheryl WuDunn, *Half the Sky: Turning Oppression into Opportunity for Women Worldwide* (New York: Alfred Knopf, 2009). Kevin Bales, *Disposable People: New Slavery in the Global Economy* (Berkeley, CA: University of California Press, 1999). Melissa D. Browning, "HIV/AIDS Prevention and Sexed Bodies: Rethinking Abstinence in Light of the African AIDS Pandemic," *Theology and Sexuality* 15, no. 1 (2009): 29–47. *The Day My God Died* (Park City, UT: Andrew Levine Productions, 2004).

   [31] Mallika Kaur Sarkaria, "Lessons from Punjab's 'Missing Girls': Toward a Global Feminist Perspective on 'Choice' in Abortion," *California Law Review* 97, no. 3 (June 2009).

influenced by a deeply ingrained cultural preference for boys; gendered economic realities related to dowry, work opportunities, and familial commitments; political instability; and so forth. What becomes clear for students in reading Sarkaria's analysis is that abortion is not simply an individual matter but a social one, and that reducing abortion mandates improving the lives of women and girls as well as attending to complex social realities.

Working with real-life cases in my courses pushes students to move beyond simplistic notions about how good is brought about in our broken world. In my sexuality course last semester, students who had a strong background in women's and gender studies but little background in theology were in conversation with students who were steeped in theology but new to women's and gender studies. Since feminism is stereotyped by some theological conservatives as "antifamily," "antichildren," and "proabortion," and since religion is stereotyped by some feminists as having mainly negative effects on women and girls, students had to work to overcome oversimplified generalizations and to see one another (as well as the academic fields of theology and women's and gender studies) as real conversation partners. When discussing the Saint Joseph Hospital abortion case and other cases, students who initially seemed suspicious of one another found ethical common ground despite differences in perspectives. In fact, theological arguments and feminist arguments often led students to similar conclusions about possible ethical responses in these cases. Open and honest discussions about real-life examples (which involved both emotion and reason) had an important twofold effect: students became more nuanced in their ethical thinking about typically divisive issues, namely, abortion and artificial contraception, and also more nuanced in their thinking about one another—meeting one another across initial black-and-white divides and building a more trustful and open learning community.

Examining Gender

To negotiate sexuality and sexual choices today, students need to critically consider gender. Magisterial teaching continues to rely on patriarchally based categories of masculinity and femininity to discuss complementarity and its appropriate roles for men and women in the church and society. In his Letter to the Catholic Bishops on the Collaboration of Men and Women in the Church and in the World, then

Cardinal Ratzinger condemns certain aspects of modern feminism, including its tendency to deny fundamental differences between men and women by viewing them as "mere effects of historical and cultural conditioning." Ratzinger claims that by emphasizing gender, feminists obscure "the difference or duality of the sexes," thereby questioning the family and its "natural two-parent structure of mother and father" and making homosexuality equivalent to heterosexuality.[32] These are weighty, and debated, claims.

Conversations about the extent to which masculine and feminine norms are socially constructed are valuable, and our students will benefit from being a part of them. As Ratzinger notes, how one thinks about sex and gender, in turn, has concrete effects on how one thinks about appropriate roles for men and women, family structures, and friendships and sexual relationships. Exciting and accessible work is being done that can help students think critically about gender and relationships. For example, extensive studies by sociologist Michael Kimmel and others on the sexual life of college-aged women and men confirm the prevalence of a hookup culture that "retains features of older dating patterns: male domination, female compliance, and double standards."[33] While men and women both participate in sexual encounters without expectations of relationship, Kimmel argues that men hook up largely in order to impress other men. Sex acts as a form of male bonding; bragging about sexual encounters affirms masculinity. Kimmel's most recent book, *Guyland: The Perilous World Where Boys Become Men*, identifies and evaluates various aspects of the social world of young men—in particular, its destructive messages about masculinity—that do not prepare them well for healthy adult relationships.

Kimmel rightly claims that young men (and certainly women as well) need more guidance negotiating their gender, sexuality, and sexual activity during late adolescence and young adulthood. He writes:

> There are virtually no trustworthy adults willing or able to talk honestly about sex with young people. Talking to their parents is far too awkward. Sex education in schools is often restricted to a

---

[32] Cardinal Joseph Ratzinger, Letter to the Bishops of the Catholic Church on the Collaboration of Men and Women in the Church and in the World (Rome: Offices of the Congregation for the Doctrine of Faith, May 31, 2004), sec. I, par. 2.

[33] Kimmel, *Guyland*, 197.

quasi-religious [or explicitly religious] preaching about abstinence. Any information that they do manage to cobble together—how it works, what to do, what women like, what they expect—comes almost entirely from their peers, and from pornography. In fact, pornography winds up being the best source of sexual information available to them, and . . . pornography is filled with lies.[34]

Educators on Catholic college campuses ought to take up this task, being trustworthy and informed adults who can help our students think carefully and critically about gender, sexuality, and relationships in a sometimes-toxic culture.

In my classes, students are eager to talk about gender and relationships. Kimmel's book, paired with the *Dreamworlds 3* film, sparks intense conversation about the stories of masculinity and femininity that are told (and not told) in our culture and about how gender norms affect relationships. My students also examine their lives as texts, drawing on their experience—in their families, friendships, and romantic relationships—to think critically about gender expectations. While they do not necessarily identify with some of the most extreme "guy behavior" described in *Dreamworlds* and *Guyland*,[35] they do connect to Kimmel's discussion of the prevalence of casual sexual encounters fueled by alcohol and of gendered double standards about sex. By and large, my students agree with Kimmel that the hookup culture and the gender norms that guide it do not train them well for lasting, intimate relationships, and they long for more mature ways of relating.

Conversations with my students about what happens when men and women step out of strict "gender boxes" on campus, and further how gender policing by peers functions to reinforce those boxes, are vibrant and informative. Particularly fruitful is an in-class activity about gender socialization that breaks students into sex-specific small groups and asks them to make two lists. The first list answers the following: When growing up, what were you taught about what it means to be a girl (or what girls are like)? The second list answers the following: When growing up, what were you taught about what it means to be a boy (or what boys are like)? When students complete the task, we compare the lists together in

[34] Ibid., 207.

[35] For example, behavior related to fraternity life, such as hazing, enforced binging, and eroticizing violence against women.

a large group.[36] In addition, we compare the students' results to a list of masculine and feminine characteristics developed by a sociologist and talk about students' impressions of the lists.[37] This flows into a discussion of the negative repercussions for students when they step out of these "gender boxes" on campus. For example, men commonly tell each other, "Don't be such a girl," when exhibiting emotion or sensitivity. Kimmel helpfully links this type of gender policing with homophobia, explaining that homophobia for "guys" is not only (or necessarily) hatred of gays and lesbians but also fear of what is feminine in themselves and fear of being perceived as gay by others.[38] Confirming this connection, a male student recently shared that his friends often use the phrase "no homo" in conversation when they complement one another—for example: "I like your shirt. No homo." His example prompted students to strategize methods of resistance to negative peer pressure about gender on campus and, further, to consider the role that authentic friends play in such resistance.[39]

Rethinking Complementarity

Since so much of the magisterium's teaching on sexuality and relationships is rooted in a theology of complementarity, a course in sexual ethics should expose students to critical questions that theologians have posed to this approach. For example, many feminist theologians have

[36] Special thanks to my colleague, sociologist Paul S. Schnorr, for suggesting this gender activity. Every time I have used it in class, it has been successful. Students love it, and inevitably the classroom is filled with energy and laughter. In addition, students find it thought provoking, even eye opening. A male student once emailed to thank me for this particular class period because it invited him to think critically about gender as he never had before.

[37] I use a list from the eighth edition of *Sociology* by John J. Macionis. The text is currently in its fourteenth edition, which was published by Pearson in 2012. The overlap between student lists and the Macionis list is consistently significant, and students' impressions of the lists are overwhelmingly negative, particularly regarding feminine characteristics. International students in my courses have added depth to these discussions, as American and international students make cultural comparisons and distinctions and think together about what makes us ideal men, women, and human beings across cultural boundaries.

[38] See chap. 3, "The Guy Code," in Kimmel's *Guyland*, especially pp. 48 and following.

[39] Michael Kimmel emphasizes the important role that friends—male and female—play in resisting the most negative aspects of hypermasculine socialization.

noted limitations of a dual-nature anthropology that is reflected in the
theology of complementarity because this understanding of human personhood construes men and women as fundamentally different by God's
design—equal but complementary, "each bearing unique characteristics
from which the other sex is excluded."[40] Feminist theologian Elizabeth
Johnson rejects this binary way of thinking about men and women,
"which rigidly predetermines the qualities each should cultivate and the
roles each can play. Apart from the naïveté about its own social conditioning, its reliance on stereotypes, and the denial of the wholeness of human
experience that it mandates, this position functions as a smokescreen for
the subordination of women since by its definition women are always
relegated to the private, passive realm."[41] In fact, some theologians argue
not only that the theology of complementarity is leveraged to promote
traditional gender roles to the detriment of women[42] but also that it no
longer adequately reflects human experience and reason. Clearly, the
dual anthropology reflected in official Catholic teaching about sexuality is not universally accepted, and students ought to be aware of this
critical engagement with the tradition as well as the construction of other
anthropological alternatives.

For example, students should be exposed to the ways that contemporary science problematizes binary thinking about sex and gender. Ethicist
Christine Gudorf points out that reliance on outdated biology limits magisterial teaching on sexuality. In order to be convincing, sexual teaching
must grapple with what biologists are telling us today about the human
person. Namely, "that there are six indicators of biological sex, and that
for many millions of people these indicators do not line up in any simple
dimorphic pattern. Not only do many millions have ambiguous genitalia,
especially (but not only) when young, but even chromosomal sex is not
dimorphic."[43] Along with scientists, the work of theologians and other
scholars included in texts like *God, Science, Sex, Gender: An Interdisciplinary
Approach to Christian Ethics* can help students wrestle with the implications

[40] Elizabeth Johnson, *She Who Is: The Mystery of God in Feminist Theological Discourse* (New York: Crossroads, 1992), 154.

[41] Ibid., 154.

[42] As noted above, this is one reason Valenti rejects a focus on women's sexual purity.

[43] Christine Gudorf, "A New Moral Discourse on Sexuality," in *Human Sexuality in the Catholic Tradition*, ed. Kieran Scott and Harold Horell (Lanham, MD: Rowman and Littlefield Publishers, Inc., 2007), 55.

of contemporary science for Christian sexual ethics. If biology is pointing to real diversity in sexualities and in gender behavior across the natural world, then Christians must reconsider the effectiveness of continuing to speak about sex and gender in binary ways. Taking seriously the scientific and sociological facts that not all persons are clearly either male or female and that sexualities and gender behaviors in nature do not neatly fit dimorphic patterns have profound implications for ethical thinking about male-female complementarity and about what "natural" and moral behavior may be for LGBTQ persons.[44]

My students are intellectually and morally engaged by discussions about complementarity in light of feminism and contemporary science. They inevitably ask, "what about" those who are excluded by rigorous theological categories of male-female complementary, such as those that undergird the theology of the body? What about gay and lesbian persons, intersex persons, and persons whose gender characteristics are not definitively masculine or feminine? Charles Curran argues that the theology of the body "clearly cannot serve as a theology for all persons and all bodies."[45] As indicated by the questions above, my students consistently notice—and express discomfort about—the exclusivity of a strictly binary theological system. They seek more theologically inclusive ways to envision sexuality and relationships, ways that stand up to experience and scientific realities, ways that include all persons and all bodies.

In a recent summer school course, I witnessed students being powerfully moved by a lesbian student who "came out" to our class. She told us about feeling ashamed and rejected as she grew up within her Catholic Church community and family because of her sexual orientation. She struggled to see herself as fully made in God's image rather than as defective. She explained that participation in this course was the first time she had an opportunity to understand and wrestle with magisterial

---

[44] See Joan Roughgarden, "Evolutionary Biology and Sexual Diversity," and Stephen Pope, "Social Selection and Sexual Diversity: Implications for Christian Ethics," in *God, Science, Sex, and Gender: An Interdisciplinary Approach to Christian Ethics*, ed. Patricia Beattie Jung and Aana Marie Vigen, with John Anderson (Urbana, IL: University of Illinois Press, 2010). On complementarity between same-sex couples, see Michael G. Lawler and Todd A. Salzman, *The Sexual Person: Toward a Renewed Catholic Anthropology* (Washington, DC: Georgetown University Press, 2008).

[45] Charles E. Curran. *The Moral Theology of Pope John Paul II* (Washington, DC: Georgetown University Press, 2003).

teaching and the wider Catholic theological tradition on sexual matters. Interacting with course materials and conversing with others in the classroom created a space for this student to consider whether and where she "fits" theologically as she never had before. She was captivated—one might argue, liberated—by resources that she never knew existed, which took her perspective and experience seriously. Ultimately, she made the claim that she, too, is made in God's image; she is made for communion, made to flourish in relationship, even if she is "outside of the box" of strict male-female complementarity. How exactly she will live that out is a matter of continuing discernment, but she has recovered a sense of her own goodness and is actively thinking theologically about herself and her relationships.

Affirming Virtues

One promising approach to sexual ethics in the college classroom is a virtue-based approach. A focus on the virtues moves away from talk about particular acts that are moral or immoral outside of context and relationship, and certainly away from an ethic that connects one's morality completely to a singular act, such as the maintenance or loss of one's virginity. The primary questions in virtue ethics are identity based, which parallel the questions perennially asked by college students: Who am I? Who am I called to be? And from the perspective of theological ethics, who is God calling me to be as an embodied person? Questions of identity, of *being*, are primary, and questions of doing, of *acting*, are secondary, because actions are understood in virtue ethics to flow from character.

Educators know well that students often express dissatisfaction with an acts-based approach to sexual ethics—for instance, when characterizing Catholic teaching as a "bunch of rules" or "dos and don'ts" that seem irrelevant to their lives. Hopefully, an in-depth knowledge of magisterial teaching as suggested above will help students to recognize the goodness and truth about the human person and relationships that exist within that tradition, beyond a simple list of rules.

Moreover, studying virtue ethics prompts students to ask foundational questions such as, what kind of person is God calling me to be? What kinds of behaviors and relationships will lead me to become my best self? How do my sexual choices reflect my character and, in turn, shape it? Are there ways of acting sexually that diminish me? That diminish others? What kinds of sexual activities and relationships will contribute to my flourishing as well as my partner's? Are my choices as a sexual person making the community better? Are there ways that persons in my community are marginalized or violated on account of sexuality or gender? If so, what is my responsibility to them? What particular virtues seem most important for living a good sexual life? Any person can ask himself or herself these questions, without distinction based on sex or gender.

James Keenan's "Virtue Ethics and Sexual Ethics" and Margaret Farley's *Just Love* serve as excellent resources to help students understand the method and value of virtue ethics and also to provide content in answering the questions listed above.[46] These theologians suggest and describe key virtues for good sexual relationships, which include being loving, just, faithful, self-caring, merciful, and fruitful. They remind us that good decision making depends on the development of prudence, or practical decision making. Keenan explains prudence as "the virtue of a person whose feet are on the ground and who thinks both practically and realistically. Prudence belongs to the person who not only sets realistic ends but who sets out to attain them. The prudent person is precisely the person who knows how to grow."[47] Students can be both empowered and challenged by an ethic that asks them to take responsibility for the development of their character, honor every other as one with equal dignity and autonomy and as made in God's image, and never stop growing. Sometimes I think the central problem is that our students simply settle for too little, for less than the best from themselves and others. It is easy to do within a culture that sexualizes girls; teaches men that masculinity depends on the use of, and domination over, women; glamorizes pornography; eroticizes violence; and too readily commodifies persons. A virtue-based ethics reminds students to ask more from themselves and their relationships. As noted above, one of the dangers of a purity ethic is that it connects one's morality to a singular act; if virginity is lost, one thinks that goodness and worth are lost along with it. A virtue-based ethic, with its focus on being rather than doing, avoids this trap. Rather, it calls students to continual growth in goodness—even when they may falter in their behavior. It is hopeful in this regard, and challenging as well, for one can never be too virtuous.

---

[46] James F. Keenan, "Virtue Ethics and Sexual Ethics," *Louvain Studies* 30, no. 3 (Fall 2005): 180–97. Margaret A. Farley, *Just Love: A Framework for Christian Sexual Ethics* (New York: Continuum, 2006).

[47] Keenan, "Virtue Ethics and Sexual Ethics," 184.

Virtue ethics affirms the autonomy and relationality of students, calling them to live with integrity and set expectations high for themselves and their relationships. The benefits of a virtue approach are manifold: it moves us beyond a simple focus on acts, particularly "taboo" acts; it takes seriously students' ability to think and act for themselves in their particular circumstances; it acknowledges that sex is more than a personal matter by linking responsibility for *social justice* to sexuality and gender; it applies to all persons—straight, LGBTQ, or questioning; it asks students to think about Christian virtues and values and how their sexual choices relate to them; and it calls students to continual growth.

Our students need help navigating the difficult territory of becoming healthy and virtuous sexual adults, a task that is particularly challenging in a campus culture, as well as a wider culture, that broadly fosters problematic messages about masculinity, femininity, and relationships. We cannot cower from frank and informed conversations with our students about the goodness of their bodies and sex. They are eager to think and talk critically about these matters in safe spaces—our classrooms, our campuses, and ideally our church traditions should offer such spaces.

In Conversation with
Michele Saracino, Manhattan College

Reading your essays on the academic vocation leaves me hopeful about what we do as theologians and why we do it, especially in a church that struggles with what Lonergan called a "classicist" worldview, one that refuses to understand experience in context. Your work shows that theology and religiosity enliven when read through story and voice, and part of your project as professional theologians is to share your stories and theological insights in an effort to make room for other women in the church to do the same. It is refreshing to see in print that while some perceive this sharing negatively, even as "touchy-feely," you claim it as indispensable to rigorous theological inquiry, as well as to creating solidarity, in a church that listens to and for other voices within the global church.

Mary Doyle Roche's analysis of voice sets the stage for the other essays by creating a distinction between listening to voices and listening for voices, which she finds in the work of Sara Lawrence-Lightfoot. While listening to voices, that is, voices of others that have been marginalized or occluded in the church and society, has been a priority of various feminist movements, Roche posits that for genuine solidarity to emerge between women, and here I believe she includes all women with a focus on female theologians, it is not enough to include multiple perspectives, but we must listen for other voices as well, paying attention to voice tone, cadences, emotional dissonance, and so on. This is the difficult work of one's vocation as a theologian, a Christian, and a human being, as it demands vigilance about the not-said, the unspoken, the silences, and the ruptures in speech due to power differentials. Practically speaking, it means not only hearing a person's story but also noticing what or who is missing and why. Moreover, for Roche, when moving toward solidarity, either locally or globally, one needs to realize that every story told potentially erases that of another, or in her words, "Their story is co-opted by mine."

This is such an important point as this volume gives voice to professional women in the church who claim a place alongside theological trailblazers of previous generations. These new voices tackle issues relevant to everyday and ordinary Christians, like dating, marriage, and family life. This is an important piece of the theological pie, especially in relation to the doctrines of anthropology and Christology. Yet there is a potential cost to listening to and including these voices—namely, obscuring and erasing the contributions of the women, often women religious, who came before them, those feminists who did not have the leeway to speak about these issues for any number of reasons. Are their stories co-opted by these?

I am thinking here about Emily Reimer-Barry's work on marriage and Bridget Burke Ravizza's work in sexual ethics and the classroom. Their essays emphasize the importance of listening to voice and listening for voice in two important sectors, marriages and the lives of our students. When Reimer-Barry speaks about how the United States Conference of Catholic Bishops' 2009 pastoral letter, Marriage: Love and Life in the Divine Plan, results in insidious assumptions that wives should be sacrificial for their families and concretizes oppressive gender roles that prevent mutuality and genuine give-and-take in some of the most intimate of our relationships, I want to cheer that this problem is given voice and that new models are being made available to our daughters and sons, nieces and nephews. However, I become uneasy when I listen for voice. I begin to wonder what effect this type of work has on individuals who either are stuck in violent relationships or perhaps choose to opt out of marriage altogether, remaining celibate or otherwise. Does this type of writing uphold the hegemony of heterosexual marriage? The same argument can be made in reference to Ravizza's work, where she outlines important guidelines for the classroom that can uplift the students' voices and needs in the midst of the "hookup" culture. While, again, I applaud her critique of purity in Catholic teaching, I want more on the diversity on sexuality. Ravizza mentions the complexities of the issues relative to GLBTQ individuals, yet somehow in Catholic culture these concerns get muted in relation to heterosexual concerns.

My concern is not with the voices that Reimer-Barry and Ravizza are listening to but rather with a skewed conceptualization of the academic vocation of theology—in terms of pieces of the pie. Each time we add a voice, it seems as if another's voice is diminished. This is especially true in feminist circles, in which we feel constrained to choose one voice as there are a limited number of pieces of the pie. Instead of vying for a piece of the theological pie, in which we are forced to compete with one another or feel guilty about having a voice, perhaps we can imagine a new type of solidarity, one without limits, and with enough pie or fish for all of us.

So I remain hopeful that more voices can be listened to and for, yet probably less hopeful than LaReine-Marie Mosely is in her essay, "For Newer Catholic Women Theologians." Mapping the theological terrain of the academic vocation and providing a balanced view of the abysses and peaks of Catholicism today, Mosely cites Elizabeth Johnson's response to the bishops as a teaching moment, a moment in which we can find hope and, I would add, imagine a new way of being church. I want to agree with Mosely, but I am worried about one-way listening. Who is truly listening for the other in this situation? Are church leaders making an effort to listen for voices that have been marginalized, muted, or just plain ignored? Beyond this particular situation, what might listening for others look like from other views of today's ecclesial panorama?

I find the need for listening for voice one of the most important spiritual activities of the twenty-first century for Christians and for anyone really who wants to be in life-giving relationships with others. This type of listening involves an openness to be wrong, to being arrogant, and, worse even, to being inconsequential. As a conversation starter, I would be interested to hear how you all envision yourselves listening for voice and about the impact that listening has on your person and your theology.[1]

Michele: As you read my written response, I found Mary's distinction between listening to voices and listening for voices helpful for moving theological conversations—especially ones that are coming from feminists and womanists—in new directions. Other essay collections have moved toward diversity by seeking out new voices and by listening to them. There is something different about listening for voices. There is a vigilance about what's missing. There is a vigilance about what's not being

---

[1] The following transcript reprints a conference call that took place on the afternoon of August 16, 2011, among the conversation starter, the contributors in this section, and the coeditors. Opening and concluding parts of the call have been edited or altogether omitted, but without altering the content of the call.

said. There is a vigilance about what's not allowed to be said, which she explains with great clarity. I think that's a good way of entering into the larger conversation today.

Emily: Michele, I really appreciated your thoughtful response. And I think it is really fascinating to see this thread of "listening" through all of the essays, and I really enjoyed reading everyone else's contributions, too. One of the things that you're picking up on in terms of the need for vigilance about what's missing and our desire to bring in new voices is the problem not only of "listening for" but of "speaking for." That may be something that we need to further explore.

In other words, there are some very difficult power differentials when you stop and think about educated feminist theologians, ethicists, and so on, who are seeking to include "other" voices in their scholarship. I know I need to be very careful about how I describe other people's stories, how I qualify my claims within my own argument, and how I struggle to remain in solidarity with the people whose voices I am trying to bring into this scholarly conversation. When we do this research, trying to contribute to the academy and the church's ongoing reflection, we must be self-reflective and self-critical. Of course, when feminist theologians, ethicists, and others engage with marginalized persons, we don't want to further marginalize those persons. And so maybe that would be another way to frame our conversation, if that rings true for other people. "Listening for" is difficult in itself, but then there is an added layer after we've listened or engaged in that process of trying to attend to more various voices. We must consider how to bring those voices into the wider theological academic debate.

And I think we need to avoid thinking that bringing my new voice is necessarily going to eclipse someone else's contribution. And so I agree with the way that you ended that part of your analysis where you questioned whether a new contribution is going to diminish someone else's. You talked about imagining a new type of solidarity with enough pie for everyone or enough fish to feed everybody. Great image! And I think that's going to take some creative new ways of engaging one another. Maybe this kind of conversation is a step towards that wider engagement, but that's one of the things that I would find more fruitful going forward instead of thinking that we shouldn't speak or shouldn't strive to bring in other voices because of the possibility that someone will be excluded. What do others think?

Michele: Emily, I think that's really helpful. It's about the power dynamic of speaking for or over others. Do any of you wish to share your perspectives on that dynamic?

Mary: When I think of this in the sense of a pie that's large enough for everyone, I think one of the things that I've uncovered or tried to discern more as I've been thinking about listening for voices is also this idea of becoming comfortable with silence. In making a space for other voices to be heard and the more that I give myself over to really authentic listening, I don't really run out of space or time for any one particular narrative to come forward. I think one of the countercultural approaches to raising voice and to listening for voice is the sense in which listening requires both an intellectual and a spiritual posture. By approaching dialogue without listening but simply being quiet until it's my turn to speak, listening becomes waiting for my turn. And I think that diminishes dialogue. What passes for dialogue in our culture of talking heads on the TV is that no one is listening. Everybody is really busy speaking and waiting to say their part in a way that doesn't suggest that they've been transformed by any of the conversation or conversation partners.

So I think that that's something that's really—if we're thinking about listening in this way—impacted the way that I am going about doing my work. And I think the other thing is—as, Michele, you said—being comfortable with the intellectual integrity of sharing narrative. I think in the field of moral theology, it is not well done unless it is really attentive to the texture of other people's narratives. But I think the other thing that feminist discourse has really brought to wider theological discourse is that in my listening to other voices, as Emily says, I am essentially also writing myself into the story. And I think that this is part of that danger, Michele, that you talk about in terms of power differentials between theologians and folks whose voices they are trying to raise. There are power differentials among theologians as well. But I am not entirely disengaged from the subject matter or the story that I am trying to narrate. I think that's a false sense of intellectual objectivity that I think it's really important for theologians to get over in many ways, which other researchers, in sociology, for example, are not afraid of being part of the story. And in that way I think that, as Emily was suggesting, I am taken out of the picture suggests that the voices I am raising have not been filtered through me. I think that danger becomes diminished when we acknowledge who we are and how we're becoming part of the ongoing narratives that we're trying to raise up to the world.

LaReine-Marie: I'd like to speak a little to the concept that listening for the voices of others is particularly important to me. I've been reflecting a lot upon issues of unconscious racism, but to racism I could also add sexism, homophobia, clericalism, male chauvinism, and colonialism. I think that there are certain mechanisms in the human person and the human mind that make us disinclined to become conscious of other individuals. And so for that reason I think "listening for" is at least an acknowledgment that everyone is not around the table and that we have to keep asking questions. And so it's important for me to listen for because someones are missing from the dialogue.

And then the other comment I wish to make has to do with so many different narratives, that listening to one narrative means that we will not attend to another. Well, personally, I think it is possible for us. We may give lip service to all the narratives, but when all is said and done, we may choose to respond to the voices that are easier to hear. And we may choose not to attend to other voices. For instance, the Catholic Church's outreach to black Catholics has been less than stellar. This goes all the way back to the 1860s, as the emancipation of those enslaved was being anticipated. The Second Plenary Council of Baltimore (1866) was called in part because Rome thought it fitting that the US bishops devise a plan for outreach and evangelization for the newly emancipated.

Well, there was enough racism among the bishops because that really never got taken care of. When I read about this in Cyprian Davis's *History of Black Catholics in the United States*,[2] it is sad that the bishops' racism, devotion to other ethnic groups, and other triggers prevented them from agreeing on a plan. There certainly were exceptions. Archbishop Spalding, the apostolic delegate, made his concerns for the black community primary. And it was only after that council concluded that a group that stayed over decided to have an annual collection for African Americans, and then Native Americans were added. This collection continues to this day. Fine. But I think what's really going on here is that they missed this golden opportunity. And what I feel is that we continue to miss these golden opportunities. And that's disappointing for me.

Michele: What do you mean by "the mechanism in the mind"? Does that mechanism in the mind prohibit us from seeing, or is it more the

---

[2] Cyprian Davis, *The History of Black Catholics in the United States* (New York: Crossroad, 1995).

case that we are so uncomfortable with what we see that we refuse to acknowledge it? I really like that phrase.

LaReine-Marie: Yes. Self-knowledge can be difficult to take, and many believe that if they do not consciously and intentionally do things that are racist, sexist, homophobic, et cetera, that they are good people. Surprise—we all have our blind spots, and at times we realize that we are not open to everyone. We could harbor those very things that we often speak out against.

Bridget: And I'd like to respond to that because I recently used Bryan Massingale's book . . .

LaReine-Marie: Great.

Bridget: . . . *Racial Justice and the Catholic Church.*[3] I used it with my masters students, and it was an uncomfortable conversation for us to have, and in particular I had one student in tears, saying, "He is calling me a racist; he is calling me a racist, and I am not a racist." And what I think is so helpful about Massingale's book is that he can point out that it's about how we define racism, that it's not necessarily one person being overtly cruel to another person based on the color of their skin, although that can happen. It's more about a system that's been set up that privileges some, how we sometimes benefit from that system, and how we can think about transforming systems. But it's hard to work with students on that, when it's so easy to take an explanation of white privilege as a personal assault, with students saying, "I am not a racist, I am a good person, I am a kind person." But I think we do have an obligation to help students really to think about that and to make those connections, that is, to think about racism in terms of systems and institutions.

LaReine-Marie: Yes.

Rosemary: If I could chime in here, in some of my own research into political psychology, I have discovered that folks who established an emotionally laden conviction will hold on to that conviction regardless of facts that oppose that conviction. And so I think when LaReine-Marie was talking about this unconscious mechanism of the mind, I think also

---

[3] Bryan N. Massingale, *Racial Justice and the Catholic Church* (Maryknoll, NY: Orbis Books, 2010).

emotions are involved in our views. And when Bridget spoke about the emotions that students expressed, I think that example shows the interconnection there between epistemology, how we know, and affectivity, what we feel.

LaReine-Marie: And that may bring me to the whole notion of what's going on in the mind and the hearts of our church leaders. It would appear that there are certain deeply held beliefs that are influencing a lot of the things that are happening in our church today. It feels like such an issue of power. So I am mindful of that; even if they wouldn't admit it to us, I think that power is at play in the United States church or perhaps abroad.

Mary: And one thing that I hear as we go through the conversation, particularly on these last few comments, is again that both the church magisterial authority and the community of scholars are hesitant to acknowledge the role that emotion and passion and one's personal connection to an idea have on the way that we think about questions, the questions that we are asking in the first place, and the kinds of answers that we get. And I think that both scholars and bishops put forward an objectivity that's dishonest. And it also then keeps us, I think, from asking those really important questions that Bridget raised about how it is we are benefiting from the systems and the structures, how the stories benefit my own sense of self-understanding, as LaReine-Marie was saying in terms of claims that I am not racist, I am not sexist, I am not homophobic.

And I think it really is this sense of owning my narrative and the ways that it has helped me, how it has secured a position of privilege for me, but then also how it has made me vulnerable, and that I bring all of that to the table around which I dialogue. And it would be false for me or for any of us to really abstract that out. That's not to say that emotion and narratives muddy good thinking, and I think that's where some of that suspicion about this practice arises. But I think that it's important for a project like this to demonstrate the ways in which it actually brings some intellectual clarity to things, as well as an investment and a commitment that isn't blinded, as Rosemary said, to facts, to developments, to other experiences.

Michele: It's worth noting that the suspicion of emotion is often tied to a suspicion of women, right? And women are more linked with emotion than men. I mean, it's the age-old dualism, that what we sometimes struggle with as part of our academic vocation is trying to present ourselves as authentic theologians or ethicists, teachers, and scholars, and that historically has meant a certain type of person, a certain type of thinking, and a certain type of body.

So when you start talking about emotion and passion and bring in psychology, you risk losing the privilege that you've attained as a theologian or ethicist. Again, that is what I find so refreshing about these essays. There is no apology. There isn't a sense that by talking about story, by reflecting on experiences in the classroom, by incorporating events and experiences on the ground, I'm any less of a theologian or an ethicist.

Bridget, you tackled some very important points about what needs to go on in the classroom for theological and ethical insights to emerge. Do you want to comment a little about how you listen for your students' voices in a respectful manner, because that could get tricky in the classroom?

Bridget: Right, well, I think part of it is related to that question at the end of your response about how we listen to voices. I think that one of the most important things that I try to do in my teaching is create a safe space. And I think that's not easy, but it is crucial. It does involve this very attentive listening, being comfortable with silences, and so on, but something very powerful happens there when people start sharing their stories. And, Mary, I loved the way you talked about how stories can be so transformative for the person speaking them.

And it can have this emotional component, also for the person who is carefully listening, which can also happen through texts. So when you, Mary, were referring to women who have HIV/AIDS and how telling their stories can be healing, I was thinking about using *Casting Stones*[4]—in the way it talks about women who are involved in sex work and how *telling* their stories can be so personally healing—and how important that is and transformative that is for my students to be *hearing* those stories, and how asking them to connect and think about their own narratives in light of those stories is so powerful. And also, as I am hearing about emotion, I do often have students in tears in my classroom. I sometimes am crying myself in my classroom, when talking about a film or a book or hearing students talking about their own stories. And if someone saw this, I wonder if they would be dismissive about the show of emotion.

---

[4] Rita Nakashima Brock and Susan Brooks Thistlethwaite, *Casting Stones: Prostitution and Liberation in Asia and the United States* (Minneapolis: Fortress Press, 1996).

They might ask, is that serious academic work that they're doing in the classroom? And in my experience, that can be the most powerful kind of classroom experience.

And I wish that we could be creating those kinds of safe spaces in our churches, where people can talk about their own stories and feel safe in doing that, and not feel like they may be punished for asking critical questions in, say, a parish setting, because that's exactly what needs to be happening around a variety of different issues, around sexual issues, reproductive technologies, and all kinds of things. So I wish we could be thinking more creatively about how to create that kind of space or environment in our churches, and not only in our classrooms.

Michele: Emily, how do you see some of this unfolding in your essay on marriage and the imitation of Christ? Is there something we could have unpacked there?

Emily: Yes, well, first of all, the analysis of self-deception that LaReine-Marie and Rosemary were talking about rings true for me. And, Bridget, I think your class looks amazing, and I'd love to see the syllabus and to talk about more about the challenge of creating safe spaces in our classrooms. Teaching sexual ethics while paying attention to students' vulnerability in the classroom has been a real challenge for me, especially when we consider the realities of gender-based violence on our campuses.

But in terms of areas that resonate with my essay, it really seems important to note—as you did, Michele, in your reflections on LaReine-Marie's essay—the problem of one-way listening in the church. It is difficult to know how best to engage church leaders in our scholarship. For example, sometimes it seems like there is a deep methodological contrast that is taken for granted but not often discussed when we compare Catholic magisterial teaching and feminist approaches. The bishops tend to start from tradition, and their role is inherently conservative. In other words, they are trying to preserve continuity with the tradition as they reflect on contemporary problems. It almost seems like their pastoral letter on marriage is written from a threatened position. They name all of these threats to marriage in contemporary culture: cohabitation, contraception, divorce, same-sex marriage, and so on. And the bishops really want to reassert norms from the Catholic tradition's teachings on marriage and simply apply those norms from tradition to today's world. Of course, in a feminist approach, the starting point is different. There is a "hermeneutic of suspicion" when feminists approach the tradition with critical questions. As Letty Russell writes, we are in search of a "usable past."[5] So, a feminist will look for both continuity and discontinuity within the tradition and pay special attention to contemporary experiences, particularly the experiences of women and marginalized persons. As a kind of liberation theology, Catholic feminism gives special attention to marginalized voices. With regard to marriage, this means listening to the experiences of married people. But I wonder if that is threatening to bishops, who cannot write about marriage from their own experience. So I'm trying to read between the lines of this latest pastoral letter on marriage, but it does seem like there is some sense of being unsettled, or a fear that dialogues could get out of hand quickly if the bishops fail to strongly reassert their interpretation of tradition.

And so by asking critical questions or naming experiences that might not resonate with the bishops' interpretation of marriage traditions, one might seem to be taking a competitive approach. And that is not necessarily the best way to approach official teaching. We want to be generous in our assumptions. We want to contribute to civil discourse, a civil dialogue. But it doesn't seem like the bishops have given much attention to feminist scholarship, like they aren't listening. So that's a real struggle for me. How do I name my voice, and how do I remain in dialogue with women whose experiences don't seem to even surface on the radar screen of the bishops' document, and at the same time try to continue to be in dialogue with the magisterium? How am I called to be a person of both integrity and fidelity?

Mary: In response to Emily, one of the things that really struck me as you were speaking is this idea: for a conversation to include everybody, lots of folks and maybe some folks (for the first time) are kept from "getting out of hand" or running amuck by shutting the conversation down altogether. And I think that's also illustrated in LaReine-Marie's piece when she talks about controversies with Elizabeth Johnson. There certainly have been a number of others where it would be our responsibility as colleagues to be in dialogue with one another, to challenge one another, to point out weaknesses in our own arguments, and to make them better. Rather than exercise that proper vocation in the church as theologians, we got cut out of that loop, and that conversation has simply ended with a statement that provides surety and security for folks who want that to happen.

---

[5] Letty M. Russell, "Search for a Usable Past," in *Human Liberation in a Feminist Perspective: A Theology* (Philadelphia: Westminster Press, 1974), 72–103.

One of the things that I think is really crucial for the vision that we're talking about to be a real possibility is more confidence that conversations are ongoing. I think the idea that a conversation will be ended once and for all is also what fuels some of that anxiety about making sure I get my voice in there, get my story in there, because the chance may never come again. So I can't cede a moment to anybody else's narrative or to anybody else's concerns or questions; the urgency to get my voice out there becomes stronger rather than having confidence that this is an ongoing story of which we are all a part. And I will have moments of silence, moments of listening, moments of speaking, moments of shouting and perhaps raising my voice in anger or in love. But I think that part of the way, Emily, as you described, the magisterium works on issues they think might get out of hand is to simply say what we can talk about and reach the conclusion that we want you to reach, or we're not going talk about it at all.

And I think it's more important for us to be comfortable with an ongoing story. I think the examples of Professor Johnson and others go all the way back to Paul, right? Women, be quiet in church. Well, obviously, they only say that because women are not being quiet in church, and the conversation keeps going on and on. To be able to trust that conversation would be welcome—I think it's really crucial.

Kathleen: I recognize that I'm interrupting the conversation, how important continuing a conversation should be, but I did want to give Rosemary a chance to present her concluding remarks. So that's acceptable to everyone?

All: Yes.

Rosemary: If there are other threads that people want to explore from your, from Mary's, comments, please feel free to do that. Or shall I go ahead?

Kathleen: Well, how do people feel? Is there someone who would like to comment, with one more comment, or follow one more strand? [Pause.] OK, then, maybe we are ready for Rosemary's comments.

Rosemary: OK. An excerpt from Monika Hellwig's inaugural lecture for the Madeleva Lecture Series will appear at the beginning of each section of the book. Her lecture was titled "Christian Women in a Troubled World," and it was published in 1985. So an excerpt from the lecture is printed at the beginning of this section, in order to provide an orienting point or on organizing frame of reference for the essays here. What I'd like to do is reread the excerpt from the lecture and then invite your responses to it.

[Rosemary reads the excerpt.]

So I'd like to invite you to respond to this excerpt. Perhaps you might think about how you would respond to any particular aspect of what I've chosen for reflection, or maybe you might consider how you would apply any of these virtues of prayer, compassion, solidarity, and so on, in your academic vocations as you try to better listen for voice.

Michele: Rosemary, was there a fourth besides prayer, compassion, and solidarity? Was it creative imagination?

Rosemary: Yes, correct.

Michele: OK. I find the quote that you read really interesting. Can I make two quick comments, and then I'll leave it open to the others? The first point is that to have the power to bully is to have some sort of privilege. And feminists have typically conflated privilege with maleness. Nevertheless, we don't want to lose sight of the fact that at times women can bully more than some men. So the concept Professor Hellwig is working with—that somehow there is something about women that makes them less apt to bully—it's something we need to think about, discerning whether we as women may be bullying, not in our words, but more in our exclusion of other voices from the conversation. Second, I think her point about creative imagination is really important and potentially fruitful and emphasizes the best of what we do as theologians and ethicists. We are always trying to think of new theological or ethical concepts for people on the ground to make sense of the world in which we all live.

Emily: I think that's a really rich segment from Monika Hellwig's address. And even if we wanted to avoid essential understandings of men and women and to disrupt patterns of racism in our work, we would still need to pay attention to the problem of bullying. I'd like to highlight the need for self-care as we think about this struggle. Unfortunately, self-care has not always been seen as a positive within the Catholic tradition because it is too often associated with selfishness and pride. But even as we think about this together, don't you think there could be more emphasis placed on self-care for women in academia? And I wonder how that could help us to speak in solidarity with other marginalized voices? But given the problem of bullying within society and the church, we can and should be attentive to our vulnerability. I think that real solidarity usually comes from a recognition of mutual vulnerability, so further reflection on this issue could be fruitful for our work as feminists. And yet, we need to remain cautious about not overextending ourselves because we need to care for ourselves as well.

Mary: It's interesting, I think, that a number of us have picked up on that word "bully." I think that's partly because it has become a real contemporary issue, especially for young people—that's what makes the news, as parents of bullies and bullying victims obviously have learned. And I think Emily's point about self-care is an important one, in part because of the way the use of power and resistance to power is understood among young people. The burden in, let's say, transforming a school environment that's characterized by bullying—and we can imagine then an academic environment, global and national settings, the church environment—for transforming those settings often falls disproportionately on the one who is bullied, so that the key or the way of transforming that logic needs to come from the victim, if you will. And I think, as Michele said, we need to think really carefully about that dynamic, and then self-care will build up a way of doing that. What really struck me about the passage from Professor Hellwig is that when one doesn't have access to power or the mechanisms of power, one can't rely on that kind of logic, the "might makes right" logic in the world, but rather needs to call on other resources. Part of what we are doing in the New Voices Seminar and in this book is trying to really cultivate those other resources for people, to cultivate the habits of another logic.

I wouldn't want to be really sanguine about the fact that folks who don't have access to power are necessarily endowed with all of those other resources. I think that part of the task is really cultivating those resources—like LaReine-Marie, what you were talking about as a part of our history of slavery, that somehow everyone was going to have all of the spiritual resources to live in freedom, however measured that was for folks, was really naïve. That is, I think saying that lack of access automatically endows one with access to a richness that is transformative is naïve. I think that's true often enough, and it's great when it happens, but I think that it is also the result of really hard deliberate work on the part of community.

LaReine-Marie: When I think about the virtues you were referring to and what you mentioned, Mary, about when we find ourselves in these unbalanced relationships as women which occupy a good portion of our life, I really appreciate that Elizabeth Johnson's response was one of tremendous integrity. And if it was one-way listening, then that doesn't take away from her graciousness. No matter what kind of response we ever get or we could ever anticipate getting, I think it's a gift for the church and the world to show how we can disagree and yet be in conversation. Elizabeth Johnson had her part of the conversation, and it would be nice to hear a response, but I really don't think this is going to happen.

Bridget: I am struck by how much virtue is coming up again and again in our essays and in our conversations. And I would say this in terms of the importance of cultivating the virtues—and Mary talked about this quite directly in her essay and so did Emily in her notion of self-care and how being a part of certain communities is essential to care for self: I think the New Voices Seminar is one of those communities that is intentionally trying to build up certain virtues that we all need. Then, as we go back into our institutions, we feel strengthened to do good work.

Rosemary: So, Kathleen, we've reached the end of the call and the end of conversation. How would you like to conclude?

Kathleen: Well, first of all, I have to say that as I sit here listening, I feel such a hope for the future to hear this conversation and to see how the conversation is so well informed by theological and ethical work. Once again, I express my deep gratitude to these young scholars who are willing to bring to the world insights that are not always easy to hear. These insights from our conversation are very valuable, and I can envision how this conversation will enhance and expand the book. So I applaud you on your work thus far. And I wish you all the best as you begin the new semester.

Michele: And you too, Kathleen.

Kathleen: Thank you.

Rosemary: OK, thanks. Bye. Thanks for today.

Mary: Bye-bye.

LaReine-Marie: Bye everyone.

Emily: Bye-bye, everyone.

Bridget: Thanks so much.

Section III

Women's Witness in Context

Religion and Public Life

From all of this there emerges the important question as to how we are to discern or identify the "usable past" that provides us with models, with insights, with warnings, with hope and challenge. . . .

When we ask whether there is a particular "usable past" for Christian women, we must acknowledge that the lives and deeds and impact of women have not been recorded and preserved for us in the same profusion as those of men. This is, of course, true of secular histories, but especially so of religious histories. . . .

Allowing for the inevitable bias in the available data, we can nevertheless draw some conclusions. Just because they were excluded from much of conventional public life, and from ordination and hierarchic authority, those Christian women who were recognized as memorable and whose lives and deeds were recorded have tended to emerge as more strongly counter-cultural in their attitudes, expectations, relationships and actions. Leadership of domination was frequently not open to them, nor were titles that inspire awe and create psychological distance. That left open the specifically Christian options of ministry, service, horizontal leadership by inspiration, invitation and community bonds of support. Similarly, conventional priestly and governing roles were usually closed to them, so it left open options for a more prophetic style than is usually possible to those who fill official positions and must play the conventional roles. And because existing offices in the

Church were not assigned to them for most of history, women were often in a better position to notice what was being left undone and who was being left out in the pastoral practice of the institutional Church.

It is not surprising, therefore, that when we do have records of the work and impact of Christian women on their societies, that impact tends to be prophetic, radical in its implications for the social structures of the society in the long run, and, in terms of social dynamics, a movement from below. . . . Such initiatives . . . commonly taken by women who saw them as expressions of faith called forth by the immediate circumstances in which they lived, also had long-term consequences which were like slow earthquakes in all of Western society, and . . . a challenge to the whole world.

—Monika Hellwig, *Christian Women in a Troubled World*, 17–23

Icons and Integrity

Catholic Women
in the Church and in the Public Square

Nancy A. Dallavalle, Fairfield University[1]

A few years ago, as I wrote an essay on feminist thought and the work of the great Jesuit theologian Karl Rahner,[2] I ran across a lecture he gave to a group of women in 1964 on the topic of "women in church and society." I read the lecture warily, concerned that I would find the spirit of his own day reflected in his approach to this topic, a topic that far too frequently served as a vehicle for male Catholic clergy to tell women who they were supposed to be and, more disturbingly, for what they should hope.

To my surprise, looking at this lecture from forty years' distance, I found great restraint in Rahner's approach to his topic in 1964. The story of women in church or in society, he suggested, should be "for the Christian woman herself to decide . . . as her primary, proper, and inalienable task."[3] Readers of Rahner will hear in those words a profound

---

[1] This essay is based on a text delivered for the Eighth Annual Anne Drummey O'Callaghan Lecture on Women in the Church at Fairfield University on October 1, 2008.

[2] Nancy A. Dallavalle, "Feminist Theologies," in Mary Hines and Declan Marmion, eds., *The Cambridge Companion to Karl Rahner* (Cambridge: Cambridge University Press, 2005), 264–78.

[3] Karl Rahner, "The Position of Women in the New Situation in Which the Church Finds Herself," in *Theological Investigations*, vol. 8, trans. D. Bourke) (London: Darton, Longman & Todd, 1971), 89.

existential command: here is a task, it is of first importance, it is yours alone, it cannot be handed off to another. Rahner presumed that women themselves would report on their own understanding of being female, instead of receiving the approved parameters of "woman" from male clergy. Even more remarkable in his approach to this question is its sense of faithful, patient, spirit-filled open-endedness. Rahner hardly presumed that "what women want" could be determined by a snap poll of "likely women believers"! Rather, he sensed that, given a favorable milieu, women would over time "live into" the vocation that is properly theirs, in a way appropriate to a renewed ecclesial sensibility.

With and without permission, women have in fact lived this renewed sensibility in the decades since the Second Vatican Council. This essay intends to lift up some characteristics of that living, on the premise that institutional life (in this case, ecclesial life) is an important but too often derided arena for women's attention and engagement. Contrary to the notion that institutional affiliation is associated too easily with the specter of false consciousness, this essay will observe that women's association with the life of the institutional church has occurred in ways that, while shaped by traditional forms, have animated these forms with renewed integrity: the form of "mother" can be seen as an icon of family life as this contributes to the social good; the form of the "cantor" can be seen as an icon of the responsive laity as people of God; and the form of "sister" can be seen as an icon of the many ways in which women animate a broad variety of social institutions. To encourage women's engagement in the "formality" of institutions and offices is not to stifle women by boxing them into dated formulas but rather to encourage women to make commitments to relational forms that are visible and dependable, because these structures, at their best, invite us to be with one another in truly human ways.

Women in Church and Society

Yet the current experience of women in the church all too often is an experience that works against women's own search for fullness and integrity. Indeed, the story of "women in the church" has undergone a curious reversal of fortune in the last few decades. Eleven years after Rahner's 1964 address, the opening paragraphs of *Inter Insigniores* did not ignore but took account of the changing social order, recognizing that the documents of Vatican II required that the church take seriously the "signs of the times" relative to women, quoting with approval the document on the laity: "Since in our time women have an ever more active share in the whole life of society, it is very important that they participate more widely also in the various fields of the Church's apostolate."[4] Two paragraphs later, *Inter Insigniores* ruled, however, that this participation would be severely limited. Noting the entry of women into "pastoral office" in the "various Christian communities stemming from the sixteenth-century Reformation or of later origin,"[5] *Inter Insigniores* recognized that such changes during a time of renewed ecumenical dialogue had put pressure on the Catholic understanding of holy orders. Nevertheless, the document rejected the notion of ordaining women, arguing that this ban is based on the church's "constant tradition" and suggesting the outlines of arguments that have since that time been further elaborated in other magisterial documents: the intention of the Lord in choosing twelve male apostles, the understanding of a sacramental sign, and the argument that the liturgical presider stands *in persona Christi.*[6]

Despite this rejection, *Inter Insigniores* maintains a striking tone that is both respectful and conciliatory. At no point does the document presume that women who seek the priesthood are deluded by secular culture or cravenly power hungry, assumptions that lurk in the subtext of many dismissals of women's ordination today. Rather, the document observes in conclusion that "women who express a desire for the ministerial priesthood are doubtless motivated by the desire to serve Christ and the Church" (no. 6). This statement stands as one of the very few on the part of the magisterium that recognizes that women who seek ordination in the church are thoughtful persons acting with integrity and in good faith.

In contrast to 1975, women in the church exist in a far different theological and practical place today. Led by the devotional reflections about "woman" by the late Pope John Paul II's "theology of the body,"

[4] Vatican II, *Apostolicam Actuositatem*, 9, http://www.vatican.va/archive/hist_councils /ii_vatican_council/documents/vat-ii_decree_19651118_apostolicam-actuositatem_ en.html.

[5] *Inter Insigniores*, introduction, http://www.papalencyclicals.net/Paul06/p6interi.htm.

[6] For a summary of the church's position, see Sara Butler, MSBT, *The Catholic Priesthood and Women: A Guide to the Teaching of the Church* (Chicago: Hillenbrand, 2007). For a critical perspective, see Elizabeth T. Groppe, "Women and the Persona of Christ: Ordination in the Roman Catholic Church," in Susan Abraham and Elena Procario-Foley, eds., *Frontiers in Catholic Feminist Theology: Shoulder to Shoulder* (Minneapolis: Fortress Press, 2009), 153–72.

positive (in the sense of "content-filled") speculation about women's "psychosexual" nature has flourished. Much of the writings in this field of theology of the body is more prescriptive than descriptive, retrieving and reifying images (such as the nuptial metaphor) that support the church's teaching on sexuality and marriage and occasionally proposing "new" ways of understanding the role of women in the life of the church.[7]

I have never championed the movement among some feminists that would dismiss the difference of gender and its profound importance for human personhood, such that gender becomes simply another difference among many, however such a silence might be understandable as an ecclesial strategy.[8] Indeed, in today's milieu, such a posture serves an even more understandable strategy of self-defense. For example, recent papal statements, while recognizing that some past descriptions of women might have been regrettable, offer a highly specific understanding of what a woman should be, an understanding that applies, in the magisterium's view, always, everywhere, and for all women.

Emblematic of the sea change between Rahner's insights and our own day is the story of the US bishops' ill-fated pastoral on women, a letter that went through four drafts between the early 1980s and the early 1990s, and then was simply abandoned. Surely, the "signs of the times" in this case were hard to read on several fronts. In the first place, the broader impetus for such a document came from the creation of national bishops' conferences, raised to the level of mandate with Vatican II's Decree on the Pastoral Office of Bishops (*Christus Dominus* 37–38). The resulting body in the US, the National Conference of Catholic Bishops, or NCCB (after 2001, the United States Conference of Catholic Bishops [USCCB]), saw as part of their role the issuance of texts on current issues, putting forward several documents that merited wide attention, particularly those on the economy and on nuclear war. Yet the newly empowered national groups

---

[7] For a critical evaluation of the theology of the body, see Susan A. Ross, "'Then Honor God in Your Body' (1 Cor. 6:20): Feminist and Sacramental Theology on the Body," *Horizons* 16 (1989): 7–27. For an appreciative evaluation, see Prudence Allen, RSM, "Philosophy of Relation in John Paul II's New Feminism," in Michele M. Schumacher, ed., *Women in Christ: Toward a New Feminism* (Grand Rapids, MI: Eerdmans, 2004), 67–104.

[8] I find the notion of "strategic essentialism" to be problematic for the same reason; see Susan Abraham, "Strategic Essentialism in Nationalist Discourses: Sketching a Feminist Agenda in the Study of Religion," *Journal of Feminist Studies in Religion* 25, no. 1 (2009): 156–61.

fell out of favor during the second half of John Paul II's pontificate, and by the early 1990s, the US group was weakened accordingly.

In addition, during the years of the drafting of this document, the possibility of the NCCB writing about women became itself an increasingly complex and even more politically loaded topic, one that, after several drafts, was finally abandoned. During the early stages of the drafting, bishops convened many groups of women to hear firsthand testimony about their experiences, testimony that was, as all such first-person accounts are, unsystematic. (Imagine trying to write such a document for the women members of even a single parish.) Interim drafts came under heavy criticism. Still, the topics tackled earlier, the economy and war, were also complex subjects that were similarly overdetermined. Why was this document, finally, impossible for the US bishops to produce and publish?

Some years later, reflecting on the failure of this effort, Bishop Francis Murphy pointed out a key difference in the process for this particular text. During the drafting process for the earlier pastorals by the US bishops, the broad public consultations featured panels of experts—military analysts, philosophers, economists, policy scholars—who were convened to provide the US bishops with the best information available on the topic in question. Yet when it came to the drafting of the pastoral letter on women, no consultation with any scholarly experts was considered necessary for the bishops' reflections. Women reported on their experience; male clergy heard with the ears they had. While it was laudable that women's voices were heard, they were heard simply as a series of personal anecdotes, easily dismissed as women's "private" experience. Thus the force of argument that might have emerged from women's expert testimony remained untapped. Insights readily available from fields such as anthropology, medicine, economics, or labor policy were not invoked; it seemed that the kind of expertise deemed necessary for an examination of earlier topics was almost regarded as antagonistic to the proper consideration of the topic of "women."[9] Within the church, in other words, women were seen as a "private matter."

[9] P. Francis Murphy, "Let's Start Over: A Bishop Appraises the Pastoral on Women," *Commonweal*, September 25, 1992.

Female and Public in the Church

This sense of women's experience as private contrasts with the shape of the early church. Early Christianity quickly arrived at the notion that its self-understanding would be not secret but public, and that its creeds would stand as public confessions of faith. In our own day, characterized by a post–Vatican II democratic, capitalist context, religion continues to play a part in the civil order in many ways—whether as a dominant story or as a counterstory, with a voice sometimes prophetic but too often triumphalist. In our own day in the United States, two sensibilities about the question of "Catholics in the public square" shape the conversation. On the one hand, many US bishops take an approach that presupposes that the tenets of democracy and religious freedom reflect important Catholic commitments and are harmonious with Catholic life. Theologically, Thomas Aquinas's optimistic view of the human person, with his sense that grace builds upon nature, can be comfortably accommodated to themes of American energy and ingenuity.[10]

On the other hand, deep currents in Catholic thought adopt a more Augustinian approach. This approach is both somewhat more pessimistic about human nature and more critical of the trajectory of American culture. While both approaches agree that grace remains God's initiative and that humans are called to actively cooperate with the divine, these approaches' working models of faith and culture differ. Most importantly, the latter somewhat more anthropologically pessimistic and culturally sectarian approach is gaining traction in the current conversation about Catholics in public life. Indeed, in his recent book *Render unto Caesar: Serving the Nation by Living Our Catholic Beliefs in Political Life*, Archbishop Charles Chaput observes that "Christianity was seen as politically subversive precisely because it denied the identification of religion and state."[11]

Negotiating these two approaches has led other theologians such as Ronald Thiemann to argue for a third path with a limited scope for church and state relations, a path that claims that religious traditions perform an important role for the civic order by socializing their adherents into the kinds of conversational practices that will nurture a rich civic

---

[10] See *Summa Theologiae* I, q. 1, a. 8, ad 2.

[11] Charles J. Chaput, *Render unto Caesar: Serving the Nation by Living Our Catholic Beliefs in Political Life* (Doubleday, 2008), 215.

life.[12] I agree with Thiemann about the value of religious conversation in general, but I think he misses the specific virtues offered by different religious traditions, as well as the potential value in having mature discussion partners who are deeply formed in an array of beliefs, an array that attempts to grapple constructively with, but does not gloss over, their points of incommensurability.

But how might the question of Catholicism in the public square be informed by an engagement with the questions of women? Rosemary Carbine notes contributions by feminist, womanist, and Latina theologians and theorists who argue for a more narrative approach that would recognize omissions in the public picture and work to include women in the story. Womanist Catholic theologian Shawn Copeland highlights the accompanying errors of commission, as she observes that women who are denied participation in the public order do not realize the full humanity to which they are called, and she argues further that racism is inextricably intertwined with the sexism of that denial.[13]

Part of the tension about women in the church and in public life derives from the gender model of complementarity that assigns women to the private sphere and men to the public sphere. Christine Gudorf names this problem well. In a 1983 article, she noted that as the church let go of the public sphere in a literal sense—when Roman Catholicism stopped being an issue of armies and territories—it began to identify its reach through families "practicing" in private homes and gathering for Eucharist at parish churches. During this shift, from the Pian era to Vatican II, as clergy continued to control the parishes, the control of family became less about inheritance and economics and more about an understanding of the family as a domestic church activated by the believing mother. The rise of Marian devotions supported and reinforced this shift, often in a privatized parallel track to the "official" church.[14]

---

[12] See his *Religion in Public Life: A Dilemma for Democracy* (Washington, DC: Georgetown University Press, 1996).

[13] See Rosemary Carbine, "Turning to Narrative: Toward a Feminist Theological Interpretation of Political Participation and Personhood," *JAAR* 78/2 (2010): 375–412. Such an assessment of women's engagement in public life rests on an understanding of the relative positions of church and state; see Mary Doak, "Resisting the Eclipse of *Dignitatis Humanae*," *Horizons* 33/1 (2006): 33–53.

[14] See Christine Gudorf, "Renewal or Repatriarchalization? Responses of the Roman Catholic Church to the Feminization of Religion," *Horizons* 10/2 (1983): 231–51.

Rahner might have had this particular tension in mind when, in the address mentioned above, he referred to the danger of a "folk-costume Christianity." Found in his earlier work, this term in Rahner's use denoted a Christianity that was too easily reduced to local ritual practices; in Catholic circles, this term might mean an elevation of culturally inflected devotional practices over core truths, or perhaps the veneration of a local saint over the worship properly due the triune God. Rahner was wary of a Catholicism that would place parochial "sacramentals"—devotions such as home altars, processions, and so forth—over the ecclesial celebration of the great sacraments. This wariness was shared by the council fathers at Vatican II, as is seen in their insistence that Mary be treated as part of the story of the church rather than in a separate document. Rahner was cognizant of the currents of his own day (and prescient about the sensibility to come) when he observed the vulnerability of the topic "woman" to the snares of "folk-costume Christianity," and he warned clearly against it.

Indeed, since Rahner's time, the church's commentary on the role of "the female" in theological anthropology, which is not without value, has put forward an idealized picture of "womanhood" that falls easily into the trap of a "folk-costume Christianity."[15] But this mistake is not confined to the church, nor to a conservative mindset. In particular, cultural tension about the role of women in public, and the way in which women's political power becomes defused, is further complicated by the role of consumerism in defining what it means to be "a woman," particularly in public.

For example, "female" as constructed by consumerism is clearly a version of the "folk-costume female," even if Rahner never imagined this story. In consumer culture (in forms that emerge from both the conservative and the progressive ends of the political spectrum), female "self-expression" has been embraced and reconstructed as a lucrative theme for media and industry, which come together to "promote" women through variously branded forms of spirituality. Even suffering and death, when women are involved, offer an occasion for the knickknacks that populate the front half of most Hallmark stores. In October, "Breast Cancer Awareness Month" is now the occasion for everyday purchases (yogurt, dish soap, cereal) to be "marked" by a pink ribbon, signifying a donor

---

[15] See John Paul II, Letter to Women (1995).

link between the corporate sponsor and an activist sense of engagement on women's behalf. In October, the "folk-costume female" thing to do is to have pink ribbons on everything, indicating a group identity that is achieved, paradoxically, by private (domestic) consumption. What could be an outward, institutionally mediated act of solidarity is turned, instead, into a privatized lifestyle choice. The "folk costume," in this case, serves to derail the genuine agency of women, under the patina of "empowerment."

Icons: Mother, Cantor, Sister

To offer a few starting points for a renewed discussion of the manifold roles of women in the church between the time of Vatican II and our own day, I am turning to three evocative images, which I will treat in this essay as "icons," with the hope that these, and others, might prove useful for feminist reflection. These images are the icons of "mother," as this image grounds the notion of female in the institution of the family; "cantor," as this image roots the laity in the institution of the church; and "sister," as this image evokes the role of the public, active, ecclesially identified woman.

In invoking these icons, we keep in mind the limits of any appeal to women's experiences, given that these experiences, in terms of both communal structure and bodily intimacy, are never available to us in some noncontextual, precritical form. Donna Teevan's discussion of feminist theological anthropology suggests that a framework for contested terms and experiences might draw on Francis Fiorenza's dynamic sense of a "reflective equilibrium" that does not yield fixed understandings of these problematic terms but rather allows these terms to "generate illuminative inferences."[16] In invoking these images, then, and suggesting that they function as icons for our reflection, I am trading on their ability to "generate illuminative inferences." Thus, they not only suggest models for relationship but they also in contemporary usage are able to helpfully destabilize relational patterns in ways that give rise to new patterns and possibilities for relationship. In other words, these "icons" can function not as blueprints that give rise to a series of norms but rather as lived

---

[16] Donna Teevan, "Challenges to the Role of Theological Anthropologies in Feminist Theology," *Theological Studies* 64/3 (2003): 595.

and living models that throw forward an evocative series of possible trajectories.

Further, these three are particularly useful because they come to us with a surfeit of resonances; they function in our world not in isolation but always hand in hand with a cloud of witnesses. In her magisterial work on the great company of saints, Elizabeth Johnson tells us that she found herself backing into this project as she theologically thought through a new approach to Mary of Nazareth.[17] Her first task, she found, was to rethink the theological understanding of the household of God in order to have a proper "house" for a theological treatment of Mary of Nazareth. So too do these icons speak to us "in company."

The task of contemporary women in the church, in my view, involves actively appropriating these icons in order to save them from precisely the kind of "folk-costume Christianity" that Rahner identified and warned against. All three remain vulnerable to such a negative use: the mother whose value is rendered only in terms of her instrumental relationship to her children; the laity whose church life consists of gathering in converted elementary school cafeterias or outdoor processions in order to be photographed for diocesan newspapers (the caption always includes the adjectives "joyful" and "grateful"); and the religious woman, too easily dismissed as "Sister." ("Sister will meet with the children, Sister knows where the records are, Sister will stay after the meeting to lock the parish hall.") "Sister" stands as the summative icon for all women who counsel, teach, organize, and heal—who do, over and over, the work of the church and the work of our world. These three icons are the heritage of Catholic women. Rahner did not propose the answer to this problem, but he saw the script written in advance. He saw the festive costumes prepared for women, and even in his day, he saw the potential for culturally reinforced narratives to be inadequate and demeaning, a caricature of the integrity they intend to bear forward.

Mother

For the institution of the family, we have the icon of the mother. US culture is deeply conflicted about the term "mother." My students ask me repeatedly about combining motherhood and having a career, and I

---

[17] Elizabeth A. Johnson, *Friends of God and Prophets: A Feminist Theological Reading of the Communion of Saints* (New York: Continuum, 1999).

have slowly realized that they are asking a question not about the logistics of childcare or career planning but about being a woman in our culture. They have watched their own mothers—those who are more perceptive have understood the struggles of those lives—and they have begun to recognize that the issues involved are not confined to scheduling.

To live this icon with integrity means to realize our deep connection to one another and to be committed to nurturing it in the domestic sphere. Here John Paul II has it partly right when he claims that mothers have a concrete experience of "making room" for another, in the same way that Elizabeth Johnson, in her work *She Who Is*, refers not only to women qua women but just as often to "women and their dependent children" as an inseparable locus for theological reflection.[18]

The economy of that primary and deep connection, the economy of the household as an institution, rests to a great extent on the mother. The way in which the icon of "mother" functions is key to this institution; thus, the changing story of women has had a profound impact on that institution. Yet this changing story has less to do with the most recent rise in US women who work outside the home during the last half of the twentieth century. Women, particularly women of color and lower-class women, have generally worked, whether in public or in someone else's private residence. Nor is raising up this icon meant to reinforce the notion that women act as the primary parent in the home. Men have often been involved in their children's lives, a pattern that is also more true of men of color and lower-class men. The notion that we have, in the wake of the swinging sixties, abandoned a social pattern in which the overwhelming majority of families consisted of a male absent breadwinner and a female homemaker is simply not true.[19]

Rather, this icon requires our attention as the institution of family itself undergoes redefinition. What will it mean to "make family," politically, in the years to come? As notions of family broaden (the percent of heterosexual "married with children" households are no longer the majority), it would be helpful for theologians to ask if this reconfiguration is merely internal and private—different groupings behind a white picket fence—or if this reconfiguration will have public, and therefore generative,

---

[18] But I would not argue, as John Paul does, that the reverse is the case—that is, that women are most fully realized in motherhood. John Paul II, *Mulieris Dignitatem*, August 15, 1988.

[19] See Stephanie Coontz, *Marriage: A History* (New York: Viking, 2005).

force. "Mother" will continue to serve, I suggest, as the foundational symbol for the domestic church. Will this institution, family, continue to be more and more privatized as it changes? Or will the icon of the mother—women and men and their dependent children—prove resonant and flexible enough to allow family to be a functionally important, that is, performative, public institution?

Cantor

The icon for the laity, as it functions in the institutional church, is that of the cantor. For many US Catholics, the image of the cantor is the image of a volunteer song leader, gamely launching into the third verse of the recessional hymn, the second half of which she will sing to their backs as the congregation streams toward the exits. At first glance, in fact, many in the pews might quickly identify themselves in opposition to this image, saying, "I can't sing."

On the contrary, the cantor's role is not "song leader," as if the role of liturgical music were to break up the action or entertain during the offertory collection or the reception of Communion; rather, the cantor's role is to lead the responses within the liturgy. The cantor signifies the church at prayer: with the cantor, the church sings the great Amen. The cantor intones, and the congregation joins in prose-like verse or song. The liturgy takes place; it is a performative event because the people respond. Indeed, over a thousand years before Vatican II's *Sacrosanctum Concilium* endorsed the notion of "full, conscious, and active participation," Augustine wrote:

> Let the cantor go up, then, but let that man sing from the heart of every one of you, and let each person be that man. For although you all say that, because all of you are one in Christ, it is the one man who is saying it. He doesn't say, "To you, O Lord, we have lifted up our eyes," but "To you, O Lord, I have lifted up my eyes." You should consider that it is each of you who is saying that, but the one chiefly speaking is that single man who is spread throughout the whole round world.[20]

---

[20] Augustine, *In Ps* 122, 1–2; PL 37:1630–31; cited by Joseph A. Komonchak on *DotCommonweal* (blog), April 18, 2011, http://www.commonwealmagazine.org/blog/?p=13062. Paul Inwood, in a comment (no. 26) on *Pray Tell* (blog), April 13, 2010 (http://www.praytellblog.com/index.php/2010/04/13/to-sing-or-not-to-sing), notes that the French tradition of the *animateur* provides a helpful model.

For Augustine, the cantor's voice was male, as were the groups of men and boys who raised Gregorian chant to a high form in the Middle Ages. While this role may now be filled by the female voice, what remains is the notion of deeply responsive prayer as a primary liturgical action.

How can women and men live this icon with integrity? First and foremost, women alongside men would claim the place of the laity within the liturgy, recognizing the dignity of the sacrament to which we are called and which requires our deep and visible engagement. Liturgy is "public work," not only limited to the public work of the clergy, but also expanded to include equally the public work of the laity as the work of the church concretized in the world. Second, women's and men's role as cantor extends to ecclesial moments outside of the liturgy because the laity should properly also take on, in a deeper, more active, and more structural way, the task of being church.[21] In liturgy, we own the extraordinary reality that our life as Catholic Christians is a response of praise and that such a response is the primary orientation of the church—and for Catholics, of one's life.

Yet this mantle of "response" as one's primary role can seem oppressive. What would a feminist understanding of this liturgical action propose? Why would a self-respecting woman (or man) want to appropriate and inhabit this icon? Daphne Hampson, for example, claims with absolute clarity that a feminist by definition cannot assume the posture of worship because such a posture turns her outside of the world, toward a (nonexistent) transcendent. For Hampson, this posture, while nonsensical for women or men, is particularly problematic for women, as it reinforces precisely what feminism seeks to overcome: the subjugation of women (and the participation of women in their own subjugation).[22] In this view, therefore, a woman can be a soloist, or a jolly choir member, but not a cantor. For the cantor's job is not to raise our consciousness about ourselves or to provide a musical interlude to distract from seemingly boring liturgical bits but to invite our gaze and our voices, to turn, with hers, in reverent and responsive worship, toward God. This understanding of human personhood is, perhaps rightly, regarded with suspicion by feminist Christians.

[21] See Paul Lakeland, *Catholicism at the Crossroads: How the Laity Can Save the Church* (New York: Continuum, 2007).

[22] See Daphne Hampson, *After Christianity* (Valley Forge, PA: Trinity Press International, 1997).

Sister

Merely invoking the icon of women religious marks these comments as the product of a specific era. For the US church at mid-century, the image of the woman religious—now mostly remembered as a late-night punch line—was of a competent, reserved woman who took things—and was taken—seriously. Within the next twenty years, this image may be eclipsed, and the resonance of this icon, for most Catholics, will be lost. Perhaps not. Perhaps this model of being an ecclesially identified woman who brings the sensibility of the church to bear on the problems of the world will take new forms, because the need to do this mediation always remains a signature feature of ecclesial life.

Certainly, many cloistered communities of women religious serve as "powerhouses of prayer" for the world. But what I have in mind here are the visible women religious (thus "sisters," not "nuns") who, over and over again, made the US Catholic Church a working reality, an institution that functioned well, a church that served generations of everyday people who needed to be educated, clothed, and cared for in hospitals, soup kitchens, and parish basements. They were, and are, Franciscans and Benedictines and Sisters of Mercy and Sisters of Saint Joseph. And they had much in common with their sisters who were not members of religious orders but were also smart, accomplished women who were intensive care nurses and middle school guidance counselors, piano teachers and social workers, librarians and frequent library patrons. As Sandra Schneiders writes,

> The protofeminist subtext under the sincere espousal of traditional Catholic pieties about the nature and role of women was supplied by the lives and accomplishments of the highly motivated, talented, well-educated, non-married Religious women who staffed the school [in this case, Immaculata High School in Detroit]. While articulating the standard expectations for Catholic women, the Religious were modeling something quite different.[23]

The mid-twentieth-century icon of the vowed religious woman had, in fact, much in common with single and married lay Catholic women; these vowed religious women were formed in an era of limited public possibil-

---

[23] Sandra M. Schneiders, *With Oil in Their Lamps: Faith, Feminism and the Future*, 2000 Madeleva Lecture in Spirituality (Mahwah, NJ: Paulist Press, 2000), 80.

ity but were deeply engaged with the fabric of their social worlds. They were intensely curious women who loved, cared, served, and cheered the accomplishments of others. They made the world go round, and we are losing them.

What would it mean for women to live this icon with integrity today? The most basic integrity about this icon is its fierce attachment to a capacious understanding of sacramentality, as well as its steely, quiet competence. In his first encyclical, *Deus Caritas Est*, Pope Benedict XVI calls for the exercise of charity in love, a love founded on faith. However, in the latter portion of the text, he states unequivocally that the first principle for those who make the world go round is "professional competence . . . being properly trained in what to do and how to do it" (no. 31). These women knew how the world and its institutional structures worked, they met those they served as Christ, and they called forth from that meeting the ecstatic fullness of their own gifts—not in a chaotic or cloudy rush, but with the precision and brilliance of love made fully visible.

Conclusion

Most women religious, or for that matter, mothers or lay ministers, openly acknowledge that their ways of life are changing. For women across the board, patterns of working shift and shift again, and family patterns shift to accommodate economic realities. New Catholic women's orders are emerging, as well as new family patterns in which men function in many new roles, too. Nevertheless, as US culture evolves, and as we shift to accommodate the new, how will we replace this connective tissue of competent women who mediated the fluid border between public and private in ways that made these structures flourish so as to serve the common good?

We cannot seem to sustain a useful conversation, in public, about "motherhood" anymore; rather, we have a trumped-up cultural conflict called the "mommy wars." We cannot seem to sustain a conversation, in public, about the role of communal worship; rather, we have individualized, consumer-inflected spiritualities. And we have not even begun to have a broad conversation, in public, in a structural way that would have real effects about what a Catholic woman is or what she might bring to the public story of the Roman Catholic Church.

There are structural impediments, of course, for women within the Catholic Church. Twenty years ago, Catherine LaCugna wrote clearly about the bifurcation of pastoral ministry and theological scholarship, noting that while women theologians increased in number, the fact that they do not also preach was detrimental to the development of feminist theological scholarship.[24] Women administrators in the church are increasing, and a number of bishops are seriously committed to bringing women into leadership roles. However, as the Leadership Conference of Women Religious observed in their 1996 report *Creating a Home: Benchmarks for Church Leadership Roles for Women*, "the relationship of jurisdiction to ordination creates a glass ceiling for women in the church. This seems markedly inconsistent with recent pledges made by the church to involve women in governance and to advance the cause of women."[25] Even when a diocese names a woman as chancellor, it will then wall off the oversight of priests from the job of chancellor. The role of chancellor (beyond its formal role as the record keeper of the diocese) can be an important role, but by moving the oversight of clergy out of its purview, it becomes oddly distorted. In all of these cases, the refusal to ordain women continues to mute and deform the contributions of all kinds of women to the institutional life of the Catholic Church. If only male voices serve as formal representatives, or trusted surrogates, about the Catholic story in the public square, this story will be told (and reinscribed) in a way that submerges the lives and contributions and critiques of women.

Women must think of themselves as playing a significant and public role in changing this institutional church life, and they must insist upon their visibility. To be sure, Catholics are not alone in understanding men as authoritative institutional representatives or as appropriate voices to shape the story of "religion in public." Most of the writing about religion in its institutional form, in the public square, is done by men (for the Catholic story on this, check out any authoritative bibliography on the topic "ecclesiology," the gender breakdown of the main articles published in Catholic scholarly journals such as *Theological Studies*, or periodicals such as *Commonweal* or *America*). Women write, but they tend to write for other women—rather than for the "generic male" of "the public." And they tend to write about private issues as private, in a manner that will guarantee that these issues will continue to be perceived as the narrow

---

[24] Catherine Mowry LaCugna, "Catholic Women as Ministers and Theologians," *America*, vol. 167, no. 10, October 10, 1992.

[25] Leadership Conference of Women Religious, *Creating a Home: Benchmarks for Church Leadership Roles for Women: An LCWR Special Report*, ed. by J. Merkel (LCWR, 1996).

purview of "women's issues."[26] Catholic intellectual life is, in fact, quite in vogue in the public square, but most of the writing that engages the issues in a structural manner are written by men and engage the writing of other men.

How well we have internalized the story that women's voices are "indoor voices" and that, when they speak in public, women's voices are to be confined to the anecdotal, the spiritualized private of daytime talk shows and niche websites that overly shape the new "folk-costume female." Even when speaking in public, all too often there is an overt or covert reversion to the narrowly experiential disclaimer "maybe it's just me," a disclaimer that preempts the extension of that reflection to the public sphere.[27]

This notion of a privatized spirituality can be tempting for a very basic reason: if I just report on my own experience, no one will hold me publicly accountable. Stepping out of that privatized spirituality and into a genuine retrieval of the icons of Catholic women's experience—mother, cantor, sister—can be an active strategy to leverage women's engagement with the important structures that shape our lives. Public accountability will be the hallmark of such an effective engagement and its leadership, drawing on the ways in which the icons of mother, cantor, and sister functioned powerfully and publicly in the institutional forms of their day. The church and world of our own day require a similar steely engagement: the mother who refuses to let "family" be reduced to the well-being of those at the table every night, the cantor who refuses to be a soloist but rather encourages the "full, conscious, and active participation" of the worshiping community, and the sister who refuses to let her fears keep her from stepping forward with authority and competence, always in company with her communion of sisters, whatever shape their lives may have. Our challenge is to retrieve this fluid yet performative sensibility so that women will continue to constructively mediate public and private realms in a world that yearns for effective institutional forms in service of the common good.

[26] See the discussion (reflecting studies for both the US and the UK) in Sarah Pedersen and Caroline Macafee, "Gender Differences in British Blogging," *Journal of Computer-Mediated Communication* 12 (2007): 1472–92.

[27] On the other hand, an excellent example of a targeted and media-savvy public engagement was the NETWORK-sponsored "Nuns on the Bus" tour during the summer of 2012, which featured religious women calling for economic and social justice for the poor and marginalized in the United States.

Bridget Jones, Cancer Patient

On Navigating the Health Care System as a Singleton

Rachel A. R. Bundang, Marymount School

On top of everything else, must go to Smug Married dinner party at Magda and Jeremy's tonight. Such occasions always reduce my ego to size of snail, which is not to say am not grateful to be asked. I love Magda and Jeremy. Sometimes I stay at their house, admiring the crisp sheets and many storage jars full of different kinds of pasta, imagining that they are my parents. But when they are together with their married friends I feel as if I have turned into Miss Havisham. . . .

"Yes, why aren't you married yet, Bridget?" sneered Woney . . . with a thin veneer of concern whilst stroking her pregnant stomach. . . .

What I should have said [was], *Because actually, Woney, underneath my clothes, my entire body is covered in scales*. But I didn't because, ironically enough, I didn't want to hurt her feelings.

—Helen Fielding, *Bridget Jones's Diary*

Many a single woman could undoubtedly identify with Bridget Jones's mixed feelings here: being simultaneously object and subject, as if under a microscope or forced to serve as informant for would-be dinner party sociologists. In comparable contemporary social settings that value couples and family life, explaining singlehood—and occasionally defending it—is certainly not as simple and tangible as having actual scales. As a result, the health care landscape is almost intelligible in comparison.

Rooted firmly in personal experience, as well as an appreciation of the conventions of both contemporary romantic comedy and women's narratives, this essay is not meant to be a typical academic article in medical ethics or theology. Rather, it is an effort at taking incarnation and lived, embodied knowledge seriously, to go beyond the theoretical and into doing ethics and theology practically. It is spiritual reflection on the experience of struggling with illness as a single person and the challenges that struggle presents to how we think about, value, and live out realities such as community and personhood, along with notions such as dignity and compassion, autonomy and relationality, respect and care, agency and flourishing.[1] All these elements are fundamental to how we may best think about and articulate medical ethics from Catholic and feminist viewpoints.

There are four perspectives in play that will provide context and counterpoint to the patient's experience. The first addresses the contemporary narrative or memoir of illness, in which authors such as Arthur W. Frank consider the process and meaning of shifting—occasionally with grace—from person to patient, and the impossibility of return to the prior "unmarked" state.[2] The second engages with scholarship on the single life in all its aspects in North America and the developed world more broadly, led by sociologists such as Bella DePaulo. Collectively, DePaulo and others make a case for reconsidering societal norms and various dimensions of personhood if we take singlehood seriously and treat it respectfully instead of dismissing it with (albeit unintended) bias.[3] The third provides practical guidance for the health care professional (HCP), as represented by Franciscan friar, physician, and medical ethicist Daniel Sulmasy. With the intuition of a doctor, the fine-tuned judgment of an ethicist, and the heart of a religious, he addresses the spirituality

---

[1] See Daniel P. Sulmasy's discussion on the dimensions of dignity as attributed, intrinsic, or derivative in "Dignity and the Human as a Natural Kind," in *Health and Human Flourishing: Religion, Medicine, and Moral Anthropology*, ed. Carol L. Taylor and Roberto Dell'Oro (Washington, DC: Georgetown University Press, 2006), 71–87.

[2] I am grateful to the late Catherine Bell for introducing me to Frank's *At the Will of the Body: Reflections on Illness* (Boston: Mariner/Houghton Mifflin, 2002).

[3] Bella DePaulo et al., "Make Room for Singles in Teaching and Research," *The Chronicle of Higher Education* (September 28, 2007), http://chronicle.com/weekly/v54/i05/05b04401.htm. See also Bella DePaulo, *Singled Out: How Singles Are Stereotyped, Stigmatized, and Ignored, and Still Live Happily Ever After* (New York: St. Martin's Press, 2006); and E. Kay Trimberger, *The New Single Woman* (Boston: Beacon, 2005).

of the relationship between the HCP and the patient and bridges that relationship with the ethical concerns involved—particularly in instances where palliative care is required or in end-of-life situations.[4] The fourth assesses the overarching role of compassionate respect in medical ethics and medical care, as esteemed Catholic feminist ethicist Margaret Farley discussed in her own 2002 Madeleva Lecture. Both compassion and respect are themes that thread through her other works, whether explicitly medical, religious, or sexual or in other categories altogether.[5] Each of these lenses and associated thinkers challenge perceptions, practices, and paradigms of what illness and healing mean, as well as what personhood means in relation to being single or a patient. Together, they lead us to consider what, indeed, are the norms we actually observe and whether we should be doing otherwise. Thus, this essay concludes in a way that outlines elements of a Catholic feminist ethics of health care for single folks and grapples with norms in health care from a Catholic theo-ethical perspective.

Patienthood vs. Personhood?

> I am more than my symptoms.
> I am more than my illness.
> I am more than my disease.
> I am more than a narrative or a checklist. . . .
> But am I more than the sum of my relationships?
>
> —from a note found in a chemotherapy clinic,
> author unknown (2008)

The first diagnosis of breast cancer occurred relatively early in my doctoral program, at a point when I transitioned from coursework to comprehensive exams. I was a single woman student in a major city

---

[4] Daniel P. Sulmasy, "Is Medicine a Spiritual Practice?" *Academic Medicine* 74 (1999): 1002–5; *The Rebirth of the Clinic: An Introduction to Spirituality in Health Care* (Washington, DC: Georgetown University Press, 2007). See also Alan B. Astrow et al., "Is Failure to Meet Spiritual Needs Associated with Cancer Patients' Perceptions of Quality of Care and Their Satisfaction with Care?" *Journal of Clinical Oncology* 25 (2007): 5753–57; Christina Puchalski et al., "Improving the Quality of Spiritual Care as a Dimension of Palliative Care: The Report of the Consensus Conference," *Journal of Palliative Medicine* 12 (2009): 885–904.

[5] Margaret A. Farley, *Compassionate Respect: A Feminist Approach to Medical Ethics and Other Questions* (Mahwah, NJ: Paulist Press, 2002).

with a sizable "urban family" comprised of friends and eventually actual relatives nearby to help. Members of and friends from the parish I attended then were particularly generous: nurses who came by after their own shifts were done for the day to assist with post-op care in the weeks after surgery; an administrator who offered a vacant apartment for my family for a month at no charge after the *third* operation; a supervisor who adjusted my work schedule to accommodate the surgeries and post-op treatments; a lawyer who let me take postradiation naps in her apartment near the hospital so that I could safely endure the long ride home; advisors and readers who were flexible with deadlines; neighbors who helped with the regular errands of daily life. Being able to stitch together a semblance of order with such incredible offers of time, resources, and presence was worth at least as much as the anointing and prayers I also accepted as gestures of care. And beyond these multiple kindnesses was the additional blessing of living in a neighborhood where almost anything could be ordered for delivery at any time.

By contrast, my encounters with medical professionals admittedly had a bumpy start while seeking a diagnosis. At first they repeatedly dismissed symptoms I brought to their attention, saying, "You're too young to be having problems like this." An accumulation of critical incidents convinced one clinician that the problem was indeed real and needed to be addressed. Then, once the cancer was actually diagnosed and the regime of care began in earnest, the first oncologist I consulted told me to "get crackin'" on the childbearing, since future chances for a safe pregnancy would likely be compromised by the kind of treatment I would need to pursue. Even under the best circumstances, such a comment would be alienating. Now imagine instead the absurdity of receiving it as a single, young woman patient. I reflected, "I already have to deal with challenges to my bodily health and integrity while I'm on the limited means of a student, and now I'm also supposed to worry about dating, marriage, and pregnancy. Oh, *and* still try to graduate." With a few further changes on the medical team, these relationships eventually improved. Ultimately, the gender of a given health care provider mattered less to me than his or her professional skill and competence, including how that HCP might manifest compassionate respect in our relationship. This cycle of surgeries and treatments lasted about two years, and during the period of remission I continued as best I could to finish my graduate degree.

When the cancer resurfaced after some years of relative quiet, I had recently transitioned into life as a new professor, but this diagnosis emerged only a few short months after a cross-country move for that job. Given two such significant manifestations of cancer under my belt before the age of forty, the team of surgeons and oncologists recommended bi-lateral mastectomy and, if I wished, reconstruction. With this recurrence, I was alone and new in the suburbs rather than in a city, far from any kind of "urban family" as I had previously experienced. Thus, I mapped out quickly how to juggle the logistics of teaching new classes while co-ordinating surgeries and countless appointments for both consultations and treatments. Luckily, my colleagues were gracious enough to adjust teaching schedules, offer rides, prepare extra meals, and run errands during the school year. The greater surprise to me was that my friends, who at that point were scattered along both the east and west coasts and had seen me through the first bout, mobilized together via e-mail and set up shared online calendars to organize a schedule of visits to care for me over the summer break, when the most invasive, potentially debili-tating surgeries were set to happen. Led by a former roommate—who was herself pregnant with her third child at the time, no less—they took turns, each coming for a week or at least a long weekend. Some were within a five-hour drive, while others made the five-hour flight. During that time, there were mercifully few gaps: the company was welcome, and I was grateful for the outpouring of support. Even those who could not participate directly in the care rotation were kind enough to send other supplies they thought I might need, such as extra linens or clothes that would allow me to dress myself easily and possibly accommodate prostheses post-op. In terms of numbers, only a small fraction of the caregivers were married or partnered; a few were members of religious communities, but this was largely women's work: single women looking after another one of their own, with help from a few good men.

Rather than mythologize illness as some kind of message or test from God, I did not question precisely *why* this illness had come my way yet again and was consuming considerable time and energy when there was already little of either to spare. Wallowing in anger, sadness, or self-pity or obsessing about the absurd arbitrariness of the sickness seemed to be a luxury hardly worthwhile, and the sentimental impulse rarely took me down. Instead, I generally accepted the whole experience as something to be borne and lived into, with equal parts matter-of-factness and, to the surprise and bemusement of my medical team, a real sense of humor to leaven and even cut through the steady stream of potential anxieties. For example, after a certain point, one of my surgeons shared in my rueful laughter that he was, by default, the most regular male presence in my personal life because I saw him so often—almost every week for months on end. Early on, especially this second time, I became conscious of having to navigate the maze back to wellness as a single person, without the same kind of accountability to another that I might have had to a spouse or boyfriend, or perhaps even a child or parent. This consciousness carried over from work life. Just as having my daily bread and not becoming what Bridget Jones would call "a tragic bag lady" depended on having and doing proper work, I took care of myself and managed this process of healing because no one else would or could do it for me, even if I wanted to delegate the power and responsibility—certainly not in the physical absence of the usual relational ties that help define us and how we are perceived. Although I clearly did not "go it alone" entirely, I nonetheless had to make different choices or arrangements and confront assumptions about community, relationships, and singlehood regularly. Thus, the "why" seemed less important than dealing with the constant present: keeping up with the parade of appointments and treatments, not to mention trying to stay on top of or to renegotiate day-to-day professional commitments as needed. Above all, I was more concerned with muddling through the whole experience without getting too derailed from the greater, ongoing, "normal" goals I had set for myself with which other young adults or single persons might identify: finding stable, meaningful, full-time work that paid fairly; making and sustaining strong personal and professional relationships of all kinds; heeding and feeding the creative part of myself by trying to stay involved in the arts as much as in academia—in short, following the imperative of choosing again and again, whenever possible, life-giving rather than life-draining things. By this point, my own life had already gone off script to such a degree; what more was illness on top of it, really?

In speaking of the spiritual disjunctions and existential pricking I experienced as a patient, I do not intend to fault at all the many HCPs—doctors, nurses, assistants, and more—who tended me at each stage of illness and healing.[6] Everyone was absolutely skilled, proficient, and professional. Despite whatever embarrassment I felt about my clear vulnerability, my

---

[6] Many people in my social (parish) and professional (higher education) community of care were Catholics, but my doctors and hospitals were not in the Catholic health care system; even if they were, I doubt my experience would have been all that different. I think the "real world" marginalization of single women is mirrored and often exacerbated in

body visibly failing me, the necessity of adjusting my own ideas about the look, feel, and meaning of womanliness, and the accompanying loss of control and freedom plus the diminishment (however real or merely perceived) of dignity, the HCPs' collective warmth balanced with matter-of-fact efficiency demonstrated their respect for my personhood, even at my worst, and called forth the dignity within me to respond and live as fully as possible. My concern actually lies more with the standard processes and practices of care in caring for patients. As Sulmasy notes, "The pragmatist and utilitarian habits of American culture have affected American medicine deeply. Everything today must be justified by outcome."[7] A patient already occupies a vulnerable position, having to surrender control to others for the sake of healing, and hence risking that her dignity and personhood will be forgotten or ignored in the process. While such standard protocols of care are understandably meant to insure patient safety and promote wellness as well as achieve certain efficiencies, as a single patient I found them alienating and at times humiliating, especially in regard to the underlying assumptions about the kinds of community and family resources that a patient would have available to assist in the recovery.

One typical routine involved the pre-op questionnaire, variations and iterations of which can be found in hospitals and clinics everywhere. The long, repetitive form requested details on everything from prior medical history, allergies, prescriptions, marital status, pregnancy status, personal health habits, symptoms or relevant issues, and so on. These questions were asked first at the intake interview, and then they were repeated prior to administering anesthesia, before the actual surgery began, during the inpatient stay at any number of points, and lastly just as discharge home became an option. Although this constant feed of disclosure and check-in was standard practice for a program and set of procedures that, by all accounts, were well coordinated and well run, the recurring questions served to emphasize the sense of isolated singularity before the knife or the chemotherapy dose (either of which already heightened my sense of contingency) and that the autonomy we are taught to cultivate and value as part of our quest for self-fulfillment as modern persons—indeed, modern women—is ultimately illusory and elusive. Despite the good and justifiable intentions that help insure healthier patients in the long run,

---

the church (beyond the proverbial stained-glass ceiling for leadership roles), and I wanted to have those two modes of being shadowing each other here in my analysis.

[7] Sulmasy, *The Rebirth of the Clinic*, 119.

and despite medical ethics' insistence that the patient should be regarded as an end unto herself, this battery and barrage of questions implies that a single person who is absent a proper family or other comparable loved ones to care for her at home has diminished standing and worth as a person. In other words, a singleton's personhood is lessened without the ordinary or obvious network of intimate relationships to frame her as a patient firmly belonging to a community of care.

During this period, I experienced complications and had to return promptly for emergency surgery. The timing did not fall neatly into the care rotation my friends had arranged, and there was no simple way to address those arrangements quickly. Several days afterward, when I was to be discharged, no one was immediately available to pick me up, and the hospital would not release me except into the care of friends or family; they would not let me take a cab home. From the patient's perspective, what is a reasonable expectation of compassionate respect here—in this case, respect for clearly articulated autonomy, tempered by the professional goal of good, compassionate care? Getting home alone, however difficult, was clearly not in the universe of safe, permissible options the HCPs could consider, perhaps legally as well as ethically.

The questionnaire was standard practice at the beginning of each major procedure, and its counterpart at the point of discharge manifested in the instructions and expectations for self-care at home. Some of those routines were either labor intensive, time intensive, or simply awkward for a patient to handle alone; in my case, it was difficult to be vulnerable with my caregivers and ask for help, despite their generosity and purpose in being present regularly. There are simply things permissible to ask an HCP to do as part of his or her job that might never be asked of a friend or family member, let alone a colleague. When is the right time to sacrifice privacy, and when is there sufficient trust, compassion, and respect to let this sacrifice happen? When is the right time to be radically, utterly human? When is the right time to surrender any pretense of autonomy so that vulnerability opens a space for a relationship and an ethic of care? When can one say that a patient is no longer exercising agency over her own illness, care, recovery, and overall well-being?

All of these incidents, of course, recalled for me two scenes in *Bridget Jones's Diary*. In the first scene, the title character—who is obsessed with surviving her life as a "singleton" with her dignity and self-respect intact and desperately hopes to find true love in the process—worries that she is doomed to die alone and not be missed for weeks, only to be discovered after wild dogs have found her first and eaten away at her flesh.[8] Attached to no person apparently responsible for her, physically or emotionally, a singleton such as Bridget is rendered marginal, forgettable, and ultimately invisible, as if sociocultural deadweight. In the second scene quoted at the beginning of this essay, the title character is the only single person invited to a dinner party otherwise populated by "smug marrieds" and other long-established couples, and she is not-so-subtly pressured there and elsewhere to be in a functional relationship with a respectable man while her biological clock ticks alongside her career ambitions, lest she become a complete spinster, Havishamesque or otherwise.[9] Both scenes assume that any pairing, even if imperfect, must be preferable to no pairing at all, at least as a form of social currency, and that a single person lacks sociocultural worth.

Farley reminds us of the unique role of religious communities and traditions in caring for the marginalized.[10] Tending intimately to the immediacy of any suffering with skill and mercy is a great gift. At the same time, caregivers in these lines of work must be able to see the larger picture; they must also be self-reflective and vigilant in asking themselves what role they may play in setting and perpetuating the conditions for marginalization. Though having to deal with the pre-op questionnaires and self-care at home are brief examples, each of those instances mushroomed into a larger-than-life indictment of the single person, especially a single woman with the misfortune of being a patient: Why wouldn't someone be at home to take care of me during the recovery period? In these instances, singlehood was deemed inherently pathological for its "unfinished" quality, or at the very least less socially visible and valuable. More importantly, the theo-ethical effects of these social practices reveal that we regard the single person primarily as preconjugal (not yet married), or the single woman especially as prematernal (not yet mother). In the calculus of care and community, friendships count less than familial relationships—which themselves give primacy to the "heteronormative," "marital-centric," or "filionormative"—and for a singleton they may be by necessity more of a lifeline. In my experience, then, health care in the United States is predicated upon belonging to and participating in a nuclear family structure that in turn has its underpinnings in traditional gender and Christian

[8] Helen Fielding, *Bridget Jones's Diary* (New York: Penguin, 1996), 18.

[9] Fielding, *Bridget Jones's Diary*, 34–37.

[10] Farley, *Compassionate Respect*, 49, 66–79.

notions of personhood and family. Though marriage does not produce a fundamental change in substance of the ones being married,[11] it does bear a different social weight as a status or identity marker. It affords the freedom of being able to slip into a category that needs no justification or explanation as singlehood does in comparison. In other words, the absence of a husband or child attached to (the rhetorical) me—or even in the case of religious, the backing and implicit support of a distinct intentional community—compromises my personhood or diminishes my dignity as singleton at least as much as illness already might.[12] With no one to claim the single woman patient as wife, or perhaps mother or daughter, what remains are the voluntary bonds of friendship, which require their own particular cultivation and sustenance. Furthermore, consider what HCPs or a community more generally owes to an utterly single patient without ties at all. To be clear, I am not (yet) proposing a wholly new anthropology of the human person. However, the ways in which health care is delivered or administered to single women patients raise questions of what we collectively value and why we proceed as we do. If autonomy is the preeminent good that the HCP and the patient negotiate between them, then the single patient, and particularly the single woman patient, enters that relationship already hamstrung.

Singlehood, Personhood, and Vulnerability

Statistics confirm popular opinion that the numbers of people who count as "never married"—that does not include divorced, separated, or widowed persons—have grown since 1990: 29.5 percent of all men and 22.8 percent of all women have never been married, increases for both genders.[13] In addition, the age of (first) marriage has also grown in that

[11] Others might argue, however, that a single person who then married has become ontologically different.

[12] For a glimpse of how the character of Bridget Jones might approach illness, see cartoonist Marisa Acocella Marchetto's graphic memoir, *Cancer Vixen* (New York: Knopf, 2006), and actress/photographer Kris Carr's resource book *Crazy Sexy Cancer Tips* (Guilford, CT: Skirt! 2007). Both authors draw upon their experience of being cancer patients as single, heterosexual women in their thirties. What is interesting in both accounts is the ways that their sexuality and marital status shape their experience and community of care during illness (each woman starts her book as a single person and is married by the end!).

[13] "Table 57. Marital Status of the Population by Sex and Age: 2009," http://www .census.gov/compendia/statab/2011/tables/11s0057.pdf. See also "Table 72. Persons

same span: twenty-six for women, twenty-eight for men.[14] Bella DePaulo and her colleagues also note that "in another striking departure from the past, Americans now spend more years of their adult lives unmarried than married."[15] A whole host of factors such as educational choices, parental expectations, and relative economic instability may account for the prolonging of singlehood as well as the extension or postponement of courtship. The window for pairing up and settling down to marry a significant other has grown longer and even sometimes open-ended. Despite valiant efforts and good intentions, single persons—especially women who are single by choice rather than by default—are judged more selfish or self-involved, less committed, more transient, and less rooted in a community, and consequently they somehow merit a different standard of care. Whatever the causes or factors, an extended, nebulous social limbo develops in which the emotional and relational lives of single persons are invisible compared to those who fit the standard categories of the nuclear family: having a spouse (or being en route to having one, via cohabitation or engagement) or having children. Effectively, a single person is always regarded as preconjugal—a puzzle piece in search of its perfect and ideal match—so that all emotional ties and relationship decisions drive toward that particular kind of intimacy and structure.

There is more to a single person than being prior to or absent from a state of marriage. Because of such expectations, however, the experience of navigating the health care system as a single person, especially when one's personal health is the matter in crisis, is fraught with emotional, logistical, and ultimately spiritual and ethical landmines. One's vulnerability is exacerbated, just as one's relationships are tested. Both the patient on the one hand and the community (including the whole range of caregivers) on the other hand are challenged to navigate that vulnerability in ways that promote and even maximize dignity, compassion, and respect. Using Farley's criterion of compassionate respect, I will

---

Living Alone by Sex and Age: 1990 to 2009," http://www.census.gov/compendia /statab/2011/tables/11s0072.pdf, and "Table 56. Marital Status of the Population by Sex, Race, and Hispanic Origin: 1990 to 2009," http://www.census.gov/compendia /statab/2011/tables/11s0056.pdf.

[14] Sharon Jason, "Dating for a Decade? Young Adults Aren't Rushing Marriage," *USA Today*, June 22, 2012, http://www.usatoday.com/life/lifestyle/2010-06-22-10year -courtship22_CV_N.htm.

[15] DePaulo et al., "Make Room for Singles in Teaching and Research," par. 1.

examine briefly four concepts—autonomy, relationality, embodiment, and totality—that are critical to a Catholic feminist perspective on medical ethics. I will also consider how they might be applied to provide care for a single patient in ways that enhance and honor personhood, that is, in ways that are more inclusive and less alienating.

> Suppose we ask, first, what it will mean to respect her precisely as a person. Central to our response to this question (at least in Western culture) is that respect for her as a person means respect for her as an end in herself. She is an end in herself because she has a capacity for free choice, for self-determination, such that it would violate who she is to incorporate her totally as a means into the agenda of another, whether of a caregiver or anyone else. This is what the principle of autonomy requires us to recognize and respect.[16]

Autonomy has multiple dimensions for Farley. In addition to looking at the single person as an end in herself, especially when she is a patient, autonomy also connotes self-reliance (though still separate from an absolute independence). In this light, it is akin to agency, defined as being able to express will or exert control over a given situation. Since the HCP is charged with assisting the patient in returning to health and full functioning as much as possible, respect for personhood includes respect for the patient's autonomy and agency at every step of the process as much as possible. Unless the patient is incapacitated and cannot make decisions in her own self-interest, the HCP is bound to honor the patient's wishes, even if they go against the HCP's best judgment or recommendation. For example, the single woman patient may decline an aggressive course of treatment that might compromise her ability to bear children in the future (should marriage and family ever become an option) and ask about alternate treatments. Or she may give priority to her own present survival and thriving and relationships to request the optimal treatment recommended and choose to deal with future relationship choices as they arise.

In caring for the single patient, perhaps the concept that gets thrown into highest relief is relationality, or our capacity to love and be loved, sometimes quite profoundly and intimately. Our personhood is shaped by those whose lives intersect with our own, and we may engage them fleetingly or commit to them again and again over time. The balance of

[16] Farley, *Compassionate Respect*, 36.

power in these relationships cannot help but shift during illness. Even if we resist, our dependence on others grows when we are weakened, and in the process of recovery or even terminal illness (as the possibility for full reciprocity grows more difficult), the persons in relation need to work their way to a new equilibrium: Will you step up to care for me as the patient, and will I surrender to that vulnerability? The HCP—and, by extension, the greater health care system—must be mindful of the different universe that such a patient occupies in her own community and culture and of the implications of singlehood in the delivery of care and the pursuit of healing. HCPs should question whether there are practices or processes that are alienating despite their good intentions and whether there are ways of being more welcoming and inclusive, more respectful of the single patient's full personhood that would also promote good outcomes. By honoring her autonomy but also treating her as part of a community of care larger than or different from the standard nuclear family (which may also encompass a different range of relationships), the health care system better embodies the ideal of compassionate respect.[17]

For the single patient navigating the health care system, embodiment raises several points to consider for HCPs. Thinking of embodiment as lived experience implies being one's fullest, quintessential self at any given moment and acting out of one's deepest motivation, whether fear, curiosity, or loyalty. Defining embodiment as the manifestation of a belief or commitment, a HCP, friend, or family member who takes the time to help care for a patient embodies compassionate respect, maybe even love. Lastly, embodiment entails the emotionally and spiritually complex terrain of dealing with one's own body—which may be disfigured or incapacitated through illness or accident, sometimes permanently—and with the changing meaning of bodily integrity, quite literally and visibly. For example, am I less of a woman if my capacity for childbearing is compromised in the long run, or if I opt to live with scars and fleshly craters instead of pursuing reconstructive surgery? How much do a patient's answers to such questions depend on her relationships, how she self-identifies, and her life's other particulars? In the choices we all make—whether as patient, HCP, or community caregiver—we embody who we are, as well as what and who are important to us.

[17] Factors such as race/ethnicity or even geography add layers of complexity to the ways that a single woman's autonomy gets lived out and understood. Culture and context matter, and they can serve as either a check on or a boost for movement.

Autonomy, relationality, and embodiment shed light on moment-to-moment decisions within the context of medical ethics. However, for truly compassionate respect to hold, each of these concepts must be viewed through the lens of totality: what an action or decision means for the totality, the whole of the life lived. Farley uses the principle of totality in sexual ethics to consider the role of love and sex within the life of a relationship.[18] Medical ethicists use that same principle to consider what range of options would make the patient most fully functional and ensure quality of life in the long term. Following Farley's line of reasoning from a moral (and not solely medical) standpoint, I would argue for *practices* of compassionate respect in care that promote the healing and flourishing especially of the vulnerable by being inclusive of all persons, regardless of social or marital status. Moreover, these practices should address the well-being of the whole patient—for example, biological health and recovery are naturally paramount in the medical context, but social and emotional health must also figure into that context, as well as implications for the wider community in which the patient lives. Alisa Carse's comments on our social shortcomings underscore the necessity of connecting in ways both targeted and broad in order to realize compassionate respect thoroughly:

> When we are thwarted or "unhinged," our flourishing becomes especially dependent on the support of others, even others with whom we have up until now shared a basic equality of dependency and need. Moreover, asymmetries of dependency and need fundamentally configure many relationships that fill our lives . . . in ways that are neither "abnormal" nor morally problematic as such. We need the protection and sustenance of others; our flourishing is threatened by others' neglect.
>
> Our attachment to impoverished paradigms of control and self-determination in human life diminishes our potential to join others in meaningful forms of connection essential to human flourishing. Acceptance of our vulnerabilities, when combined with the virtues of empathy, compassion, and solidarity, can ground and motivate a moral call to provide all people with needed forms of sustenance and support—to ameliorate the isolating impact of suffering, to help

---

[18] See Margaret A. Farley, *Just Love: A Framework for Christian Sexual Ethics* (New York: Continuum, 2008), 48, 278.

in the work of "healing" among those facing chronic disability or terminal illness, to sustain contexts in which those left shaky or terrified in the aftermath of trauma can regain trust and self-respect, and—most fundamentally—to ensure minimally decent conditions necessary for the realization and expression of those capacities for evaluative reflection, commitment, and generous-hearted collaboration that mark human beings as unique in the universe of creatures.[19]

Practices of compassionate respect should serve to embody the love, inclusion, and skilled care we claim to value in tending to the needs of the patient. Already sidelined by illness, we need not magnify the patient's vulnerability unduly by exacerbating that sociocultural marginalization as well.

Making Room for the New Normal

> To be human is to be patient, but to be patient is not necessarily to be sick.
>
> —William Desmond, "Pluralism, Truthfulness, and the Patience of Being"[20]

Just as any patient has to negotiate a new equilibrium in her relationships during and after illness, so too does the single patient need to work out a new balance in the delivery of care in order to maximize compassionate respect. (Ultimately, this balance would be reciprocated and shared with the HCP and the extended community of care.) To imagine what compassionate respect would look like and mean to the single patient—and how one might respond in faith—let us step back briefly to consider that particular experience of suffering and vulnerability.

Psychiatrist Arthur Kleinman makes some valuable distinctions between illness, disease, and sickness. He regards the scientific, psychological, and sociocultural dimensions of each term in ways that are useful for my argument. First, illness, seen primarily from the patient's perspective, is "the innately human experience of symptoms and suffering," as well

---

[19] Alisa L. Carse, "Vulnerability, Agency, and Human Flourishing," in *Health and Human Flourishing: Religion, Medicine, and Moral Anthropology*, ed. Carol L. Taylor and Roberto Dell'Oro (Washington, DC: Georgetown University Press, 2006), 47–48.

[20] William Desmond, "Pluralism, Truthfulness, and the Patience of Being," in *Health and Human Flourishing*, ed. Taylor and Dell'Oro, 66.

as "how the sick person and the members of the family or wider social network perceive, live with, and respond to symptoms and disability." Next follows disease, which privileges the HCP's perspective; it is "what the [medical] practitioner creates in the recasting of illness in terms of theories of disorder. . . . In the narrow biological terms of the biomedical model, this means that disease is reconfigured *only* as an alteration in biological structure or functioning. . . . In the broader biopsychosocial model now making headway in primary care, disease is construed as the embodiment of the symbolic network linking body, self, and society." Sickness has the broadest scope as "the understanding of a disorder in its generic sense across a population in relation to macrosocial (economic, political, institutional) forces."[21]

Kleinman further teases out four meanings of illness, two of which are important for our consideration. On the one hand, illness is a particular kind of suffering with its own cultural salience or significance (e.g., leprosy, bubonic plague, AIDS); we experience and respond to it as "a distinctive moral or spiritual form of distress" with biomedical and/ or psychological roots.[22] On the other hand, illness is also an event (or series of events) that "transfers vital significance from the person's life to the illness experience."[23] The process of healing and recovery involves the patient—and sometimes her extended community of care—in trying to make meaningful sense of what is happening, how one should be treated, and how it all should be understood.

> The meanings of chronic illness are created by the sick person and his or her circle to make over a wild, disordered *natural* occurrence into a more or less domesticated, mythologized, ritually controlled, therefore *cultural* experience. . . .
>
> Thus, patients order their experience of illness—what it means to them and to significant others—as personal narratives. The illness narrative is a story the patient tells, and significant others retell, to give coherence to the distinctive events and long-term course of suffering. The plot lines, core metaphors, and rhetorical devices that structure the illness narrative are drawn from cultural

[21] Arthur W. Kleinman, *The Illness Narratives: Suffering, Healing, and the Human Condition* (New York: Basic Books/HarperCollins, 1988), 3–6.
[22] Ibid., 26.
[23] Ibid., 31.

and personal models for arranging experiences in meaningful ways and for effectively communicating those meanings. Over the long course of chronic disorder, these model texts shape and even create experience. The personal narrative does not merely reflect illness experience, but rather it contributes to the experience of symptoms and suffering.[24]

For the single patient, then, the particulars of her community and context cannot be forgotten. For example, greater attention to maximizing autonomy (within safe and reasonable bounds, of course), would go quite far in promoting compassionate respect. HCPs would do well to remember that for any patient, really, illness and recovery are not one-size-fits-all experiences that every procedure will suit. Pursuing greater flexibility in the care sought and received is possible—again, within safe and reasonable bounds.

Illness is a disruptive spiritual, bodily event or state that transforms a person into a patient. This disruption upends established habits and routines and forces finding a new equilibrium to accommodate the challenges and changes. The path to "the new normal" is unknown to the patient, and possibly unscripted altogether. The single person undergoing major illness here confronts vulnerability most squarely, for she is more vulnerable in a society or system that assumes safety in numbers and comfort in the embrace of heterosexual family and community—which is always available to take care of you. This loss of power is not the same as loss of agency, but it also challenges the autonomy and independence we are expected to value and embrace as US women of relative privilege, with access to health care, education, and other relevant resources. As Sulmasy reminds us,

> Illness is a spiritual event. Illness grasps persons by the soul as well as the body and disturbs both. Illness ineluctably raises troubling questions of a transcendent nature—questions about meaning, value, and relationship. These questions are spiritual. How health care professionals answer these questions for themselves will affect the way they help their patients struggle with these questions. . . .[25]

> Patients struggle with all the big questions: What is the meaning of my illness? Why must I suffer? Is there anything about me that

---

[24] Ibid., 48–49.
[25] Sulmasy, *The Rebirth of the Clinic*, 17.

is valuable now that I am no longer "productive"? What is broken in my relationships that I somehow feel called to fix now that my body is broken? Can my doctor possibly understand what I am really going through?[26]

If illness reveals the disruption of right relationships—within the patient's body, between her body and the surrounding environment, or between the individual and her community—then healing is about restoring right relation in each of those places. Both illness and healing have spiritual implications.[27]

Throughout this essay, I have used the word "community" to mean a group of people who share a common goal, purpose, interest, or commitment, in this case, the well-being of a patient from their circle. Having to deal with illness outside the usual ways—that is, beyond the conjugal or nuclear family model—opens possibilities for imagining alternate ways of providing health care and embodying community. Not having to rely on the marital-centric or the filionormative circle will undoubtedly raise issues of gender and other contextual markers in a rearticulated anthropology of the human person because other understandings of community, relationships, and singlehood will emerge in the process.

Returning to Fielding's novel, much is made of Bridget Jones's ultimately being loved "just as she is," even with quirks and imperfections that are at times maddening and endearing. With clear eyes rather than sentimentality or cheekiness, Farley's notion of compassionate respect pays careful attention to "the concrete reality of persons"[28] and the demands that personhood makes on us. In the process, she provides the space to call earnestly for more inclusive practices of community in the health care setting so that all can care for the patient, especially the single one, "just as she is," as an end in herself rather than as a sociocultural afterthought, even within uncomfortable or difficult situations. When the personhood of all involved in the healing process is recognized and honored through practices of compassionate respect, models of singlehood, personhood, community, and care emerge that counter dominant ways of being. Through compassionate respect, Farley lays the groundwork for a constructive, generous notion of "just love" yet to come, in both

[26] Ibid., 22.
[27] Ibid., 125.
[28] Farley, *Just Love*, 209.

substance and methodology. Compassion and respect are inseparable, as are justice and love, and having all these elements in play are fundamental to recognizing the personhood of the human before us in any situation, not only in health care crises. The best possible care addresses the reality and well-being of the whole person while also being mindful of the wider community and context in which the patient lives.

Reservoirs of Hope

Catholic Women's Witness

Kristin Heyer, Santa Clara University

At a time when temptations to despair abound in the church and world alike, the prophetic courage of Catholic women offers a source of hope.[1] For centuries, women religious worldwide have witnessed to God's reign amid life's complex realities through their various ministries. Even under the scrutiny of concurrent Vatican investigations,[2] women religious in the United States continue to model integrity and a commitment to defend the vulnerable. A recent example from NETWORK Social Justice Lobby's forty-year history of tireless Catholic advocacy through changing political seasons conveys life-affirming triumph despite deterrent risks. Thrust into the national spotlight due to their role in the health care reform debate, the women of NETWORK have consistently brought their prophetic vision to Capitol Hill and beyond. Their advocacy and internal operational witness alike reflect the deeper religious traditions in which they are rooted, offering fruitful insights for understanding conscientious discernment and prophetic fidelity.

---

[1] This essay is adapted from the Annual Anne Drummey O'Callaghan Lecture on Women in the Church delivered at Fairfield University, October 6, 2010.

[2] In December of 2008, Cardinal Franc Rodé, CM, prefect of the Vatican's Congregation for Institutes of Consecrated Life and Societies of Apostolic Life, announced a three-year apostolic visitation investigating the lifestyles of women religious. In 2009 the Congregation for the Doctrine of the Faith launched a doctrinal inquiry into the Leadership Conference of Women Religious, charging the conference had failed to sufficiently promote the church's teachings on the male-only priesthood, on homosexuality, and on the primacy of the Roman Catholic Church as the means to salvation, as warned eight years prior.

The Courage of Lobbyists with a Conscience

In March of 2010, US popular opinion credited American nuns with saving health care reform amid contentious debate within the Catholic community and the halls of Congress. As the debate over health care reform began, the Catholic community prioritized several objectives: universal access to affordable care, expanded access to health care for immigrants, and maintaining the Hyde Amendment's prevention of federal funding for elective abortions. As the Senate version of the bill moved to the House for consideration, where pro-life critics charged that it allowed for abortion funding, Catholic Health Association president Carol Keehan (Daughter of Charity) broke with the United States bishops' opposition and issued a statement adding CHA's support to the bill. As Keehan indicated, she had become convinced that abortion coverage language in the Senate version could be resolved, as mechanisms were in place to isolate coverage from government-regulated health care markets, and that the legislation presented a historic opportunity to extend the "human right" of universal and affordable health care to millions of Americans.[3]

When Sister of Social Service Simone Campbell, executive director of NETWORK Social Justice Lobby, read Sister Keehan's statement, she decided Keehan needed strong Catholic support. Since its founding almost forty years ago, NETWORK has advocated for "accessible, affordable, quality, universal healthcare." Grounded in Catholic social teaching, the group understands "access for all to quality healthcare [to be] a fundamental social good . . . as well as a human right."[4] Campbell immediately issued a statement on behalf of NETWORK praising the Catholic Health Association's stand and expressing the view that health care legislation's extension of access to millions would reduce the number of abortions. Campbell also drafted a letter to members of Congress signed by the president of the Leadership Conference of Women Religious (LCWR) and over seventy-five heads of orders of women religious. The letter urged members to "cast a life-affirming 'yes' vote" on the health care bill, acknowledging it was an "imperfect measure" but a crucial next step in realizing universal coverage. They explicitly noted that, "despite false claims to the contrary, the Senate bill will not provide taxpayer funding

[3] Sister Carol Keehan, DC, "The Time Is Now for Health Care Reform," (March 15, 2010), available at http://www.chausa.org/The_time_is_now_for_health_reform.aspx (accessed September 24, 2010).

[4] http://www.networklobby.org/issues/healthcare (accessed September 22, 2010).

for elective abortions." The letter underscores the apostolic context for their advocacy:

> As the heads of major Catholic women's religious order[s] in the United States, we represent 59,000 Catholic Sisters in the United States who respond to needs of people in many ways. Among our other ministries we are responsible for running many of our nation's hospital systems as well as free clinics throughout the country.
>
> We have witnessed firsthand the impact of our national health care crisis, particularly its impact on women, children and people who are poor. We see the toll on families who have delayed seeking care due to a lack of health insurance coverage or lack of funds with which to pay high deductibles and co-pays. We have counseled and prayed with men, women and children who have been denied health care coverage by insurance companies. We have witnessed early and avoidable deaths because of delayed medical treatment.[5]

On the basis of this tireless commitment and the bill's potential to dramatically extend access to care while upholding conscience protections and investing significantly in pregnant women's support, NETWORK and others cast their position as "the real pro-life stance." As other pro-life Catholic organizations endorsed CHA's position despite the bishops' conference's continued opposition, several pro-life members of Congress—including a few key Catholic Democrats—supported the bill, convinced that ambiguities in the proposed law concerning abortion would be resolved, given the March 24, 2010, presidential executive order promising to ensure no federal funds would be spent on abortion.[6] Campbell noted that during the signing ceremony for the Patient Protection and Affordable Care Act, President Obama credited her and NETWORK's allies with the bill's passage.[7]

---

[5] Full text of the letter is available at http://www.americamagazine.org/blog/entry. cfm?blog_id=2&entry_id=1799 (accessed October 8, 2010).

[6] March 24, 2010, presidential executive order "Ensuring Enforcement and Implementation of Abortion Restrictions in the Patient Protection and Affordable Care Act," available at http://www.whitehouse.gov/the-press-office/executive-order-patient -protection-and-affordable-care-acts-consistency-with-longst (accessed April 25, 2011).

[7] Jerry Filteau, "Pro-life, Social-Justice Catholics Gain Traction on Hill," *National Catholic Reporter*, April 16, 2010, available at http://ncronline.org/news/politics/pro -life-social-justice-catholics-gain-traction-hill (accessed April 30, 2010).

As NETWORK staff reflected subsequent to the act's passage and signing in March 2010, "The new law does not have everything we wanted, but it is a historic step. . . . [It] promotes quality healthcare that is more accessible, affordable, universal and pro-life."[8] Yet they maintain that their support of the new law does not indicate complete satisfaction, and they continue to advocate for additional steps needed, in their view, to improve the US health care system. For example, NETWORK continues to push for policies that permit undocumented immigrants to purchase health care coverage on the exchange with their own funds, to "eliminate the five-year ban for documented immigrants to be eligible for government health care benefits (Medicaid, federal subsidies, etc.)," and to provide adequate subsidies for low-wage workers and their dependents still unable to afford health insurance.[9] The Pregnancy Assistance Fund announced by the Obama administration in summer 2010 offers one step forward in an abortion reduction strategy that addresses root causes.[10] $250 million was authorized over ten years to assist "pregnant and parenting women and teens with child care, housing, education and services for those victimized by domestic or sexual violence." Such comprehensive support is particularly crucial for women who lack access to basic resources to raise a healthy child and consider abortion their only option. As Campbell reflected at the time, in contrast to soaring public rhetoric about protecting family values, these funds for holistic support (from baby food to postpartum counseling to parenting classes) "extend a compassionate hand of support to women rather than a judgmental finger waved in condemnation."[11]

[8] http://www.networklobby.org/issues/healthcare (accessed September 22, 2010).

[9] Ibid.

[10] The Affordable Care Act provides $25 million for each fiscal year from 2010 through 2019 and authorizes the secretary of health and human services, in collaboration and coordination with the secretary of education, to establish and administer the fund. As its first disbursement, the Department of Health and Human Services awarded $27 million for the support of pregnant and parenting teens in states and tribes nationwide on September 28, 2010 (see the HHS press release at http://www.hhs.gov/news /press/2010pres/09/20100928d.html [accessed April 14, 2011]).

[11] Peg Chemberlin and Sister Simone Campbell, "Health Reform Will Help Reduce the Number of Abortions," *The Hill's Congress Blog,* July 14, 2010, available at http:// thehill.com/blogs/congress-blog/healthcare/108747-health-reform-will-help-reduce -the-number-of-abortions (accessed September 22, 2010).

NETWORK's willingness to risk support for imperfect legislation that will provide a historic step toward universal coverage and anticipated abortion reduction reflects the too-seldom-glimpsed integrity of a Catholic comprehensive ethic that attempts to unite pre- and postbirth commitments. Whereas internal Catholic disagreement persisted over the means of reducing abortion rather than the morality of abortion per se, many have noted that "industrialized countries that achieve universal or near-universal coverage have demonstrably lower abortion rates" than does the United States.[12] Too often a Catholic political ethic isolates life and justice issues or elevates "nonnegotiables," whereas strategies in this vein of pregnancy assistance toward abortion reduction interconnect life issues with just social contexts, enhancing integrity and credibility for Catholics promoting the fullness of the gospel of life.

Former Michigan congressman Bart Stupak (D-MI), credited with forging a compromise that allowed pro-life allies to support (and thereby ensure) the health care bill's passage, has remained optimistic that the executive order will continue to protect the Hyde language. He notes that in three instances in the law's first year, President Obama and Health and Human Services secretary Kathleen Sebelius have upheld the order's provisions. They have required states' high-risk pools to exclude federal funding for abortion, ensured that community health centers cannot perform or advocate for abortions, and stipulated that related grant applications comply with Hyde language. Stupak notes that as a result of refusing to "look the other way" in these instances, fewer abortions have occurred due to the executive order and the health care bill than if neither had come to pass.[13]

[12] T. R. Reid, "Universal Health Care Tends to Cut the Abortion Rate," *Washington Post*, March 14, 2010, A19.

[13] Chris Good, "Bart Stupak, a Year after Health Care: Getting 'Bitched Out' in Airports, How the Deal Went Down, and More," *The Atlantic*, March 23, 2011, available at http://www.theatlantic.com/politics/archive/2011/03/bart-stupak-a-year-after-health-care-getting-bitched-out-in-airports-how-the-deal-went-down-and-more/72938 (accessed April 1, 2011). Whereas insufficient time has lapsed since the Affordable Care Act's passage to measure abortion rates, there is data on such rates in the state of Massachusetts after the passage of its health care reform act, which, unlike the Affordable Care Act, requires abortion coverage for all publicly subsidized health insurance plans. An analysis published in the March 2010 *New England Journal of Medicine* indicates that the abortion rate dropped in Massachusetts after the state adopted its own health reform law. It shows the number of abortions declined 1.5 percent from 2006 to 2008, with

Whereas many Catholic citizens arrived in good faith at different conclusions about the potential impact of health care reform on abortion prevention, the gap between antiabortion rhetoric and concrete efforts to reduce abortions calls for ongoing vigilance. Nearly a year after the passage of health care reform, Campbell bemoaned the hypocrisy of Republican leaders who targeted Planned Parenthood amid congressional budget debates while attempting to shred the social safety net. Campbell criticized such lawmakers who "tout their pro-life bona fides [and] then blatantly undermine life with budget proposals that will hurt pregnant women, mothers and children and likely lead more poor women to end their pregnancies."[14] The disconnect between antiabortion rhetoric and action in the 2011 budget debates recalls a 2004 study by Harvard economists on politicians' use of "strategic extremism." Their analyses showed that, with respect to religious values, we can typically determine whether a politician is motivated to take a particular extreme policy stance due to conviction or to strategy: "If the stance arises from personal conviction ('nonstrategic extremism'), then actions taken in support of it will typically be more extreme than the rhetoric of the campaign. If a stance arises from strategy, though, the campaign message will be more extreme than the policy actions ultimately taken."[15] Theologians and political analysts alike have suggested that the ongoing impasse on abortion serves politicians whose rhetoric or appearance of working toward a solution advances political interests without delivering results.[16]

---

the number of abortions obtained by teens decreasing by 7.4 percent. During this time period the birthrate increased and the population grew. Patrick Whelan, "Abortion Rates and Universal Health Care," *New England Journal of Medicine* (March 2010): 362, e45.

[14] Simone Campbell, "When Budgets Are Not Pro-Life," *The Hill's Congress Blog*, March 2, 2011, http://thehill.com/blogs/congress-blog/economy-a-budget/147047 -when-budgets-are-not-pro-life (accessed April 27, 2011).

[15] Daniel Finn, "Hello, Catholics: Republicans and the Targeting of Religious Voters," *Commonweal*, November 4, 2005, 14–17, at 16. Finn's article analyzes Edward L. Glaeser, Giacomo A. M. Ponzetto, and Jesse M. Shapiro, "Strategic Extremism: Why Republicans and Democrats Divide on Religious Values," National Bureau of Economic Research Working Paper No. 10835, *Quarterly Journal of Economics* (November 2005): 1283–330.

[16] Finn, "Hello, Catholics," 17. "The number of abortions has remained about the same under Democratic and Republican presidents, even apparently rising somewhat since George W. Bush's election. Republicans remain perennially the champions of Christians opposed to abortions—without actually bringing about any change. (Even partial-birth legislation doesn't reduce the number of abortions; it just requires another method be used.)" Finn, "Hello, Catholics," 16. For example, during the April 2011

Campbell insists that "if lawmakers are really serious about building a culture of life, rhetoric is not enough." She warns that such budget cuts would only encourage abortions because low-income women are "less likely to have abortions when they have access to quality health care and strong social safety nets," as demonstrated in countries that offer robust pre- and postnatal care.[17]

Prophetic Obedience and Prudential Discernment

In the wake of their support of the health care reform bill, the motives and competencies of certain groups of women religious were impugned, with the USCCB issuing an official statement charging those who differed from the bishops' interpretation of the health care bill with causing "confusion and a wound to Catholic unity."[18] Archbishop Charles Chaput of Denver accused the "self-described 'Catholic' groups" as committing "a serious disservice to justice, to the church, and to the ethical needs of the American people by undercutting the leadership and witness of their own bishops."[19] Bishop Lawrence Brandt of Greensburg, Pennsylvania, forbade any religious community that signed the aforementioned letter supporting the bill from using the diocese's offices, parishes, or newspaper to promote vocational programs that encourage young people to consider religious life.[20]

The focus in this fallout centered around the nature and limits of the bishops' authority on matters of faith, morals, law, and policy.[21] Important

---

budget debate, Sen. John Kyl (R-AZ) claimed that Planned Parenthood (one of the organizations targeted for funding cuts) devotes 90 percent of its resources to abortion provision, whereas in reality the figure is 3 percent. When questioned, Sen. Kyl issued a press release indicating he had not intended that figure to be a "factual statement." Under the pressure he received in response, he ultimately had the comment stricken from the Congressional record.

[17] Campbell, "When Budgets Are Not Pro-Life."

[18] Cardinal Daniel DiNardo, Bishop William Murphy, and Bishop John Wester, "Setting the Record Straight," May 21, 2010, available at http://www.usccb.org/comm/archives/2010/10-104.shtml (accessed October 8, 2010).

[19] Archbishop Charles Chaput, "A Bad Bill and How We Got It," *Denver Catholic Register*, March 24, 2010.

[20] Editors, "Courage of the Sisters," *New York Times*, May 1, 2010, A18.

[21] See Thomas Weinandy, OFM, Cap, "The Bishops and the Right Exercise of Authority," available at http://old.usccb.org/healthcare/11-01-10-commonweal-response.

distinctions were revisited, such as the application of universal moral teachings and specific moral principles to concrete policies. Particular strategic applications of principles are more fluid in character, and hence our grasp is "necessarily more tentative than [our] knowledge of principle[s]."[22] As Thomas Aquinas cautions, certainty about moral truth and obligations diminishes as we descend to contingent particulars from general principles.[23] In the case of the divergence of some women religious from the bishops on health care reform, the debate occurred nearly entirely at the level of prudential judgments about technical legislative language. The disagreements arose not over the morality or legality of abortion but "whether specific legislative provisions in fact did what the drafters of the legislation insisted they did—namely, prohibit federal funding of abortions in accord with the principles of the Hyde Amendment."[24] By contrast, Cardinal Francis George, then president of the USCCB, cast the matter less in terms of prudential judgment than in terms of ecclesiology, concerned with the nature of the church and its legitimate spokesmen.[25]

The virtue of prudence is what helps guide the conscience in such practical moral judgments, including how citizens should vote. Attending to means, not ends, prudence carefully considers human experience, others' counsel, anticipated consequences, and the discernment of God's invitation to reach a decision that best fits the complexities of a given situation.[26] While concerns about lack of unity are understandable, then, at the level of general principles, in their exercise of practical wisdom at this level of contingent applications, NETWORK and others claimed a legitimate space to witness to Catholic values in concrete circumstances.

---

shtml (accessed April 27, 2011); John L. Allen Jr., "Health Care: Transcript of Cardinal George June 16 NCR Interview, *National Catholic Reporter*, June 22, 2010, available at http://ncronline.org/blogs/ncr-today/health-care-transcript-cardinal-george-june-16-ncr-interview (accessed April 27, 2011); and Daniel Finn, "Uncertainty Principle: The Bishops, Health Care and Prudence," *Commonweal*, March 25, 2011.

[22] See Charles E. Curran, *Catholic Moral Tradition Today: A Synthesis* (Washington, DC: Georgetown University Press, 1999), 152n71.

[23] See Thomas Aquinas, *Summa Theologiae* II-II, q. 47, a. 2.

[24] Richard R. Gaillardetz, "The Limits of Authority: When Bishops Speak about Health Care Policy, Catholics Should Listen, but Don't Have to Agree," *Commonweal*, June 30, 2010.

[25] Allen, "Health Care."

[26] See Richard Gula, *Reason Informed by Faith: Foundations of Catholic Morality* (Mahwah, NJ: Paulist Press, 1989), 316.

In so doing, they demonstrated an understanding of conscientious obedience that departs from blind acquiescence. From a certain point of view, the prudential discernment that played out amid the health care reform debate could be interpreted as a success story—whereas not every member of the Catholic community arrived at identical conclusions regarding how to best protect the same values, the public reasoning and communal conscience formation ultimately influenced pending policy to better reflect and protect such values, as indicated by the executive order on abortion funding.

In her series of essays on religious life as prophetic life form in which she builds upon her 2000 Madeleva Lecture,[27] Sandra Schneiders, IHM, differentiates the hierarchical definition of obedience as "total and absolute submission in thought, word, and deed, interiorly and exteriorly, to office authority" from the prophetic definition of obedience. Prophetic obedience entails "the prayerful listening for the will of God and all relevant 'voices' and the search for that will in the 'signs of the times,' followed by careful discernment [of] . . . the good of real people in concrete situations."[28] Analogously, Anne Patrick, SNJM, distinguishes between a fundamentalistic understanding of obedience, which understands it primarily as submission such that conformity with official teaching and interpretation of moral obligation rests with authority figures, and a revisionist understanding of obedience. The latter emphasizes hearing rather than submission (*ob audire* as "hearing toward"), and consequently obedient discipleship entails "listening with care for clues to the divine will" rather than submitting to the voice of authority per se.[29] The obedience characteristic of women religious profiled here recalls the under-

---

[27] Sandra M. Schneiders, *With Oil in Their Lamps: Faith, Feminism and the Future* (Mahwah, NJ: Paulist Press, 2000).

[28] Sandra M. Schneiders, "Tasks of Those Who Choose the Prophetic Lifestyle," part 4 of a five-part essay, *National Catholic Reporter*, January 7, 2010, available at http://ncronline .org/news/women/tasks-those-who-choose-prophetic-life-style (accessed October 8, 2010). She notes that in the wake of Vatican II, "obedience ceased to be understood as blind submission to divinely empowered, absolute, and non-accountable official 'authorities.' Rather, corporate obedience meant the full and free cooperation of all members of the community with congregational leaders and each other in co-responsibility for their life and mission. . . . [This was a transition] from divine right monarchy to a discipleship of equals."

[29] Anne E. Patrick, SNJM, *Liberating Conscience: Feminist Explorations in Catholic Moral Theology* (New York: Continuum, 1997), 103–4.

standing of the moral life that H. Richard Niebuhr and James Gustafson articulate as discerning what God is enabling and requiring us to be and do.[30] Addressing the LCWR in August of 2010, ecclesiologist Richard Gaillardetz noted that women religious' responses to the ecclesial tensions they face—not only in light of their stance on health care but also amid the doctrinal investigation and apostolic visitation—would be a witness to all Christians who also inevitably experience tensions. Theirs, he suggested, is a model of creative fidelity.[31]

The Catholic tradition enjoys an ambiguous history regarding the relationship of individual conscience to official church teaching.[32] Whereas an understanding of conscience as conformity to the teaching of the hierarchy remains in tension with the shift to a more personalist model at the Second Vatican Council, the discernment of Catholic groups at the health care reform moment demonstrates a response to the call to actively discern responsibility in light of the gift and challenge of God's law of love. As Carol Keehan put it, "This was a bill that, for the first time in the lives of 32 million Americans, gave them a chance to have decent health insurance. . . . That was a heavy burden on my conscience, and on our organizational conscience. . . . We did not differ on the moral question, or the teaching authority of the bishops."[33] In *Gaudium et Spes*, the council fathers characterize conscience as that "secret core and sanctuary of a [person]" where he or she "is alone with God, Whose voice echoes in his [or her] depths."[34] This "encounter with the divine basis of moral obligation is mediated through [a person's] agency, and hence through

[30] See H. Richard Niebuhr, *The Responsible Self* (Louisville: Westminster John Knox Press, 1999, orig. New York: Harper and Row, 1963), 149–78; and James M. Gustafson, *Christ and the Moral Life* (Chicago: University of Chicago Press, 1968), esp. 265–66.

[31] Thomas C. Fox, "Women Religious Experiences Have Implications for Entire Church," *National Catholic Reporter*, August 12, 2010, available at http://ncronline.org /news/women-religious/women-religious-experiences-have-implications-entire-church (accessed October 4, 2011).

[32] See Linda Hogan, *Confronting the Truth: Conscience in the Catholic Tradition* (London: Darton, Longman and Todd, 2001).

[33] John L. Allen Jr., "Minding the Gap between the Bishops and Catholic Health Care" *National Catholic Reporter*, June 16, 2010, available at http://ncronline.org/news/politics /minding-gap-between-bishops-and-catholic-health-care (accessed October 8, 2010).

[34] Vatican II, Pastoral Constitution on the Church in the Modern World (*Gaudium et Spes*), no. 16, http://www.vatican.va/archive/hist_councils/ii_vatican_council /documents/vat-ii_cons_19651207_gaudium-et-spes_en.html.

the spirit, reason, affections and relationships that constitute human agency."[35] In this vein, the women religious profiled here witness to an understanding of conscience that entails the capacity and willingness to pursue the truth about doing the right thing in concrete, complicated circumstances, rather than having all the answers.[36] Their efforts to seek the good and thereby encounter God witness to the capacious character of the church and the agency Christian discipleship invites and demands.

The etymology of "conscience" (knowing together with) highlights the social dimension of moral knowledge. Understanding conscientious discernment as inclusive of multiple sources of moral wisdom—including the riches of Scripture, the wisdom of the Catholic community over the centuries, natural law, insights of church officials and theologians, and moral exemplars, as well as the reflective experiences of those immersed in health care ministries and the details of legislative analysis, as in the case at hand—calls disciples to a more complex and proactive endeavor than assumptions that restrict such sources to the teaching authority of the hierarchy alone.[37] Further, as Patrick has observed, attending to the fact that "God's Spirit is given to all the faithful and not only to those in positions of hierarchical office" not only impacts one's understanding of conscience but, more broadly, raises normative considerations regarding authority. The sacramentality of the church, she cautions, does not insulate ecclesiology from questions of justice.[38]

Outside observers have perceived the diverse manifestations of discipleship flowing from some of these underlying differences. In the aftermath of the health care act's passage, *New York Times* columnist Nicholas Kristof detailed accounts of the "two Catholic churches" he encounters through his international travels: one is the rigid, all-male Vatican hierarchy obsessed with dogma and rules (that he deems "out of touch"), and the other supports life-saving aid organizations and operates "superb

---

[35] David E. DeCosse "Conscience Issue Separates Catholic Moral Camps" *National Catholic Reporter*, November 10, 2009.

[36] According to the Catholic tradition, conscience entails a three-part structure involving conscience as innate capacity, process, and judgment.

[37] DeCosse, "Conscience Issue Separates Catholic Moral Camps."

[38] Anne E. Patrick, SNJM, "Authority, Women, and the Church: Reconsidering the Relationship," in Patrick J. Howell, SJ, and Gary Chamberlain, *Empowering Authority: The Charisms of Episcopacy and Primacy in the Church Today* (Kansas City, MO: Sheed & Ward, 1990), 17–33, at 17.

schools that provide needy children an escalator out of poverty." He highlighted the Maryknolls' work in Central America and the Cabrini Sisters' work in Africa, concluding, after a terrifying ride visiting AIDS orphans in Swaziland with an American nun with a "lead foot," that "the very coolest people in the world today may be nuns." Kristof's bifurcated depiction may resonate with those who prefer to retreat to either the hierarchical or the "grassroots" versions.[39] Yet Gaillardetz fittingly lifts up the unity of the faith that Catholics profess, concluding that there must arise a place where "the doctrinal teaching of the bishops and the dirt-stained testimony of those who experience God's grace on inner-city streets, in prisons, hospitals and immigration advocacy centers, can meet."[40] Discerning the promptings of the Spirit in the church and world demands that these different routes not only encounter but mutually inform—and transform—one another.

NETWORK's Operational Witness

This understanding of conscientious discernment reflects the particular models of authority women religious have adopted in response to Vatican II. Schneiders characterizes these models as marked by "egalitarianism, collegiality, . . . dialogical procedures, [and] discernment processes."[41] NETWORK has long embodied such consultative processes. In December of 1971, forty-seven religious sisters from a variety of orders and twenty-one states convened in Washington, DC, to discuss organizing a network of women religious concerned about public policy issues. At that meeting, they decided to form a network for political education and action and with that step became the first registered Catholic social justice lobby in the United States.[42] From its origins, the group set out to be "women-led, linked to the economically exploited, rooted in the social justice tradition of the church, reflective of experience, centered around working collaboratively, and dedicated to educating and organizing grass-roots

[39] Nicholas Kristof, "A Church Mary Can Love," *New York Times*, April 18, 2010, WK11.

[40] Thomas C. Fox, "Women Religious Experiences Have Implications for Entire Church."

[41] Schneiders, "Tasks of Those Who Choose the Prophetic Lifestyle."

[42] Patrick Connor, SVD, "NETWORK, A Politician's Nightmare," *Word* (publication of the Divine Missionary Brothers) 50, no. 1 (January 2001): 24–25, at 24.

constituencies for political lobbying."[43] That mission accurately describes the group's work forty years later. Today NETWORK educates, lobbies, and organizes to influence federal legislation to promote economic and social justice, as the health care reform example illustrates.[44]

In order to lobby for public policies that will enable all people to have their basic human needs met, the organization strives to be in solidarity with the economically exploited.[45] Hence, Catholic social teaching helps NETWORK to describe its vision of a just society and analyze policy issues, yet it also influences how they construct lives together, modeling within their organization what they want to see in the world. For example, NETWORK's participative decision making and its collaborative management style are marked by power sharing rather than domination. Also, the uniformity of staff salaries (regardless of position, time served, or education level) emphasizes the fact that the work that everyone does enhances the achievement of the mission. Reminiscent of *Justitia in Mundo's* maxim that those who speak about justice must first be just, NETWORK's efforts to institutionally model its values stand in contrast to the internal challenges authoritarianism or sexism can pose to Catholic social witness. NETWORK regularly presents priority issues and then polls its membership to determine on which issues they would like to see NETWORK focus its energies. This "consultation/affirmation process" holds significance as a means of ensuring that NETWORK both represents the concerns of its members and lives out its commitment to collaboration and participation. The organization also works assiduously to get input from people who are poor, especially when drafting position papers.[46] NETWORK's connection

[43] Ibid., 25.

[44] As it approaches its fortieth anniversary, NETWORK's advocacy areas (beyond health care) focus upon economic justice, immigration reform, peacemaking, ecology, ex-offenders, and problems facing the Gulf Coast region in the wake of hurricanes Katrina and Rita and the Deepwater Horizon oil spill. See http://www.networklobby.org/issues (accessed April 25, 2011).

[45] 1998 NETWORK membership survey, archives available at NETWORK's national office, Washington, DC. For a more detailed analysis of NETWORK's history and theological self-understanding prior to the health care advocacy profiled here, see my *Prophetic and Public: The Social Witness of U.S. Catholicism* (Washington, DC: Georgetown University Press, 2006), chaps. 4–5.

[46] For example, NETWORK gathered economists, ethicists, and social workers, along with staff and participant representatives, from four direct service agencies to generate their "Economic Equity Statement."

to service agencies operated by women religious and to its membership
helps to keep them in touch with those "on the receiving end" to facilitate
such participation, as illustrated in their three-part TANF Watch Program
over the past fifteen years, in which they interviewed thousands of patrons
in various emergency facilities around the country to examine the short-
and long-term effects of the 1996 welfare reform legislation.

Beyond consulting its membership, service providers, and recipients,
NETWORK staff value coalition work, not only strategically but also
theologically, because they perceive God at work in other human rights
movements. Veteran NETWORK lobbyist Catherine Pinkerton, CSJ,
notes NETWORK staffers continually ask, "How do we find God at work
and cooperate with that work of God dancing across the world?"[47] Thus,
their ministry on Capitol Hill is characterized not by a triumphalistic
imposition of Catholic beliefs but rather by a mutual engagement with
an active openness to the presence of God outside of the church and to
learning from the other.

NETWORK understands its ministry as rooted in a prophetic stream
of the Catholic heritage; its history, leadership, and membership situate
NETWORK within broader traditions of women religious putting their
bodies and their financial resources in support of their rhetoric—whether
as pioneers in establishing hospital networks and schools or in investor
responsibility.[48] Schneiders characterizes the ministerial identity of women
religious as modeled on Jesus' prophetic words and work, bearing witness
to God's compassion in concrete contexts. In her words, "Prophecy is
about telling the absolute future of God, what Jesus called the Reign of
God, into the present. The prophet is immersed in the life of the people
in a particular place and time and is commissioned by God to interpret
that situation in the light of God's dream for this people and the whole
of humanity." As a result, she notes, women religious search out those
places—often on the margins of the church and society—"where the need
for the Gospel is greatest," and there they preach the Gospel "freely as

[47] Personal interview with Catherine Pinkerton, CSJ, Washington, DC, July 23, 2002.

[48] Approximately one in six hospital patients in the United States was treated in a
facility founded by Catholic women religious in 2005. Thomas C. Fox, "Women Religious
Honored by University of San Francisco," *National Catholic Reporter*, December 18, 2010,
available at http://ncronline.org/news/women-religious/women-religious-honored
-university-san-francisco (accessed April 27, 2011).

Jesus commissioned his itinerant, full time companions to do."[49] Prophets are not merely disruptive iconoclasts; rather, they are attuned to the divine pathos and thereby seek to console and defend those who suffer.[50]

Former NETWORK director Kathy Thornton similarly articulates NETWORK's ministries as fostering the fullness of life that Jesus came to inaugurate for all people in the here and now. She reflects that the organization's founders viewed their efforts as influencing society's structures and systems so that they do not exclude new ways to bring about God's reign here on earth, or a movement toward that vision.[51] Hence, as they take up the Christian call to announce and instantiate "release to the captives" and "freedom to the oppressed," NETWORK stands in a prophetic tradition that "empower[s] people to a practice of justice that will make God's compassion the normal state of affairs." Whereas some insist the "sausage making" of legislative advocacy is the last place such lofty efforts belong, NETWORK staff members perceive politics as "a ministry of justice," not a compromising enterprise to be avoided.[52] Prophetic ministries in any venue risk posing a threat, as the aftermath of the health care debate illustrates. As Schneiders puts it, "It is precisely because the prophet is addressing the actual situation, publicly lamenting current oppression as contrary to God's will, and energizing real people to imagine and begin to strive for an alternate future, that the prophet is often perceived as dangerous to the status quo."[53]

[49] Sandra M. Schneiders, "We've Given Birth to a New Form of Religious Life," *National Catholic Reporter*, February 27, 2009, available at http://ncronline.org/news/women/weve-given-birth-new-form-religious-life (accessed October 8, 2010).

[50] See Abraham J. Heschel, *The Prophets*, 2 vols. (New York: Harper and Row, 1962), I, 24; and Catherine E. Clifford and Richard R. Gaillardetz, "Re-Imagining the Ecclesial/Prophetic Vocation of the Theologian," *Proceedings of the Sixty-Fifth Annual Convention of the Catholic Theological Society of America* 65 (2010): 43–62 at 48–49.

[51] Personal interview with Kathy Thornton, RSM, Washington, DC, July 26, 2002.

[52] Interviews with NETWORK staff members, July 26, 2002.

[53] Sandra M. Schneiders, "Religious Life as Prophetic Life Form," part 1 of a five-part essay, *National Catholic Reporter*, January 4, 2010, available at http://ncronline.org/news/women/religious-life-prophetic-life-form (accessed October 8, 2010). She notes later in the series, "Jesus' prophetic ministry of word and work was not merely a threat to the particular domination systems of Rome and Jerusalem. . . . It was this definitive subversion of the violent human way of running the world by God's loving way of luring creation, including us, toward union with Godself that was the ultimate threat Jesus represented." Schneiders, "Tasks of Those Who Choose the Prophetic Lifestyle."

Conclusions: Living inside Hope

Internecine Catholic divides cannot be reduced to fault lines between bishops and nuns. Nor do the women religious ministering within the United States today comprise a monolith; their diversity exceeds their different congregations' charisms, ministries, theologies, and members' idiosyncrasies. Furthermore, the divergent ecclesiologies implicit in the disagreements outlined above, whether understood in terms of sect and church or more nuanced descendants, predate and far exceed the US health care reform debate.[54] Ilio Delio, OSF, diagnoses the internal divergences between those women religious perceived as embracing modernity and those who emphasize communion through a clear Catholic identity (Timothy Radcliffe's *Concilium* or Kingdom Catholics and *Communio* Catholics[55]) as rooted in fear of change rather than in different interpretations of Vatican II.[56] Drawing upon Pierre Teilhard de Chardin's understanding of the universe as the coming to be of Christ and of adoration as seeing the depths of divine love in ordinary realities and loving what we see, Delio reflects upon the evolution of women religious in recent decades: "The women of LCWR have risked their lives in the pursuit of authentic Incarnation and have proclaimed prophetically that the love of God cannot be exterminated or suppressed. . . . Congregations may die out, but the paths inscribed in history by the women religious of Vatican II are nothing less than the evolutionary shoots of a new future. [As] part of the evolutionary process . . . isolated structures must give way to more complex unions."[57] Whereas the future of religious life as presently constituted may face challenges, the very attributes explored above, from posture to practices, augur an enduring and fertile future for the charisms of many congregations.

[54] As Finn argues, "Those who take a more sectarian position might have refused to endorse the compromise embodied in the Hyde restrictions out of a false sense of moral purity. But ours is a church, not a sect. The Catholic Church engages the secular world in order to transform it; it does not simply judge the world sinful and walk away." Finn, "Uncertainty Principle."

[55] See Timothy Radcliffe, OP, *What Is the Point of Being a Christian?* (London: Burns and Oates/Continuum, 2005).

[56] Delio generally maps the divergence between traditional and progressive religious life onto the Conference of Major Superiors of Women Religious (CMSWR) and Leadership Conference of Women Religious (LCWR), respectively. Ilia Delio, OSF, "Confessions of a Modern Nun: The Vatican Visitation Prompts Reflection on a Religious Divide," *America*, October 12, 2009.

[57] Ibid.

The prophetic obedience and creative fidelity exhibited by women religious profiled here reflect Catholic feminism's bridging of moral objectivity and universal values with an "inductive and communal model of reasoned moral insight." Rather than posing a threat to Christian faith or pluralism, this tradition can help save genuine feminist concerns from relativism and restore public discourse in the wake of postmodern critiques.[58] Bringing the concrete suffering of those marginalized into moral discernment and policy formulation, Catholic feminists both stake a principled religious claim and invite collaboration. As women exhibit bold and humble compassion rather than fearful legalism, they narrate the Christian story. For women religious faithfully minister with undocumented immigrants, with torture victims, with the homeless, on Capitol Hill, and "in myriad other situations in which there [are] no easy answers and the stakes for real people [are] as high as they were for the woman taken in adultery to whom Jesus proclaimed the Reign of God as compassion redefining justice."[59]

Inside the Beltway and in the trenches, women religious seek life for the vulnerable in the face of significant risk. NETWORK and the women religious profiled here provide models of personalist conscience formation, of creative fidelity that transcends narrow notions of acquiescence, and of collaborative leadership that counters hierarchical power dynamics. Their example witnesses to an understanding of agency that surpasses obedience to law or authority and that is rooted in discernment and responsibility.

Hallie is a character in my favorite Barbara Kingsolver novel, *Animal Dreams*, who at one point in the story corresponds with her sister while working in the cotton fields of Nicaragua. She tries to explain to Codi (in Tucson, AZ) why she is truly not some "martyr off saving the world." Hallie writes: "The least you can do in your life is to figure out what you hope for and the most you can do is live inside that hope. Not admire it from a distance but live right in it, under its roof." Hallie's is a not a

[58] Lisa Sowle Cahill, *Sex, Gender and Christian Ethics* (Cambridge: Cambridge University Press, 1996), 12. See also Cristina Traina, *Feminism and the Natural Law: The End of Anathemas* (Washington, DC: Georgetown University Press, 1999), 158. These elements of Catholic natural law feminism are cited together in James F. Keenan, SJ, *A History of Catholic Moral Theology in the Twentieth Century: From Confessing Sins to Liberating Consciences* (New York: Continuum, 2010), 189.

[59] Schneiders, "Tasks of Those Who Choose the Prophetic Lifestyle."

religious or eschatological hope in any explicit or thematized sense—she names "enough to eat, enough to go around, the chance for children to grow up to be neither the destroyers nor the destroyed." Her letter continues, "Right now I'm living in that hope, running down its hallway and touching the walls on both sides. I can't tell you how good it feels."[60] Amid temptations to retreat into cynicism or despair, or to advance tentatively down safe and well-trodden avenues alone, may the women we have considered herein embolden us to inhabit hope, hope both in what is seen and in what is unseen (2 Cor 4:18).

---

[60] Barbara Kingsolver, *Animal Dreams* (New York: HarperCollins, 1990), 299.

The Beloved Community

Transforming Spaces for Social Change and for Cosmopolitan Citizenship

Rosemary P. Carbine, Whittier College

Public life is often envisioned as a civil society arena of reasoned debate among citizens about socially significant issues that reaches for consensus about the common good.[1] However, as the mid-twentieth-century United States Civil Rights Movement demonstrates, US public life construed under this model of deliberative democracy fails to realize its egalitarian vision of communicative practices in civil society; instead, it operates in an exclusionary way with roots in race, gender, class, and other social constructs of what determines rational discourse, who counts as a political actor, and what defines the common good. Currently, US immigration reform activists within the New Sanctuary Movement contest an increasingly exclusionary antidemocratic trend in US public life based on ethnic, religious, national, and other identity-marking criteria.

---

[1] In Catholic social thought, the common good encompasses "the sum total of social conditions which allow people, either as groups or as individuals, to reach their fulfill-ment." It thus opposes a rugged individualistic or exclusivist group notion of rights and responsibilities. See Pastoral Constitution on the Church in the Modern World (*Gaudium et Spes*), December, 7 1965, in *Vatican Council II: The Basic Sixteen Documents: Constitutions, Decrees, Declarations*, ed. Austin Flannery, OP (Northport, NY: Costello Publishing Co., 1996), no. 26; and Donald Kerwin, "Rights, the Common Good, and Sovereignty in Ser-vice of the Human Person," in *And You Welcomed Me: Migration and Catholic Social Teaching*, ed. Donald Kerwin and Jill Marie Gerschutz (Lanham, MD: Rowman and Littlefield, 2009), 93–121, esp. 101–5.

Speaking of US immigrants as "undocumented workers" or "illegal aliens" reduces persons to their labor and often to singular racial, ethnic, and national identities of citizenship guarded by military or metaphoric territorial borders. Religious groups in both movements make religio-political interventions to critically rethink and remake status quo notions of political community and belonging. Womanist studies of the black church as a mediating institution in early African American women's movements as well as in the Civil Rights Movement[2] and feminist studies of subaltern counterpublics that counteract a hegemonic US public sphere[3] provide theoretical and theological grist for the prophetic mill to interpret the ways that both movements challenge and reconceptualize political community—and thereby imagine and begin to enact an alternative, radical democratic space and membership in it. As these studies demonstrate, subordinated groups marshal religious resources to raise collective consciousness about social injustice and simultaneously remake a hegemonic public/political sphere by creating, embodying, and momentarily modeling alternative publics with a more just vision and practice of our shared life together. In keeping with these studies, twentieth- and twenty-first-century US social justice movements, such as the Civil Rights Movement and the New Sanctuary Movement, resemble such mediating institutions and counterpublics because they engage in prophetic praxis, relying on religious resources to challenge—both rhetorically and actively—an unjust political status quo as well as to reimagine and remold it for more just possibilities.

The term "prophetic" holds much potential for critical theory in religious studies to interpret both historical and contemporary US religio-political movements and engagement for social change. Prophetic work defined by biblical scholars[4] involves religiously inspired efforts to both criticize an unjust political status quo and simultaneously imagine as well as begin to actualize a more just alternative possible future. Moreover, prophetic practices within the Christian tradition often draw on Christology as a theological justification to critically engage with and constructively

[2] Evelyn Brooks Higginbotham, *Righteous Discontent: The Women's Movement in the Black Baptist Church, 1880–1920* (Cambridge, MA: Harvard University Press, 1993), 7–13.

[3] Nancy Fraser, *Justice Interruptus: Critical Reflections on the "Post-Socialist" Condition* (New York: Routledge, 1997), 81–82.

[4] Walter Brueggemann, *The Prophetic Imagination*, 2nd ed. (Minneapolis: Fortress Press, 2001), 1–19.

reshape US public life. Following more contemporary political theology,[5] imitating Jesus functions as a christological praxis, or "a Christian theatrics," that parodies the countercultural life, ministry, and death of Jesus. Just as Jesus wielded the cross for the purpose of life rather than for imperial Roman purposes of punishment, repression, and death, so too US Christian social justice movements emulate the way that Jesus "steals the show" by subverting a state-backed culture of oppression at the risk of retribution. Both the CRM and the NSM illustrate biblical and theological understandings of prophetic praxis in their respective attempts to build the beloved community through various modes of public engagement, either by taking nonviolent direct collective action or by providing hospitality.

Using an interpretive lens shaped by feminist, womanist, and biblical studies cited above, this essay explores the role of prophetic vision and praxis in US social justice movements that pursue a more just public life. Drawing on some salient literature and episodes from the US Civil Rights Movement (CRM) and the New Sanctuary Movement (NSM), this essay examines underlying religious claims and practices that support prophetic work in both movements, especially to transform political and religious spaces, such as the National Mall or local churches nationwide, into counterspaces that edge toward a more just society and citizenship in it. More specifically, this essay examines the emergence of the notion of the beloved community in the Civil Rights Movement and the reemergence of this notion in the New Sanctuary Movement, with particular attention to how both movements appeal to this religious rhetoric as a means to inform and motivate a prophetic vision and praxis that ultimately transform political and ecclesial spaces into alternative models of more just political community and membership.

The Civil Rights Movement

Martin Luther King Jr. (1929–68) recounted in sermons, speeches, letters, and other political writings the brutal realities of African American life under US legalized segregation from the late nineteenth century through the mid-twentieth century.[6] To educate the American and wider

[5] Mark Lewis Taylor, *The Executed God: The Way of the Cross in Lockdown America* (Minneapolis: Fortress Press, 2001).

[6] In his 1963 "Letter from a Birmingham Jail," King described major racist episodes and experiences in the African American community with an increasingly breathless

global public about the sociopolitical and economic racist realities of segregated social institutions during the US Jim Crow era, King and CRM activists utilized nonviolent direct collective action to "dramatize" or perform the social sin of racism and its attendant "evils of our society" on the local and national public stage.[7] CRM activists engaged in prophetic protests at personal and collective risk of jail, beatings, and even death. And the state's systemic, physical, and violent retaliation to such protests—manifested in the beatings of the freedom riders in 1961, in the police dogs and fire hoses used against Student Nonviolent Coordinating Committee (SNCC) demonstrators in Birmingham in 1963, and the police pushback against voting rights marchers from Selma to Montgomery in 1965—served the pedagogical purpose of raising public awareness about US racism and the state's means of enacting it. These events aroused the public conscience as well as garnered presidential support for African American citizenship rights,[8] especially the 1964 Civil Rights Act and the 1965 Voting Rights Act.

King drew on and modified a traditional Christology of redemptive suffering to theologically articulate the reasons for and the risks entailed in nonviolent protests.[9] The cross provided a religious motivation for boycotts, sit-ins, marches, and other protests and for their goal of achieving an egalitarian society.[10] In line with this traditional theology, King stated in his writings on nonviolent methods of social change that the CRM identified with and emulated the "sacrificial spirit" of early Christian

---

rhythm in order to defend the CRM and its aim to regain African Americans' God-given and civil rights. King, "Letter from the Birmingham Jail (1963)," in *I Have a Dream: Writings and Speeches that Changed the World*, ed. James Melvin Washington (San Francisco: Harper Collins, 1992), 88–89.

[7] Ibid., 86; cf. King, "Nonviolence: The Only Road to Freedom (1966)," in *I Have a Dream*, 131.

[8] King, "The Social Organization of Nonviolence," in *I Have a Dream*, 53.

[9] Roger Gottlieb, *Joining Hands: Politics and Religion Together for Social Change* (Cambridge, MA: Westview Perseus Press, 2002), 101–28. For a more extensive study, see Brian E. Brandt, "The Theology of the Cross and the Ethic of Redemptive Suffering in the Life and Work of Martin Luther King, Jr." (PhD diss., Loyola University of Chicago, 2002).

[10] Joanne Marie Tyrell, *Power in the Blood? The Cross in the African American Experience* (Maryknoll, NY: Orbis Books, 1998), 77–83, 96; and Charles Marsh, *The Beloved Community: How Faith Shapes Social Justice, from the Civil Rights Movement to Today* (New York: Basic Books, 2005), 45.

martyrs[11] to "put an end to suffering by willingly suffering themselves."[12] However, King revised this traditional theology of redemptive suffering to avoid an uncritical acceptance of African American suffering from racist-based retaliatory violence as in itself christic. To do so, King reflected on the cross as a possible outcome of nonviolent direct action: "Stand[ing] up and protest[ing] against injustice . . . will mean suffering, . . . going to jail, . . . fill[ing] up the jail houses, . . . even . . . death."[13] As James Cone contends, the cross symbolized divine agency in reconciling broken relationships as well as "an inherent part of the Christian life in the struggle for freedom."[14] Nonviolent direct collective action, then, does not reinscribe racism, negate the agency of CRM activists by reducing them to victims, or eschew the pain of activists or the culpability of state and local perpetrators of these horrific acts. On the contrary, nonviolent direct action highlights and resists the evils of racism, reinforces the agency of activists who participated in preparatory workshops for such protests, and underscores the responsibility of local and national actors and systems in perpetrating and perpetuating racist violence. As later feminist and womanist theological criticisms of redemptive suffering have argued, enduring personal or social suffering is in itself not christic but carries christic implications as a costly consequence of taking prophetic action.[15]

In addition to confronting a racist status quo by reenacting and resisting it on a public stage in a christic way, major demonstrations within the

[11] King, "Letter," 97.

[12] King, "Nonviolence," 134, cf. 129–30. According to Gottlieb, redemptive suffering led to limited victories for the CRM because this tactic lacked its putative moral purpose; it mobilized collective sociopolitical and economic pressure to empower African Americans rather than sparked a *metanoia* in US morality. See Gottlieb, *Joining Hands*, 116–17, 119, 124.

[13] King, "Facing the Challenge of a New Age (1957)," in *I Have a Dream*, 26.

[14] James H. Cone, *Martin, Malcolm, and America: A Dream or a Nightmare* (Maryknoll, NY: Orbis Books, 1991), 127–28.

[15] Rosemary P. Carbine, "Contextualizing the Cross for the Sake of Subjectivity," in *Cross-Examinations: Readings on the Meaning of the Cross Today*, ed. Marit A. Trelstad (Minneapolis: Fortress Press, 2006), 91–107, 287–90; and Arnfridur Gudmundsdottir, *Meeting God on the Cross: Christ, the Cross, and the Feminist Critique* (New York: Oxford University Press, 2010), 124, 148–49. I thank Rosetta Ross for probing the points in this paragraph with me when I delivered an earlier version of this essay in the Theology of Martin Luther King Jr. Consultation at the American Academy of Religion annual meeting, October 30–November 1, 2010.

CRM, such as the 1963 March on Washington, served as prophetic action because they incarnated, at least fleetingly, a more fully participatory democracy, a political instance of what King envisioned as the beloved community. The beloved community offers a rich and expansive account of King's political vision. In King's theological terms, the CRM aimed to eliminate segregation through faith-based prophetic social witness, that is, nonviolent direct action, and to establish the beloved community, a racially reconciled society anchored in the theological moorings of divine justice, agape or altruistic love, and shared power, or what King called alliance politics, that is, the ability of multiple groups in solidarity to effect sociopolitical and economic change through nonviolent action.[16] In his study of the origins and historical legacy of this term, Charles Marsh chronicles the emergence of the beloved community in King's writings during the 1955 Montgomery bus boycott.[17] King continually reminded CRM activists that nonviolent direct action accomplishes the political goal of disobeying and repealing unjust segregation laws that diminish human dignity, and the religious goal of converting an oppressive society: it "is merely a means to awaken a sense of shame in the oppressor and challenge his false sense of superiority. But the end is reconciliation, the end is redemption, the end is the creation of the beloved community."[18] One year after the bus boycott, King spoke at a gathering of the Institute on Nonviolence and Social Change at Holt Street Baptist Church. In this 1956 speech, "Facing the Challenge of a New Age," King brooked two worlds and tried to usher in a world that globalized the beloved community into "a new world of geographic togetherness" characterized by communion, peace, distributive justice, and respect for human dignity.[19]

King further developed and elaborated the notion of the beloved community in subsequent civil rights campaigns. During the March on Washington in 1963, which addressed racial and economic inequalities faced by poor blacks and whites, King joined religious and constitutional principles of human dignity and equality and thereby reconceptualized US public life to embrace African American citizenship rights. In his renowned "I Have a Dream" speech, King relied on biblical prophetic

[16] King, "Social Organization," 52–53; cf. "Black Power Defined," in *I Have a Dream*, 159, 161–62.

[17] Marsh, *The Beloved Community*, 11–50.

[18] King, "New Age," 22.

[19] Ibid., 19, 27.

visions of justice from Amos and Isaiah to reclaim and radicalize US constitutional citizenship rights, and thus advocated for African American political equality.[20] Moreover, in his last sermon during a Memphis sanitation workers' strike in 1968, King reinterpreted the exodus story and mapped it onto overcoming contemporary racist and economic inequalities that similarly plagued whites and blacks. In that sermon, "I See the Promised Land," he closed with an almost mystical vision of the kingdom of God, of the beloved community, stylizing himself as another Moses on the mountaintop looking at but not yet reaching the promised land of universal human equality.[21] King avoided political theories of gradual, inevitable progress to instantiate the good society, the beloved community, and he also eschewed an otherworldly eschatology that encourages a complacent, status quo–supporting church with an irrelevant ministry.[22] In using this phrase, King fused Social Gospel idealism with Niebuhrian Christian realism[23] to advocate for African American rights in a world embedded in the social sin of racism. He opted for and promoted a realized eschatology that involved human response to and cooperation with God as "coworkers" in local and global freedom movements in order to actualize the beloved community, a this-worldly just society modeled on divine love and justice.[24] In his 1967 sermon against the Vietnam War at Riverside Church in New York City and in his 1967 presidential address to the Southern Christian Leadership Conference (SCLC), King emphasized divine love present in all world religions as a moral basis for a more expansive scope of the beloved community that paralleled his

---

[20] King, "I Have a Dream (1963)," in *I Have a Dream*, 102–6.

[21] King, "I See the Promised Land (1968)," in *I Have a Dream*, 203.

[22] King, "Letter," 92, 97, and "Promised Land," 198.

[23] In his 1968 sermon "The Drum Major Instinct," King characterized the human condition, similar to Niebuhr, as beset by a rugged individualism that severs social relationships and responsibilities. He observed the dangers of this egoistic instinct, in which individuals, the church, and the nation succumb to a narrow parochial contest for power. Also similar to Niebuhr, resolving this individualistic instinct for King involved both emulating the life-ministry of Jesus and strengthening African American democratic power and institutions. See King, "The Drum Major Instinct (1968)," in *I Have a Dream*, 180–92.

[24] King, "Letter," 92, and "Promised Land," 194–95. King's theology of social change is rooted in theological anthropology. Humanity enjoys the capacity to be coworkers with God in reshaping society based on creation in the *imago Dei*. See Richard Wills, *Martin Luther King Jr. and the Image of God* (New York: Oxford University Press, 2009), 139–64.

increasingly widening structural analysis of and resistance to "the triple evils" of racism, poverty, and militarism.[25]

Ultimately, the beloved community in the CRM carried ecclesiological implications for US public life, standing in as a secular term for the theological notion of the kingdom of God, and for a political vision of restored American democratic life. It both captured and constructed his vision of redemptive social change in a racist society: an eschatological hope in divine justice that undergirds rather than undoes human efforts to realize that justice, at least partly, through moral and spiritual forces of transformational love. The beloved community, as utilized by King, pointed out the antidemocratic, sinful nature of American society and was partly instantiated by resistance to that society via boycotts, marches, and strikes. In other words, these nonviolent direct action demonstrations not only countered a racist status quo but also embodied what Roger Gottlieb calls a praxis of "world making," or constructing a more just alternative shared common life.[26] Specifically, the March on Washington transformed whitewashed (architecturally and socially) public spaces, especially the National Mall, into alternative religio-political spaces that all too briefly enacted racial equality and solidarity.

This religious rhetoric and praxis associated with the beloved community in the US Civil Rights Movement later motivated the prophetic praxis of the New Sanctuary Movement. Religious groups involved in immigrant advocacy movements also serve as a prophetic leverage point both to challenge dominant notions of political subjectivity and public life and to perform an eschatological ideal of the beloved community— which in turn both justifies religious dissent from an exclusionary public life and performs a religiously based just alternative to it.

The New Sanctuary Movement

The NSM began in spring 2007 after an initial meeting of representatives from eighteen cities, twelve religious traditions, and seven interdenominational organizations in Washington, DC.[27] But the NSM traces its

---

[25] See King, "A Time to Break Silence (1967)," in *I Have a Dream*, 150, and "Where Do We Go from Here? (1967)," in *I Have a Dream*, 176–77.

[26] Gottlieb, *Joining Hands*, 4–6, 9, 19–21.

[27] Louis Sahagun, "L.A. Church in Forefront of Sanctuary Movement," *Los Angeles Times*, March 23, 2007; Sahagun, "Churches Unite to Provide Immigrant Sanctuary,"

origins further back to activist churches and synagogues that sheltered and supported Central American civil war refugees in the 1980s.[28] Between the 1980s and the 1990s, nearly three thousand churches, synagogues, and Quaker meetings in Tucson, Arizona; San Francisco, California; and throughout the United States declared their communities public sanctuaries for nearly one million refugees seeking political asylum from civil war–torn Central American countries.[29] These faith communities drew on biblical tradition, classical Greco-Roman and medieval European law, and US abolitionist movements to form the Sanctuary Movement (SM), a movement based on religious convictions about practicing civil disobedience against unjust US immigration laws, which morphed later into a civil initiative to uphold the US government's asylum laws.[30] The US government infiltrated the movement in 1985 via an undercover investigation and indicted sixteen and eventually convicted eight sanctuary workers on seventy-one counts of conspiracy to transport and harbor (conceal or shelter) illegal immigrants.[31]

Latin American liberation theologian Jon Sobrino justified the SM on theological, ethical, and practical grounds: to encounter the divine

---

Los Angeles Times, March 28, 2007; Ysmael D. Fonseca, "The Catholic Church's Obligation to Serve the Stranger in Defiance of State Immigration Laws," *Notre Dame Journal of Law, Ethics, and Public Policy* 23, no. 1 (2009): 291–316.

[28] Inspired by the faith-based Sanctuary Movement, nearly one hundred "sanctuary cities" across the US have passed ordinances since the 1980s that limit the use of local and municipal officials, especially police, in immigration law enforcement. The history of the city Sanctuary Movement with a particular focus on San Francisco is explored by Jennifer Ridgley, "Cities of Refuge: Immigration Enforcement, Police, and the Insurgent Genealogies of Citizenship in US Sanctuary Cities," *Urban Geography* 29, no. 1 (2008): 53–77.

[29] For the history of this movement, see Gary MacEoin, "A Brief History of the Sanctuary Movement," in *Sanctuary: A Resource Guide for Understanding and Participating in the Central American Refugees' Struggle*, ed. Gary MacEoin (San Francisco: Harper & Row, 1985), 14–29; Ignatius Bau, *This Ground Is Holy: Church Sanctuary and Central American Refugees* (New York and Mahwah, NJ: Paulist Press, 1985); Susan Bibler Coutin, *The Culture of Protest: Religious Activism and the U.S. Sanctuary Movement* (Boulder, CO: Westview Press, 1993); and Hilary Cunningham, *God and Caesar at the Rio Grande: Sanctuary and the Politics of Religion* (Minneapolis: University of Minnesota Press, 1995). See also Pamela Begaj, "An Analysis of Historical and Legal Sanctuary and a Cohesive Approach to the Current Movement," *John Marshall Law Review* 42, no. 1 (2008): 135–63.

[30] Bau, *This Ground Is Holy*, 124–61; Renny Golden, "Sanctuary and Women," *Journal of Feminist Studies in Religion* 2, no. 1 (Spring 1986): 131–49, esp. 133–34; cf. Begaj, "An Analysis of Historical and Legal Sanctuary," 137–41.

[31] Bau, *This Ground Is Holy*, 83–87.

in supporting the life of refugees in the face of death; to provide safe haven for refugees who fled governments and wars funded by US Cold War foreign policies to curtail the spread of communism in the region; and to model a utopia or alternative just form of public life, grounded in solidarity, hospitality, and the inalienable rights of all citizens in a democracy.[32] The SM's central goal was to build solidarity with Central American political refugees and thereby denounce US immigration policies that denied asylum to those refugees as well as deported them at the risk of further persecution.[33]

While the SM provided asylum for Latin American political and wartime refugees, the NSM focuses on Latin American economic migrants seeking to improve their families' lives. Current anti-immigrant attitudes in the US are fed and spread by nativist and nationalist opponents of economic migration.[34] Because immigrants are defined mainly by socioeconomic, political, and legal constructions of US citizenship,

---

[32] Jon Sobrino, trans. Walter Petry Jr., "Sanctuary: A Theological Analysis," *Cross Currents* 38, no. 2 (Summer 1988): 164–72; cf. Miguel De La Torre, *Trails of Hope and Terror: Testimonies on Immigration* (Maryknoll, NY: Orbis Books, 2009), 11–13.

[33] Golden, "Sanctuary and Women," 131–32, 143, 146; cf. Hilary Cunningham, "Sanctuary and Sovereignty: Church and State along the US-Mexico Border," *Journal of Church and State* 40, no. 2 (1998): 371–86, esp. 377.

[34] Although the 1952 and 1965 immigration acts overturned nineteenth- and twentieth-century race-based criteria in US immigration policy, and although the 1980 Refugee Act removed the link between foreign policy and US immigration policy, nativism and civic nationalism have contributed to US restrictionist immigration policies since the mid-1980s. Nativists focus on race, ethnicity, religion, and other inherited attributes to define US national identity, and thus they often oppose birthright citizenship for children of undocumented immigrants, which runs contrary to the Fourteenth Amendment to the US Constitution. See Donald Kerwin, "Toward a Catholic Vision of Nationality," *Notre Dame Journal of Law, Ethics, and Public Policy* 23, no. 1 (2009): 197–207, esp. 197–99. The nativist political agenda underlies repeated but eventually tabled bills in the US House of Representatives (H.R. 1940 in 2007, H.R. 1868 in 2009) to contravene the US Constitution and eliminate birthright citizenship. Conservative civic nationalists ground US national identity in shared ideological values related to religion (Christianity), language (English), European heritage (such as the Protestant work ethic), the rule of law (a.k.a. law and order), and so on. They prioritize assimilation to this definition of American identity and oppose birthright citizenship or paths to citizenship that flout the rule of law. See Kerwin, "Toward a Catholic Vision of Nationality," 199–201. For more on restrictionist immigration policies implemented at the federal and state level after the 9/11 terrorist attacks on the World Trade Center and the Pentagon, see Pierrette Hondagneu-Sotelo, *God's Heart Has No Borders: How Religious Activists Are Working for Immigrant Rights* (Berkeley

"undocumented workers" or "illegal aliens" are all too easily criminally caricatured, stereotyped, and labeled as terrorists, drug dealers, or *reconquistas*[35]who threaten US national security, sovereignty, and economic stability by draining jobs and social services without paying taxes. Such reductive racist and nationalist stereotypes dehumanize immigrant peoples and thereby absolve the US government from legal or ethical responsibility for multiple human rights abuses of immigrants during border crossings, work, workplace raids, arrests, detentions, and deportations.[36] For example, militarizing border fences via Operation Gatekeeper in 1994 and Operation Safeguard in 1995 symbolically secured US borders and assured national sovereignty. However, immigrant crossings shifted from cities like San Diego, California, and Nogales, Arizona, to more treacherous desert and mountain regions of Southern California, Arizona, New Mexico, and Texas, thereby leading to the US-caused tragic human rights crisis of more than three thousand to four thousand and rising immigrant deaths.[37]

But do these fears that spark human rights abuses of economic immigrants hold water? Undocumented workers in low-skilled jobs that account for less than 5 percent of all US jobs do pay income, property, sales, and corporate taxes, alongside their nonreciprocal contributions to

---

and Los Angeles: University of California Press, 2008), 9–13; and Fonseca, "The Catholic Church's Obligation," 300–304.

[35] Motivated by manifest destiny, the US territorial expansionist Mexican-American War (1846–48) concluded with the 1848 Treaty of Guadalupe-Hidalgo, in which the US annexed nearly half of Mexican territory and created the nearly nineteen-hundred-mile southwesterly US border from California to Texas. See De La Torre, *Trails of Hope and Terror*, 9–11.

[36] See Coutin, *The Culture of Protest*, 93–96, 99–102; Miguel De La Torre, "For Immigrants," in *To Do Justice: A Guide for Progressive Christians*, ed. Rebecca Todd Peters and Elizabeth Hinson-Hasty (Louisville: Westminster John Knox Press, 2008), 73–84, esp. 77–80; De La Torre, *Trails of Hope and Terror*, 60–70, 90–91, 109–14; Robert Gittelson, "The Centrists against the Ideologues: What Are the Falsehoods that Divide Americans on the Issue of Comprehensive Immigration Reform?" *Notre Dame Journal of Law, Ethics, and Public Policy* 23, no. 1 (2009): 115–31; Daniel G. Groody, "Crossing the Divide: Foundations of a Theology of Migration and Refugees," *Theological Studies* 70, no. 3 (2009): 638–67, esp. 642–44, 656–57; and Kristin E. Heyer, "Strangers in Our Midst: Day Laborers and Just Immigration Reform," *Political Theology* 9, no. 4 (2008): 425–53, esp. 426–32.

[37] Hondagneu-Sotelo, *God's Heart Has No Borders*, 138–41; De La Torre, *Trails of Hope and Terror*, 14–15.

Social Security, Medicare, and so on, to the extent that their taxes more than offset their use of social services.[38] Moreover, migrant pay performs an important social service in offsetting global poverty. In 2009 the World Bank reported that migrants sent over $414 billion in remittances to their home or sending countries, not accounting for remittances sent through more informal channels.[39] Scholars in sociology, anthropology, and religious studies along with legal and other advocates rely on such statistics to counter recurring populist scapegoating of economic immigrants for US social and economic woes,[40] but without stemming the tide of racist and nationalist xenophobic fears of race, culture, language, and other differences that lead to a dehumanizing belief that "closing the border becomes a strategy to minimize the 'browning' of America."[41]

Building on this prior movement and these ongoing sociopolitical realities, the NSM raises public awareness about immigration reform through prayer vigils, educational literature, and hospitality to immigrant families, and women in particular, by giving them sanctuary in participating US churches. The NSM keeps immigrant families together by advocating (at least in highly profiled cases) for women with US-born and therefore citizen children who have come to signify the urgency of US immigration reform.[42] Both the SM and NSM gained and galvanized public attention around high-profile cases of women and children.[43] Sanctuary workers Stacey Merkt and a Roman Catholic sister, along with

[38] De La Torre, "For Immigrants," 78; De La Torre, *Trails of Hope and Terror*, 61–65; Gittelson, "The Centrists against the Ideologues," 122–26.

[39] Migration Policy Institute, *MPI Data Hub: Migration, Facts, Stats, and Maps*, http://www.migrationinformation.org/datahub/remittances.cfm (accessed September 26, 2010).

[40] Latino/a immigrants and US citizens with Latino/a backgrounds were deported during the Great Depression in the 1920s and during Operation Wetback in the mid-1950s. See De La Torre, *Trails of Hope and Terror*, 42–43.

[41] De La Torre, *Trails of Hope and Terror*, 114, cf. 116–19.

[42] Alexia Salvatierra, "Sacred Refuge," *Sojourners* 36, no. 9 (September/October 2007): 12–20; Sasha Abramsky, "Gimme Shelter," *The Nation* 286, no. 7 (February 25, 2008): 24–25. See the documentary film about the sanctuary of Yolanda and her teenage daughter Anabella at Immanuel Presbyterian Church in Los Angeles, titled *Sanctuary's Daughter*, by Mason Funk and Leanna Creel (Los Angeles: Channel Road Films, in process); the film's trailer is available at http://www.sanctuarysdaughter.com (accessed September 26, 2010).

[43] Justice for migrants in a globalized context increasingly focuses on women and the interface of gender, race, and class in the exploitation of women's sexual, familial, economic, and other forms of labor. See Gemma Tulud Cruz, "Between Identity and

a newspaper reporter, were arrested in 1984 for transporting Salvadoran Brenda Sanchez-Galan and her two-year-old child Bessie Guadalupe from Casa Oscar Romero in San Benito, Texas, to a Lutheran church in San Antonio, Texas.[44] Similarly, the NSM was sparked by three major events related to immigrant advocacy for women and families: rallies in major US cities during spring and summer 2006 to contest US House of Representatives bill H.R. 4437, which criminalized providing basic services (e.g., humanitarian aid and medical or legal services) to undocumented immigrants;[45] the sanctuary of Elvira Arellano in Adalberto United Methodist Church in Chicago between August 2006 and August 2007 to avoid deportation and separation from her US-born son, Saul;[46] and the fragmentation of families during workplace raids in Massachusetts, Nebraska, and Iowa in 2006 and 2007.[47]

The NSM constitutes an interfaith coalition of congregations in nearly thirty-five cities from Los Angeles to New York that provide hospitality in the form of legal, humanitarian, and spiritual aid to undocumented families who face deportation and separation from their US-born citizen children.[48] The NSM is grounded in Christian sacred texts that contain multiple moral injunctions and imperatives not to oppress but to provide institutional and individual hospitality to the accused (Exod 21:12-14;

Security: Theological Implications of Migration in the Context of Globalization," *Theological Studies* 69, no. 2 (June 2008): 357–75.

[44] Bau, *This Ground Is Holy*, 76–79; Golden, "Sanctuary and Women," 143.

[45] Roger Cardinal Mahony, "A Nation That Should Know Better," *Los Angeles Times*, June 1, 2005; "The Gospel vs. H.R. 4437," *New York Times*, March 3, 2006; and "Called by God to Help," *New York Times*, March 22, 2006.

[46] Louis Sahagun, "A Mother's Plight Revives the Sanctuary Movement," *Los Angeles Times*, June 2, 2007. Arellano was arrested and later deported after attending a Catholic Mass and speaking at an immigrant rights rally at Our Lady Queen of Angels in Los Angeles on August, 19, 2007. See Randal C. Archibold, "Illegal Immigrant Advocate for Families Is Deported," *New York Times*, August 21, 2007; N. C. Aizenman and Spencer S. Hsu, "Activist's Arrest Highlights Key Immigrant Issue," *Washington Post*, August 21, 2007.

[47] De La Torre, *Trails of Hope and Terror*, 84–89, and the testimonies by a teacher and a Roman Catholic sister involved in providing sanctuary during those raids in both schools and churches, 95–98, 139–42. See also Kerwin, "Rights, the Common Good, and Sovereignty," 112.

[48] Salvatierra, "Sacred Refuge"; Antonio Olivo, "Illegal Immigrant Sanctuaries Set," *Chicago Tribune*, May 9, 2007; Grace Dyrness and Clara Irazabal, "A Haven for Illegal Immigrants," *Los Angeles Times*, September 2, 2007.

Num 35:10-15; Deut. 4:41-43)[49] and to the alien or stranger, at times with identity (Exod 22:21-23; 23:9; Lev 19:33-34), legal (Deut 10:17-19; 24:17-22), and salvific (Matt 25:35-40; Luke 10:25-37) implications. Jesus' ministry of table fellowship exemplifies such hospitality; Jesus' meals not only signify salvation (Luke 22:30) but also constitute new communities across racially, economically, religiously, and other socially constructed divisive borders (see Luke 7).[50] In addition, papal apostolic constitutions, pontifical councils' instructions, and national bishops' conferences' letters since the mid-twentieth century consistently emphasize hospitality to migrants—whether humanitarian, legal, pastoral, or social services—as central to the praxis of Christian discipleship.[51] To do otherwise not only contributes to unjust structures, ideologies, and actions associated with the social sins of the current US immigration system[52] but also fails to recognize the *imago Dei* or the shared humanity and consequent inalienable human rights that transcend (and in this case transgress) social, political, and national borders. In Catholic social thought, *imago Dei*–based rights—to food, clothing, housing, state of life, family life, education, work, good reputation and conduct in accord with conscience, respect, knowledge, privacy, and freedom, especially of religion (*Gaudium et Spes* 26)—cannot be restricted by socially constructed hierarchies of race, ethnicity, gender, class, sexuality, religion, ability, politics, or nationality.[53]

The NSM's praxis of giving sanctuary is prophetic because it challenges and seeks to transform dominant US notions of public/political life and thereby risks various forms of financial, legal, and religious retribution. Similar to the SM, the US government warned NSM congregations against interfering with federal immigration laws and enforcement,[54] but with different results. Rather than arrest, prosecution, and conviction, the United Church of Christ in Simi Valley, California, was warned by

---

[49] Bau, *This Ground Is Holy*, 124–29; Cunningham, *God and Caesar*, 68–83.

[50] Groody, "Crossing the Divide," 657–58.

[51] Fonseca, "The Catholic Church's Obligation," 295–97; Groody, "Crossing the Divide," 641.

[52] Kristin E. Heyer, "Social Sin and Immigration: Good Fences Make Bad Neighbors," *Theological Studies* 71, no. 2 (June 2010): 410–36, esp. 413–14, 425–29.

[53] De La Torre, "For Immigrants," 82; De La Torre, *Trails of Hope and Terror*, 137; Groody, "Crossing the Divide," 642–48.

[54] James Barron, "Congregations to Give Haven to Immigrants," *New York Times*, May 9, 2007; cf. Audrey Hudson, "Chertoff Warns Meddling 'Sanctuary Cities,'" *Washington Times*, September 6, 2007.

the city not to practice sanctuary and then later was billed (or fined) forty thousand dollars by the city to subsidize police presence at an anti-immigration protest in mid-September 2007. The city effectively restricted and then failed to protect the church's constitutional rights to freely exercise its religious obligations and provide hospitality to women and their families.[55] The US courts have not ruled whether sanctuary is incorporated into the US constitutional right to the freedom of religion protected under the First Amendment.[56] Nonetheless, Christian theology and ethics are centrally (but certainly not only) concerned with encountering God in the stranger (Gen 18; Heb 13:2; Rom 12:9-13), with encountering Christ in providing just hospitality to the stranger (Matt 25:34-35), and with affirming our common humanity and equal dignity: "To welcome the stranger is to acknowledge . . . a human being made in God's image."[57]

Existing ethnographic studies of the NSM in the southwestern US show that the NSM theologies and churches function prophetically both as life-supporting mediating institutions and as life-sustaining counterpublics to the dominant militarist and xenophobic US public square. Faith-based sanctuary movements "compensate for the lack of public institutional mechanisms to protect human rights and care for the well-being of unauthorized journeying migrants."[58] Not only do these churches constitute a substitute sociopolitical body, but in so doing they also offer an alternative, possible model of US public life. For example,

[55] Anna Bakalis, "Simi Valley, Calif., Won't Charge Church for Future Protests," *Ventura County Star*, September 25, 2007; Brent Hopkins and Angie Valencia-Martinez, "Simi Valley Bills Church for Cops' Time at Protest," *Los Angeles Daily News*, September 20, 2007; cf. Ben Daniel, *Neighbor: Christian Encounters with "Illegal" Immigration* (Louisville: Westminster John Knox Press, 2010), 119–32.

[56] See Bau, *This Ground Is Holy*, 90–91, 111–12; and Begaj, "An Analysis of Historical and Legal Sanctuary," 151–55, 161. In the trials of SM workers in the mid-1980s, the judges either barred the defense from presenting any evidence related to the SM's religious freedom and beliefs, dismissed the defense's motion to drop the charges on the grounds that they violated Sanctuary workers' constitutional right to freedom of religion, or ruled that the US government's interests in protecting its borders from criminals, enemies of the state, and the like outranked the religious principles of SM workers. See Begaj, "An Analysis of Historical and Legal Sanctuary," 155–59.

[57] Ana Maria Pineda, "Hospitality," in *Practicing Our Faith: A Way of Life for a Searching People*, ed. Dorothy C. Bass (San Francisco: Jossey-Bass, 1997, 2010), 29–42, esp. 30, 34–35, 39–40; quote at 38.

[58] Jacqueline Maria Hagan, *Migration Miracle: Faith, Hope, and Meaning on the Undocumented Journey* (Cambridge: Harvard University Press, 2008), 83.

252 Section III Women's Witness in Context

the earlier 1980s SM filled the gap created by the US government's failure to abide by national and international refugee laws by developing a "civil initiative" that substituted for the failed US immigration system. SM activists upheld refugee rights by screening, crossing, sheltering, and publicizing the stories of Central American immigrants.[59] Moreover, SM workers stood in solidarity with immigrants when they traveled to various Central American countries and shared their risks of political violence; they also enacted that solidarity in lobbying for and winning US asylum hearings.[60] Also acting as mediating institutions that supply state-withheld services and as counterpublics that model an alternative political order, the NSM assists immigrants with sustaining material, spiritual, and political resources and thus "challenge[s] state institutions and their regulatory activities" of narrow border-based notions of citizenship rights.[61]

Moreover, recent sociological and theological studies show that faith-based immigration reform activists advocate for social inclusion and justice for immigrants and in doing so use religion to forge a counterspace to conventional nation-state–based notions of citizenship and rights.[62] For example, the US and Mexican conferences of Catholic bishops issued a joint pastoral letter in 2003, Strangers No Longer, that affirmed US national sovereignty via the right to control its borders but simultaneously challenged US border protection strategies that violate human dignity and rights, particularly the right to work and to migrate for work within and beyond one's country in order to meet minimum conditions for earning a decent livelihood and for leading a dignified life.[63] Also, annual Latino/a Catholic posada rituals performed at the San Diego–Tijuana border

[59] John Fife in De La Torre, *Trails of Hope and Terror*, 170–75.

[60] Screening refugees by the SM churches unfortunately reinscribed imbalanced power relations between US congregations/citizen-subjects and Central American refugees/noncitizen objects. Also, pigeonholing Central American refugees in the category of the oppressed contravened a main purpose of the SM, namely, solidarity. See this critique in Coutin, *The Culture of Protest*, 107–30, 183–87; cf. Coutin, "The Oppressed, the Suspect, and the Citizen: Subjectivity in Competing Accounts of Political Violence," *Law and Social Inquiry* 26, no. 1 (Winter 2001): 63–94, esp. 63–66, 67–74.

[61] Hagan, *Migration Miracle*, 83.

[62] Hondagneu-Sotelo, *God's Heart Has No Borders*, xi, 8.

[63] Conferencia del Episcopado Mexicano and United States Conference of Catholic Bishops, Strangers No Longer: Together on the Journey of Hope, January 22, 2003, nos. 34–39, available at http://www.usccb.org/issues-and-action/human-life-and-dignity /immigration/strangers-no-longer-together-on-the-journey-of-hope.cfm (accessed Septem-

reenact the search of Joseph and Mary for housing in Bethlehem and act as an allegory for the search of immigrants for posada (a shelter) amid rejection, suffering, and death at the US-Mexico border.[64] This ritual both commemorates border deaths and builds solidarity between white Americans, Latino/a Americans, and Mexican peoples through shared hands and gifts across a chain-link border fence that extends into the Pacific Ocean, and in so doing, "symbolic racial-ethnic and denominational borders are crossed."[65] As a counterpublic, this ritual bears religio-political significance as a locus of "a new civil society of biblically inspired social action groups . . . [who] create a momentarily sacred space that symbolically violates the divisions imposed by nation-state borders."[66] This ritual effectively reconfigures our body politic by restoring a common *imago Dei*–based dignity to all humanity rather than reinforcing divisive nationalistic borders and attendant legal citizenship–based rights.

This binational bishops' statement and this transnational border ritual, together with interfaith movements that supply humanitarian aid (food, water, and medical care) to immigrants in southern Arizona deserts (e.g., Humane Borders, Inc., the Samaritans, and No More Deaths),[67] constitute a new civil society grounded in prophetic hospitality, solidarity, and common humanity for the purpose of "imagining and calling for a more just future, . . . a utopian vision of antiborderism, a postnational unity of humanity."[68] These movements not only incarnate a new ecclesiological model of "a borderless church"[69] that resonates with the

---

ber 26, 2010). For commentaries, see Hagan, *Migration Miracle*, 88–92; Heyer, "Strangers in Our Midst," 433–40; and Kerwin, "Rights, the Common Good, and Sovereignty," 97–99.

[64] Hondagneu-Sotelo, *God's Heart Has No Borders*, 133–35. Posada is also regarded as a place, a shelter itself, provided by individuals and communities, whether by entire cities or by particular organizations, such as those community kitchens that feed and advocate for homeless communities. See Pineda, "Hospitality," and Christine D. Pohl, *Making Room: Recovering Hospitality as a Christian Tradition* (Grand Rapids, MI: Eerdmans, 1999).

[65] Hondagneu-Sotelo, *God's Heart Has No Borders*, 136, cf. 157–63.

[66] Ibid., 144, 150, cf.164–66.

[67] Hagan, *Migration Miracle*, 103–9.

[68] Hondagneu-Sotelo, *God's Heart Has No Borders*, 167–68, 169.

[69] Hagan, *Migration Miracle*, 93. Bishops in Tucson and Phoenix, AZ, together with bishops in Hermosillo, TX, created Diocese without Borders in 2002. Bishop Gerald Kicanas traveled across these dioceses in order to raise public awareness about immigration ministries that offer care, broadly construed, to migrants in the southern Arizonan and northern Mexican deserts. See Hagan, *Migration Miracle*, 95.

decentralized, nonhierarchical, social justice praxis-based, and transnational ecclesiology of the earlier 1980s movement.[70] They also advance a more expansive notion of US religio-political identity—public life as well as citizenship rights and responsibilities in it—around a common humanity (and implied inalienable rights) that consequently problematize and contest the conventional contours of the nation-state and its associated nativist and narrow nationalist notions of citizenship. "One nation under God" with its exclusivist views of membership based on common race, ethnicity, religion, language, or culture is now reconfigured as "one family under God" committed to "human rights, the common good, solidarity, and cultural diversity."[71]

In providing sanctuary, NSM churches prophetically refigure religious spaces via hospitality to immigrants in order to embody a more expansive twenty-first-century version of King's beloved community. Alexia Salvatierra, director of Clergy and Laity United for Economic Justice (CLUE), California, and an early leader in the NSM, explicitly referred to King's notion of the beloved community to interpret the NSM.[72] The beloved community serves for the NSM as a theological benchmark for promoting equal dignity and rights regardless of country of origin, for determining moral responsibilities in the face of suffering peoples, and for supporting the congregations in nearly thirty-five cities at that time in the movement that house "prophet families—families who are willing to tell their story publicly—[as] a religious witness and a moral voice on the immigration issue."[73] Similar to the CRM, the NSM expands the borders of the beloved community via the church into the civic sphere as a means to break citizenship rights beyond the narrow box of the nation-state. In other words, King appealed to a common humanity as a theo-political reason to justify US citizenship rights for African Americans and later human rights for all people oppressed by the triple evils of racism, poverty, and militarism. The NSM appeals to a common humanity as a theo-political reason to protect and promote human rights for immigrants that transcend nation-state defined rights,

[70] Cunningham, "Sanctuary and Sovereignty," 378–79, 383–84; cf. Cunningham, *God and Caesar*, 110–14, 130–37.

[71] Kerwin, "Toward a Catholic Vision of Nationality," 203, 206–7.

[72] De La Torre, *Trails of Hope and Terror*, 163–70.

[73] Ibid., 164, 165, 167.

that break the nation-state box of determining such rights,[74] and that express "the global citizenship enjoined on Christians."[75]

Toward a Christian Cosmopolitanism

Based on the multiple waves of forced and voluntary immigration that characterize US history, the US is shaped and reshaped by displaced peoples who lack familial, economic, social, political, and other marks of identity. The CRM and the NSM occupied and refigured public and ecclesial spaces, respectively, in order to open up a space in US society and politics for such displaced peoples, to expand the circle of welcome particularly to African Americans and Latino/a immigrants, and to advocate for their basic political recognition and rights. As this essay has argued, both the CRM and the NSM participate in prophetic action—national gatherings of racial solidarity or long-term hospitality for immigrants in churches nationwide—that contests and remakes political and religious spaces in an effort to model and make a more just public life.

Going beyond simple inclusion of formerly excluded peoples in US democratic politics and daily life, the CRM and NSM aim through prophetic praxis—nonviolent direct action or hospitality, respectively—to remake long-standing notions of public life and political subjectivity. The religious rhetorical vision and praxis of the beloved community in both movements carry implications for edging political belonging and membership toward cosmopolitan citizenship. As Peggy Levitt observes in her rich ethnographic study of immigrant religious groups' attitudes to US citizenship, US political sovereignty is often interpreted from a Christian doctrinal perspective: "one land, one membership card, and one identity is a secular version of the Holy Trinity."[76] By contrast, these groups

[74] The SM and the NSM can be considered a form of liberal civic nationalism that links US national identity with ideals such as freedom, equality, rights, justice, opportunity, and democracy. See Kerwin, "Toward a Catholic Vision of Nationality," 201.

[75] Heyer, "Strangers in Our Midst," 439. Some Christian theologians also claim a dual citizenship, or earthly citizenship en route (or on pilgrimage) to the future kingdom of God, which similarly "challenges any form of ideological, political, religious, or social provincialism that blinds people from seeing the interrelated nature of reality." Groody, "Crossing the Divide," 659–64, at 663.

[76] Peggy Levitt, *God Needs No Passport: Immigrants and the Changing American Landscape* (New York and London: The New Press, 2007), 68.

have created "religious space [that] transcended its political counterpart, encompassing people and places across the world and complementing, if not superseding, the nation and its significance."[77] In my view, the CRM and NSM fall into Levitt's category of faith-based global or cosmopolitan citizenship because, as Levitt states, "religion is the ultimate boundary crosser. God needs no passport because faith traditions give their followers symbols, rituals, and stories they use to create alternative sacred landscapes. . . . [Religion helps] to trade in a national lens for a transnational one . . . [that] begins with a world that is borderless and boundaryless."[78] Both movements have claimed and promoted divinely given human rights that by definition transcend exclusionary logics and limits of the US nation-state. Prophetic praxis in both movements have reconfigured and recast national and religious spaces into alternative arenas with religio-political implications for recognizing inalienable human rights that transcend borders of race, gender, birth, legal residence, and so on. Feminist theorist Seyla Benhabib explores these basic human rights under the Kantian category of the right of hospitality as a cosmopolitan right of respect and egalitarian reciprocity associated with our common humanity.[79] Cosmopolitan or universal rights for Benhabib evoke a new notion of political belonging, what she names a "postnational solidarity," that supersedes but does not replace the nation-state and that is in fact rooted in nation-states' and other political entities' respect for human qua human rights, not human qua citizen rights.[80]

Rather than disregard political borders or call for borderless nation-states, cosmopolitan rights require a basis for recognizing human rights of the other as human, as participating in a shared humanity. Benhabib grounds the legitimacy of human rights by appealing to UN Human Rights conventions and to other supranational sources that express and embody a "context-transcending appeal" for such rights.[81] Likewise, both the CRM and the NSM appeal to the nation-state in order to safeguard but not define human rights.[82] The CRM and the NSM question the

---

[77] Ibid., 84.

[78] Ibid., 12–13, 21–22.

[79] Seyla Benhabib, *The Rights of Others: Aliens, Residents, and Citizens* (Cambridge: Cambridge University Press, 2004), 2–3, 13, 26–27, 36.

[80] Ibid., 17, 21.

[81] Ibid., 10–12, at 19.

[82] While nation-states protect identity, government, and rights within their borders as well as the integrity of their borders, "from a Christian perspective sovereign rights are

political nonbelonging of African Americans and immigrants under then-contemporary US laws and policies, and thus define the rights of these groups via a religious appeal to an imprinted divine image within all humanity. Luke Bretherton designates such an appeal Christian cosmopolitanism, which opposes narrow-minded notions of rights coterminous with national borders and instead promotes the common as well as cosmic good against a theological horizon of the *imago Dei*.[83] Following Luke 14:15-24 (a tale of radically inclusive table fellowship) and Galatians 3:26-28 (early Christian baptism that creates radical equality in the Body of Christ), a Christian cosmopolitanism emphasizes the basic human dignity and rights of all people when viewed against an eschatological horizon of hope in a future fulfillment of all creation in God's image. The *imago Dei* trumps national or territorial borders, legal-political categories of identity, or ethnic, linguistic, and social indexes of citizenship.[84] As Elie Wiesel contends, "Any person by virtue of being a son or a daughter of humanity, is a living sanctuary whom nobody has the right to invade."[85]

In keeping with these theoretical, political, and religious movements toward cosmopolitan citizenship and rights, the CRM and the NSM rely on the religious vision and practice of the beloved community in order to transform political and religious spaces into an altogether transfigured form of human life together. Inaugurated in the CRM and reconceptualized in the NSM, the beloved community, in my view, exemplifies a Christian cosmopolitanism because it questions an existing exclusionary sociopolitical order and incarnates another alternative, possible *polis* or way of being and living together beyond existing borders. In both movements, the beloved community helps cultivate a transcendent and transnational identity based on religio-political appeals to and praxis of hospitality, solidarity, and shared humanity, and it thereby overcomes

---

subject to a larger vision of human rights [and] the common good." Groody, "Crossing the Divide," 666. In other words, nation-states enjoy legitimacy by safeguarding and upholding human qua human rights, not human qua citizen rights.

[83] See also *Gaudium et Spes*, no.75.

[84] Luke Bretherton, *Hospitality as Holiness: Christian Witness amid Moral Diversity* (Aldershot, England, and Burlington, VT: Ashgate, 2006), 121–51; Bretherton, *Christianity and Contemporary Politics: The Conditions and Possibilities of Faithful Witness* (Malden, MA, and Oxford: Wiley-Blackwell, 2010), 126–60.

[85] Elie Wiesel, "The Refugee," in MacEoin, ed., *Sanctuary*, 50, quoted in Letty M. Russell, *Just Hospitality: God's Welcome in a World of Difference* (Louisville: Westminster John Knox Press, 2009), 87.

"the sin of exceptionalism engrained in the nation's social psyche."[86] It transforms public and ecclesial spaces into alternative societies that gather folks together for the purpose of recognizing the inherent human dignity of each person, not as instrumentally valued and dehumanized commodities or objects of the state, the market, or other organizations.[87] It marks and creates a politically safe space that in turn becomes a sacramental sign of that togetherness which seeks and signifies, at least in part, the common good, the good of our common humanity.

Although underwritten by and linked to a Christian theological perspective, the beloved community does not require uniformity under a Christian umbrella; that is, it does not require confessional consent to Christian beliefs about creation in the image of God. A faith-based vision and practice of the beloved community legitimates respect for common humanity from a Christian perspective, but this does not preclude other religious traditions or other folks with no religious tradition from articulating their supranational reasons for such respect. As the late Letty Russell remarked about welcoming the other in a pluralistic society, "Hospitality is an expression of unity without uniformity, because unity in Christ has as its purpose the sharing of God's hospitality with the stranger, the one who is 'other.'"[88] As exemplified in both movements, prophetic praxis of enacting the beloved community "will not make us safe, but it will lead us to risk joining in the work of mending the creation without requiring those who are different to become like us."[89] Indeed, this praxis only requires eschewing "us and them" ways of thinking and living, and instead finding ways of thinking and living about "us" as inherently interrelated with "them."

---

[86] Heyer, "Social Sin and Immigration," 435.
[87] Bretherton, *Christianity and Contemporary Politics*, 215.
[88] Russell, *Just Hospitality*, 80, cf. 118–23.
[89] Ibid., 123.

In Conversation with
Mary J. Henold, Roanoke College

I want to begin by extending a welcome to everyone and by thanking you for your thoughtful and evocative essays. I also ask for your indulgence as a historian in a virtual room with two theologians and two ethicists. As I read the essays, I was often struck by my own difference, from an academic standpoint, but that very difference prompted me to seek common ground as a Catholic woman academic who moves in and among the themes present in this work, if from a different perspective. I am a historian by training, with research interests in the history of American Catholicism, Catholic laywomen, and the history of Catholic feminist movements. I also teach in the field of spatial history—that is, the study of the creation of spaces, public and private, and how perceptions of those spaces change over time. These interests shape my response, and I will use them to start our conversation.

There are certainly many common themes that run through these papers. First, they highlight the efforts of individuals, primarily Catholic women, and organizations to advocate for those who are poor, the victims of injustice, and those who find themselves marginalized and vulnerable in American culture for a variety of reasons. A second common theme is that these advocates make a conscious choice to enter public spaces in order to promote justice and human flourishing. These spaces—political, sacred, and institutional, all designed ostensibly to promote the greater good—are contested, fraught with risk, and permeated by the assumptions that both guide and undermine the unfolding of our communities. Finally, each essay—and I think this is what marks them as products of theology and ethics and not history—offers a construct for continued fruitful advocacy. I certainly want to address these efforts to provide

259

guidance for the future, but I'll begin with some central questions that these essays raise for me both as a historian and as a Catholic woman.

I'll begin with Nancy's essay, which I read first, and her central question colored my reading of the other three. Nancy suggests that Catholic women be encouraged to reengage in public life, particularly the institutions of the church. She fears that contemporary Catholic women will retreat into the private sphere, marked by an unwillingness to claim authority beyond personal experience and by the foolhardy reliance on consumption to provide meaning and a sense of belonging. Underlying this is the fear that the shrinking sisterhoods will cost the Catholic community models of how to live a rich, engaged, and meaningful spiritual life in both public and private spaces. (We know, of course, that spaces are rarely one or the other. Consider Rachel's single patients who experience extreme vulnerability in public medical institutions, or sacred spaces that become homes for refugees in Rosemary's analysis of Sanctuary movements.)

So Nancy hopes that Catholic women will risk a return to these public spaces and, to some extent, be inspired by past female archetypes that echo through them. These hold the promise of life and support even though she knows well, as all of you express at one point or another, that public spaces—particularly Catholic public spaces—have historically been very risky places for Catholic women to inhabit.

I would throw out to the group this observation: if we are going to encourage Catholic women to engage with Catholic institutional life in the public sphere, we must do so with great caution, even though it has the promise of so much good, as we can see from the examples of NETWORK and the Civil Rights and Sanctuary Movements. What is clear from these articles is that when women enter the Catholic public sphere, the institution not only believes it has the right simply to pass judgment on what is and is not correct, or what is or is not just; it also reserves the right to define personhood, Catholic identity, and marginal status.

We see it most obviously, and most chillingly, in Kristin's essay. Here we are faced with authoritarian bishops who do not hesitate to crack down on those who step out of their place. For the purpose of this discussion, though, I would argue that they do more than that. They take on the power to *disown*, questioning the women of NETWORK's right not only to act as spokespeople for church teaching but even to call themselves Catholic. And then there's the worst threat of all: removal from the diocesan newspaper! This is tantamount to having your photos cut from the family photo album. They insist: you may not name yourself, you may not claim to be part of us.

From Nancy's essay we see the limits placed on women's identity through the promotion of carefully defined archetypes over time: the private and self-sacrificing mother, the quietly competent sister, the lay-woman cantor who leads, but only through response. These archetypes are valued by the institution because they preserve order in private families and in public ritual, and it is therefore in the church's best interest to maintain them.

Though Rachel's essay is not specifically about Catholic single women, I could hardly help drawing some connections. From Rachel we have the image of single women who face multiple vulnerabilities that come first from practical limitations but also from cultural assumptions. The most striking of these is the assumption that single women are unfinished and in-waiting. If the medical establishment is obtuse on this issue, then the institutional Catholic Church has been even worse. Historically, American Catholic single women have been exhorted to seek the wholeness they lack by throwing themselves into service to others. From the nineteenth century through the 1960s, single women were told to fill the emptiness of their lives by teaching Sunday school or babysitting their sisters' children. Within Catholic public and ritual life, single women receive virtually no affirmation of whole personhood, because the sacraments that take place in public liturgy revolve mostly around the milestones of families or vowed religious. When was the last time you heard the milestones of a single person's life acknowledged with affirmation or blessing in a Catholic church? Practically speaking, in the rituals of the public church, singleness is perceived as wholeness only in the person of the celibate priest, whose singleness is viewed as sacred choice and thus confers authority rather than marginalization.

And finally, from Rosemary we have a story that should be uplifting, but that I perceived—in part—as heartbreaking. She shows us the vision of what the institution can do when it officially deems a group marginalized: then we see the insistence on hospitality, welcome to the stranger, acknowledgment of a wholeness and humanity not dependent on borders, states, and labels. We see the joy of acting in the image of Christ to love one's neighbor and the power of enacting Christ's sacrifice interpreted as entering into and subverting status quo powers. For me, this only throws into sharp—painful—relief the institutional church's refusal to offer such generous love to its women because it does not recognize them as marginalized or its own role in perpetuating injustice against them.

All of the essays, then, suggest the risks of negotiating official Catholic public space either as advocates for others or simply as whole persons attempting, in Kristin's words, to "inhabit hope" or, in Rachel's, to choose life-giving rather than life-draining things. I know we all face the risks ourselves every time we step into a sanctuary for Mass or talk to a young Catholic woman struggling with her church. I confess that when I read about hard-line authoritarian bishops, I wonder if it's time to walk out as so many Catholic feminists have done before me.

But it is, of course, the stories of prophetic witness that call me back, and that's what these essays offer. We have a number of constructs presented as means of simultaneously negotiating and transforming public institutional space. From Rosemary we have "Christian cosmopolitanism" and from Rachel, "compassionate respect." These are concrete ways of modeling an approach to the world that values both human flourishing and justice. They call on advocates to challenge the trappings of culture that convey insider status—citizenship, marriage, race—and use institutions to promote autonomy and full personhood.

Kristin and Nancy also offer ways forward, but they are dealing more specifically with a Catholic institutional context. Their essays raise the perennial question of how advocates can successfully use a tradition to promote justice when they themselves are marginalized within it. Kristin draws on the experiences of NETWORK to highlight a redefining of obedience as a strategy for how to simultaneously challenge the church and use it as a platform for justice. "Conscientious obedience" promotes listening and discernment as a means of honoring personhood while discerning God's will. Nancy also asks Catholic women to reevaluate the archetypes of the past so that the best of each may not be lost.

Yet seeing the risks involved (and the bruised heads from continually banging them against brick walls), I think it's fair to ask if those who would advocate for the marginalized gain more from an engagement with Catholic institutional/public life than they lose. Do the battles over Catholic identity and authority simply take too much energy from the work at hand?

I'm also concerned about the perpetuation of tropes about Catholic women's identity. For example, there's a rosy glow emanating from the women religious in these essays. Are we in danger of glorifying women religious as their numbers decrease, forgetting the ways they exercise power over others as well as demonstrate the church's best principles? Will we neglect their full humanity going forward by painting halos on them? I'm also concerned about retrieving a mid-twentieth-century understanding of Catholic women negotiating public/private life. We need to remember that both laywomen and women religious choose paths of action based on their lack of power. We must take care that we continually challenge that lack of power lest we simply duplicate the conditions that forced women to circumscribe their behavior and ambitions in Catholic institutional and liturgical life.

To conclude, I'd like to promote a much more modern, autonomous, and yet fully human "icon" for women, as suggested by Rachel and by using terms analyzed by Rosemary. The number of single women is growing in the United States, and even those of us who eventually marry are forever marked by the experiences we had as long-term singletons. By necessity in a world of mobility, these women (and men) must pour enormous energy into community building and maintenance. In doing so, they can create a profound model of the beloved community, ministering to each other's needs as friends, confidants, caregivers, ride givers, movers, ministers, and, on occasion, lovers. To be a member of such a community is to embrace God's call to be present to each other in the moment where we are, in public and private spaces. It's a role that is largely unrecognized by the institutional church, which lacks models to understand it and rituals to celebrate it.[1]

Mary: Let's open it up for discussion. I want everyone to feel that they have the ability to take the discussion where they'd like it to go. So, I don't want you to be limited to my response.

Rachel: I have an initial thought that I want to say about my essay. When I was writing it, I kept in mind the conversations we have had as a group, especially those informal conversations over dinner. And I remember a number of occasions in which the mothers in the group talked about how they integrated motherhood and its notions, ideas, and tropes into the way they do theology. And so that point acted as a background conversation partner in my head. And I thought about why and how it

---

[1] The following transcript reprints a conference call that took place on the afternoon of August 23, 2011, among the conversation starter, the contributors in this section, and the coeditors. Opening and concluding parts of the call have been edited or altogether omitted, but without altering the content of the call.

is that they—the ones who are mothers—get to be more themselves in a way, more than single persons do.

Rosemary: To pick up on the mothering angle, or the motherhood angle, Mary, in your longer response, and today in your abbreviated response, you mentioned that some of these icons or tropes that we're trying to reclaim can risk further privatization of women—and by implication that if women are representing the church, then we risk the privatization of the church as well. And so I was thinking about the women that figure centrally within the Sanctuary and the New Sanctuary Movement. And both of those movements, at least in highly profiled cases as I've researched them, tend to focus on mothers, but those mothers don't fit the icon or trope of the idealized mother that's promoted in official magisterial documents about the maternal "genius" of women. The churches in which these women and children and sometimes whole families receive sanctuary are not viewed as homes, but they really function as an alternative polis or civil society, or the kind of society we want to see politically that's more just, inclusive, and so on. So I think that it all depends on how the icon is harnessed and interpreted. And in this case, both of those movements avoid the risk of privatization.

Mary: They might, however, thinking of the Sanctuary Movement—you know this better than I do—but they might actually highlight the trope of the suffering mother.

Rosemary: Yes. You're right—but it's not the suffering, self-sacrificial, kenotic type of mother, willing to give all for her children. While that might have been their reason for coming to the United States, . . .

Mary: Right.

Rosemary: . . . the suffering that they are undergoing in the United States has to do with being severed from family due to deportation, raids, and so on, due to their undocumented status. So it is a different kind of political suffering, and it is a different box, I guess for lack of a better term, to put mothers into.

Kristin: I agree, Rosemary, that perhaps both of those echo this suffering, kenotic mother, but they also embody challenges to those traditional tropes in their steely resilience, creative resourcefulness, and other ways in which they are in fact challenging cultural norms that are mixed with religious assumptions about women's roles and men's roles. So I agree that it problematizes and challenges—maybe as much as it replicates—some of those gendered roles in some ways that are fruitful for the church and society.

I was going to also add, Mary, that your point about perhaps canonizing the women religious as they come out in some of these tropes in the essays is an important one. I think particularly as I continue to talk to different women religious, which it would be very dangerous to generalize about it, but there is this acknowledgment that what I've profiled here is perhaps a hopeful movement that broke open some new space and new understandings even, but that there is really a mixed climate right now, maybe one of fear and fatalism. I think at the end I tried to touch on this, and while I wouldn't want to generalize, I think that ambivalence is important in terms of thinking about obedience. Another member of our New Voices Seminar, Colleen Mallon, commented on a panel at the CTSA regarding the visitation experiences that by virtue of baptism we can't really "take all our marbles and go home."

So I think understanding obedience not only as vows taken or in terms of vowed women religious per se but also as how the actions of certain single women or vowed women religious or married women can break open what's become a narrow understanding of discernment or obedience, is more what I'd like to look to.

Nancy: Running along with that, one thing I was hearing in what you were saying, Kristin, was what I wondered about when we were talking about women religious, especially when we use these icons or these tropes about women. But there is a difference between evaluating people morally and evaluating people functionally in the hagiography that goes on, whether with regard to traditional women religious or with regard to people active in social justice movements.

I don't think we want to extend the moral haze to any of these or even to our fellow feminist sisters. It's not about an individual morality that is better than others. There are ways it seems to me when we talk about how women are working or working in public that we can separate that out a little bit and talk about how they are functioning. And what their roles are, how they function in those roles, and how that moved or doesn't move the church along. And so, for example, I was very interested in your essay, Rachel, about the question of singles in the church or singletons or I am not sure how precisely to refer to this. Probably because one of the problems—I don't mean it is bad—but one of the problems is how a single person is understanding himself or herself to be institutionally connected, which of course is what it means to be institutionally defined. I mean these are questions. So we have this vocation called marriage in which at one point you say yes, and then we understand this to be a life-long commitment which of course sometimes doesn't work and then gets refigured with the idea of vowed religious, with clergy. Assuming single-hood isn't the provisional state in which one is waiting to be something else, how should we institutionalize it in a way that respects what it is?

Rachel: Yes, and that . . .

Nancy: Or is institutionalizing it a death sentence?

Rachel: Well, yes, that's an important question. I wrestled with how we think about personhood in the context of the institution, especially if we cast singletons as waiting in a limbo state until marriage or motherhood or something else. And that waiting state implies that a single person is not a whole person or is somehow deficient, which goes against so much of the social and cultural message that I think a lot of contemporary single women imbibe every day.

Nancy: If I can say one more thing . . .

Rachel: Yes.

Nancy: Karl Rahner has this writing, forgive me for how this is going to sound at the beginning—he has writing about children which says we should not see children as in some way merely provisional but in some ways that they have an integrity about themselves as a person.[2] And I'm hearing—in the weird status we have attributed to single persons—an extended childhood too.

Rachel: Right.

Nancy: It seems that there might even be a corrective there. Again, these are not the same thing; one is a provisional reality, an extension of this understanding of a child. But it is this idea of the person's status that holds until one is married.

---

[2] For a full exposition of Karl Rahner's treatment of childhood, see Mary Ann Hinsdale, "'Infinite Openness to the Infinite': Karl Rahner's Contribution to Modern Catholic Thought on the Child," in Marcia Bunge, ed., *The Child in Christian Thought* (Grand Rapids, MI: Eerdmans, 2001), 406–45.

Rachel: Right. I also didn't want to forget what status religious life might have in that equation. Does going off the ramp, so to speak, into religious life redefine singlehood in some way that being ordinarily single does not?

Mary: Can I jump in? I am going back to the question that Nancy asked earlier about how would you institutionalize—and it sounds horrible, but you know what I mean—the single person and whether it's desirable. I want to tell a little anecdote. I was in a wonderful parish up in Rochester, New York, and they were very attuned to blessings. So they would bring families up, and it was almost always families, for a blessing for a child being born or whatever. And so as a single person at the time it was very striking to me that it was always families who were formally being blessed by the church. But there was one instance where single people received a very significant blessing, and that's when they moved away.

And that may sound harsh, but for me it was a really beautiful thing, because one of the markers of a single person's life, particularly when you're in your twenties, is that you move all the time. And it's very significant because you have to put so much energy into this community building, and when you leave you have to start all over again. And so for me to be called up on the altar of that parish and receive a blessing from that community when I had to leave—it was something that was very special and moving to me. So this is an example of what might be possible.

Rachel: On the one hand, I think that is a beautiful image. On the other hand, what are churches doing for the people who will be there long term?

Mary: Right. [Pause.] Can I call the group back at this moment and ask you to address this question of—as I put in my response—a rosy haze around women religious? Do you think that as we move forward and the numbers (as they seem to be doing) continue to diminish—do you think as scholars we are at risk of turning towards hagiography?

Nancy: There is the trope out there "honor the troops" that has come under fire in a similar way. Yes, we do that with women religious. And what will be interesting, though, I think, is to tease out why is that—why do they get this particular status? Is it simply because we felt that for so long they were taken for granted? Is it simply because we need to name something that has an institutional imprimatur and say, "See, we're good." For example, someone mentioned Nicholas Kristof in here, with whom I have a debate. He does this all the time; he likes to divide the church, separating the "bad" institution from "good" things like those stalwart nuns caring for the poor—I always want to note that those nuns are Catholic.[3]

Kristin: Yes, that was my quote, and I had a similar distaste. I think I ended that section with a plea to bring these two together, so they are also understood as an emblem of the institutional church, not some radical offshoot that has nothing to do with the institutional church. So I do think that that's problematic as well, and too convenient, I think, for outside commentators to throw out the baby with the bathwater amid headlines about scandal.

Nancy: The positive stories are used to ward off the charge of being anti-Catholic.

Kristin: Exactly, yes, to cover themselves.

Nancy: It is not a solution to the problem, period.

Kristin: Exactly. I think I prefer this sense that I think I added at the end of the essay that I had recently read about—not seeing the diminution of vocations as the end of an era but as an evolutionary offshoot. How do these charisms get passed on or institutionalized? I was struck by a *New York Times* piece this week on the head of another Catholic health care system stepping down and being replaced with a lay counterpart, not with the sense of "there goes the store," but I thought, actually a pretty thoughtful piece talking about not only her competence but what she brings in terms of presence and modeling nonviolent and gender-inclusive language. No "bullet points," no "blown-up" photos, but I thought it was an interesting commentary not on "we're nothing without women religious in these roles," but on "here is their legacy, and how will this evolve in that case in terms of lay leadership?" So I think I would caution against both the hagiography you're talking about but also the kind of fatalism that I hear a lot.

Rosemary: Some of that fatalism came through in one of the questions that Mary had for us in her response, in which she said that she

---

[3] One example would be Nicholas Kristof, "A Church Mary Can Love," *New York Times*, April 17, 2010, available at http://www.nytimes.com/2010/04/18/opinion/18kristof.html (accessed October 2, 2011). Kristof assumes that the social justice Catholics he praises would want to distance themselves from the institution he condemns, possibly a false assumption.

wonders whether it's time for yet another exodus from the church that
has happened in the past, made most famous by Mary Daly and others
who exited Harvard Chapel.[4] And I was really struck by that in your
response, Mary, because I think you're right that the church's public
ministries with marginalized folks come at the cost of failing to recognize
the marginalized within the church itself.

And so I don't know if it's time for an exodus from the church unqualified as church, but maybe it's time for an exodus from the institutional hard-line church notions of identity and authority and so on that
lead to, as you said, disowning women religious as Catholic or preventing
them from talking about themselves as Catholic or preventing them from
talking about themselves in the diocesan newspapers and so on.

So I don't think it's time for an exodus from the church qua church
but an exodus from certain interpretations of what the institutional
church looks like, how it operates, and so on. And so maybe part of the
hagiographic tendency for talking about women religious is that they do
embody alternative ways of being church, as Sandra Schneiders has so
well analyzed in her interpretation of women religious, as leading toward
these prophetic ways of being church. So I think it's an exodus from a
type of church to another type of church, but not from the church itself.

Nancy: There is a nostalgia for that, thus that hagiography, because they
are dwindling. And as a recent piece by John Allen shows—something
we've all observed—those who are attracted to not only the priesthood
but also religious life and lay ministry tend to be very comfortable with
strong public Catholic identity markers.[5]

Mary: And part of the trouble of course is that if you can separate your
notions of church, then that only works if you're not working in the
institutional church as public sphere. Part of my research and writing

---

[4] Mary Daly, "The Women's Movement: An Exodus Community," *Religious Education* 67, no.5 (September/October 1972): 327–33. See also Susan Henking, "Beyond
Radical: Mary Daly, Feminist Theologian, Changed Worlds," *Religion Dispatches*, January 6, 2010, available at http://www.religiondispatches.org/archive/atheologies/2163
/beyond_radical%3A_mary_daly,_feminist_theologian,_changed_worlds (accessed September 26, 2011).

[5] John L. Allen Jr., "Big Picture at World Youth Day: 'It's the Evangelicals, Stupid!'"
National Catholic Reporter, August 19, 2011, available at http://ncronline.org/blogs/all
-things-catholic/big-picture-world-youth-day-it%E2%80%99s-evangelicals-stupid (accessed October 2, 2011).

addresses that response, because I wrote a book on the Catholic feminist movement, and it ends with much of this exodus. And as I was writing it in my life at that time, I was completely committed, and I would talk to these women in their seventies saying to me, "Why, why, why? It's time to go." And I wasn't there yet, and now ten years later I understand them better. Ten or more years of being in parishes that are not ideal—it's hard; it wears a girl down. So that's what you're hearing in my response—at some point, when do we stop throwing energy into engaging with all of the rigmarole in the public sphere, if we don't need to? Now this is not to say I am about to march out the door because I'm really not, but I have to throw that question out there.

Nancy: Yes.

Rosemary: Well, part of the way I resolve that tension is that in my own research and writing, I tend not to focus on intrachurch realities. In my teaching, I help students process internal church questions, but in my own research and writing, I tend to focus more on the public church. Now very often, the public church in the United States defaults to bishops and other male spokesmen for the church, which connects to priestly authority and so on. But the public church is bigger than its institutional representatives, and we have a long history of social movements and so on which do represent a more complex face of the public church.

So when I do ecclesiology in my own research and writing, I am not focusing on intrachurch governance issues but rather on how folks think about the church's advocacy roles, credibility, and so on, in public. So that's how I resolve some of that tension. I still live it, but that's how I resolve some of it, so that I still have energy to work with that creative tension.

Kristin: Right. That is so interesting, Rosemary, to hear you reflect on that, because I think I am finding the opposite, not by any design, but I find myself worried that leaving my students to get the party line from the media or the official spokesmen, as you said, will let them think that exhausts "church." And so as uncomfortable and difficult as it is, I find myself engaging more in intrachurch debates even in ethics classrooms, or even over the multiple historical contexts that I seem to be teaching inevitably, to give students a sense of the dialogue and the disagreement. For example, in the health care debate I don't think about the church's internal disagreement as a failure, but actually this is what it's about—

we are better fulfilling its redemptive mission through contestation than through false unity or uniformity or perceived fortitude.

Also, to give students hope, that the meaning and felt understanding of church is broader than the hierarchy alone. So maybe I am working out my own stuff on my poor students rather than what I am "trained" to do as an ethicist, not a systematic theologian.

Rachel: I have a question for Kristin. What sorts of questions from your students set you thinking, "Oh, I need to address this," or "Oh, I need to correct that," so that they have a more nuanced view of what's possible for the church?

Kristin: Sure, comments such as "the church says ObamaCare is pro-abortion" or "the church says homosexuals are intrinsically disordered and therefore I must be wrong," or the understandings of women some of you have articulated in your essays prompt me to work with the students on a more nuanced view of the church. So, the students understand there is actually at least a dialogue or conversation around some of these issues, or at least some theologians are writing in different terms about sexual ethics. In terms of this book chapter, I haven't really taught on health care, but I try to convey to the students that members of these movements understand themselves to be Catholic but depart from the bishops' position on this legislation as a matter of conscience.

Also, in terms of Rosemary's point, I think even teaching those movements often supplements students' vision of the church as concerned with maybe two to three nonnegotiable issues that don't really figure into most of the movements that Rosemary discussed and profiled. How about you, Rachel or Nancy or Mary? Does this come out in your teaching in different ways?

Rachel: Which part?

Kristin: I am sorry; I am not asking the questions. Sorry, Mary—back to you.

Mary: No, please do. Go ahead.

Kristin: I was thinking if others of you have this tension coming out in your teaching at all, in ways that Rosemary and I spoke about.

Nancy: So the tricky thing is that the tension cannot come out if our students have only experienced Catholicism from the pew fitfully and occasionally in a headline, right?

Kristin: Yes, absolutely.

Nancy: So our job as teachers is to make this story thick and complex, and our job as teachers is to teach the history of why something that seems so straightforward has never ever, ever, ever—that's three *evers*—ever been like this in the history of the church. And so I think that—so there is a way, yes, in which we have to make these things problems for our students. They may come up to us with a fairly flat yes or no, saying, "I am gay; the church has a problem with this; therefore, I don't belong to the church."

Kristin: Right.

Nancy: But then you need to take apart those notions—gay, church, sexuality—and make all of those much more complex questions and invite them to think about themselves in a much more complex way.

Rosemary: And to pick up on that point, Nancy, I would tell the students from the history of social movements that do still identify themselves as Catholic—whether the institutional church recognizes them or not as Catholic with a capital *C*—to go explore the possibilities of Dignity USA, or go explore the possibilities of other open and affirming Catholic communities that maybe not are affiliated with Dignity but are moving in that direction. In addition to all of the discerning work that you laid out, I would also want to introduce students to the history of social movements that do "own" that Catholic identity differently, whether the church disowns it from them or not.[6]

Nancy: Well, absolutely, and to see in those movements where the Catholic has reverberated.

Rosemary: Right.

Nancy: So it's not a question of "Is this Catholic?" but we also have to realize that there is stuff outside that we also need to take in, in terms of justice. No, "Catholic" in fact has, in its long history—has been much more complex, and certainly the question of same-sex relations has been very complex in the church and continues to be.

---

[6] Michele Dillon, *Catholic Identity: Balancing Reason, Faith, and Power* (Cambridge and NY: Cambridge University Press, 1999).

Mary: I would add to that. I don't actually teach a lot of Catholicism, believe it or not—I teach mostly American history—but when I do, I think about it as analogous to teaching feminism, because for students, Catholicism and feminism are both things that are calcified in their minds.

Nancy: Right.

Mary: So feminism is this, Catholicism is this—it's "I buy into this" and for feminists "I don't buy into that," right? But so, when I teach feminism, the first thing, the very first thing, that I do is present the diversity of feminism. And that's when everything breaks open because they can see it's not all of those crazy radicals and admit, "Oh, I actually believe that." And I think the same thing can be done in Catholicism to show them the great diversity of how one can be Catholic, whereas, as Nancy was saying, for those who have received their Catholicism from the pew, they would have no idea that there is a diversity of ways of being Catholic.

Nancy: That's where I would bring up again Rahner's notion of "folk-costume Christianity." And that he is warning women clearly about that as a possibility, that there may be a rather cartoonish scenario that you will put on what you think of as folk-costume Catholic motherhood. And in the same way, I think probably, in order to be self-critical, there may be a folk-costume feminism that our students are reacting against, that doesn't get the fullness of the story out there. And these are things that as they arise, they complexify, they calcify, then we rethink.

Mary: At this point, given that we have five minutes left, I want to open the floor for anyone who wishes to take this conversation in a different direction, who had other themes or other questions, to please bring them forward at this point.

Kristin: This is not fully formulated, but I actually appreciated your question, Mary, that we were talking about—this exit. I think I am with Rosemary, who asked how we can think of church in a much more capacious way, but I do think a more urgent sense which that question raises really stuck with me as a more pressing task to unmask this age-old injustice within the church and the treatment of women. I was thinking of your charge to us, and reading some commentary on these freedom of conscience clauses as Health and Human Services (HHS) tries to spell out what health care reform will look like. The commentator noted that the institutional church is so worried about these Catholic institutions' conscience being respected, yet not about their female employees, or females who practice contraception for therapeutic reasons, or the recent polls that report 98 percent of Catholics conscientiously condone its practice.[7]

So when you raise that question of exit, it helps intensify the urgency rather than shaking our heads and saying, "This is to be expected, oh well," especially for future generations or in light of that calcification. Maybe there is a folk-costume version of the resigned, resentful Catholic feminist in some ways which we can break down as well.

Mary: One of the things I was thinking about as we were talking is that question of when you stop, when you get tired of a bloody head from banging your head against the wall. And being an Americanist, I think of the suffrage movement, because seventy years' worth, several generations' worth, of women had to make this choice—well, let's stop; it's not getting us anywhere. But there were so many who kept it going. Are we in danger of giving up? As I was reading over my own response, I kept thinking this sounds so old—injustice, women's role in the church—oh my goodness, are we going to go back there again?

But in the end, yes, we have to. It may be getting old because we're not getting anywhere. And so we're in a lull because we're tired. But we can't stop. That gets me back to my response to Nancy, which is if we go back to the old tropes, we can't stop talking about justice because we're in danger if we promote "traditional" archetypes without pointing out the injustices buried in them.

Nancy: Yes, we don't have to figure this out now. I certainly don't think we should go back to that. I think we need to revision them and see how they effectively engaged with the church in ways that are eluding us right now.

Rosemary: I think another way of interpreting the perennial cycle of return to these questions in the history of the church, whether we're talking about women in the church or feminist and womanist engagement in the church, is to think of it as the kind of work that traditions do. This is the kind of work that religious traditions do in each era. They go back. They ask the same (or new) questions again in light of different

[7] Jamie L Manson, "The Church's War on Women's Health and Child Welfare," *National Catholic Reporter*, August 16, 2011, available at http://ncronline.org/blogs/grace-margins/churchs-war-womens-health-and-child-welfare (accessed August 16, 2011).

resources, look at what past traditions have to offer both for good and for ill, and decide what to carry forward, what to rethink, what to leave to the side, and so on.

So I take the fact that these questions keep getting raised as a good sign that women scholars in the study of religion are doing the hard work of tradition as a verb, not as a noun at some static deposit that gets protected, preserved, and promoted for all times, in every place, and for everybody.

Kathleen: Right. Thank you, Rosemary, as the last speaker. If there is no other comment, may we move to the ending reflection? Would that be acceptable to everyone?

Most respond: Sure.

Kathleen: OK. Rosemary, will you take it from here?

Rosemary: Sure.

Kathleen: OK.

Rosemary: So, as you know, the New Voices Seminar emerged out of the Madeleva Lecture Series, and the inaugural Madeleva Lecture was delivered in 1985 by Monika Hellwig. She was a long-time professor at Georgetown University for almost thirty years and served as the executive director of the Association of Catholic Colleges and Universities for a very important decade when the American Catholic bishops were modifying and implementing *Ex Corde Ecclesiae* across Catholic institutions of higher education. And Monika fought for academic freedom as much as possible for those folks in Catholic higher education.

But the quote that I have for us to consider today comes from her inaugural Madeleva Lecture. And she, in that lecture which is titled "Christian Women in a Troubled World," says the following about some of the themes we talked about today, a usable past, the work of being prophetic, and what she calls small, slow earthquakes. So that takes us back to the beginning of our call, and some of us who had earthquakes today, but not on the West Coast. So, I will read this excerpt, which comes from the lecture, and then invite your responses to conclude the call.

[Rosemary reads the excerpt.]

So I know that's a lot to take in, but what spoke to me about that quote or that excerpt about the usable past was that Monika stresses that perhaps expecting prophetic ministry from those who fill institutional roles is misplaced, and that those who fill official positions are called, as she says, to play conventional roles. And so prophetic voices and praxis necessarily come from elsewhere. So that's what spoke to me, but I'd be very interested in how you all respond.

Rachel: My immediate reaction to that reading is that (a) there is a lot of truth to it but especially about a usable past, but (b) on the flip side, I think it extends the window of tension and marginalization. And, in the process, are we saying that there will always be prophetic voices doing heavy lifting from the outside? Is that, in the long run, the kind of church—the kind of community—that we should strive to build?

Nancy: Well, I'll jump in. What I was struck by when I was listening to that was the way in which for those who are marginalized from institutional structures, their private selves often become the locus of their public actions. And that has pluses and minuses. We certainly saw in the women's movement the recognition of "the personal is political," and I think that is true to a great extent. But I would simply like to argue at least for a reexamination of how institutionalized roles do serve a function of allowing us to have private lives that are not about our public functions. I hasten to add that that has gone massively awry in the contemporary Roman Catholic Church. But I would like us to notice that the fusion of private selves and public actions also has some downsides for women.

Kristin: I think I would resonate with the caution sounded by both Rachel and Nancy, and I am now trying to think of something hopeful to add. In terms of the image of the slow earthquake Rosemary mentioned, I think, on the one hand, of the rupture that any earthquake causes. It's helpful to remember that it shouldn't be that astonishing that it's threatening to the status quo of the church or of the society, that it's unsettling—that's to be expected. Yet the slow or gradual sense could also give hope in terms of the "banging our head against the wall" efforts or the traditioning that you each mentioned—perhaps even if it seems to go nowhere in the short term. But I would be cautious about consigning presently marginalized voices or bodies to awaiting their reward, as it were.

Kathleen: Well, let me in this moment of silence—let me thank you as you have such fine minds, all of you, and you're putting them to such good use. I am very impressed with the quality of the conversation. So since we are a little bit over time now, unless there is something to add, shall we waive adieu for now?

Mary: Thank you so much. Thank you all.

Kristin: Thanks, all.

Rachel: Bye.

Nancy: Bye-bye.

Rosemary: Thanks, everyone.

Kathleen: Bye for now.

Afterword

Dialogue, the Pearl of Great Price

Colleen M. Griffith, Boston College

Its roundness and smooth surface provided shape and texture. It had a mysterious inner glow that gave it beautiful luster. The iridescent pearl evoked such joy and delight. The worth of the gemstone extended well beyond the merchant's efforts and expectations. Here, at last, was something of lifelong value. In the miniparable found in Matthew 13:45-46, the kingdom of heaven is likened to a precious pearl. The seeker who discovers it has both the eyes to recognize the pearl's significance and the wisdom to cherish it. The perspective of the seeker changes forever because of the pearl, and acknowledgment of its unique worth carries with it a summons for a way of life. The pearl in Matthew 13:45-46 holds the possibility of many things for the merchant: the justice, mercy, and truth of the reign of God. In our own time, one hallmark of that reign, something sought ardently by contemporary seekers, is meaningful dialogue, the kind of genuine conversational exchange that holds the possibility of people and communities being rendered more present to one another. Experiences of it, like the pearl, are of lasting value.

Today we are forever coming up short in the dialogue department. A paucity of opportunities for dialogical exchanges is a troublesome "sign of the times" in our churches. Too often what passes for "dialogue" in communities looks more like warring monologues than anything else. Lament is a common enough practice in a nondialogical ethos. Theologian Bradford Hinze views lament to be a most appropriate response to how exchanges that pass for conversation get conducted. He notes,

278

"There are many reasons for lament concerning how power and status have been exercised in dialogical practices."[1] Questions multiply in our churches regarding unjust uses of power in conversational exchanges, and there is a lack of attention paid to the inadequate communication skills of persons in leadership.

In contrast with the nondialogical melody line that is all too dominant today, the woman authors in this volume offer refreshing counterpoint. Their writings emerge from contextual standpoints in the global church, the academy, and the public realm where they have been engaged in substantive, rich conversations. The theologians and ethicists represented here stand committed to a dialogical approach to doing theology; each puts the Christian tradition that she prizes in lively conversation with a specific locality, a real context, all the while turning a special eye of care toward women and their specific life concerns and struggles. The fruits of the labor of these women, so evident in these essays, are already the outcome of vigorous, sustained dialogue and real conversations.

The authors here share a common hope that further dialogue will erupt as readers engage these texts. They extend an invitation to us to join a conversation begun by them. A fresh layer of dialogical exchange becomes possible, one that holds the promise of new levels of meeting and dynamic solidarity with one another—author, reader, and those written about. Engaged in this further conversation, we as readers are walked toward new doorways and pointed outward to what lies beyond old and familiar reference points. In the back-and-forth movement of wider conversation between the texts presented and ourselves, we experience what David Tracy calls a being "carried along, and sometimes away, by the subject matter itself into the rare event or happening named 'thinking' and 'understanding.'"[2] The questions and struggles highlighted by authors here turn into the ones to which we as partners in dialogue now are oriented.[3] We are not the passive recipients of these essays; we are those caught up in dialogical interaction with them instead.

What does this kind of conversational exchange demand of us as readers? It requires a decision on our part to stretch our listening, to

---

[1] Bradford E. Hinze, *Practices of Dialogue in the Roman Catholic Church* (New York: Continuum, 2006), 248–49.

[2] David Tracy, *The Analogical Imagination* (New York: Crossroad, 1981), 101.

[3] See Hans-Georg Gadamer, *Truth and Method*, 2nd ed. trans. Joel Weinsheimer and Donald G. Marshall (New York: Crossroad, 1992), 367.

"attend with the ear of the heart," as the great fifth-to-sixth-century Christian monk Benedict of Nursia suggests in the opening of his Rule.[4] It asks that we be both hospitable enough to hear the plight and word of the "other" and open enough to receive the "beckon" in another's word. Doing so involves (1) a particular kind of listening, (2) a willingness to allow the word of another to resound in us, and (3) an ability to hear the summons in what is new sound.

A Way of Listening

To listen, observes the French philosopher Jean-Luc Nancy, is *tendre l'oreille*—literally, to incline the ear—a reference that points to the movement and stretch of the pinna of the human ear. In hearing, sounds travel to the ear as vibrations, moving down the ear canal to the eardrum in the middle ear. A complex network of bones and membranes send vibrations to the inner ear that then are changed into electrical signals carried to the brain. The brain interprets the messages and we hear them as sounds. The pinna, the outer part of the ear also known as the auricle, is what "collects" and "filters" sound. It performs as a funnel, amplifying sound and ushering it to the auditory canal. The pinna is also able to indicate mood and radiate heat.

The human ear that hears becomes a rich organic metaphor, at once powerfully suggestive in coming to understand the components of attentive listening in conversational exchange. In the act of listening, "hearing" something becomes a matter of understanding the sense of it. As Nancy notes, listening in both a figurative and a proper sense is to be "straining toward a possible meaning."[5] The sensory register of the ear according to its nature and function operates precisely this way. The reverberation chamber in the ear that makes listening possible posits relationship to potential meaning (*sens*), "a tension toward it," as Nancy claims, "but toward it completely ahead of signification."[6] The biomechanics of hearing serve as a wonderful reminder that listening is "inclined toward the opening of meaning."[7]

---

[4] See Benedict, *The Rule of Saint Benedict*, ed. Timothy Fry (New York: Vintage, 1998), 3.

[5] Jean-Luc Nancy, *Listening*, trans. Charlotte Mandell (New York: Fordham University, 2007), 6.

[6] Ibid., 27.

[7] Ibid.

Attentive listening, that which can happen when engaged in conversation with people or texts, assumes the posture of stretching toward meaning. Generosity and openness to the presence of the truth in the words of an author who is "other" makes real dialogue possible. In conversation with a text, observes Tracy, "we find ourselves by losing ourselves in the questioning provoked by the text."[8] A new "between" emerges that is fertile yet untilled dialogical space, one that enables the exploration of possibilities in the cultivation of truth.

To be open in a hospitable way to the insights, observations, and pleas of authors as found in their texts involves more than the bringing of focused attention to specific words on a page. It entails taking into account the tacit dimensions of the words expressed, something for which we are likely to have only a vague feeling. Tacit dimensions of texts are their powerful unwritten aspects that include the passions, affects, and commitments of authors that lie beneath their words and have influenced their writing. This level of listening requires "an inclination of the ear of the heart" indeed. It further presumes a basic acknowledgment that "*all* thought," as the physicist David Bohm underscores, "is actually a subtle tacit process."[9] To listen well, therefore, we must get underneath texts in order to hear what is being communicated at a tacit level.

Embodied senses give rise to multiple forms of verbal expression; putting effort into understanding those senses from which a text's words spring is one way of sensing its tacit ground. Paying attention to the tacit dimensions of our reception and processing of texts is also vital. Thoughts and affect are observable in the words of texts and in us as well. Listening for the tacit dimensions of both the texts themselves and our reception of them depends very much on our willingness to allow what we have heard to resound within us.

Letting Words Resound

The willingness to let thought and the tacit ground of thought resound within us requires a certain epistemological humility. Comparative theologian Catherine Cornille offers helpful guidelines for engaging in a kind of dialogue that has transformative impact. She asserts: "A first

---

[8] David Tracy, *Plurality and Ambiguity: Hermeneutics, Religion, Hope* (Chicago: Chicago University Press, 1987), 19.

[9] David Bohm, *On Dialogue*, ed. Lee Nichol (New York: Routledge, 1996), 14.

condition for genuine dialogue is *doctrinal* or *epistemic humility*. Any possibility of change or growth indeed presupposes recognition of one's own fallibility and imperfection."[10] Epistemological humility involves recognition of the finite and limited perceptions we carry and awareness that the truths we hold dear, however fine and orienting they may be, have been grasped and articulated within the frameworks of our own social, cultural, and institutional contexts.

The Christian tradition has a long history of reflecting upon and advising the virtue of humility. Rooted in truth, humility, in a Christian understanding of it, involves sensing both our and God's true proportions. In Christian discipleship, humility gets expressed not only in relation to God but in relation to fellow/sister human beings and the created order as well, all made in the image and likeness of God. One characteristic result of humble persons is the ability to let go of absolutist holdings of one's own assumptions. Approaching the word of another humbly means being genuinely open to the potential for truth in that word, even if it is particularly challenging. For real dialogue to occur, participants need to be aware of their assumptive tendencies in order to hear the word of another.

We aren't always adept at catching sight of the assumptions that affect our hearing, our interpretation of and responses to texts. Bohm offers a reminder: "Assumptions affect the way we see things, the way we experience them, and consequently the things that we want to do."[11] Being more aware of what our assumptions are, and understanding if and how they impede dialogue with another, makes it possible to move beyond them, thereby enabling the creation of a new moment, "the making of something *in common*"[12] rather than ongoing "necessary" protection of one's own turf.

Once we are willing to allow the word of the other to resound in us, we are able to observe the directionality of our own being in response to it. Sense, as Jean-Luc Nancy describes it, "is first of all the rebound of sound."[13] In conversational exchanges with texts, the presence of the other unfolds in words that rebound, opening up a sonorous exponent. Words of texts stretch out in space, carrying into dialogical territory,

---

[10] Catherine Cornille, *The Im-Possibility of Interreligious Dialogue* (New York: Crossroad, 2008), 4.

[11] Bohm, *On Dialogue*, 69.

[12] Ibid., 2

[13] Nancy, *Listening*, 30.

vibrating outside of the confines of the pages on which they are found. The sound of the other is amplified in genuine exchanges with texts as words spread in the act of resounding. Words that evoke dialogical encounter and conversation reverberate and expand. They are either received and engaged, or else deferred or silenced.

Sonorous insights are like waves on a swell, not points on a line.[14] They create interconnection whereby the wisdom of another is viewed as related to and relevant for our own ways of thinking and living. Riding the swell of waves of sonorous insights, we come into more than a fuller intellectual understanding. We come into a sense of the "summons" in what is new sound.

Hearing the Summons in New Sound

What resounds in genuine dialogue with a text promises to expand our reality and not diminish it. Resounding sounds evoke thought and can emit an existential summons. Not only is the listening ear inclined *toward* meaning; it is stretched and fashioned *by* meaning and *beckoned* in accord with it. In the evocation that ensues, there is what Nancy describes as "breath, exhalation, inspiration and expiration."[15] The summons in new thought ensures that the dialogue underway, from which the new thought springs, not only informs but also forms and transforms us as well.

Detecting the summons in what resounds as a result of conversational exchange with texts is like "panning for gold."[16] We dip into words that resound, pulling up sand as well as some nuggets of gold. We move the waters of thought around with our mind's hands, emptying out the sand and saving the nuggets. Within the gold, we find the summons, the invitation to new levels of knowing and being.

Avoidance of the summons in the word of another is ever a possibility, but the grace to respond to it in truth is ours for the receiving. We engage in genuine dialogue and all real conversation accompanied by God's Spirit. Recognition of this divine accompaniment brings a tone of reverence and expectancy to the activity of dialogue; it shapes every conversation. In the summons iterated in the resounding word of

---

[14] This is an image used by Jean-Luc Nancy to describe "sonorous time." See *Listening*, 13.

[15] Nancy, *Listening*, 20.

[16] For this image, I am indebted to Janet Ruffing, RSM, who utilizes it very effectively in her book *Spiritual Direction: Beyond the Beginnings* (New York: Paulist Press, 2000), esp. chap. 3.

the other, we are edged anew in the direction of God's reign. Like the merchant who recognized that his perspective was forever changed by the presence of the pearl, we too have recognized the unique worth of our dialogical exchange with the texts shared here. Like the merchant, we seek to attend to the summons rising from these essays for our lives. In doing so, we honor the fondest hopes of the authors included in this volume and pay tribute to the activity of dialogue as one hopeful sign of the reign of God in our midst, a pearl of unparalleled value. Having alighted upon the summons rising from our dialogue with this text, we are spurred on by it. The grace of this summons is not something we possess. It claims us, awaiting our response.

Pearls

You are pearls.
You began
as irritants.

The ocean pushed
your small, nearly
invisible
rough body
through an undetected
crack in the shell.
You got inside.

Happy to have a home
at last
you grew close
to the host,
nuzzling up
to the larger body.

You became
a subject
for diagnosis:
invader, tumor.

Perhaps your parents
were the true invaders
and you were born
in the shell—
no difference—
called an outsider
still.

You were a representative
of the whole
outside world,
a grain of sand,
particle of the Universe,
part of Earth.
You were a *growth*.

And you did not go away.

In time
you grew
so large,
an internal
luminescence,
that the shell
could contain
neither you nor itself,
and because of you
the shell Opened itself
to the world.

Then your beauty
was seen
and prized,

your variety valued:
precious, precious,
a hard bubble of light:
silver, white, ivory,
or baroque.

If you are a specially
irregular and rough
pearl, named baroque
(for broke),
then you reveal

in your own
amazed/amazing
body of light
all the colors
of the Universe.

—Alla Renée Bozarth[1]

[1] Alla Renée Bozarth, "Pearls," in *Womanpriest: A Personal Odyssey* (New York and Mahwah: Paulist Press, 1978; rev. ed., Luramedia and Wisdom House, 1988); *Water Women*, audio-cassette (Wisdom House, 1990); Alla Renée Bozarth, Julia Barkley, and Terri Hawthorne, *Stars in Your Bones: Emerging Signposts on Our Spiritual Journeys* (St. Cloud, MN: North Star Press of St. Cloud, 1990); and *Accidental Wisdom* (iUniverse, 2003).

Contributors

Susie Paulik Babka is assistant professor of theology and religious studies at the University of San Diego. She received her PhD from the University of Notre Dame, specializing in trinitarian doctrine and Christology. Her research interests have turned to intersections between these subjects and visual art, and she has published several articles in this regard. She is currently working on a book entitled *Suffering, Kenosis, Presence: Exploring the Incarnation through Visual Art*. She hopes to later work on how theological aesthetics may serve interreligious dialogue.

Rachel A. R. Bundang earned her PhD in constructive theologies, praxis, and ethics at Union Theological Seminary. She is on the religious studies faculty at the Marymount School in New York, where she also serves as the director of retreats and social justice initiatives. Besides teaching and writing in the area of Catholic feminist ethics, she works as an experienced liturgist and musician, with occasional pastoral duties in young adult ministry.

Rosemary P. Carbine holds master's and doctoral degrees in theology from the University of Chicago Divinity School and is currently visiting assistant professor of religious studies and director of fellowships at Whittier College, a Quaker-inspired liberal arts college in Southern California. She specializes in historical and contemporary Christian theologies, with a particular focus on theological anthropology; public theology; comparative feminist, womanist, and *mujerista* theologies; and teaching and learning in theology and religion. She has published on these topics in major reference works, scholarly journals, and books, including *Monika Hellwig: The People's Theologian* (Liturgical Press, 2010), *Frontiers in Catholic Feminist Theology* (Fortress Press, 2009), and *Prophetic Witness: Catholic Women's Strategies of Reform* (Crossroad, 2009). She currently serves as the coconvener of the Women's Consultation on Constructive Theology in the Catholic Theological Society of America.

Nancy A. Dallavalle is associate professor of religious studies at Fairfield University, where she has taught since 1993, following doctoral work at the University of Notre Dame, and has chaired the department since 2008. Her scholarly interests include systematic theology (especially trinitarian theology, theological anthropology, and ecclesiology), the conversation between science and religion, and the popular discussion about the role of Catholics in the public square. On these topics, she has published "Resilient Citizens: The Public (and Gendered) Face of American Catholicism," in *Inculturation and the Church in North America* (Crossroad, 2006), and "Feminist Theologies," in *The Cambridge Companion to Karl Rahner* (Cambridge University Press, 2005).

Mary Doak is associate professor at the University of San Diego. She received her PhD from the University of Chicago, and her main areas of research include political theology, theological method, eschatology, and ecclesiology. She has published a book and several articles on aspects of public theology, and she is currently writing a book on the global mission of the church in the twenty-first century.

Kathleen J. Dolphin, PBVM, completed her MA and PhD at the University of Chicago Divinity School and holds two additional master's degrees: MST, University of Montana, and MChSP, Creighton University. Kathleen is in her eleventh year as director of the Center for Spirituality at Saint Mary's College, Notre Dame, Indiana, where she also teaches in the Religious Studies Department. Prior to Saint Mary's, she was on the graduate faculty of the Institute of Pastoral Studies at Loyola University Chicago for ten years. Her main area of research is the integration of theology and spirituality. She serves on the Women's Advisory Committee at the Woodstock Theological Center at Georgetown University and on the advisory board of the Catholic Common Ground Initiative at the Bernardin Center at Catholic Theological Union. She is a member of the Congregation of the Sisters of the Presentation of the Blessed Virgin Mary.

Colleen M. Griffith is associate professor of the practice of theology at Boston College's School of Theology and Ministry, where she serves as faculty director of spirituality studies in the DREPM Department within the school. Her research and writing interests lie in the areas of theological

290 Women, Wisdom, and Witness

anthropology, theological method, and the relationship between theology and spirituality. Her most recent publication, *Prophetic Witness: Catholic Women's Strategies for Reform* (Crossroad, 2009), was awarded first place in the gender category by the Catholic Press Association in 2010.

Mary Henold is associate professor of history at Roanoke College, a liberal arts college in southwest Virginia. She is the author of *Catholic and Feminist: The Surprising History of the American Catholic Feminist Movement* (University of North Carolina Press, 2008). Her research interests include the history of American Catholicism, particularly in the post–Vatican II era, and the history of American Catholic women. She is currently researching the responses of moderate and conservative laywomen to the Second Vatican Council.

Kristin Heyer holds the Bernard J. Hanley Chair in Religious Studies at Santa Clara University. Her books include *Kinship across Borders: A Christian Ethic of Immigration* (Georgetown University Press, 2012), *Prophetic and Public: The Social Witness of U.S. Catholicism* (Georgetown University Press, 2006), and the edited volume *Catholics and Politics: The Dynamic Tension between Faith and Power* (Georgetown University Press, 2008). She serves as an editorial consultant for *Theological Studies* and is a member of the planning committee for Catholic Theological Ethics in the World Church.

LaReine-Marie Mosely is assistant professor of theology at Loyola University Chicago. Her research interests include Catholic theology, black theology, black Catholic theology, womanist theology, all other liberation theologies, the theology of Edward Schillebeeckx, and the collaboration of theologians of various perspectives. Her publications include "Womanist Ways of Being in the World," in *Frontiers in Catholic Feminist Theology: Shoulder to Shoulder* (Fortress Press, 2009), and "Daniel Rudd: The Civil Rights Leader and Black Catholic Lay Animator," in *American Catholic Studies* (Winter 2011). Her upcoming monograph is tentatively called *A Heart as Wide as the World: Shared Theological Sensibilities*.

Maureen H. O'Connell is associate professor of theology at Fordham University, where she teaches social ethics, religion and politics, and theological aesthetics to undergraduate and graduate students. She authored *Compassion: Loving Our Neighbor in an Age of Globalization* (Orbis Books, 2009), and coedited the College Theology Society's most recent annual volume, *Religion, Economics, and Culture in Conflict and Conversation* (Orbis Books, 2011). Her current research, funded in part by the Louisville Institute and the Wabash Center for Teaching and Learning in Theology and Religion, explores the arts as a source of ethical wisdom and a catalyst for moral action. She has published on this topic in the *Journal of the Society of Christian Ethics* and in an image-laden manuscript titled *If These Walls Could Talk: Community Muralism and the Beauty of Justice* (Liturgical Press, 2012). She currently serves on the board of the Society for the Arts in Religious and Theological Studies and chairs the Committee on Race, Diversity, and Pedagogy for the College Theology Society.

Anne M. O'Leary, PBVM, is assistant professor of New Testament at Saint Mary's University, San Antonio, Texas. She is author of the book *Matthew's Judaization of Mark* (Continuum, 2006), as well as chapters in edited volumes, such as "Creative Use of the Bible in Religious Education," in *Exploring Religious Education: Catholic Religious Education in an Intercultural Europe* (Veritas, 2008), and "An Introduction to the Christian Scriptures," in *An Introduction to Theology* (Veritas, 2007). Her research interests include the study of the Johannine corpus, composition of the gospels in the context of the use of sources in Greco-Roman antiquity, Mary and religion, and Presentation spirituality.

Nancy Pineda-Madrid is associate professor of theology at Boston College, where she teaches at the School of Theology and Ministry. She holds a doctoral degree in systematic and philosophical theology from the Graduate Theological Union (Berkeley, California). She recently published a book entitled *Suffering and Salvation in Ciudad Juárez* (Fortress Press, 2011), taking the feminicide there as the context for developing a theological interpretation of suffering and salvation from a Latina feminist perspective. She does constructive work in Latina feminist soteriology and has published in several edited collections and in theology journals. She has more than a decade of professional experience in pastoral leadership and ministry at the national, archdiocesan, and parish levels.

Bridget Burke Ravizza is assistant professor of religious studies at Saint Norbert College in De Pere, Wisconsin, where she directs the peace and justice minor and contributes to the program in women's and gender studies. In addition, she teaches Christian ethics in the college's master of theological studies program. Current areas of scholarly interest are the ethics of marriage and family and sexual ethics. Recent publications include "Ministering to Moral Pioneers: Prenatal Testing and Christian Parenting," *New Theology Review* (August 2011).

Emily Reimer-Barry is assistant professor in the Department of Theology and Religious Studies at the University of San Diego. Her research interests include ethnography and ethical method, feminist ethics, and sexual ethics. She is currently working on a book project with the tentative title *HIV Prevention for Vulnerable Populations: A Contextual Approach*. She teaches undergraduate courses in Catholic theology, Christian ethics, and Catholic social thought.

Mary M. Doyle Roche is assistant professor of religious studies and Edward Bennett Williams Fellow at the College of the Holy Cross in Worcester, Massachusetts, where she teaches courses in Christian ethics. She is the author of *Children, Consumerism, and the Common Good* (Lexington, 2009) and lives with her husband and two children in Westborough, Massachusetts.

Michele Saracino is associate professor of religious studies at Manhattan College in Riverdale, New York. Her books include *Being about Borders: A Christian Anthropology of Difference* (Liturgical Press, 2011), *On Being Human: A Conversation with Lonergan and Levinas* (Marquette University Press, 2003), and most recently, *Clothing: Christian Explorations of Daily Living* (Fortress Press, 2012). She teaches on the intersections among theology, culture, and ecology.